W9-AQN-987

GAL 9.86

310-3
6
MAY 1981
RECEIVED
OHIO DOMINICAN
COLLEGE LIBRARY
COLUMBUS, OHIO
43219

REFORM and the CITIZEN

SHERMAN LEWIS
California State University, Hayward

REFORM and the CITIZEN

The Major Policy Issues of Contemporary America

DUXBURY PRESS
NORTH SCITUATE, MASSACHUSETTS

309.173
L676r
1980

Reform and the Citizen: The Major Policy Issues of Contemporary America was produced by the following people:

Copy Editor: Beverly Harrison Miller
Cover Designer: Joanna Snyder
Cover photographs: Owen Franken, Stock Boston (top & left); Charles Gatewood, Magnum Photos, Inc. (right)
Art Coordinator: Joanna Snyder
Production Coordinator: Elizabeth Patterson

Duxbury Press
A Division of Wadsworth, Inc.

© 1980 by Wadsworth, Inc., Belmont, California 94002. All rights reserved. No part of this book may be reproduced, stored in a retrieval system, or transcribed, in any form or by any means, electronic, mechanical, photocopying, recording, or otherwise, without the prior written permission of the publisher, Duxbury Press, a division of Wadsworth, Inc., Belmont, California.

Library of Congress Cataloging in Publication Data

Lewis, Sherman.
Reform and the citizen.

Includes bibliographies and index.
1. United States—Politics and government—1945–
2. Political participation—United States.
I. Title.
JK274.L563 309.1'73'092 79-21088
ISBN 0-87872-214-9

Printed in the United States of America
1 2 3 4 5 6 7 8 9 — 84 83 82 81 80

Contents

114222

Preface

This book is about the problems of American society in the 1980s. It describes them and suggests solutions for all major areas of policy except national security. Its purpose is to contribute to an emerging subfield of political science: citizen policy. Citizen policy is concerned with substantive analysis of issues, distinguishing along a spectrum from those policy issues likely to be decided by experts and insiders, and, at the other end, those issues for which the opinions of citizens are or should be important. Citizens cannot be experts; and experts may be poor citizens. Citizens need a broad knowledge of the issues yet get little guidance from any profession that is disinterested in the issues. Some professionals and popularizers try to communicate their own expertise to the general population, but it is generally from a point of view reflecting socialization into the profession and its self-interest. Even political scientists tend to stay with traditional topics of the discipline.

The vast complexity of the problems I have included is reason enough not to try to master some knowledge of them all. This world rewards specialization, which is very challenging in itself. The result is that students and other people in general pick up some understandings of the problems and solutions over time swayed by the latest simplistic ideologue to gain media attention. Academics in general and political scientists in particular can do better. Someone needs to give people a broad and sophisticated introduction to our larger society that can shape their behavior as citizens for years to come. Citizens do not need to know most details about most issues, but they do need to know the central understandings and facts.

I also hope to develop within the field of citizen policy the approach of complex advocacy. Some textbooks can be impressively objective, but this one is not; it is committed. However, my commitment is not one that I like to put a label on. I use the concept of reform to pull together all of the ideas and give the book some coherence. I feel it does have some coherence, but at a deeper level of general principles that are not discussed in the book. These principles are in tension with each other, producing what I hope will be perceived as an intelligent pragmatism. One aspect of advocacy is not *that* I advocate but *how* I advocate: with a mixture of self-confidence and respect for opposing views. Too often a purely objective approach teaches objectivity, which is relevant for science but impossible for citizens, who by action and inaction, in ignorance or knowledge, must make immediate decisions on issues too large for the experts.

Reform can be defined generally as a change for the better in society accomplished by our own conscious, collective efforts. What is considered better involves a value judgment and thus is different for each person. Any book on American problems and public policy inevitably has some such value judgments, and this one is no exception. I will use my sense of values, generally widely shared, as to what constitutes reform. But specific definitions are always subject to debate and are never simple, and how we should seek reform is equally controversial.

Each period has some idea called *reform* and people called *reformers.* Some common historical themes of reform include equality of opportunity, equality before the law, civil liberty, voting rights, public safety, conservation, democracy, world peace, fair taxes, employment, free markets, fair wages, stable currency, and strong families. One reason that the concept of reform is so complex is that it seeks not one or a few of these values but several or even all of them. In each era, reformers must necessarily focus on the excesses of their time, pushing reforms aimed as simply as possible at those problems and operating within the political, social, and economic restraints of their times.

In looking at reform in the present, our attitudes are shaped by our understanding of reform in the past. It is currently intellectually fashionable to take a harsh, even contemptuous, attitude toward reform ideas and reformers of the past. There are three major criticisms of the past reform efforts, each with a degree of truth. First, we can say that the reformers had the wrong idea to begin with, that they did not really understand their times. To the extent they were successful, their reforms "backfired" with unintended consequences, often doing more harm than good. Second, we can say that even when they were right about what needed to be done, they had too little power to effectuate their solutions. Thus it may be said—to summarize the first two criticisms—that reformers are either stupidly powerful or wisely impotent. A third criticism is that to the extent change for the better actually occurred, it resulted from forces other than the reformers.

This criticism makes reformers irrelevant. Historians can find good cases where some or all of these criticisms apply to some extent, but as a comprehensive assessment, they are too narrow. We know that some reformers and reform movements have had significant and positive influence on history.

The criticism also fails at a deeper level: it does not correspond to the way that most of us perceive our times and our own roles. We experience choice and have some sense that our choices will make a difference. Despite our ignorance, our weaknesses, and the strength of forces beyond our control, we retain a sense that history is made by individual human beings. We fight to retain this sense against the powerful forces of a complex society that is molding us in certain directions.

This book attempts to sketch what reform means in our place and time—America of the 1980s—for the sake of those willing to make their individual effort for a better world. The book necessarily reflects my own opinions, and those who disagree with what I advocate will consider this book biased and unbalanced. I admit to the possibility of being wrong and invite you to think your way through to your own solutions. I reserve the right to change my mind as I learn more. I also trust you, the reader, to recognize when I am presenting relatively factual material and when I am presenting opinion.

This book is aimed at citizens who need information about major problems relevant for the kinds of actions they can take. I will try to avoid generalizations that are vague or that do not help us make choices among politically possible approaches. I will also avoid problems of detail likely to be handled by specialists and in which the role of citizens is not likely to be important. I am thus aiming at a middle level of generalization: what the educated citizen needs to know. This knowledge covers the substance of the issues themselves and how the citizen can act on them. No specialists will be satisfied with the necessarily brief coverage of each issue, nor is it possible to cover all issues. National security and other foreign policy issues, for example, are not included.

Social scientists who write textbooks on the American political system and those who require their students to read them are specialists, too, in their own way. They have tended to teach students what they know about—the workings of the system as such, abstracted from its specific issues. An introductory course on the U.S. political system, for example, typically covers the development of the Constitution and some history of other aspects of the political system, the nature of American values and public opinion, voting, campaigning and parties, interest groups and lobbying, federalism and state and local government, the Congress, the president, the Supreme Court, and possibly the bureaucracy and something on civil liberties. But even those longer texts with a chapter or two on broad policy areas do not cover real citizen choices or suggest changes or indicate how to get them. The information these books provide is valuable, but they overlook why it is that we should be interested in politics in the first place.

The reason that all of the information about institutions and leaders is important is because what they do affects us and we can, if we will, affect them. The economy, environmental problems, social problems, and institutional problems have a profound effect upon us. We need help in thinking through the trade-offs among values just as much as we need the information about institutions. The realities of the problems motivate us to participate, and our participation can be an excellent education about the institutions. This book is designed carefully to complement texts or readings on the American political system. It is aimed at making the issues alive and important.

Chapter 1 summarizes how the American political system works, the nature of the average American in this system, and the dynamics of reform. Chapters 2 through 5 discuss substantive problems—the economy, the environment, pervasive social problems, and major social institutions—and chapter 6 concentrates on procedural or systemic problems. Each chapter summarizes the fundamentals of the problem, suggests moderately ambitious reforms, and describes successful and unsuccessful attempts at reform. The purpose is not so much to describe actions that individuals can take as to motivate people to seek out their own ways to be effective. Such motivation springs from an understanding of a problem and of the relevance of our actions. Chapter 7 looks at reform more comprehensively, at public interest groups, and at the actions and attitudes of committed citizens.

Our age seems to suffer from a lack of purpose; there is no hot war to win, no depression to fight, no single sustained focus for national attention. Many people seem lonely and without purpose; many others confuse purpose with following the latest fads and fashions being hyped by the media, the corporations, and self-promoting saviors. Yet beneath this surface are many people with mature and stable historical commitments. For students seeking some purpose in life, this book offers many possible challenges. I have tried to use an interesting writing style so that the vitality and meaningfulness of these challenges can shine through.

The chapter notes sometimes provide more information than is academically required to give students a better idea about where to find more detail. They are all the more important because I have not included a bibliography; the reason is that I want to emphasize continuing sources of information and continuing involvement through public-interest groups. It is, in fact, somewhat contradictory to try to use a book to accomplish something better done by years of gentle nudges. In that same vein, I have tried to use sources for tables that could be updated by students who, until they get some sense of historical continuity, tend to assume that just because something was true last month does not make it true now. In particular I have used the Bureau of the Census's *Statistical Abstract of the United States,* and where data are not referenced, that is usually the source.

The major parts of the chapters are written to stand alone for the convenience of reading assignments that may need to cover only some of the topics or do them in a different order.

Acknowledgments

Bernie Hennessey deserves first acknowledgment for the great role he played in bringing this book into print. He saw merit in the 974-page version of 1976, his praise going beyond my own realistic self-assessments and articulating my hopes. His support was critical in finding and keeping a good publisher. The publisher deserves a lot of credit too, for this is an unusual kind of "textbook" and therefore a high-risk project.

Several friends and colleagues have read parts of drafts; I wish to thank Jim Nichols, with whom I shared office and counsel for many years and who never gave up on me; Emily Stoper, also of the department of political science at Cal State Hayward, for her comments; and Dane Smith, college roommate and now Foreign Service officer, for his long letter.

Hundreds of students have been exposed to these ideas in my classroom over the last decade, and many of them helped with questions and comments. Carl Pope of the Sierra Club, the Oracle Collective, and Common Cause made useful comments on particular chapters. I also acknowledge the comments and suggestions of reviewers: R.J. Snow, University of Utah; Dan Barber, California State University, Long Beach; Ray Johnston, Wayne State University; and Jeffrey M. Berry, Tufts University. I hope I have answered their questions.

I have been working on this so long I have lost track of whom to thank. I appreciate all the journalists and writers who have supplied me with a continuing flow of facts and ideas; I have borrowed much more material than I created.

Finally, I am grateful for the support of my family, Alison, Sherm

Junior, and Eleanor. Because I am very inefficient, my work often had to compete with my time to help and enjoy them.

None of the above are responsible for any mistakes or interpretations in this book; I am reasonably sure that a few may not even want to be associated with it. I do hope, nevertheless, that *Reform and the Citizen* is the best in its field on the market and needs only, like the Union, to be made more perfect. I hope those who enter into the spirit of this enterprise will feel free to communicate their comments to me.

I

The System and the Citizen

The American Political System

A *system* is a pattern of behaviors that relate to each other and fulfill a function. A *political system* is the set of behaviors used by a society to make overt decisions that shift the distribution of values in the system as a whole. These decisions achieve commonly shared values, adjust conflicts of values by compromise, and enforce dominant values against deviant behavior. The related behaviors can be called *roles* or *institutions*. *System* also refers to the underlying assumptions of the behavior—that is, the political culture.

The United States has a relatively democratic political system. One attribute of democracy is that there usually occur some meaningful differences between at least two candidates in campaigns for election on the major issues of the day. Research on the House of Representatives indicates that the United States meets the requirements for candidate differences. In 1966, for example, significant differences were found on issues in about two-thirds of the districts. In the other districts, 13 percent of the candidates had no opponent, and 20 percent at most had two candidates with little net differences on issues. The choices were usually between a so-called conservative Republican and a so-called liberal Democrat who differed over foreign affairs, civil rights, and welfare.[1] Research on voting patterns in Congress reveals similar differences between the parties on key votes. Speeches, news reports, periodicals, and so on provide more evidence of differences. The popular idea that there are no real differences between candidates is usually wrong. The differences may not be extreme, but they are usually meaningful to most participants in the political system.

Similarly the popular idea that politicians say one thing and do another is wrong as a generalization; once elected, they closely follow the positions they held as candidates.[2] Occasional dramatic cases of switching should not obscure the underlying reality of consistency: politicians are no more hypocritical than the rest of us. Their thinking, like ours, changes over time, and sometimes they may change on the issues in response to changes in popular thinking.

Democracy by some definitions also requires that people vote for leaders who best conform to their notion of a public interest. It follows logically, then, that the public must have knowledge about issues and candidates and an ability to relate their vote to their values. Most evidence, however, shows the general failure of the American people to vote knowledgeably, meaning that we do not have a full democracy in this sense. Most Americans (about 70 percent) do not vote in most elections, and most of those who do vote know little if anything about the issue differences of candidates. Most Americans also are politically inactive and have a low interest in politics.

Pluralism

In world context, the American system is clearly some kind of democracy, nevertheless. We can call it a *procedural democracy* because the system does follow the procedures of democracy and because popular opinion plays an important role. The politically active class that uses the procedures to exercise power can be called the *plural elite*.

The system is plural in that it has many centers of autonomous power, each making decisions within a specialized policy area, and it is far more open and competitive than that of most other countries, even most other procedural democracies. Within the national government, power is divided constitutionally by a system of checks and balances among separate institutions—Congress, the legislative branch (further divided between House and Senate); the presidency, the executive branch; and the Supreme Court, the judicial branch—and these institutions share power. The method of selecting officials of one branch cannot be controlled by the officials of another.

This national government, divided within itself, is further limited by federalism, the philosophy of giving much power to the states. The state governments are themselves divided like the federal government and in turn delegate significant powers to a multitude of local governments. A philosophy and system of law maintains a system of limited government and individual freedom, which limits these many governments in controlling the private sector, made up of individual citizens and their associations. The private organizations are of two general types, economic and noneconomic, ot which the economic is much bigger. Major examples of economic associations are corporations and unions, and there are many of them, further increasing pluralism. Noneconomic groups include the religious, charitable, fraternal, home-owner, academic, and political types. A few associations mix economic and noneconomic interests. (See table 1–1.)

The pluralism does not end here; the units themselves have internal divisions of political importance. For example, even in one branch—like the executive branch of the federal government—there is frequent and open competition among its component agencies. An agency itself may not be unified. A big agency like the Defense Department has serious internal divisions.

Freedom of the press, essential to the whole democratic political process, inhibits secrecy and the suppression of interests. The press is, in fact, a power resource in the competition. Such openness pulls in more participants as allies on one side or the other and as referees. This pluralism contrasts starkly with the politics of most other nations, which hide conflict and limit participation.

Elitism

A system so plural is threatening to itself. Similar constitutional systems have failed in many countries from an excess of competition, resulting in a loss of *legitimacy,* the consensus among participants and people supporting the system itself. Typical forms of collapse include executive dismissal of legislatures and of judges and military coups, usually with civilian support.

The elite can be defined as those people who occupy the positions of power of the pluralistic system just described. There is no sharp line between elite and people. Elite status is correlated with the authority or legal power of the position held; with the number of employees, amount of money spent, and prestige of the institution under a given position; with the centrality of a person within a decision-making process; with reputation; and with personal forcefulness.

The pluralist divisions of power are to a great extent overcome by a consensus among the members of the elite. Some observers believe that this consensus fundamentally destroys the potentially democratic nature of the system; they can be called *elitists.* Others believe the consensus allows meaningful competition over issues in a fairly democratic way; they can be called *pluralists.* Pushed too far, neither view makes much sense. Elitists do not generally see perfect unity among the elite, and pluralists do not pretend that the system is close to an ideal democracy.

The American elite has been one of the most durable in world history. Only once has a major segment tried to break the rules of procedure in a major way. That one exception, which resulted in the Civil War, ended

Table 1–1 American Political Institutions

	Public Sector: A Federal System	
	National	*State and Local*
Legislative	Congress	State legislatures County supervisors * City councils * School boards * Special district boards *
Executive and Administrative	Presidency	Governorships, other state elective offices
	Federal departments and agencies	State administrations Elected mayoralty County and municipal administration
Judicial	Supreme Court Federal courts	State supreme courts State and municipal courts and justices of the Peace
	Private Sector	
	Economic	*Noneconomic*
	Multinational corporations, Other large corporations, mostly publicly held Smaller corporations, many privately held small businesses, farms Wealthy entrepreneurs, partnerships, proprietorships The mass media Occupational associations: labor unions, professionals Industrial associations, Trade associations: Chambers of Commerce, National Association of Manufacturers, the Business Roundtable	Political parties Public interest groups Other interest groups: veterans, ethnic, religious, racial, cultural, hobby, sports, fraternal, homeowner, civic Private schools, universities, colleges, nonpolitical academic associations Foundations, research institutes Hospitals, other health groups if nonprofit Religious groups, charities Families

* May also have executive functions.

in a stronger union and a stronger federal government than before. This historical continuity makes it hard to find events in which one elite has lost to another dramatically as in a revolution or a coup d'état. Yet elites have changed greatly over the decades. Similarly, it is difficult to assess the improvements and decays in the representation of popular interests. Further, there may be overlapping interests between elite interests and popular interests, and these overlaps may not always be compatible with democratic requirements to protect individual and minority rights. In this complex and often confusing reality, it seems fair to say that in an important sense there is an elite in the United States that has a pervasive and disproportionate influence. For good or for ill, its myths and values dominate.

In choosing this approach, I must not go too far in the direction of a unified elite. Some observers claim to find such an elite, whose members know each other, who are aware they are the elite, who coordinate their efforts, and who are predominant over all issue areas of importance. However, this kind of elite does not exist. The American elite is far too numerous for its members to know each other; what is possible for a tribe or city-state is not possible for the biggest developed democracy. Members of the elite are usually aware that they are well off but often sense no particular separation from those lower down. Their sense of social equality can help maintain their leadership. Members of the elite often feel less closeness to others in the elite (with whom they compete, or of whom they disapprove, or whom they do not even know) and more closeness to others in their own groups regardless of rank. Given these limitations, coordination of effort among the elites is similarly limited. There is a certain predominance of an elite in the American system, but it manifests itself in more subtle and complicated ways than overt unity and coordination. We need to avoid the monolithic connotation of one elite without going to the other extreme of confusing pluralism with full democracy. I will try to do this by talking about *elites*.

The American elites and their pluralistic system must deal with two very important kinds of challenges: interelite conflict and popular discontent. The American elites have avoided the peril of any one elite's gaining total power and the opposite peril—loss of power to popular interests. Such a balance is exactly the results hoped for by the framers of the Constitution in 1787. Both goals require that the autonomous elites find some way to cooperate across the institutional barriers of pluralism. For example, both chambers of Congress and the president must agree on identical wording to make a law. Agreement has been possible because of consensus on basic democratic values and a strong commitment to compromising differences. There has also been the knowledge that without compromise, the system would collapse.

The consensus is taught by one generation to the next. The dominant culture is Anglo-Protestant, educated, and middle class in its values. Elite and middle-class children are generally socialized to venerate the system, especially the presidency, giving the government legitimacy. The initial and most powerful instrument of socialization is the family. Later come schools, colleges, and graduate schools. Then initial work experience takes over, and along the way skills and contacts critical for success are established. The children of the elites and, to a lesser extent, the middle class pick up advantages that cumulatively give them a head start. The most obvious kind of advantage is inherited wealth, characteristic of a sizable and stable part of the elites. Most members of elites, however, base their power on the social and educational advantages of family and educational background. American elites are generally competitive and allow a fair amount of upward and downward mobility. They are working elites. Many have so much money they could stop but continue working long days. Young adults are expected to be successful on their own merits.

Influence and Control

A major factor, perhaps the major factor, in the excessive influence of elites is *cooption,* uncritical support for the system by people who misperceive the best means to obtain their values. They may be influenced by the personal qualities—considerateness, fairness, intelligence—of a prominent person they know. They may have experienced meaningful improvement, good income, and job security. They are likely socialized to a certain way of thinking. They may overgeneralize from their own family and work experience.

Cooption includes weakening the emerging leaders of popular interests with minor concessions, well-paid jobs, and the prestige of participation. But in a broader sense, it includes a large number of people not very interested in politics who can be manipulated or influenced to have views favorable to the elites. The idea of cooption is tricky because it involves some assumption about what the popular interest "really" is.

The *mass media* help perpetuate the system. They generally propagate the most easily gathered news, since this focus satisfies the elite members who are producing the news, the media-owning elite who want to produce news cheaply, and the people, who assume that the news presented to them is newsworthy. The media are objective, but usually about things that are not important. Rarely do the media help their audiences understand where they fit in or how they can influence events. Most people's ideas about what is going on "out there" are molded over time by the media, and are very limited. "Out there" refers to the reality presented to us by the media, as contrasted with "here" where we can see and hear more directly.

The *law* is a major instrument of influence and control, partly because of the way the laws are written and partly because the elites can more easily afford lawyers. The law works both to regulate popular excesses and to regulate interelite conflict. Elites influence the way the laws, which impose taxes, create bureaucracies, and regulate all other institutions, are written. They not only possess political skills; they also use *money* to run for office. The elites give money to candidates they agree with and who can win. They are not always happy with whom they have to support, but they have far more influence than the average person, who gives no support at all. Once a candidate is elected, *lobbyists* will ensure that elites get their views put across. There are no lobbies of the people, and relatively few and weak lobbies speaking for the people or for reform.

Campaign money is especially interesting because it propagandizes voters and is one of the few action-oriented political messages that people get from any source. This propaganda is usually not the major force determining an election, but it can be decisive in a close election. Elites vary in the degree to which they depend on government, but they are all dependent in some measure. Some find political investments to yield higher returns than any other.

Influence over the system through politics also uses *secrecy,* which includes proprietary (private) information about who owns corporations, the profits and other accounting data of firms with several product lines and of closely held firms, the contents of packages, pollution, chemical compounds, and energy reserves. Frequently bureaucracies make decisions without people's even knowing, and when they find out, it is too late to affect the decision. The government does not know, does not have time to analyze the information it has, or will not reveal it. Values on privacy and national security allow secret decisions with far-reaching public consequences. The money and secrecy patterns help overcome the apparent pluralistic divisions of power.

In any given national issue area, there is typically a triangle of intimate relations among three elites: affected interest groups, a congressional subcommittee, and an agency of the executive branch. The interest group perspective tends to dominate through campaign and lobby influence over congressmen on the subcommittee and through appointment to the political positions over the agencies. People move among these institutions in predictable patterns. Thus, the economic private sector, especially large corportions, has disproportionate influence in most of the official centers of power in the public sector.

A large part of the competition within the private sector (between unions and corporations or among businesses, for example) is like competition in the political arena: it is not over fundamental issues. Many important interests worth representing are represented; the problem is that too many interests are left out. The clash of interests does not add up to a reasonable appproximation, in terms of reform values, of the public interest. Much private competition is more apparent than real because of the way banks, producing firms, suppliers, unions, transportation firms, insurers, accountants, law firms, utilities, and commercial firms often work together in a stable pattern, a coherent but not sharply competitive business system. These links dull competition, and when a large firm (or a few large firms) dominates its market, competition is further reduced. Working relationships even extend to overlapping boards of directors; a typical director of a major corporation often serves on several boards. Successful business people also tend to dominate the nonprofit private sector, such as foundations, universities, charities, and cultural organizations.

Similarly, the political parties, despite some important differences, do not differ extensively or over fundamental issues. The parties to a great extent are large groupings of the business interests just mentioned.

In several ways the fundamental issues are raised, but the elites have so much influence that they can relatively easily prevent serious threats to their power, prestige, and wealth. Reform candidates can run for office but tend to get defeated. A legislator can introduce a reform bill, but the committee chair may have power to kill it or the committee may refuse to consider it. A legislature may weaken a bill; an executive can veto a bill. Even if the legislation is passed, there may be too little money to make the law work or ineffectual administration. Legal procedures may slow enforcement to a snail's pace. The government may decide not to take cases to court, and judges may not side with the public interest view.

The media tend to focus on conflicts within the elites, overlooking or playing down reform decisions. The news seems to be important but hides the reality of no change and painfully slow change. It becomes, then, more difficult to mobilize resources to overcome the obstacles, because few people know what is going on or recognize its importance. The ability of elites to ignore fundamental issues is something called *nondecision making*.

The prospect of failure is discouraging. Many would-be reformers give up before they start, even though if they tried they might succeed. This problem, called *anticipated reactions*, greatly reduces the number willing to try for reform and makes it easier for elites to resist the few who do.

The American political system is sufficiently complex to lend itself to different but plausible interpretations. It is a plural elite system using the procedures of democracy. It has great pluralism: many centers of power, significant internal differences, some degree of openness, and some degree of responsiveness to public opinion. Yet the American political system also has many features of elitism. The elites have consensus on fundamental issues, durability, an effective system of socialization, an ability to coopt much of their support, control over the media, law, money, and information, linkages among different interests and institutions within and between public and private sectors, and the power to stop and discourage attempts at fundamental change.

A Closer Look: Political Strata

A closer look at the American political system reveals more specific levels or strata both in politics and in society. Political stratification concerns general levels of power or influence of individuals. Such a generalized concept is hard to measure, and there are many ways to do it. The following is meant to be suggestive rather than definitive and uses the positions or wealth people have, their volunteer activity and level of overt political activity, their levels of conceptualization, their memberships, campaign contributions, voting and information intake.

The *top elites* constitute less than one-tenth of 1 percent of the adult population. Top elite members hold positions of public and private power or possess great wealth, yielding them high authoritative power. They are more than 95 percent white male and generally of Anglo or Northern European extraction. They have special and superior sources of information in their areas of specialization but are not exceptionally well informed in other areas. They are very busy and hard for the average person to reach. Access to them is screened by others, who also help them get information, organize their time, and carry out their decisions. While small in percentage terms, the number who might be considered in the top elites is fairly large, about 150,000.

The *secondary elites* constitute a few percent of adults. They hold positions just below the top elites and have some political content and discretion in their jobs. Alternatively, they may have wealth or autonomous power of some kind but not enough to be considered at the top. Some high-level volunteers should also be included. The secondary elites are busy but more reachable. They are as well informed as the top elites but generally have less power.

Looking at the positions held is a first and simple step toward identifying members of the elites and distinguishing between top and secondary levels. However, many top officeholders are essentially passive in carrying out their functions. The real "movers and shakers" are often in lower positions, hustling to implement their ideas and parlaying their limited power resources into significant influence. A definition that looks for this kind of behavior is better but harder to implement than a positional analysis. Elites of both levels belong to many organizations and contribute to them and to candidates; they are usually to some extent politically active and nearly always vote. Many additional distinctions can be made about the various kinds of power and shifts of power among elites.

The distinction between secondary and top elites, while vague, is nevertheless very important. In our desire to understand reality, we are constantly tempted to oversimplify it to make our task easier. We may seek to explain how things work by attributing great power to a few people—the president, a few congressmen, the corporate leaders, the military brass. It is more difficult to understand how their actions are tightly constrained by other top elites and by the capabilities of their secondary elites and their institutions. Power resides not in individuals but in organization. The secondary elites supply the top elites with information and ideas needed to make decisions; they carry out the decisions made. While the top elite can usually choose who will be under them, they are also constrained by the abilities of those chosen. For example, the chief executive of a large organization can get as frustrated in trying to influence it as a complete outsider. Conspiracy theories imply great power to a few people acting in secrecy; they miss the point about how important the political environment is.

It is too easy to blame our problems on a few people. In reality, the few with power are an integral part of a larger consensus that legitimizes and effectuates their decisions. The style and character of an age are not set by a few personalities but by a much larger group: the secondary elite. This group, still small in percentage terms, adds up to several million people. They make history as much as, perhaps even more than, either a top elite or the lower strata.

The *active citizens* are about a fifth of the adult population, or possibly a fourth of adults if the elites are included. As a separate stratum, however, active citizens come between the elites and the average Americans. They conform to several features of the ideal of democratic citizenship. They hold jobs with less political content than the elites, although it is impossible to draw a precise line where one leaves off and the other begins. Active citizens are fairly well informed in terms of what the media present, and some have special sources of information, making them well informed in certain areas. Like the elites, active citizens have some ability to understand the political issues of the times using a liberal-conservative spectrum. They usually belong to politically active groups and contribute small amounts to them and to candidates. Being interested in politics, talking politics with others, and voting are the hallmarks of the active citizen. Some go beyond this with volunteer activism, varying from the moderate, steady kind to intense involvement in an election or lobby effort, followed by political inaction.

The *average Americans* make up about two-thirds of the adult population and will be discussed in the next section. Briefly, they hold jobs with low political content. They are unevenly to poorly informed, with low or passive information intake. They are generally uninterested in politics; it has to intrude in some obvious way to get to their attention. They vote irregularly or rarely or without thinking too much. They use group interest, party loyalty, or candidate image in voting. They may be members of groups that take political positions, but their role is passive. They do not talk politics very much and rarely give to candidates. Their attitudes may range from loyalty to alienation, but they all have low levels of understanding and participation.

The *apoliticals,* about 10 percent of the adult population, rarely or never vote, have low to no information intake on politics through the media, and have no interest or particular awareness of state or high-level politics. They have few, if any, political discussions. They tend to be isolated by disabilities, in rural areas, by institutions, and by families that take care of their needs. They tend to be poor, uneducated, and members of minorities.[3]

A Closer Look: Socioeconomic Strata

The levels or strata of society are concerned with the same people, but describe different characteristics. Socioeconomic stratification deals with social and economic class. The "social" and the "economic" can be separated, but I will combine them for simplicity, as in the concept of socioeconomic status (SES). SES is a major result of the political system; it concerns the major values society has to distribute and is a way of keeping score in the struggle for prestige and wealth. SES is based mainly on income, occupation, and formal education; it can also include ethnic, religious, racial, and geographic characteristics and even family origins.

SES correlates with political stratification. Higher SES individuals are likely to be higher in political level; however, the correlation is far from perfect. For example, a greater portion of the rich are in the elites than any other SES, and they have the least who are apolitical. Most of the rich, though, are not politically active; they fall into the active citizen and average American strata. Conversely, the poor may have the most apolitical members compared with any other group, but most of them are average Americans and a few are active citizens.

The *rich* are about 4 percent of the population. They can be defined using Internal Revenue Service data on inheritances, which indicate 4 percent of the adult population owning 33 percent of all personally held assets. Other definitions might be a net worth of $100,000 or more, or an income above $40,000 in 1977 for a family of four. The rich typically have at least some income from wealth (rentals, stock, loans, and business ownership) as opposed to income from labor (salaries, wages, and fees). The rich include the hereditary plutocracy, who make up about 20 to 30 percent of this stratum. The rich also include top executives, top professionals, top independent business people and their spouses, and some politicians. The rich are high in education, have prestigious occupations, and enjoy social prestige. Like the top elites, they are usually white and of Anglo or Northern European extraction.

The *upper middle class* is about 15 percent of the population and has a cut-off of about $25,000 for a family of four in 1977. The upper middle class derives most of its income from labor, usually from well-paid jobs in management, the professions, and technical work with corporations, government, their own business, or nonprofit institutions. They are also highly educated and usually white. Many attain this level by having both husband and wife working.

These two groups, the rich and the upper middle class, constitute about 20 percent of the population. Taken together, they can be called the *affluent*.

The *middle class* includes over half the population, with 1977 incomes ranging from $10,000 to $25,000 for a family of four. These are general estimates. A family at the top end in a low cost of living area who owned their own home could be considered upper middle, while a family at the low end in a high cost of living area should really be considered near poor. Most of the income comes from labor in white-collar and blue-collar occupations paid well above the minimum wage. Often both spouses work, though one may only be employed part time, part year, or at a low wage. Educational levels range from high school through college. More minorities are included in this category than in the previous two.

The *near poor,* perhaps a fifth of the population, had 1977 incomes of $6,000 to $10,000 for a family of four. The near poor are really poor by the standards of those better off but do not suffer absolute deprivation and are doing well by world standards. The near poor earn most of their money at poorly paid jobs and part-year or part-time work. There are higher levels of disability, physically and mentally, and higher rates of dependency—that is, the number of children, the elderly, and disabled in relation to the number employed. Employment is less likely to be unionized and more likely to be at or near the minimum wage in blue-collar, service, and farm jobs. Education levels tend to be high school or less, and the number of minorities and female-headed households is disproportionate to their number in the general population.

The *poor* are less than 10 percent of the population and probably only about 6 percent. Their 1977 income for a nonfarm family of four in 1977 was below $6,000 including welfare, food stamps, Medicare, and Medicaid income. This income, called *transfer income,* puts many families into the near-poor category. Most of the poor are children, the old, women heads of households with preschool children, and the disabled. Unemployment rates are high. Education is typically less than high school. There is a disproportionate number of minorities. The poor suffer absolute deprivations, such as inadequate food, unhealthy housing, poor sanitation, ineffective schools, minimal health services, and high rates of victimization by crime.

The Average American

Politically, the elites are characterized by what they do; the people, by what they do not do. The hallmark of elites is political action; of the people, political inaction. The average American is characterized by a lack of interest in politics, which results in low levels of political conceptualization, little effort to seek information, minimal knowledge, apolitical attitudes and values, nonvoting, and low political activity. The data presented below come from academic research and opinion polls, but a similar impression can be obtained by going door to door campaigning for a candidate or ballot issue.

Political apathy does not mean that average Americans are apathetic in general. Quite the contrary, Americans are actively committed in many ways. However, these commitments are primarily nonpolitical. They include family, work, education, church, health, leisure pursuits, and so on. Our lives are so full of these commitments that political concerns are crowded out. Young people are especially busy getting educations, earning money, growing up, forming families, pursuing recreation and entertainment, and generally discovering themselves and the world. Yet even among young adults, it is evident that such commitment is a result of learning to be interested in some things rather than others. This section will examine various aspects of the political thinking and behavior of the average American.

Political Conceptualization

One way to evaluate the political competency of citizens is to ask them their reasons for supporting a particular party or preferring a particular candidate in presidential elections. These reasons can be categorized into several types of conceptualization or ways of thinking about politics. See table 1–2.

Ideology means use of a liberal-conservative spectrum for understanding many differences among policies, candidates, and parties. *Near ideology* is a fragmentary or partial use of such ideology. Some notion of a liberal-conservative spectrum is essential to an understanding of American politics. The liberal and conservative labels are used extensively by participants and in the media, and they reflect a major, perhaps the major, general policy division among elites. The number of people able to use ideology seems to have increased steadily since 1956, probably because of an emphasis on ideological differences in the elections of 1964 and 1972 and the increasing education of the electorate. However, these people are mostly those in the participant strata of elites and active citizens, not average Americans.

These figures must be used with caution, however. The data for 1964

Table 1–2 Citizen Conceptualization for Candidate Preference

	1956	*1968*	*1972*	*1964*
Ideology	3%	6%	7%	16%
Near ideology	10	17	20	
Group benefits	44	33		
Nature of the times	25	25		
No issue content	18	20		

Sources: 1956 and 1968: Philip Converse, "Public Opinion and Voting Behavior," in *Nongovernmental Politics,* vol. 4, *Handbook of Political Science,* Fred Greenstein and Nelson Polsby, eds. (Reading, Mass.: Addison Wesley, 1975), p. 102. 1972: Arthur Miller and Warren Miller, "Ideology in the 1972 Election: Myth or Reality—A Rejoinder," *American Political Science Review,* September 1976, 844. 1964: John Pierce, "Party Identity and the Changing Role of Ideology in American Politics," *Midwest Journal of Political Science,* February 1970, pp. 25–42. See also Angus Campbell et al., *The American Voter* (New York: Wiley, 1964), chap. 9, and Norman Nie et al., *The Changing American Voter* (Cambridge: Harvard University Press, 1976), chap. 7.

in the table were derived from a methodology different from that of the other years. The interviewers asked people to define "conservative" and identify which party was more conservative. At a maximum 16 percent were able to do so, similar to the results four years before and four years later.[4] Furthermore, in other research when people who used ideology in thinking about politics were asked to guess which party was more conservative, 10 percent of the near ideologues and 4 percent of the ideologues were unwilling to do so, and 9 percent of the ideologues who did so guessed wrong.[5] Much recent research seems to exaggerate the ability of voters to use ideology effectively.

Group benefits conceptualizes the reason for candidate preference in terms of benefits to the voter's group, such as farmers, poor people, workers, businessmen, or housewives. This approach is rational but has little room for some concept of the public interest or other diverse and important issues.

Nature of the times is another phrase to describe how voters think about their political decisions. A voter may refer nebulously to the nature of the times; for example, a voter who thinks the times are "good" votes for the incumbent, or if they are "bad," votes for the challenger. Other nature-of-the-times voters are concerned with solely a personal issue—perhaps their social security check, graft, mudslinging, or stopping tests of bombs—and can think of no other reason. Many people in this category simply plead ignorance of politics, and many are unhappy with the parties for criticizing each other.

No issue content voters cannot relate their votes to issues at all. Some are party loyalists but are unable to explain why. Others like a candidate's image—perhaps his or her appearance, voice, religion, family, apparent sincerity, or popularity. Some mix these two reasons. Some can think of no reasons for a vote at all. They are not hostile to the interviewer; they just cannot think of anything to say.

In summary, about 20 percent of American adults at most seem able to use ideology, the highest level of conceptualization. About 40 percent use a rational but narrow group-benefits approach. And about 40 percent are vague, idiosyncratic, or have reasons unrelated to issues.

Political Knowledge and Information

Most people lack information about politics that could lead to effective action, or they are misinformed and act against their own values. Lengthy interviews have revealed that most people have fairly coherent, complex, and meaningful world views for their immediate situations, but they lack much perception of the larger political system.

Thirty-eight percent of Americans, for example, do not know that the Congress is composed of the House and the Senate.[6] Fifty-nine percent do not know the name and party of their representative in Congress. Most people can identify themselves on a liberal-conservative spectrum but do not know what the terms mean. Sixty percent feel uninformed about what is going on in Washington and 72 percent feel uninformed about state politics. Sixty-three percent do not try to keep up on politics. Sixty-four percent do not know the names and parties of their two senators. Even larger numbers do not know who their state legislators, city council members, county supervisors, school district trustees, or special district representatives are, or where any of them stand, or what the issues are. In May 1976, after four months of campaigning by presidential candidates, over half of the voters could not identify their favorite candidate's position on any of the five major issues.[7] It seems likely that even more knew no positions of the other candidates.

Information on challengers is even lower than that on incumbents for congressional races, decreasing the ability of voters to compare candidates. If people care about an issue, however, they are likely to get information and use it in voting. A major example of citizen effectiveness is white opposition to school busing. Racial issues often have this unusual salience.

The problem is still larger, however. About 75 percent of the people cannot name any provision of the Bill of Rights, and few would sign it if asked. Sixty percent hold the mistaken belief that the Constitution guarantees a college education. Fourteen percent of the people cannot think of any problem facing government, and only 23 percent can think of more than three problems. People tend not to know how much taxes they pay, for what services, or with what benefit, but they nevertheless believe that taxes are too high and that all government is inefficient. This attitude, based on lack of knowledge, does a disservice to the reality. We also tend to be unaware of how rich we are in relation to less-developed countries and unaware that our control over world food exports is greater than OPEC's control over world oil exports.

No one person is really well informed about what is going on; there is simply too much happening. Yet even when we try to set a low criterion, it is still too demanding for most Americans. Unless citizens have information, they cannot hold elected officials directly accountable.

Attitudes and Values toward Politics

"Politics" has a bad reputation with most Americans, fostered by elites and the media who put the label on politics they do not like. *Business* conveys useful work rather than profiteering, but *politics* suggests manipulating others for one's own political and pecuniary advantage rather than public service. Politicians are seen as untrustworthy and unprincipled, as glib but shallow human beings.

We have a natural tendency to assume that the problems with which we are not familiar are somehow much simpler than the ones we know firsthand at home, at work, and at school. It is easy to assume that there must be good people who can solve the problems were it not for "politicians" and "bureaucrats." These feelings are especially common when people have strong but one-sided opinions and feel that the political process is frustrating them.

People tend not to blame themselves. For example, polls show that the number of people who believe that government is "run by a few big interests" rose from 29 percent to 70 percent between 1965 and 1975. An index of feelings of powerlessness rose from 29 percent to 55 percent between 1966 and 1973. But the polls did not find out what people were doing to remedy the situation.[8] With the Vietnam War and Watergate behind us, there may be some recovery of confidence, but there is little indication of any large increase in the kind of seriousness and permanence of commitment to solving problems that would produce the reforms most people want.

Some additional attitudes of Americans are brought to bear in voting; the most important are partisanship and candidate image. Party identification alone can predict 77 percent of the votes, although this includes people who have issue reasons for candidate preference.[9] Usually party feelings, often vague and weak, play a powerful role, especially for the less-publicized partisan offices of the House of Representatives, state legislatures, and some local governments. Party identification is a kind of shorthand; it simplifies politics and makes it seem manageable. However, party identification does not relate at all well to people's feelings about where they think they stand on a liberal-conservative spectrum. See table 1–3.

For many reasons not well understood by political scientists, Republicans have been declining in numbers. In 1977 only 20 percent of the population identified themselves as Republicans. Conversely the Democrats have been rising gradually in number, getting support from 49 percent of the population in 1977. Independents have risen a little faster, reaching 31 percent by 1977.[10] At the same time, the number of people calling themselves "liberals" has declined, and the "conservatives" have increased. There are many other aspects of party identification, but the problem here is to try to find any strong connections with issues.[11]

An additional reason for candidate preference emerges at the presidential level where media coverage is sufficient to develop candidate images in voters' minds. Some research indicates that image—a perception of personal qualities like honesty, ability, or popularity—is even more important than partisanship.[12] Issues are important in voting but seem to come third after partisanship and candidate image.

Voting and Other Behavior

Voting is the most widespread, clearly political act committed by most Americans. It is also important as the means by which the elites will accept

Table 1–3 Partisanship and Affective Ideology, 1972

Affective Self-Identification	*Party Identification*			
	Democratic	*Independent*	*Republican*	*Total*
Liberal	13%	11%	3%	27%
Middle of the road	15	12	8	35
Conservative	10	12	15	37
Total	38	35	26	99

Note: Most people cannot define *liberal* or *conservative*.

Source: William H. Flanagan and Nancy H. Zingale. *Political Behavior of the American Electorate,* 3d ed. (Boston: Allyn and Bacon, 1975), p. 114.

change in leadership without bloodshed. Historically, voting has expanded to include more kinds of people—women, youth, and minorities—and more offices, and it has become easier, more efficient, and more honest. Now top executive and legislative officials at all levels of government, and even some state and local judges, are elected by the people.

Most people, however, do not vote in most elections. Only in the presidential elections do almost two-thirds of the number eligible vote. This figure, of course, means that one-third of the voters can determine the majority will. Yet the fact that about two-thirds turn out for presidential elections does not mean that average Americans are voting at that rate. Since the participant one-fourth is voting at a very high rate, the rate for average Americans is somewhat lower.

The elites also understand better than the average American where their self-interest lies, and thus concentrate their votes. The active-citizen group is generally higher in SES than the average Americans and therefore more coopted by the elites. As a result, their voting, combined with other efforts to influence elections, can usually succeed in electing a favorable candidate.

Presidential primaries and elections for governors of large states, mayors of big cities, and congressmen usually have much lower turnouts than do presidential elections. Local elections and lesser other races have still lower participation. Ironically, the further government is from the people, the more interest they seem to take in it. Local government, supposedly closest to the people, is often controlled by 5 to 10 percent of the voters, a kind of voting elite, and state legislatures may be controlled by little more.

This irony seems best explained by the mass media: the more it pays attention to an institution or office, the greater the turnout. People see and hear more about the presidency than any other office, and thus they know and care more about it. Congress as a whole is paid a lot of attention, but its individual members get on average far less, creating a strong awareness of Congress but little awareness of congressmen. The mass media cannot easily cover 535 members of Congress. The problem is that people do not seek out or even know how to find specialized sources on their representatives.

Perhaps the most important political act of most people is *not voting*. Nonvoters can be identified by examining voter turnouts, which are exceptionally low for blacks and Spanish-origin people. In 1974, 46 percent of whites voted, but only 34 percent of blacks and 23 percent of Spanish origin did so. Nonvoters also tend to be unemployed, with a lower income, lower occupation, less educated, from single parent families, women, the old, and the young. In 1972 60 percent of those eighteen to twenty did not vote; in 1974 the percentage was 79.[13] Most nonvoters (70 percent) tend to have a low net preference; that is, their likes and dislikes, if any, about candidates and parties tend to cancel each other out.[14] For example, a like for the Republican party might be canceled by a dislike of Nixon's image. People who lean to one party are less likely to vote than those who identify more strongly, and independents vote even less. There is no evidence that non-voting is correlated with knowledge or information; in fact the reverse is true. Those who most need to vote to improve their socioeconomic status are least likely to do so.

People give various reasons for not voting. In November 1976, 11.5 percent of adults said they were registered but did not vote because of illness, an emergency, were not at home, had to work, lacked transportation, did not want to stand in long lines at the polls, or were faced with delays because of broken voting machines (in that order of importance); 25.1 percent were unable to register to vote, mainly because of lack of citizenship but also because of residency requirements, "not getting around to it," illness or disability, lack of transportation, inconvenient registration office hours, not knowing where or when, and lack of English. The reasons of 36 percent, mostly unregistered, were not ascertained; 27.3 percent, mostly unregistered, were not interested, did not like the candidates, or for some other reason did not want to vote.[15]

Voting is an easily measured action, but the act itself is a result of a much larger and harder to measure matrix of action and thought. The quality of voting depends on information. We really know very little about *information habits*—what people see, how much time they take, what they are interested in, what they remember.

We have not thought much about how to evaluate the adequacy of information intake. There is far too much information available; we could spend all of our time reading and cover only a fraction of it. What is a reasonable amount of time? What are the best sources of information? These questions receive attention in chapter 7 but for now we will look at what people actually do.

About two-thirds of the people rely on television news.[16] But television rarely covers candidates for minor offices, and even candidates for major offices often get only a few minutes of exposure. Because of the brief exposure, candidates rely on trying to project an image. They can, of course, buy time on the networks to put across their position, but media time is expensive. Similarly, special broadcasts may help, but fewer people are watching.

Television news is, essentially, a kind of headline service. But even its headlines are largely useless for issue voting. The most popular news programs in the San Francisco Bay Area consist of 22 percent commercials, 13 percent sports, 10 percent weather, 9 percent chat among newscasters such as "teases," "leadins," and "happy talk," and 46 percent international, national, state, and local news. Each news story lasts an average of twenty-nine seconds, and 55 percent of news time relates to sex, fire, crime, and other human-interest stories. Serious news takes up about a fifth of programming time.[17] One study found that 72 percent of the evening news from January through October 1976 on the presidential campaign focused on who was winning or losing, strategy, crowds, campaign events, and other events not related to issues. Only 27 percent was on candidate issues and backgrounds and issue-related items.[18] Finally, what little coverage there is on issues is often biased by the mild liberalism that is the milieu of the national television news society.

Newspapers are a more adequate source of information; they have much more news at all levels. We know that about half of the population says it uses newspapers "a great deal," but we do not know any details (for example, how thoroughly they read them, what items they read, or even how much "a great deal" is).[19]

About a fourth of the population claims to use news magazines "a great deal" for political information, but circulation figures indicate that only about 10 to 15 percent of households actually subscribe to them. This group probably overlaps heavily with the elite and active citizen strata. Only 13 percent claim to use special reports and publications a great deal. This category includes opinion magazines, public interest group mailings, newsletters, and bulletins, probably the best sources of detailed information. Lower percentages of people use other sources.[20] In general it seems that the elites and active citizens have information habits that allow them to be effective, while average Americans do not. At best, the media are erratic searchlights—illuminating first one, then another problem—but usually passing on before effective action can be mobilized.

Group membership is another activity that has potential for political effectiveness. Most people belong to something: 55 percent belong to churches, 26 percent to social groups, 23 percent to school organizations, 21 percent to charitable groups, 14 percent to fraternal orders, 11 percent to sports groups, 9 percent to cultural or arts groups, and 7 percent to fan or boosters clubs, all of which are usually nonpolitical. Economic self-interest is the most powerful motivator of politically relevant group memberships—14 percent in professional organizations, 10 percent in business organizations, and 16 percent in labor unions—which combined makes upwards of 40 percent of the population.[21] However, many of these groups are relatively nonpolitical, and many members, especially in unions, join but do not participate. About 14 percent join civic groups and 12 percent join political clubs.[22] Statistics are not available on public-interest group membership, but it is probably less than 5 percent and may be as low as 1 percent. The vast majority of Americans do not join voluntarily any group for political purposes. Such memberships seem to be largely confined to the elite and active citizen strata.

Another political activity is *giving money to candidates*. Small amounts from even half the population would be greater than the money the elite usually raises, but most people give nothing. Only 11 percent give any money to presidential candidates every four years.

Other activities such as writing to the editor or to an officeholder, actively campaigning, attending a political coffee, dinner, rally, or other meeting, or even wearing a button or having a bumper sticker are activities generally confined to the top 20 percent or so of political stratification. At the most informal level, less than a third have tried to persuade someone else how to vote.[23] Most people at some time in their lives may do one or more of these things, but participation is sporadic.

In what way do you fit into these statistics?

Reform

Our attitudes toward the American political system, elites, and average Americans are strongly influenced by how well we think the system is performing. Many people, especially those higher in SES, are relatively content, even complacent, about the system because they feel it is doing well, at least as far as their immediate concerns go. There are grounds for self-congratulation. The American system by world standards has perhaps the highest general standard of living and of civil liberties of any nation and has made the greatest contributions to science, technology, social science, and even the arts and humanities. America is still the land of opportunity, so much so that millions of people come here illegally to seek their fortunes. We have more educational opportunity for more people than any other country. We have great social, geographic, and occupational mobility. We have huge programs to assist the needy. The vast majority of people are happy with the health services they receive and with the quality of their neighborhoods. Little wonder, then, that radical ideologies have so little appeal.

By other standards, unfortunately, the system is doing poorly. The United States (and the Soviet Union) are by far the most militaristic countries in the world. The rich enjoy arbitrary privileges, allowing many of them, perhaps most, to escape fair and effective taxation. We suffer from chronic inflation and serious hard-core unemployment, lack of free competition, and inadequate consumer protection. Overpopulation, resource extraction, overconsumption, pollution, and poor planning are destroying our environment. Poverty, racism, sexism, crime, health, and education are serious problems. Our civil liberties were severely endangered by war and Watergate. Our institutions still allow excessive influence by monied interests. They need to be far more democratic and efficient.

The roots of these problems lie in characteristics of the elites and the people. The vested interest elites are preoccupied with material gain. Making money and the bottom line (profits) is of primary importance not only for elites as business people but also for elites as people. Human and environmental suffering and the quality of our culture and society are of secondary importance. The people are similarly materialistic but less successful at it. Institutional aggrandizement is a dominant value of the nonprofit and public sectors. When a powerful institution is unchecked, problems occur, whether it be excessive power of military elites or a big hospital complex or a university expanding into a disadvantaged or middle-class neighborhood. The power of the military, though, is additionally strong because of the militaristic anticommunism of the far right, the fearfulness and machismo of elites and people, the vested interest of defense contractors, the foreign policy influence of the multinational corporations, and Soviet militarism. But there are other root causes also, such as our ignorance in many policy areas, the inertia and prejudice of human thinking, and the problems that individuals create for themselves.

It is fashionable to attack the elites for all the ills of our system, to blame the corporations, the unions, the government. In a milder form, elite politicians proclaim that other elite politicians have failed and that they, the good leaders, will restore public confidence. These approaches reaffirm the centrality of the elites. Many reformers and academics fall easily into the same trap, identifying where the superstructure needs repair.

Ironically, hardly anyone in this democracy talks about the responsibility of the people, as if whatever goes wrong can be blamed on someone else. The people, of course, are not totally responsible; that would go to the opposite extreme.

This book is based on the idea that only the citizen can protect the citizen. It is not useful to blame elites for the characteristics of the people. The passivity of most people provides a vacuum in which elites implement their myths and values, despite their own many nonpolitical members and internal conflicts.

Another premise is that successful reform does not require that everyone be active. Reform occurs even now. Getting more may be possible with small increases in the number of people willing to work for it. The way to turn average Americans into committed citizens depends not so much on exhortation as on information and on learning from successful reforms.

Our system allows small but meaningful changes, which can be generated by reformers using both elite and popular attitudes. Popular apathy itself allows those who do act to have more impact. Elite positive values can win general elite support for change when publicity reveals hypocrisy or misbehavior by specific elites.

Would-be reformers have their own problems: oversimplifying, paternalism, self-righteousness. If the problems had more obvious solutions, they would probably be solved. Reformers are probably most helpful when they present information and ideas that allow others to develop their thinking. The public does not think too deeply about many public problems. For example, many people say that they are against welfare but in favor of aid to needy children and the aged. This type of aid identifies most of the welfare program. Many people are also critical of what they label "social programs"; but at the same time, they think that government should be the employer of last resort, itself a costly social program. Most people favor gun control but do not know where their elected representatives stand on the issue. And most want to close tax loopholes but not "destroy incentives" for business and employment.

When asked to balance values, people produce interesting answers. On the question of whether we prefer to pay more for goods to end pollution or prefer lower prices and pollution, 60 percent supported environmental reform and only 22 percent lower prices. This was asked in the midst of the 1975 recession. Do we want pollution control devices or lower car prices? Forty-eight percent for control, 38 percent for lower prices. Do we want to regulate strip mines or lower electrical rates? Forty-three percent for controls, 41 percent for cheaper electricity.[24] This kind of balancing is what reformers do: they look at both sides of an issue and make informed, difficult choices. In the examples just given, the plurality of opinions supported the reform position.

In 1971 the National Urban Coalition published *Counterbudget,* which struck a balance among a large number of reform goals and showed in a practical way how they could be achieved. The coalition is a large group of organizations concerned with urban, racial, and poverty issues, and its proposals mainly dealt with those issues. The proposals were expressed in terms of an alternative budget for the federal government. They were moderate ideas widely discussed in the United States and were law in many European countries. *Counterbudget* programs included public-service jobs, training, less military spending, welfare reform, national health insurance, programs for the aged, education reform, revenue sharing, tax reform, urban development, mass transit, ending subsidies, environmental reforms, family planning, criminal justice reform, civil rights enforcement, consumer protection, antitrust, and foreign aid.

By improved taxes and cutbacks in some programs, the overall impact on the economy was minimal. Federal spending would not have increased as a percentage of gross national product, except for three percentage points increase to pay for national health insurance, which was mostly money previously channeled through private health insurance schemes. *Counterbudget* manifested a consensus among a large number of reform-oriented activists, though not necessarily a majority. It is now out of date but provides some indication of the kinds of improvements that reform could bring. Middle-class family income, for example, would have been about $1,000 a year higher, and poor families, about $2,000. We can speculate that these figures are one way to measure the price of political apathy or the cost of letting the elites manage politics.[25]

The Problem of Intensity

We do not have simply a problem of apathy. A more objective approach uses the important concept of *intensity*. As citizens, dozens, even hundreds, of issues that affect us are being processed by dozens of governmental institutions. A few interests, usually not particularly political (like family, work, and education) have high intensity for us. This means that they are very important to us and demand our priority attention. Even active citizens can follow only a few issues with medium intensity. Hence, while most of us might like to see a change made, it may be too unimportant in relation to our other priorities to motivate action. Meanwhile, those few who feel intensely (usually those with a narrow economic gain) take effective action. Even the elites' consensus is not always strong enough to police single elites, who may differ from the general elite and popular values. Elites and people alike have an intensity problem.

Reformers partially overcome the intensity problem in a number of ways. The first step is to enlarge our understanding of how we fit into the system and how the system affects us. Reformers have an expanded concept of their self-interest. There may be some altruism involved, but more important is the enlightenment of their selfishness. Effective action flows naturally from their understanding.

Defining the Reformers

Just as elites and people have many diverse interests, so do reformers. Some are primarily concerned with security issues, trying to counterbalance the power of the military-industrial complex and thus reduce the probability of nuclear war, conventional war, and wasted resources. Others are more concerned with economic problems like taxation, inflation, unemployment, or consumer protection. Still others spend their time on an environmental issue—saving wilderness, controlling population, reducing pollution, or regulating urban and transportation developments. Others concentrate on poverty, racism, sexism, crime, health, or education. Some focus on institutional issues like civil liberties, campaign finance reform, or governmental reorganization. Some concentrate on local affairs, others the state, the nation, or international affairs. Some are campaigners, others lobbyists. Active citizens may have time for none of the above but still are conscientious in seeking information, writing letters, voting, and other less time-consuming activities.

Just as the degree of consensus among elites is elusive, so is the degree of consensus among reformers. It is common to find people who favor a reduction in military spending, the reform of taxes, fiscal restraint against inflation, an increase in public service jobs, the development of better information for consumers, environmental protection, population control, welfare reform, affirmative action, and so on down the list of problems that we will be discussing. However, there are not enough such people to form an identifiable group. Although there is a kind of conservative consensus for business and the status quo and a kind of liberal consensus for various reforms, there are many exceptions and much diversity of views.

The elites-reformers-people distinction becomes much more useful when discussing each issue area. Then there is more of an identifiable elite contending with more specific reformers who specialize on the issue.

Politically, reformers are found in the participant strata (active citizens, secondary elites, and top elites). Some are in the elites in the sense of participation but not in the sense of supporting dominant policy. We need to introduce a new distinction, a new spectrum from left to right, to overlay on the stratification system. There are many ways of defining this spectrum. The dominant one is liberal-conservative, which is especially applicable to economic and social policy but less so to security and environmental policy. Reformers are generally liberals, but the term is too elusive for us to use. The content shifts as conditions and leading ideas change. Some conservatives advocate reform on particular issues. Some liberals specialize in criticizing liberalism.

We will use an "elites-reform" distinction, in which *elites* refers to dominant or power-holding elites who defend institutional and economic vested interests, and *reformers* refers to those seeking what will be defined as reform in each issue area. On the periphery of struggle in each issue area are the other elites, other reformers, and the people.

Just as there is partial conflict and partial agreement among the interests of elites and people, so also are there overlaps among reformers and elites and among reformers and people. But because of the intensity problem, overlaps of interest among all three do not necessarily produce corresponding policy. The elites and reformers agree, for example, on the rule of law and on democratic procedures, but specific elites have violated them. In these cases, reformers seek to activate values of the general elite to discipline a specific elite. The people, while supporting law and democracy in principle, do not understand them well enough to make them work. The elites know how these principles work in practice because they use them in their internal competition and political activities. In other cases, reformers may try to activate popular values in elections to achieve a reform unpopular with the elites. Examples could come from the antiwar movement of the late 1960s and early 1970s and from the environmental movement. Yet another variation is to mobilize both general elites and popular sentiment against abuses of a specific elite. Examples could come from the civil-rights movement of the late 1950s and early 1960s and from the environment.

Reformers lack the power to be effective alone or in the normal course of events. They cannot counter both elites and people at the same time, and they often suffer the frustration of being ahead of their times. They have to maximize their leverage by finding as many allies as possible and taking advantage of events. Fundamental change is too difficult for them to achieve, but the possible marginal changes can be meaningful. They can use leverage for gradual change.

Think about how we are spending our time and what our values are. With all of our commitments, it is probably extremely difficult to include politics among our activities. For younger people in college, this may be very appropriate; it is a good time to gain self-confidence and maturity and to do the extensive learning desirable to get some impression of how everything works and what is worthwhile. This fundamental understanding can motivate long-term effective commitment. But it is fairly easy never to become involved. Commitment takes too much time, we cannot really be sure we are right, and we are not sure what to do. The problem is not elite power, but how we almost willingly allow ourselves to be neutralized.

Reform requires not just more participation but participation of a higher quality. Elites, people, and reformers are all up against the very real limits of human nature—our energy, our intelligence, our openness to ideas, our compassion, our capacity for growth and commitment.

No capsule description of the system can capture its complexities and ambiguities. Radicals would emphasize instead the elite power, elite consensus, discrepancy of elite interests from the people's, the selfishness and militarism of those interests, and the potential for and virtue of popular power. Moderates might stress the opposite—the depth and relevance of elite divisions for popular choice, the inherent intractability of the problems themselves, and the influence, sometimes negative, of popular forces.

American democracy falls short of the ideal because people are generally unaware of the choices they have, do not vote or vote with impoverished conceptualizations and little knowledge, do not undertake other citizen activities, and are not much concerned beyond their own immediate personal problems. We have a procedural democracy in which the vote plays an important role, but as part of a plural elite system. The elites have a consensus on the rule of law and compromise, which allows coherent policy to be made despite pluralistic institutions and conflict. The elites use a number of mechanisms to influence the people, such as cooption, the media, law, politics, nondecision making, and anticipated reactions. But fundamentally most people do not take much interest in politics.

Reform-oriented people do not let rationalizations about the difficulty undermine all participation. Instead they take advantage of conditions of the elites and people to attain useful reforms that improve their own and others' lives. Although it might seem desirable to change the people, it is more realistic to try to increase the number committed to reform, thus producing significant leverage for more reform. The system is complex; it has much stratification and overlaps of interest, as well as conflict among elites, people, and reformers. Reform involves a complex balancing of values, to which we now turn.

Notes

1. John Sullivan and Robert O'Connor, "Electoral Choice and Popular Control of Public Policy," *American Political Science Review*, December 1972, pp. 1256–1268.
2. Ibid.
3. Kenneth Prewitt and Sidney Verba, *An Introduction to American Government*, 2d ed. (New York: Harper and Row, 1976), present a different political stratification. They identify 11 percent as complete activists, 15 percent as campaign activists, 20 percent as active locally and socially but not very political, 4 percent as regular voters who may contact officials on personal problems, 21 percent as voters who take no other part in politics, 22 percent as irregular voters and politically inactive, and 7 percent as unclassifiable. The first two categories, however, seem too large. See Sidney Verba and Norman Nie, *Participation in America* (New York: Harper and Row, 1972).
4. Informational ideologues from John Pierce, "Party Identity," *Midwest Journal of Political Science* (February 1970): 32. Consistency from 1960 to 1968 is indicated by Pierce according to Philip Converse, "Public Opinion," *Nongovernmental Politics*, vol. 4, *Handbook of Political Science* (Reading, Mass.: Addison Wesley, 1975).
5. Arthur Miller and Warren Miller, "Ideology," *American Political Science Review*, September 1976, p. 845.
6. Louis Harris and Associates, *Confidence and Concern: Citizens View American Government* (Cleveland: Regal Books, 1974), pp. 17–18. This study, performed for the Committee on Government Operations, was based on a poll of 1,596 people in two hundred locations in September and October 1973. Unless otherwise noted, the figures cited here are from this source.
7. *Hayward* (Calif.) *Daily Review*, June 3, 1976, from Associated Press.
8. Harris and Associates, *Confidence and Concern*, p. 6.

9. Stanley Kelley, Jr., and Thad W. Mirer, "The Simple Act of Voting," *American Political Science Review,* June 1974, pp. 575–576.
10. *San Francisco Chronicle,* August 22, 1977, from the Gallup Poll.
11. There are connections, but they seem weak to me. These issues are debated in the January 1972 issue of the *American Political Science Review,* in which several authors argue for stronger conclusions than seem justified by their figures.
12. David Repass, "Issue Salience and Party Choice," *American Political Science Review,* June 1971, p. 400, and *Hayward* (Calif.) *Daily Review,* June 3, 1976. Repass found standardized regression coefficients of 0.39 for candidate image, 0.23 for issues, and 0.27 for party identification, in each case controlling for the other two variables. The higher the coefficient, the greater its explanatory power.
13. *San Francisco Chronicle,* January 4, 1973; U.S. Bureau of the Census, *Current Population Reports,* Series P-20, no. 275 (January 1975) and no. 304 (December 1976).
14. Kelley and Mirer, "Simple Act," p. 577.
15. Bureau of the Census, *Current Population Reports,* Series P-20, no. 304, p. 6.
16. Harris and Associates, *Confidence and Concern,* pp. 19–20.
17. *San Francisco Bay Guardian,* November 7, 1975, pp. 6–10.
18. Thomas Patterson and Robert McClure, *The Unseeing Eye* (New York: Putnam, 1976), p. 41.
19. Harris and Associates, *Confidence and Concern,* pp. 19–20.
20. Ibid.
21. Ibid., p. 21.
22. Ibid.
23. Survey Research Center, University of Michigan, poll of 1964 election; Lester Milbraith, *Political Participation* (Chicago: Rand McNally, 1965), pp. 18–19.
24. Brock Evans, "Backlash? What Backlash?" *Sierra Club Bulletin,* November-December 1975, p. 19, using an Opinion Research Corp. poll of August 1975.
25. National Urban Coalition, *Counterbudget* (New York: Praeger, 1971), p. 10.

2

The Economies of Vested Interests

All problems have economic aspects, but some seem more economic than others. We can call these *macroeconomic* questions. All problems also have international aspects, but we will focus largely on domestic issues. First, we will look at the overall system of taxes and transfers, which is the major way government reallocates resources between public and private sectors and among and within levels of personal income. We will ask whether the tax system is fair and efficient. Second, we will look at inflation and ask how we can stabilize prices. The third issue is unemployment. We will look at the relationship between inflation and unemployment; try to determine what the unemployment rate really measures; and ask what should be done about hard-core unemployment. Finally, we will examine the degree of competitiveness in the free marketplace and address the issue of what needs to be done to enhance competition and protect consumers.

Subsidizing Some of the Affluent

The major element of unfairness in the redistribution of income by taxes and transfers is that a large number of affluent people escape effective taxation. The affluent *on average* pay about the same portion of their income to all taxes as those of moderate and middle incomes, and the very highest in income pay just a little more. *Some* of the affluent, however, use loopholes and other inequities to pay less, often far less, in taxes than the average working family. Some of the affluent, by the same token, seem to be paying far more than the average in their income category.

Reformers do not want taxes to level the rich down to middle-class levels, but they do favor *progressive* taxes, which means that as income goes up, the percentage of income paid in taxes should go up. The primary principle should be ability to pay. Taxation can also be *proportional,* where all incomes pay the same percentage in taxes, and it can be *regressive,* where the percentage paid in taxes goes down as income goes up. Conservatives generally favor proportional or regressive systems, liberals favor some degree of progressivity, and radicals favor leveling. Progressivity attempts to balance two values: preserving the incentive to work and raising tax money from those who can afford to pay.

The tax system is vital for the kind of society we have. America is distinctive for its sense of social equality even though incomes may vary. Disparities of wealth—especially those that go on year after year and decade after decade and are not based on ability, work, or luck—arouse ill feeling. These feelings can deepen into class divisions dangerous for democracy, especially if the worse off believe that the affluent are not paying their fair share of taxes.

All societies have sizable disparities of income regardless of their economic organization. In China, for example, public officials have high incomes, they drive limousines, attend banquets, frequent special shops, use recreational facilities, are provided privileged seating on trains and planes, and are paid salaries five to ten times higher than workers receive. Monthly salaries in China in 1975 ranged from $14 to $285.[1] Yet this reality does not seem to inhibit the Chinese from thinking that they have an egalitarian society, and it does not seem to prevent the rest of the world from seeing China in this way. Sweden probably has the greatest equality of income of any country, and most of us have heard complaints about its tax system. Yet Sweden also manages to preserve the incentives that have made it one of the world's richest countries.

The American tax system includes *transfer payments.* Transfer payments are income transferred from government to individuals because of entitlement programs. *Entitlement* means getting the income without having to work directly for it. The major examples are social security, welfare, unemployment compensation, veterans' benefits, food stamps, and Medicare-Medicaid. These programs are services, paid for by taxes, but unlike most other services, they represent personal income to the recipient. About 13 percent of all personal income is transfers.

Market income is not a simple concept. Most of us think in terms of earned income from wages and salary, and this is two-thirds of all personal income. But income also includes other categories: business, professional, and farm income (6.4 percent), rentals (1.6 percent), dividends (2.7 percent), and interest (9.6 percent). Market income should also include inheritances, certain gifts, and the gains from selling property and other capital goods. Most of these are counted as income in table 2–1.

The second column in the table shows the *effective tax rate*: the average amount of taxes people in that income category pay as a percentage of total income. The taxes subtracted from income are not just income taxes but also sales and excise taxes, property taxes, social security taxes, corporate income taxes, and estate and gift taxes. Sometimes it is difficult to determine who really pays various taxes. Income taxes are subtracted from the income of the person paying the tax; that seems obvious enough. Sales taxes, however, are not subtracted from the income of the business collecting the tax; they are subtracted from the income of the customer who buys the merchandise. But who pays the property tax—renters or owners? And who pays the corporate income tax—the owners of the corporation or the customers who buys its products? Ideally it would be desirable to know if, for example, the corporation dominated its market and was able to pass on its tax costs to consumers, or, on the other hand, if it sold less and made less profit because of the tax. The question of which income the tax should be subtracted from is the problem of *incidence*. The table assumes that about half of corporate income taxes are passed on to consumers and the other half paid by stockholders and that about half of property taxes are passed on to consumers, with the other half paid by property owners.

The analysis reveals that the American tax system is progressive at the top 0.2 percent of taxpayers, regressive for the bottom 9.9 percent of taxpayers, and proportional for everyone in between—averaging 25.3 percent for everyone from $3,000 a year to $200,000 a year income.[2] The progressiveness at the top is relatively minor and affects few taxpayers. The regressiveness at the bottom is of more concern because it involves a large number of low-income people.

The third column of the table indicates that over half of the income of this lowest category comes from transfers. Transfer income is not subject to federal income tax, and those with low incomes pay very low income tax rates, so it is interesting that the poor pay so much in taxes. One reason is that they cannot escape paying sales taxes and property taxes and, if they earn income, social security taxes. Another reason is that some people have low apparent incomes because they are living off savings, and the spending of savings is not shown in the table.

The Process of Market Income, Taxes, and Transfers

Table 2–1 shows the result of a process that has several steps. The first step is the distribution among income levels of market income before transfers. Most market income is produced by labor in the form of wages and

Table 2–1 Income, Taxes, and Transfers

Income, Including Transfers [a]	*Effective Tax Rates (% Total Income)* [b]	*1964 Transfers (% of Income)* [c]	*% of Units* [d]	
			1971	*1976*
$100,000 and over	29.9% *	0.3%	0.2%	1.5%
$50,000–99,999	26.4	3.3 *	0.8	
$30,000–49,999	24.4	2.2 *	2.4	6.3
$25,000–29,999	24.3	5.3	2.4	5.7
$20,000–24,999	25.1	6.2	5.1	10.0
$15,000–19,999	25.3	4.9 *	12.3	15.5
$10,000–14,999	25.5	5.3 *	23.4	18.7
$5,000–9,999	25.9	7.4 *	31.2	21.9
$3,000–4,999	25.3	18.9 *	12.1	10.2
$0–2,999	28.1	51.8 *	9.9	10.3

Note: Figures marked with an asterisk are estimates.

[a] Pechman and Okner define income as "adjusted family income," which includes earned income, farm and nonfarm proprietors' income, rental income, corporate earnings, interest, transfer payments; accrued capital gains on business inventories, farm assets, and nonfarm real estate; and imputed rent on owner-occupied residences. Excluded are gifts, reported capital gains, and receipts from pension funds. Excluded from "family" are the institutionalized population (usually poor), pension funds, nonprofit organizations, and fiduciaries.

Radner and Hinrichs define income as "family personal income," virtually the same as Pechman and Okner, but there are probably some technical differences, and they included estimates for Medicare and food stamps that Pechman and Okner did not.

[b] Pechman and Okner, p. 59. Variant 3b of the incidence assumptions, which is the maximum case allowed by Pechman and Okner of owners passing taxes on to renters and buyers, is used. They raise the issue of market power (allowing owners to pass taxes on to buyers) but do not make an estimate as to its extent. For several reasons, 3b is the most adequate of their projections. An estimate was made for the top income category by averaging the rates of the top three categories of their table covering the same range of income.

[c] Radner and Hinrichs, pp. 28–29. Estimates from their table average the rates where one of the above categories is represented by two or more of theirs. (*Notes continue on page 37.*)

Table 2–2 Impact of Taxes and Transfers on Income, 1976

Quintile	*Share of Market Income*	*Share of Income after Certain Taxes and Transfers* [a]
Lowest 20%	0.3%	7.2%
Medium low 20%	7.2	11.5
Middle 20%	16.3	16.6
Medium high 20%	26.0	23.4
Highest 20%	50.2	41.3

[a] "Certain taxes" refers to state and federal personal income taxes and employee share of social security taxes.

Source: *Focus,* Fall 1977, p. 6. *Focus* is published by the Institute for Research on Poverty at the University of Wisconsin.

salaries. Some is produced by capital in the form of dividends from stock, interest from credit, rents from property, and gains from the sale of assets. See table 2–2.

Market income is sharply skewed to the high incomes; the affluent receive over half of all of the income. The next step in the process is to tax this income. Taxes amounted to $477 billion in 1976. An additional $95 billion came to government from public utilities, state liquor stores, postal service, education, sewerage, and other sales and charges, interest earnings, and other nontax sources. The gross national product (GNP) was $1,707 billion in 1977, indicating that about 28 percent of it went for taxes. The other sources were 5.6 percent of GNP, making about one-third of GNP altogether. The major taxes are personal income, corporate income, sales (including excise), property, and social security. These were the major sources of governmental taxes in 1976:

Federal and state personal income taxes	33 percent
Social security, employee retirement, unemployment compensation, and other insurance trusts	25 percent

[d] "Units" combines families and unrelated individuals. I have broken down the $25,000–$50,000 incomes by extrapolating from the Bureau of the Census, *Current Population Reports,* p. 19.

Sources: Daniel Radner and John Hinrichs, "Size Distribution of Income in 1964, 1970, and 1971," *Survey of Current Business* 54 (October 1974): 19–31; Joseph Pechman and Benjamin Okner, *Who Bears the Tax Burden?* (Washington, D.C.: Brookings Institution, 1974); U.S. Bureau of the Census, *Current Population Reports,* Series P–60, no. 107 (1977), p. 2.

Sales taxes, including gasoline, alcohol, tobacco, utilities, federal custom, and excise taxes	16 percent
Property taxes (state and local governments only)	12 percent
Federal and state corporate income taxes	10 percent
Inheritance, gift, and death taxes	1.4 percent
Other	2.8 percent

The federal government received 57 percent of all revenues, the states, 25 percent, and localities, 19 percent. The federal government, however, transfers much of its income to the states and localities, leaving it with 42 percent of all revenues.[3] This second step of taxation lowers everyone's income, some more than others, so already some redistribution is taking place.

The third step is to allocate the transfer payments to their recipients according to income level. Some high-income people receive transfers, but most go to the middle- and lower-income groups. The transfer programs cost $176 billion in 1976, or about 37 percent of all taxes. (In sum, about a third of GNP goes to government, but over a third of that comes right back again as transfer income.)

How much do these transfers benefit the poor? Table 2–2 shows that after certain taxes and transfers, the affluent 20 percent are down to 41 percent of total income and the poor 20 percent have come up to 7.2 percent of total income. These 1976 data indicate that the higher-income half of the population is down $142 billion after paying income and social security taxes and receiving transfers, while the lower half has come up $119 billion after the same taxes and transfers. Conservatives typically think that this amount to low-income sectors is enough, even too much; liberals think it too little, especially for the very lowest incomes. We redistribute income enough to place us ahead of France, but we still have a more inequitable distribution than the other Western European countries.[4]

Horizontal equity is fairness within a given level of income, defined as people with a similar income paying a similar amount of taxes. The challenge of reform is to lower taxes on some high incomes and increase taxes on other high incomes by closing loopholes in such a way as to improve horizontal equity and increase moderately the average tax paid. Moderate increases of taxes paid by higher incomes will make the current proportional system into a moderately progressive one. Moderate progressivity is the goal of *vertical equity,* or fairness among different levels of income. Thus, the reforms aimed at horizontal equity can also be used for vertical equity.

Personal Income Taxes

The income tax is the most important tool for achieving horizontal and vertical equity. The task is complicated by the impact of inflation on earned income. The rates of income tax have not been fully adjusted to reflect the loss of purchasing power. Government has been taking a windfall gain. The extra money has gone into many governmental programs people want and to make up for revenues lost because of the increased use of loopholes by persons and corporations.

The income tax is highly progressive. Without it, the system would be highly regressive because state and local taxes are highly regressive. Localities, for example, take 14 percent of incomes under $3,000 but only 4 percent of incomes over $1 million. The federal income tax, on the other hand, takes 14 percent of incomes under $3,000 and 25 percent of those over $1 million.[5]

Yet the progressivity of the income tax is much less than its rates indicate. The actual rates, called the *effective rates,* are much lower than those shown on the tax forms. At $1 million of annual income, the stipulated rate is 68 percent, but the effective rate is only 32 percent. More taxes are, on average, escaped than paid. On average, incomes of $1 million pay 32 percent, but some pay much less and some pay much more. Reformers believe that the stipulated rate can and probably should be lowered from 68 percent; it is too high. They believe that by closing the loopholes, they can actually increase the amount of taxes paid. For example, a fully effective stipulated rate of 40 percent would collect more taxes and be more progressive than the current effective rate of 32 percent. About a third of those with incomes over $30,000 a year pay less taxes than the average rate paid by those in the next lower category. Every year about 20,000 rich families pay less than the average working family. The reason is that they can take advantage of tax loopholes.

The tax system should count as income all earned and property income, allowing deductions only for legitimate nonpersonal business expenses necessarily incurred in obtaining that income. Any deviation from that principle can be called a *loophole.* Officially, loopholes are called *tax expenditures.* The government creates each loophole to achieve some public goal. It thus forgoes that tax income in order to achieve that goal, on which the tax avoider presumably spends the money. How well this system works is rarely asked. The average American does not pay much attention to the problem, and each elite likes the loopholes that benefit it, altogether an excellent illustration of the intensity problem.

For example, the largest government housing program by far has the purpose of encouraging housing investment and home ownership. It subsidizes middle- and upper-income housing, and the more expensive the house, the greater the subsidy. This occurs because home owners can deduct expenses of home mortgage interest and local property taxes on schedule A of form 1040. For years no one knew how much was being spent on this program. Finally reformers were able to require the Treasury Department to collect the necessary information. In 1975 it was revealed that this program cost about $10 billion. The 1980 budget put the cost at $16 billion.

The largest and possibly least justified of loopholes is for long-term capital gains. If you buy something, hold it over one year (six months for commodity futures), and sell it, only 40 percent of your profit counts as income. Included are land, buildings, machinery and equipment, stocks, bonds, and other business assets, including livestock and timber. An example illustrates the loophole, though it is unlikely to occur in real life. Suppose two taxpayers, each married and with four deductions for dependents, file a joint return. One has a salary income, the other only long-term capital gains. Each has an income of $50,000, with no other complications: the salaried worker pays 29 percent; the capital gains worker, only 9 percent. See table 2–3.

One justification for the loophole income is that it provides an incentive to invest, stimulating employment and the economy. But reformers reply that before the loophole, there was no lack of investment and after it, no identifiable increase. The incentive to invest, they hold, should be the free market, not tax subsidies. The actual operations of capital gains stimulate a

Table 2–3 *How Capital Gains Works*

	Salary	*Capital Gain*
Personal income	$50,000	$50,000
Less deduction for capital gain of	0	30,000
Adjusted gross income	50,000	20,000
Less exemptions of	3,000	3,000
Taxable income	47,000	17,000
Tax bracket (rate on last dollar of taxable income)	48%	25%
Tax liability	13,784	2,530
Effective tax rate (% of income paid in income taxes)	28%	5%

Note: This is based on the filing of a joint return with four exemptions for dependents in 1978.

Source: Derived from Internal Revenue Service, *Your Federal Income Tax: 1979 Edition* (Washington, D.C.: Government Printing Office, 1979), pp. 130, 138, 159, 160, back cover.

lot of financial manipulation to deduct expenses from regular income and realize income from a capital gain. The people benefited are those who already have capital; those on salary have to pay such high taxes that they find it much more difficult to save to invest. The loophole essentially disrupts free markets, discriminates against one kind of work and in favor of another, and defends the rich. These arguments against capital gains are derived from basically conservative notions about free markets and equality of opportunity.

Defenders of loopholes also talk about the need for an incentive to work, saying that higher taxes would reduce the incentive. This argument overlooks the equally important role of nonmonetary incentives and the fact that many high-income people pay very high taxes with no evident loss of incentive. Closing loopholes would allow a reduced rate on high incomes, increasing the incentive for some. And basically, the marketplace, not the tax code, should be the incentive to work. The incentive to beat the tax code already wastes the time of able accountants, lawyers, government tax collectors, and others, time that could be spent productively.

In a progressive system, the tax rate rises with taxable income. The *tax bracket* is the rate of tax on the last dollar earned, rising to 70 percent for the highest incomes. Loopholes often involve a deduction, exclusion, or exemption that reduces taxable income. Since higher income people are in higher brackets, they save more than lower income people using the same loopholes. When a rich person gives ten dollars to charity, he or she may save seven dollars in taxes; a middle-income person might save only two or three dollars in taxes. One simple way to reform such loopholes is to allow *credits*—amounts that can be deducted from the tax itself and not from the taxable income. Tax is figured first on the full income. Then ten dollars of credit for charity is the same for all incomes paying ten dollars or more in taxes. This reform could be applied to other loopholes, also.

Each loophole has a special constituency that defends it. For example, interest income from state and local bonds is not taxed at all. This bond-interest exclusion is defended by state and local governments, who benefit $4.5 billion in reduced interest payments while the federal government loses $6 billion in income taxes.[6] The real beneficiaries are wealthy bondholders, who can annually receive a million dollars or more free of income taxes. Another example is the deduction of interest payments on mortgages from taxable income. Middle-class home owners get a $23 tax benefit on average, not realizing that eliminating the loophole could collect more from the affluent, so much more that their tax bill could go down $61. These are classical illustrations of cooption, in which lesser interests are persuaded that they benefit from certain policies. Yet these policies do not really benefit the lesser interests and greatly benefit the affluent. Making reform more difficult, the coopted interests intensively defend what they think is in their interest. Combined with low intensity of popular interest, the politics of tax reform are extremely difficult.

There are many other loopholes. The Treasury Department study revealed the staggering costs of the loophole system and the tremendous benefits to high-income people. (See table 2–4.) Low-income people benefited $267 per taxpayer from the fifty-seven loopholes studied. Middle-income people who earned about $20,000 per year received $901 in benefits. But people with $200,000 and over averaged $45,663 in benefits. The Treasury analysis did not include two important loopholes: split income benefits and business expense account abuses. The split income benefit allows a high-income person with a low-income spouse to get a break, but at very high incomes the break get very large. Business expense abuses allow business people to deduct luxurious restaurant meals, travel, entertainment, and lodging for business-related work. At least forty of the fifty-seven items studied are clearly regressive and cost about $58 billion in lost taxes. Eleven of the loopholes cost over $1 billion a year, and the tax code is riddled with smaller special-interest abuses.[7] In 1980 the tax expenditure budget reached about $150 billion as compared with budget outlays of $530 billion, and it included eighty-five special exceptions to the tax laws.

Table 2–4 Tax Expenditure Budget, 1974

Adjusted Gross Income	*Total Benefit per Individual*	*Average Capital Gain* [a]	*% of Taxpayers in Class*
$0–2,999	$ 267.44	$ 18.73	6.1
$3,000–4,999	229.32	4.49	11.3
$5,000–6,999	284.90	9.79	12.4
$7,000–9,999	385.28	13.83	17.1
$10,000–14,999	556.36	19.06	23.8
$15,000–19,999	901.08	28.61	14.7
$20,000–49,999	1,933.60	126.25	13.4
$50,000–99,999	9,337.40	1,479.39	1.0
100,000 and over	45,662.50	19,431.25	0.2
Apparent cost to U.S. Treasury	58,175.00	6,150.00	100.0

[a] Excludes farming and timber.

Source: *People and Taxes,* June 1975, pp. 9–10.

Corporate Income Taxes

Corporations file their own returns and are supposed to pay 48 percent of their profits in taxes. However, like the individual income tax, the corporate tax has become so riddled with loopholes that it does not work well. Revenue from this tax is declining and is now only one-third as important as the income tax. For example, in 1971 a new loophole, the investment tax credit, cost other taxpayers $4 billion. The credit allowed a percentage of the cost of new investment to be deducted from taxes. It failed to stimulate the economy as planned but has not been repealed. It was successful at another purpose, though; it functioned as a favor from incumbent politicians to the interests who helped get them elected. Also in 1971 the asset depreciation range loophole was created, reducing asset life for tax purposes and costing $4.2 billion; it also eliminated some practices that had controlled the abuse of depreciation deductions. Corporations were able to reduce their share of federal revenues from 34 percent in 1944 to 15 percent in 1974.

The principle that should guide the corporate tax system should be to allow a free market. In fact, business taxation favors big over small, and petroleum, banking, and real estate over other industries. (See table 2–5.) Many of the loopholes for individuals also apply to business, but the results for business in general are hidden by secrecy and lack of analysis. In 1975 about 4,000 corporations had assets of $100 million and over. They earned almost $100 billion in income subject to tax, but paid only 22 percent of it in taxes. Firms with under $1 million numbered 1,882,000 and paid 26 percent in taxes. Firms with assets in the $5 million to $10 million asset range were unable to take advantage of the special rates for small firms and the loopholes for big firms; they paid 43 percent in taxes. The big firms owned 73 percent of all corporate assets; the smallest ones, 6 percent; those with $5 to $10 million in assets, about 2.4 percent.[8]

Direct Subsidies

The preferred method of elite power is loopholes because they continue forever with little oversight or evaluation. A relatively small amount goes to elites directly in the budget where it more obviously competes with other priorities.

Agriculture and transportation receive subsidies that mostly benefit the affluent. In 1978 a record $7.9 billion was budgeted for federal aid to farmers, many of whom are affluent. The chronic problem of American agriculture has been overproduction, which leads to low prices, although the world food shortage of 1973 temporarily altered this situation. A new law in 1973 was designed to avoid methods that had failed in the past by using a new

Table 2–5 Federal Corporate Income Taxes, 1973

Industry	*U.S. Tax Rate on World Income*	*World Tax Rate on World Income*	*Lowest Rate Paid*
9 largest nonoil corporations [a]	22.0%		2.8%
6 largest oil corporations [b]	6.3		0.9
10 next largest oil corporations	11.5	37.0% [c]	0.6
10 biggest metals and mining	17.3	25.5	– 2.1 [d]
12 largest commercial banks	3.6	16.1	–19.3 [d]
12 largest drug companies	22.1	36.7	7.3
10 largest conglomerates	24.5	29.3	4.6
12 largest chemical companies	24.4	35.2	15.0
11 largest retailers	29.4	33.5	0.5
10 largest food processors	28.4	41.5	12.3
44 largest other (electronic, steel, timber, trucks, and equipment)	32.6	40.3	6.5

Note: The official tax rate was 48.0 percent.

[a] GM, Ford, Chrysler, General Electric, IBM, ITT, Western Electric, U.S. Steel, and Westinghouse, in that order. There is little variation year to year.

[b] Exxon, Texaco, Mobil, Gulf, Standard of California, and Standard of Indiana.

[c] Includes royalties disguised as income tax.

[d] The government owes them money, deductible from future tax bills.

Source: National Committee for Tax Justice, *Tax Justice Act of 1975* (Washington, D.C.: The Committee, 1975), p. 3.

technique of "target prices" for cotton, feed grains (like corn), and wheat. When the market price falls below the target price, the government buys the commodity. Costly subsidies continue for peanuts, rice, tobacco, tung nuts, honey, milk, barley, oats, rye, sorghum, wool, and mohair. Some benefit goes to small farmers, but big farmers benefit the most. The programs tend to encourage more production than can be consumed. Billion-dollar irrigation projects provide many farmers with heavily subsidized cheap water. Too often those who benefit are corporate farmers and large holders in violation of the 1902 Reclamation Act, which requires residency on the farm and limited acreage. Legal and social problems of organizing farm workers and the employment of illegal aliens also provide a kind of labor subsidy. All of these aspects interact with farm-related tax loopholes and too often seem to hurt small farmers in the name of helping them.

Dam building and other water projects also subsidize interests in electric power, still water recreation, and water transportation. Keeping alive noncompetitive shipbuilding and ship-operating businesses costs about $300 million a year. Federal subsidies go to bankrupt eastern railroads and a few local airlines. Tariffs, export subsidies, and import quotas have subsidized a number of businesses, such as textiles, sugar, milk, oil, and wheat.

These and other subsidies to the affluent generally are ignored, but occasionally scandal brings one to light, as in the case of the Russian wheat deal in 1972. The U.S. government was subsidizing a few large grain-elevator firms to export wheat, making up the small difference between the low world price and the high American domestic price, in order to keep up prices at home and promote exports abroad. The program, undesirable to begin with, was mismanaged. For example, forecasts of rising world wheat prices were ignored, and the delay of claims allowed companies to inflate their subsidy. For a while, the Russians were paying $1.63 a bushel when Americans were paying $2.10 plus a $.47 subsidy for each bushel sold to the Soviet Union.

Adverse publicity can stop the extreme cases, and steady criticism can limit the usual kinds of subsidy, but most of them persist, like loopholes. But unlike loopholes, subsidies are more visible and, possibly for that reason, much smaller in dollar volume. Their visibility is created by their inclusion in each year's budget. They are mentioned here because they act like loopholes; they fulfill a nominal public purpose but in unpublicized ways give money to the affluent.

Case Study:

Oil Depletion

The petroleum industry is the largest industry in the country and until recently has had one of the most obvious giveaways in the tax code, the *depletion allowance,* which allows a percentage of gross income to be deducted from that income before it is taxed. The existence of this loophole was a demonstration of the influence of this elite; its repeal was an illustration of the influence of reformers. Designed to provide an incentive to find oil, it produced about a dollar's worth of reserves for each ten dollars in lost taxes. The allowance even applied to foreign oil production from reserves not owned by the companies. For many years, an oil quota kept foreign oil stimulated by the depletion allowance out of the United States.

By 1973, the elites were ready for reform. The loophole benefited only the oil elite and adverse publicity was making it an embarrassment. People were also favorably disposed to reform because of the oil boycott and price rise.

The depletion allowance eventually was reduced partly due to a strong citizen reform effort. Common Cause, a public-interest group supported by 240,000 citizens, and reformers in Congress had been working for years to accomplish the procedural reforms necessary to get the depletion reform bill considered. Historically, depletion reform had been blocked by the simple refusal of the House Ways and Means Committee to consider it; such was the power of the key tax committee. (In addition, oil and politics have always mixed closely. Senator Russell Long received $329,151 in U.S. tax benefits from 1964 to 1969 and said he saw no conflict of interest in his support for the loophole.[9] In 1979 there were thirty-two congressmen with income from oil companies.)

The first reform required Ways and Means to hold meetings in public, so when the tax reduction bill came along, noncommittee members could keep track of it. Second, Ways and Means, with all the other committees, was required to hold its votes in public. An amendment to the tax reduction bill for oil depletion reform was defeated by a committee vote of 22 to 14. However, the majority was the typical coalition of conservative Dixiecrats and Republicans; among the Democrats on the committee, a majority favored reform.

Third, the House Democratic caucus voted 152 to 99 to allow the tax reduction bill to be amended on the House floor, a power given the caucus by another recent procedural reform. The chairman of Ways and Means decided to yield to the wishes of his party and allow the reduction bill to come to the House floor. A few weeks earlier, three of his fellow chairmen had lost their positions, voted out as unresponsive, also a result of another procedural reform and the addition of new reform-oriented Democrats to the House in 1975. The House voted 248 to 163 to uphold the caucus and reform over the committee; it approved depletion reform. In the Senate a filibuster threatened to kill the bill, but it was cut off because a procedural reform a few days earlier had lowered the number of votes to end a filibuster from sixty-seven to sixty. Because President Ford wanted the tax reduction more than he opposed depletion reform, he signed the bill.

But it was not an unambiguous victory. A billion-dollar loophole was written into the bill for smaller firms, most of which were already using the full panoply of loopholes to escape all taxation and were making huge profits on new oil (the price on old oil was controlled). The public justification was to help these small firms compete with the giants, although they were actually doing better than the large firms. More realistically, the inclusion of the loophole was an interesting expression of power by less visible junior members of the oil elite at a time when the senior members were suffering the embarrassment of being so successful that the public was beginning to realize what was happening. Nevertheless the reform did raise $1.7 billion in taxes, and now only $1.8 billion per year is being lost in taxes through depletion.

The reform of the oil depletion allowance illustrates many very important features of the reform process. It showed that citizens simply cannot keep track of all the myriad details necessary to know who is responsible for what and when to do what to get a reform. Citizens had to employ professionals on their side—in this case, Common Cause—which provided the extra pressure necessary, on top of work by reformers in Congress and stories in the media, to make some reform happen. Another factor was the extensive popular concern over the power and wealth of the oil companies. Middle-of-the-road politicians felt that they had more to fear from voters finding out about their position on the issue than from oil interests. But third, the reform could occur without basically affecting the power of the oil industry, which is not harmed by the loss of a couple of billion dollars. Therefore, the reform satisfied the average citizens, who believed they were being benefited, and the oil industry, which can recover the loss for less than a penny a gallon extra. Fourth, notice how important procedural reforms were for getting the substantive reform. Procedural barriers had prevented reform legislation from even reaching the floor, so most congressmen could avoid going on record. Five important procedures had to be changed to get the reform, but once made subsequent reforms may be easier.

Other Taxes

Our discussion so far just scratches the surface of tax policy. Other important taxes include the property tax, sales tax, social security tax, and wealth taxes. The property tax acts as a highly regressive sales tax on housing of about 24 percent nationwide. It also has a major impact on education because public education is financed primarily from these taxes. Low-wealth school districts often receive less money per pupil despite a higher tax rate than high-wealth districts do. Owners can deduct property taxes from income tax; renters cannot. The wealthy and industries tend to congregate in their own enclaves, with low tax rates. Local governments are forced to compete in a kind of warfare to attract industry to their area and to keep low-income people out. Local governments—counties, cities, school districts, special districts—depend on the property tax for about 82 percent of their tax revenues.

The property tax is one of the most poorly and unfairly administered taxes in the system. One reform may be to institute more county-wide and statewide property taxes, which could even out disparities of wealth and systematize administration. The California property tax is among the most fairly administered, so it is ironic that there was a rebellion against it. Yet its very fairness meant that assessments of property value kept up with inflation, and urban residential property values were inflating in the mid-1970s even faster than the consumer price index. Local governments then applied their tax rates to the assessment. Locally elected officials could avoid raising rates and even lower them while increasing their budgets faster than inflation because the assessments were increasing so much. In 1976 while the rest of the nation was paying $266 per capita in property taxes, Californians were paying $415, almost the highest in the nation, and in 1977 they paid even more. It was too much, and at a critical juncture the legislature failed to act.

Proposition 13, a poorly drafted, relatively extreme measure, was put on the June 1978 ballot by popular initiative. That spring assessments shot up again, the state government announced a huge, multibillion dollar surplus, and a moderate initiative by the legislature was never adequately explained to the voters. "Prop 13" passed by a two to one margin, reflecting a desire for lower taxes, frustration in influencing government, and a belief that mainly waste would be eliminated. The legislature cushioned the shock by cutting cost-of-living increases and distributing the surplus; some waste was eliminated; and governments found new sources such as building fees for replacement revenues. Although not as bad as predicted, the number of public employees has been substantially reduced and many social programs cut.

Mostly without realizing it, voters greatly reduced the power of local governments and increased the power of the state. Restrictions on increasing assessments will gradually shift the property tax burden to home owners and new property owners. Local and state governments have shifted from an expansionary to a siege mentality, worrying about funding when the surplus is gone. On the positive side, California has a statewide property tax and is more in line with national property tax levels, though on the low side. The property tax is the only one that many people pay with a large check once or twice a year, making it stand out as a target. Equally serious problems with other taxes fail to rouse the same intensity, apparently because their impact is more hidden.

Citizen Profile:

State and Local Tax Reform

Getting politically involved with an issue as complex as tax reform is something that happens gradually, not overnight. My first political involvement came in high school with student government. I went to a Catholic, Jesuit-run school with about 1,200 students. When someone bet me a quarter I couldn't be elected to office, I bet and won. Thereafter followed four years in a variety of offices. I began to identify with the progressive wing of the Democratic party, including the antiwar movement, despite a family background entrenched in the Republican party.

In college at the University of California, Davis, I was determined to get involved in "real" politics, not just student government. Virtually ignoring classes (I was majoring in political science and sociology), I got involved in every local and state race that came along. After the 1974 election, a group of students started a progressive political group, the Student Democratic Coalition, all around California, and I became its president. So when the presidential campaign of 1976 rolled around, I was lucky enough to have the best list of progressive, politically active students in the state.

After a little research, Fred Harris, a former Oklahoma senator, seemed like the best candidate in the Democratic primaries. Shortly, my wife and I found ourselves working full time for him. First San Francisco, then Los Angeles, after that east to Washington, Pennsylvania, New York, Chicago, New Hampshire, Boston, etc. During the campaign I went "professional" for all of about $300 a month "salary."

My thinking changed in perspective. I realized that money is always the bottom line. Spending questions usually dominate the day. How can we get more effective programs? I was developing a greater sense of how economic issues underlay all other issues.

After the Harris campaign folded, I came back to California and worked for a string of political campaigns and causes. First it was the antinuclear initiative, proposition 15 on the June 1976 ballot, with a lot of former Fred Harris people. During the summer it was for the California Democratic Council, and in the fall it was for John Tunney's campaign. Having supported Tunney's opponent, Tom Hayden, in the primary, working for Tunney was difficult, but I figured he was a lot better than S. I. Hayakawa. Hayakawa won.

I was 0 for 3 in the first three campaigns I worked professionally. Harris, Nuclear Safeguards and Tunney all lost. For the next year and a half, I worked for a variety of political groups at very low wages—$300 to $650 a month. These included environmental groups, students coalitions, and local housing organizations.

Throughout all this, the importance of tax issues became clear to me. Fundamental to our current economics is a very regressive state and national tax system. Therefore, when the California Tax Reform Association was looking for an organizer, I jumped at the chance.

CTRA had tried to pass a liberal property tax reform bill in the state legislature, but the legislature fell two votes short of passing the bill. Then Howard Jarvis and the conservatives wrote proposition 13, an extreme measure opposed by every progressive group in California.

Prop 13 passed, and now the tax system is even worse. We are fighting to clean up the new inequities created by proposition 13, to increase the renters' credit, and to close tax loopholes. Having become CTRA's lobbyist in Sacramento, it is my job to sell the program to the legislature. The frustration of this job is to see the vested interests (big business and real estate investors, among others) so well represented, and the average taxpayer underrepresented.

In 1959 California business paid 57 percent of all taxes paid to state and local governments, excluding user fees. That includes property, sales, cigarette, alcohol, gas, and income tax. Now business only pays 36 percent of the tax burden to state and local government. Meanwhile, the legislators hear probusiness tax arguments all week long in their offices. The public is seldom represented. While CTRA can't see every legislator even once on all the issues, our opponents, because of the greater number of lobbyists, can see legislators as often as they want.

Of course, CTRA has something the special interests don't; we have broad, citizen, local-based support. The reward of the job is when, by informing the citizenry and mobilizing that support, or by talking to legislators and convincing them, CTRA can beat a tax loophole bill or help pass a new, progressive tax law. Recently we helped defeat an income tax loophole for multinational corporations worth over a hundred million dollars. When you consider that without CTRA's presence that bill may have passed, it all becomes worthwhile. That is why CTRA is so important and tax justice so exciting to work for.

Steve Smith
Davis, California

Sales taxes tend to be better administered but are still very regressive. They should be reduced in favor of using a fairer income tax. Excise taxes, on the other hand, are aimed at specific commodities—such as tobacco, alcohol, and gasoline—and can usefully and simply discourage their consumption.

Social security taxes are more important for the average wage earner than income taxes. They take 5.85 percent of income up to $16,500 of income (as of 1977). The rate and the income ceiling will increase to 7.15 percent and $42,600, respectively, by 1987. Since 1973, over half of all taxpayers have paid more in social security than in income taxes. This tax is highly regressive above the income ceiling, but the benefits are highly progressive, making a tax-transfer system that is generally proportional. The system is supposed to be an insurance scheme, and it largely is. Payments in balance payments out, both for the system year to year and for the family over its lifetime (though much depends on adjustments for inflation). Benefit improvements have made social security important for millions of retirees, disabled, and survivors, who are a potent political force. Recent tax increases have put social security on a sound financial basis, but there are still problems of excessive increases of benefits with inflation and of "double-dipping." Since the federal employee retirement system is separate from social security, some people have been able to qualify for pensions under both systems, a "double dip."

The distribution of private wealth is even more skewed to the wealthy than the distribution of income. Wealth includes corporate stock, bonds, real estate, mortgages, cash, and life insurance. The taxation of wealth transfers has even more loopholes than the income tax. There is much unknown about who owns private wealth because of secrecy. Federal inheritance data, finally released by the Internal Revenue Service in 1973, indicates that 4 percent of the adult population owns 33 percent of personally held assets.[10] Institutionalized inheritances are passed down through the generations, protected by a cadre of business managers, lawyers, and accountants, the modern retainers of an entrenched plutocracy. Estates of about a million dollars are supposed to pay 33 percent in taxes; because of loopholes, they actually pay 17 percent. In 1969 Ailsa Mellon Bruce died leaving an estate of $570,748,725. The heirs paid a little over 1 percent in taxes: The system is more loophole than law. Possible reform might be a small tax on net worth levied every five years, eliminating the current gift, estate, and trust system of taxing wealth. The current system loses about $10 billion a year in special treatment of capital gains at death.[11]

System Reform

The tax system has become so complex that we do not really know how it works, what parts of the law really mean, or how to administer it. The Internal Revenue Service (IRS) has greatly weakened its auditing of complex and large returns over the years. Tax error and tax fraud are on the increase. The IRS is understaffed, its compliance efforts misdirected, its procedures cumbersome. Simplification is now a reform goal almost as great as closing loopholes. In June 1973 the IRS told President Nixon that his returns were correct; they later proved to have $432,787 due but not paid in taxes.

Tax reforms at all levels depend on more citizen attention. Vague alienation needs to be replaced by specific knowledge. Most people do not know where their representatives stand on the issues. Many others accept arguments of the rich about how much good their tax breaks do. Committed citizens are needed to edge the system back toward simplicity and fairness.

In 1978 tax reform efforts were rebuffed by a Congress that instead expanded the capital gains loophole to 60 percent. To balance the budget in 1980 attention focused on cutting school lunches rather than on the $1 billion spent on executives' food and drink, on cutting medical research and training rather than on the $1.5 billion tax expenditure on health by those with incomes over $50,000, on cutting social security rather than on the $3 billion in tax expenditure for private pension funds of those with incomes over $50,000, and on cutting public service jobs instead of on tax credits going to business for a similar purpose but without results.[12] The power of elites is nowhere more evident or so easily measured as in the tax system.

Inflation

Inflation is a rise in the general level of prices. We view it as a problem. Generally, incomes are also increasing during inflation, which is not considered a problem. However, if prices and incomes rise at the same rate, there is no loss of purchasing power. If incomes rise even faster than inflation, there is an increase of purchasing power, making inflation a minor inconvenience. But the nature of inflation in our accounting sytem makes business more difficult to conduct, and inflation tends to outrun gains in income of vulnerable groups like the old and the unskilled. In fact, increasing incomes themselves may be a major cause of the inflation. Such increases are inflationary if they are made possible by an excessive increase in the supply of money. Indeed, the supply of money is the common theme underlying all discussions of inflation. Apparent causes of inflation are always a manifestation of some increase in the supply of money faster than the rate of real economic growth.

In relation to a goal of inflation below 3 percent per year, we have had excess inflation since 1968, and the inflationary momentum began to build even earlier, in 1966. The dollar of 1966 was worth only fifty cents in 1978. On the other hand, compensation (wages, salaries, fringe benefits, and

Table 2–6 Inflation versus Compensation (% Annual Change)

	1960–1965	*1965–1970*	*1970–1975*	*1976*	*1977*	*1978*
Consumer prices	1.3	4.5	6.9	4.8	6.8	9.0
Compensation per hour [a]	4.0	6.4	8.2	8.5	7.6	9.8
Net gain in purchasing power	2.7	1.9	1.3	3.7	0.8	0.8

[a] Private nonfarm business, all persons.

Source: *Economic Report of the President* (1979), p. 56. See also *Statistical Abstract of the United States, 1978,* p. 11 (percentage net increase in population), and p. 447 (annual percentage change in real disposable personal income).

employer contributions to social security) has been increasing even faster. On average we may be gaining, but some are falling seriously behind, and the stability of the economy is seriously threatened. (See table 2–6.)

Business suffers from inflation. It must raise prices to cover wage increases; wages are about 70 percent of the cost of production. Our system of accounting creates artificial profits from underdepreciation of assets and overvaluation of inventory, increasing taxes and decreasing real profitability. Lenders find their loans being repaid in depreciated dollars and must charge higher interest to recover losses and anticipate future inflation. At some point in an inflationary cycle, the interest rate on Treasury bonds may rise above that on savings accounts, leading big investors to take their money from one to the other. The lenders then lose the money they need for construction loans, and that industry slumps.[13] With business less profitable, stock prices slide; the bear market (falling stock prices) of 1974–1975 was one of the worst in American history.

If we cannot control inflation, we should allow adjustments for it in the accounting and taxing systems. Brazil has had some success with *indexing,* as such adjustments are called. Indexing would be preferable to tax loopholes, which in some ways accomplish the same adjustments.

The underlying cause of inflation is simple: there is an excessive increase in the supply of money, defined in many ways, but most simply as currency in circulation and demand deposits (checking accounts) in commercial banks. The federal government controls the supply. The Congress and the president set general policy, and the Department of the Treasury and the Federal Reserve System carry it out. This elite could control and prevent inflation, if that were its top priority. But from time to time, other goals, especially economic growth, employment, and market power, are given a higher priority. The relationships among money supply, these other goals, and the economy are extremely complex, making it difficult to trace the causes of inflation to money supply. The two leading economic schools of thought can be called the *monetarist* and the *Keynesian.* The monetarist school believes that the money supply should increase no faster than the economy itself and tends to oppose using federal deficits to stimulate the economy. The Keynesian schools holds that the government can stimulate the economy without causing inflation under certain circumstances.

Circumstances allowing stimulus without inflation are slack in the economy: workers are willing to work at existing wages, businesses are willing to sell at existing prices, and some resources of capital and labor are not being used. Then the extra money puts people to work and enables them to spend, getting the economy going again (called *priming the pump*), so that it can continue on its own. Keynesians, or liberals, are more willing to stimulate a sluggish economy and even put up with a little inflation to get more production and more employment. Monetarists fear that such stimulation gets out of hand, requiring painful deflationary policies.

There are three ways to expand the money supply: monetary policy, fiscal policy, and private debt. Fiscal and monetary policy are determined by the federal government and can permanently expand the supply. Private debt is more temporary and limited in its potential.

Monetary Policy

Monetary policy is controlled by the Federal Reserve System, whose board of directors holds fourteen-year appointments, the longest outside the judiciary. Once appointed, the members can follow their own philosophies free of short-term political influence. "The Fed" operates through twelve banks, the most important of which is in New York City. These banks are used by nationally chartered or state-chartered commercial banks, with which most of us do business.

The most important method of controlling money supply is by *open market transactions*, guided by the Fed's Open Market Committee, one of the most powerful and least visible agencies of government. The Fed's banker in New York City has the power to write a check without funds to cover it. If we owned a bank and wrote a check on it without funds, we ultimately would come up short of cash. The Fed's check, however, cannot bounce, because the Fed has the power to create and destroy money. Its check thus creates money. The Fed uses the check to buy Treasury bonds, and the person (or investment house) that sold the bonds gets the check. That person now has, say, $100 million more. The money supply is increased by that amount. The person could take the Fed's check to a commercial bank and legally demand actual currency for the full amount. In practice, the system works more indirectly and creates even more money. The person with the check usually deposits it in a bank, which typically puts about 16.5 percent back into the Federal Reserve Bank as required reserve and loans out the rest. Now the amount of money in circulation is the $100 million the person deposited plus the $83 million the bank has loaned. But economics is never simple, and the recipient of the bank loan is likely to deposit that loan in another bank, so through this multiplier effect of a chain of deposits and loans, $100 million becomes almost $600 million. Similarly the Fed can destroy money by selling bonds, removing the money that it gets from circulation. The people who buy the bonds have to reduce their checking accounts to pay for the bonds, which reduces the amount the bank can loan out, and so on.

The Fed has goals besides preventing inflation, such as stabilizing interest rates. When it buys bonds, the Fed may have to pay a higher price or interest rate for them; when it sells, it may have to take a lower rate and bring rates down. Its open-market transactions affect the *federal funds rate,* the interest rate that banks charge each other, which is the most sensitive rate for loans to everybody else. Money supply and interest rates can work at cross-purposes. When the Fed buys bonds to increase the money supply, it may have to offer a premium that increases interest rates. Problems like this create well-paid employment for economists. Monetary policy acts directly on the private financial system, which in turn affects the economy.

Fiscal Policy

Monetary policy does not increase debt, but fiscal policy and private debt do. Fiscal policy concerns federal government spending, the revenues it collects, and management of the resulting deficit (or surplus). Since World War II, the federal government has gone deeply in debt and goes deeper every year. From 1960 to 1970, the gross federal debt increased at about $9.17 billion per year, from 1970 to 1975 at about $32.3 billion per year, and from 1975 to 1980 at an estimated $71 billion per year, for an estimated total debt of $899 billion in 1980.[14] Going into debt allows the federal government to spend money that it has not collected, thus increasing the money supply. It risks inflation but can stimulate the economy and reduce unemployment. Deficit spending has been far more important for causing inflation than has monetary policy, although to some extent they work in tandem. Fiscal policy can primarily benefit recipients of federal spending, which since 1975 has been the military, energy programs, and transfer programs. Fiscal policy also benefits recipients of federal tax cuts. Democrats have favored cuts to middle and low incomes; the Republicans, to upper middle and high.[15]

How do fiscal deficits increase the money supply? The Treasury Department, anticipating more bills than it can pay, borrows from ordinary citizens through savings bonds, but since these have too low an interest rate to attract serious investors, it must borrow more at higher interest through short-term bills (under a year), medium-term notes (one to seven years) and long-term bonds (over seven years, but "bonds" or "paper" can be used to refer to all types). They pay higher interest than savings bonds do but lower than commercial paper because they are risk free. (A business may go bankrupt, but the government can print more money when it needs to.) Investors need $100,000 and multiples thereof to participate.

If the Treasury cannot obtain money at a low enough interest rate, it can offer a higher rate, but that then drives up interest rates across the board and "dries up" or "crowds out" available money for private investing, and is inflationary. In this case the Treasury can persuade other parts of the government, like the Social Security Administration, to invest in its bonds, or it can turn to the Federal Reserve Banks. The Fed can "buy" a Treasury bond from the Treasury in the same way that it does from a private party: it uses its special "checks," which the Treasury deposits in its bank accounts. With its accounts increased, the Treasury can write checks that will be cashed and redeposited with the same multiplier effect described earlier.

One problem with the national debt is the cost of paying interest on it—about $65.7 billion in 1980, about 9 percent of the national budget and 2.6 percent of GNP. The interest rate averages 7.3 percent, but this mixes low interest on savings bonds with high interest on long-term paper. If we decided that it was important to eliminate the debt, we could raise the money by higher taxes. Although the taxes would depress the economy, they would be canceled out by the stimulation from people spending the money from selling their bonds. If the debt has any useful role, it is to stabilize financial markets and provide a secure place to put short-term funds. Almost two-thirds of the interest is paid to government and ordinary citizens; only about one-third goes to business and the wealthy. Even then the interest payments may reduce the cost of business and get passed on to consumers.

Fiscal policy acts directly through tax cuts, federal spending, and interest payments, which in turn affect the economy. Monetary policy tends to be stable, expanding money at 5 or 6 percent a year, while fiscal policy is more dynamic, and used so much in recent years as to cause inflation. Recent efforts to require a balanced budget could in the short run reduce fiscal policy as a cause of inflation. However, if we were constitutionally locked into it, we would be unable to pursue a policy of stimulus in a depression and unable to have a surplus when needed to dampen excessive inflation. The real solution is to gain a better understanding of unemployment and market power, which would then be the basis for intelligent policy.

Other Debt

A third factor is state, local, and private debt, which has a short-term influence on money supply. Corporate, farm, mortgage, commercial, consumer, and nonfederal government borrowing can expand and contract within limits wide enough to affect short-term money supply through the same multiplier effect as fiscal-monetary policy. Thus, an increase in consumer confidence increases borrowing and the money supply.

Nonfederal debt helps put the federal or "national" debt in perspective. From 1958 to 1978, the federal debt grew by a 5 percent average annual compound rate, but the debt of states and localities grew by 8.3 percent and private debt by 9.8 percent. As a percentage of total debt, the national debt has been steadily falling, from a high of 70 percent in 1945 due to the depression and World War II to a low of 19 percent in 1978 due to the growth of other debt.[16]

The Problem of Inflation

In these ways—fiscal policy, monetary policy, and nonfederal debt—money supply can be permanently or temporarily expanded and contracted. The most important of them for causing inflation in recent years has been fiscal policy. By 1965, deficits had stimulated the economy to a relatively high level of employment without causing inflation; there was no slack. President Johnson decided not to raise taxes during the war in Vietnam. His large deficits caused inflation, which acted as an indirect tax to pay for the war. This episode contrasts sharply with World War II, in which taxes were raised, bonds were sold, and other savings were encouraged, taking money out of the consumer economy, with wage and price controls on top of that.

The 1965 war-caused inflation initially increased defense worker wages, leading other workers to try to catch up with them and reestablish traditional wage relationships among industries. Businesses followed suit with prices. But these are secondary causes. If the money supply is not expanded, the money will not be there to buy the goods and services at the higher prices, and there will be recession, unemployment, and bankruptcies until new price relationships are worked out. It is possible that one segment of the economy may be strong enough to insist on its higher wages and prices, but the weaker segments will have to lower their wages and prices correspondingly. Inflation is not the rise of one price but of the general level of prices.

If some prices go down as others go up, there is no inflation. Some segments of the economy have enough power to insist on their price or wage much longer than others, who are thus forced to suffer most of the costs of adjustment. This is part of the problem of market power. Rather than allow this suffering and unwilling to attack market power, the fiscal policy elite has preferred to cause some inflation in the name of stimulating the economy. Some of the stimulus helps employment, but too much subsidizes market power and causes inflation.

The war inflation was followed by wage-push inflation, and this was followed by commodity shortages acting similarly to wage-push inflation. In 1972, a world food shortage occurred. And in 1973–1974, the Arab oil boycott and the OPEC (Organization of Oil Producing Countries) price increase of 400 percent occurred. Other commodity shortages appeared. The food and fuel crisis alone seemed to explain about 80 percent of inflation during this period. Restraint in the money supply, however, could have forced an adjustment: less oil use, less food consumption, alternative methods of food and fuel production, and so on. This adjustment would have been extremely difficult, especially in the short run. It was easier to have inflation, which allowed other prices to catch up more or less. Food production rebounded, lowering relative food prices. Even oil prices have been eroded by inflation. OPEC has a new concern that higher prices would so disrupt Western economies that they would not be able to buy enough oil at the higher price. Nevertheless, price erosion and unrestrained American demand are causing some increases.

After inflation for several years, an inflationary psychology develops. Everyone starts anticipating it with wage and price increases.

The money supply increased so much that inflation shot up to 11 percent in 1974. Finally, inflation became so important that it took priority over other goals. Money growth was cut, partly because of policy and partly because of other factors. The fiscal deficit had been $14.8 billion in 1973; in 1974 it was only $4.7 billion. By mid-1975 inflation had been cut dramatically to about 6 percent a year. But the reduction in money supply reduced aggregate demand and resulted in the worst recession since the Great Depression and in high unemployment rates. Recession triggered automatic transfer programs like welfare, food stamps, and unemployment insurance, producing a deficit of $45 billion in 1975. This spending caused more inflation, which has continued to the present in a pattern of big deficits, excessive increases in money supply, and high inflation.

In conclusion, federal deficits seem to have too little effect on unemployment while causing inflation. Fiscal-monetary policy can work, but it takes time for expansions and contraction to work their way through the economy. A decision to spend may not produce actual expenditures in time to deal with conditions before they have changed so much that the expenditure is undesirable. Changes in consumer tastes, new technologies, international factors, shortages, and other public policies further complicate the picture. Fiscal-monetary policy is like a small rudder on a huge ship trying to steer between the rock of unemployment and the whirlpool of inflation. A few billion dollars, even $50 billion, is only a small part of the total economy.

Fiscal-monetary policy seems able to control inflation but unable to deal with other problems, unemployment and market power, at the same time. Conservative economists are making a strong case for a new approach to unemployment, and liberal economists are making an equally strong case for public service jobs and for control of market power.

Unemployment

Conservative economists have tended to argue for low budget deficits and moderate monetary growth as the best way to have price stability and moderate, steady economic growth. In their view, such growth provides the securest source of new jobs and thus reduces unemployment. Liberal economists have tended to favor higher budget deficits and greater monetary growth as the best way to stimulate the economy and increase employment. In their view, such stimulation provides the best way to generate the economic growth by using otherwise wasted labor. Conservative policy is willing to tolerate a higher rate of unemployment, and liberal policy a higher rate of inflation. Both views have tended to emphasize fiscal-monetary policy as the major tool to attain both employment and price stability. Until the mid-1960s, there seemed to be a fair trade-off between inflation and unemployment. Then in the late 1960s and 1970s, the relationship deteriorated; we appeared to be having both high inflation and high unemployment, and fiscal-monetary policy seemed unable to manage either.

There are two major reasons for the ineffectiveness of fiscal-monetary policy in helping unemployment. One is the inappropriate way in which we have defined unemployment. The second, discussed in the next section, concerns economic concentration, which allows large corporations and unions to resist fiscal-monetary policy and to capture ever larger pieces of the economic pie.

The huge budget deficits of 1975 and 1976 meant that the recession, the worst since the 1930s, had relatively mild social consequences. Food, medical, welfare, and unemployment insurance spending; increases in social security benefits; and tax cuts gave millions of people enough to get along on. There is even statistical and anecdotal evidence that unemployment benefits prolonged the time that people stayed unemployed. The deficits also helped fuel the demand that slowly brought us out of recession in 1976–1977.

These deficits did not cause as much inflation as smaller deficits had in the mid-1960s because then the economy was tighter. A *tight economy* is one in which industrial capacity is almost fully utilized and the experienced labor force is almost fully employed. In a tight situation, extra money coming in mainly produces increased wages and prices—inflation. A *slack economy* has unused capacity and unemployed experienced labor. In a loose situation, stimulation (deficits fueling demand) can have the intended pump-priming effect by getting the economy going without inflation. The problem is that in a complex economy, some parts are relatively tight and others loose, and much depends on where the demand is placed.

Those who are unemployed, for example, may or may not have the skills to work for the industries that are trying to respond to demand. If skilled, experienced people are not available, the costs of training increase the costs of production. A business may decide that the costs and risks of training new people are not worth the benefits and simply raise prices. Theoretically, competition could develop if the price rises too high. In practice in many industries, this does not happen unless prices are so high that they overcome the extremely high risks of starting a new business. Implicit in this process is a high rate of inflation as the number of easily employable people declines.

Defining Unemployment

The unemployment rate does not measure just the number of easily employable people; it also includes the difficult-to-employ inexperienced and untrained workers also. It includes people who are not really looking for work but have to say so to get benefits, and those who are choosy about what they will do. These problems are more than fiscal-monetary policy can solve. The unemployment rate, in fact, is probably the most misleading of the important economic indicators. All it measures is the number of people in a survey each month of 57,000 households who say they are looking for work. The labor force consists of those with jobs plus those looking for jobs, and the unemployment rate is the percentage looking for work in the labor force. In many households, one spouse holds a job while the other is looking. In other households, the income may be below the poverty line, but an adult member is discouraged and not looking. The first case increases the rate of unemployment; the second does not, yet obviously the second case is the more serious social problem.

Students, homemakers, the disabled, the retired, and others have not been considered part of the labor force. Yet historically the number of women seeking work has steadily increased as they leave the pure homemaker role. Women have a higher rate of unemployment than men do, thus increasing the overall rate. Historically, many youths could find farm work or work in a family business. Those sources have declined, and more youths have sought work in other areas. They also have a higher rate of unemployment, again increasing the overall rate. Meanwhile, the rate excludes those not looking and tells us nothing about the needs of those households.

The economy, contrary to popular belief, has been tremendously successful in creating jobs and has done so significantly faster than the rate of population growth. Let us try a less arbitrary definition of unemployment, one not based on seeking work. We will define it in terms of the number of people aged eighteen to sixty-four who do not have paid jobs in relation to the total number aged eighteen to sixty-four. Both numbers exclude the institutionalized population (in prisons, for example) but include students, homemakers, the disabled, and others found in households. This definition yields a very high unemployment rate. The important thing about it is how it changes over time. We can relate this rate to the conventional unemployment rate.

Figure 2–1 shows that unemployment as a percentage of the population aged eighteen to sixty-four has been declining, with some ups and downs, since World War II. The line starts at 38.2 percent not working in 1948 and goes down to 31.5 percent by June 1977. The recession thus did not seriously affect the decline in unemployment according to our definition. But the unemployment rate as officially defined shows just the opposite; it starts at 3.8 percent in 1948 and moves up, with some fluctuations, to 7.1 percent in June 1977. Perhaps the major failing of fiscal-monetary policy has been to pursue the wrong definition of unemployment. We have been much more successful than we give ourselves credit for. Unemployment is not as serious a social problem as the way we define it.

Kinds of Unemployment

The unemployment rate contains four distinct kinds of unemployment.

The first is *cyclical.* It refers to unemployment created by a recession, by an actual falling off of existing production, by a failure of the economic structure to keep going. Layoffs rise above normal; unemployment compensation increases. Workers generally stay unemployed until called back. Unemployment benefits are fairly generous for this kind of worker, who also tends to be more affluent and hopeful about recovering his or her job. Benefits may last as long as sixty-five weeks, during which time the workers find odd jobs, perform bartered work, work on the house, or vacation. Their benefits are tax free, and they have no commuting or other work-related costs. Requirements to look for a job in order to receive benefits are not meaningfully enforced. Some northern workers have their benefits sent to

Figure 2–1 Alternative Measures of Unemployment

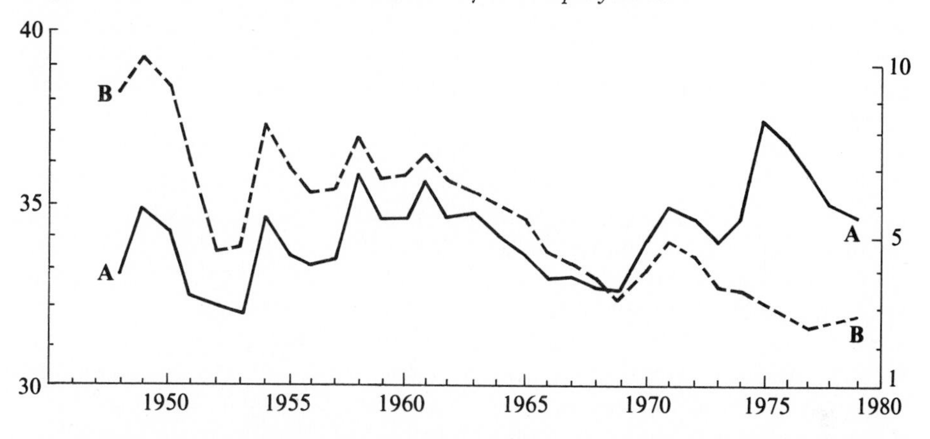

A The Official Rate: defined as looking for work as a percentage of total labor force. Labor force includes those employed and those looking for employment.

B The Alternative: defined as total noninstitutional population age 18–64 years minus total employed age 18–64 years, including armed forces as a percentage of total noninstitutional population age 18–64 years.

Note: Government data do not permit better definitions.
Source: 1948–1973: letter of January 29, 1975, from Bureau of Labor Statistics and *Employment and Earnings*. 1974–1977: *Employment and Earnings*, 26(April 1979):25, 37.

Florida. Some may actually look for work. The unemployment insurance system is a complex mosaic of different benefits by states and by industry—in some cases too generous, in others too stingy or nonexistent. Cyclical unemployment is best measured by variations in the *job loser* rate. The decline of job losers from June 1975 to June 1977 measures our recovery from the recession. Since cyclical unemployment involves existing capacity and experienced workers, it is the most responsive of the four kinds to fiscal-monetary policy. The trend from 1975 to 1977 shows that the fiscal stimulus worked.

The second kind of unemployment is *frictional*. It refers to the inevitable amount of unemployment in a dynamic economy caused by the natural shifting around of workers, seasons, technologies, consumer taste, and so on. The rate is about 1 to 3 percent. Not much needs to be done about this kind of unemployment except to have some system to prevent extreme suffering of individuals and their families who are temporarily out of work.

Unemployment due to choosiness is the third kind. It occurs when a person is not under severe economic pressure to work and wants a particular kind of job to meet special requirements about when to work, how far to travel, their training and interests, whom they will work with, how much they will be paid, and so forth. Typically married people whose spouses have good incomes are in this category. They are serious about finding a job, but their search may take a long time, increasing the rate of unemployment. Other times people will quit a job they do not like, especially if times are relatively good, in order to get a better job. Unemployment due to choosiness is best indicated by the rate of job leavers and of reentrants, which form about 3 percent of the unemployment rate. Another statistic that tends to confirm the importance of choosiness is that about 56 percent of the unemployed have at least one person in their family employed full time. Over 80 percent of unemployed wives and other relatives (mainly working age children) have at least one full-time earner in the family (usually the husband and father). Another aspect of choosiness is the great increase of workers on voluntary part-time schedules. This kind of unemployment is not a serious problem as far as government policy is concerned.

The final category consists of the *hard-core unemployed*. They can be defined as those ablebodied of working age who cannot find work after fifteen weeks or more of looking, who do not have serious responsibilities to care for dependents, and who are in moderate- to low-income households. Many such people work only part time or part year or for low pay. Part of the hard-core problem is measured by new entrants to the labor market, but many of these find work and are not really part of this category. Even when the economy is good, the hard-core unemployed are still out of work. We do not have statistics on the hard-core unemployed because the data on individual employment tend to be separate from those on household income.

Those who make up the hard-core unemployed tend to lack the culture, education, or skills desired by employers. Statistics allow us to define them indirectly by breaking down the rate of unemployment by characteristics. (The data are for June 1977.) The rate was 7.1 percent overall, but only 3.4 percent of married men were out of work and only 4.3 percent of household heads. Males twenty and over were doing fairly well at 5.0 percent, and whites at 6.3 percent were below the national average. Females twenty and over were at the national rate. Blacks had a 13.2 percent rate and teenagers an 18.6 percent rate. Combining adverse characteristics usually accentuates a rate. Black teenagers, for example, had an extremely high rate: 49 percent.[17] The figures for those of Spanish origin generally come out between blacks and whites. By occupation, the highest rate is for blue-collar laborers and by industry, for construction and agricultural wage workers. Rates are also somewhat higher for youths aged twenty to twenty-four and people over fifty-four. They are higher for the disabled and for people who live alone or with nonfamily members.

Although not included in the unemployment rate, some people not in the labor force also should count as hard-core unemployed. In the second quarter of 1977, there were almost 59 million people not in the labor force; 9.8 percent of them wanted a job and were not looking. This smaller number, under 6 million, was further broken down: 25 percent were students, 14 percent were sick or disabled, 23 percent had home responsibilities, 18 percent thought they could not get a job (probably mostly hard core), and 19 percent "other." Treating those who thought they could not get a job as 100 percent, the data can be further broken down: 15 percent thought that employers would think them too young or too old, 12 percent cited lack of education, training, or other personal handicaps, 45 percent said they could not find a job, and 28 percent thought no job was available.[18] The usual unemployment rate thus is unrealistic because it does not include these poor, discouraged workers.

Every month the Bureau of Labor Statistics publishes many tables based on monthly interviews with a carefully structured sample of 54,000 households. The Bureau of the Census publishes income-related data in its current population reports (series P–60). But none of these include the number of hard-core unemployed, defined as above or in any other way. In 1975 there were about 11.8 million persons aged eighteen to sixty-four in poverty, but most of them had home responsibilities or jobs and many were in school or were disabled. Making guesses about these numbers leaves perhaps 3 to 5 million hard-core unemployed, or about 2 to 4 percent of all adults aged eighteen to sixty-four. This figure includes those looking and not looking. It is the most important part of the unemployment problem and the part that government has done the least well with.

Policies for the Hard-core Unemployed

Policy in four areas affects hard-core unemployment: the minimum wage, illegal aliens, training, and public-service jobs. The *mimimum wage* of $2.65 an hour in 1978 affects about 6 million workers—mostly farm workers, domestics, local government employees, and retail clerks—in a labor force of about 90 million. It has risen unevenly but steadily with inflation. One person working forty-eight weeks a year at the minimum makes $5,088 annually, an income that is below the poverty line for a family of four (but well above it for smaller families). If both parents work full time at minimum wage, they can be defined as middle class. A teenager working in the same family at minimum wage could raise the family income even higher or could be considered above the poverty line if he or she lived alone.

The minimum wage is a two-edged sword. It helps the bargaining power of low-wage workers by forcing employers to pay more than they otherwise would, but it also makes it too expensive for employers to use unskilled labor, especially teenagers.[19] Lowering the rate for these youths might put adults out of work. In the apparel industry, for example, the minimum wage in the antiunion South brings up labor costs enough to allow union labor in the North to survive. One-fourth of those earning minimum wage are members of families with income at or above the median of all families. For example, about half of the teenagers working at the minimum wage come from families at or above the median income. Raising the minimum wage from $1.60 to $2.65 reduced the number of families in poverty by only about 5.5 percent.[20] Because of these counterproductive impacts on teenage unemployment, benefits to the middle class, and marginal results reducing poverty, the minimum wage has to be managed very carefully. It is a limited tool but can help. For example, it might be useful to allow employers to pay below minimum wage to inexperienced workers in trainee positions.

Illegal aliens are living contradictions to the problem of unemployment in the United States. They are here basically because they will work for less money than Americans at jobs Americans do not want. They are laborers, domestics, and service workers. Some even start new businesses and employ Americans. The problem is aggravated by the lack of sanctions against employers who knowingly use and exploit illegal immigrants, by the lack of enough border patrol manpower along the Mexican border, by an understaffed Immigration and Naturalization Service, by lack of effective sanctions against those who are caught, and by the need to avoid procedures that could harass Americans because of their speech, race, or manner of dress. About 6 to 12 million illegal aliens are in the United States—no one can be exact—and they are coming in at the rate of about 2.5 million to 4 million a year.[21] (A large number also leave each year.) Some come across the border; others fly in with temporary visas for students and visitors and then disappear. Fraudulent documents are also used. The Southwest has the greatest number of illegal aliens, but they are found throughout the nation.

The problem is that many take jobs that Americans want. Half of the employable illegal aliens apprehended in 1975 were making over $2.50 an hour in industry. On the other hand, automatic payroll deductions collect taxes from them. Many do not use tax-supported services. They are afraid, usually, to claim services for fear of being caught, so probably they pay more into the tax system than they get back on the whole. In California, the deportation of illegals during 1977 made available 2,154 jobs. But the state employment agency was unable to fill them. Americans eligible for welfare and other aid refuse these jobs for laborers, service workers, and domestics because of low pay, long hours, and low prestige.[22] Many things can be done to get Americans to work. For example, better enforcement of the minimum wage would ensure a certain level of pay, making the jobs more attractive. Very few ablebodied working age people without young dependents are on welfare, but those few who are can be required to take jobs or at least be denied benefits if they do not. Abuses of unemployment insurance, veterans' benefits, and other programs are serious. The common expression, "if you really want to find a job, you can," has a lot of truth in it.

Many people, however, are not qualified for many of the available jobs. About 1 million to 2 million jobs are unfilled even in recession. Many people need *job training and experience* and related placement and counseling services. Existing educational programs, state employment offices, vocational rehabilitation, and the veterans' programs help a great deal in this area. In 1973 federal manpower programs were reformed by the Comprehensive Employment and Training Act (CETA) to provide instruction, on-the-job training, and work experience. CETA is now the major source of funding in this area of special short-term help for the hard-core unemployed. In 1978 about $4.2 billion was spent to reach about 3.9 million program participants.[23] In 1975 CETA and the related WIN (Work Incentive) program for welfare recipients helped over half a million people get jobs.[24] Some CETA programs are at the national level; they are designed to aid disadvantaged youth (Job Corps), migrant workers, prisoners, non-English speakers, older workers, Vietnam veterans, and native Americans. Most CETA money, however, goes to about 460 local manpower agencies. These local agencies have citizen advisory boards, which can play a vital role. Job training for the hard-core unemployed is inherently difficult because they tend to be the least educated, least able, often most poorly motivated people in the labor force. The mixed record of training programs should not be surprising. The better programs show that job training can work.

The fourth area of policy related to hard-core unemployment is *public-service jobs*. Successful implementation in the other three policy areas will not solve the whole problem. Most reformers and even most other citizens believe that the government should be the employer of last resort. The idea is gaining increasing acceptance in the elites. Essentially, we have to admit that there is a category of persons who cannot compete effectively in the existing job market but can be expected to work and should not be eligible for welfare. Without any means of support, such people may turn to crime or be part of families with too little income to support them above the poverty line and thus live a marginal and unhealthy existence. Reformers generally feel that any able adult from a low-income household should have the right to a job.

A major question is how much these jobs should pay. The more they cost, the more taxes they will use, the fewer people can benefit, and the more people with other jobs will be pulled away from them by the public-service jobs. Conservatives have tended to oppose such jobs, and liberals have tended to make them too expensive. The jobs should probably have a rate of pay that is low enough to maintain incentive to enter the competitive job structure yet be high enough to allow one person to live above the poverty level. This guideline would seem to call for pay somewhat below the minimum wage, with supplementary benefits to the family if it is still poor. Most of the beneficiaries will be single people, especially teenagers, or couples without children. They will be people with little or no training or experience, whose labor is not worth the minimum wage in the job market. Or they will be people with negative work attitudes, personality problems, low education, convicts, drug and alcohol abusers, and other marginal citizens. For some, public-service jobs would simply be a means to earn an existence; for others, they could be a step toward self-respect, self-confidence, better attitudes, experience, more training, and a better job.

Probably about a million or more such jobs would be needed, with many vacant at any given time. The number would vary with need. Then unemployment among the poor would be voluntary, and anyone from a low-income household who wanted a job could have one.

The kinds of jobs would have to avoid using cheap labor to substitute for existing jobs. It will not be easy to draw the line between regular jobs and public-service jobs, but it probably can be done by avoiding the types of jobs that already exist and by not reducing funding for existing regular jobs. The kind of work likely to be approved for these jobs includes reforestation, clean-up, watershed protection, trail development and maintenance, fencing, inventories of public lands resources, other information collecting, traffic direction and some clerical aspects of police work, clean-up and landscaping of city streets and parks, minor public-works and road maintenance, school monitors and teachers' aides, community health aides in hospitals, nursing homes, and private homes, day-care workers (allowing parents time for training, job search, and working), recreation aides in parks and school grounds, and some community social work. There is potential for boondoggle and waste, but probably less than the existing system, which denies funds to many who need them, gives to those who do not, breaks up families, fails to do needed work, encourages dependency on a bureaucracy, and pays people without work in return. The public-job system could have many problems and still be much better than the current welfare system.

How much would it cost? Some money could be saved from the existing welfare, food stamp, and unemployment benefit system. A million jobs paying $5,000 annually to each worker would cost $5 billion, a small part of the federal total budget. Some savings would accrue because those able but unwilling to work would not be eligible for any welfare. Closing any one of the eleven largest tax loopholes would raise all the money needed, yet another reason for tax reform. This scheme would take from those with the highest-cost jobs and create numerous low-cost jobs, thus creating more jobs within the same economy. Since no new money is being created, it is noninflationary. The rich-serving part of the economy would decline a little, and the low income-serving part would correspondingly increase. Eliminating hard-core unemployment is much more of a political than an economic problem.

Federal efforts have been timid so far, though the Carter administration has expanded previous efforts. By 1978 the CETA program was funding 672,500 public-service jobs, costing $5.9 billion. One problem is the high cost per job, $8,220 per year in 1975.[25] Nevertheless, research so far indicates that public-service jobs are more efficient in increasing the number of jobs than are other programs. The other programs are aid to states and localities, accelerated public works, government purchases, and income tax cuts.[26]

This discussion of job creation has been limited to a program for the most needy and difficult group. In a broader context, the private economy generates most jobs for the general population and produces the surpluses taxed by the government for public employment. The executives who rescue floundering corporations save and create many jobs. Government regulations may also create jobs. Sometimes individuals make their own jobs. The ability of the economy to create public-service jobs depends on the working vitality of society as a whole. Inflationary deficits and a poorly defined unemployment rate distract us from a focused effort on solving the most socially important unemployment problem—that of the hard-core unemployed.

Market Power

Market power is the term economists use to describe how much a firm or group of firms can control their marketplace. It is closely related to the concept *economic concentration* (how much of the sales in a market are controlled by the largest firm and the other large firms). The extent and importance of market power are among the most hotly debated subjects in economics today. Market power interacts with the equally complex problems of unemployment and inflation. Reform economists tend to feel that there is so much market power that it contributes to unemployment and inflation.

The ideal of market competition requires a large number of firms, with some being created and some failing, none of which are dominant. As a general rule, the ideal fails if there is a "four-firm concentration ratio" of 50 percent or more. In other words, if the four largest firms selling a product line have 50 percent or more of the total sales in that line, market power exists. It is also possible to have market power with far less concentration, as in the case of oil. Market power is complex; it is a matter of kinds and degrees running from loose oligopoly (ratio under 50 percent) to monopoly. Labor unions may also have market power. Tables 2–7 and 2–8 lay out

Table 2–7 Market Power of Corporations, 1975

Industry	*National Income (billions)*	*Portion of National Income under Market Power* [a]	*Concentrated Major Markets* [b]
Agriculture, forestry, and fishing	$ 44.7	0%	
Mining	16.4	38	Major metal ores (see Manufacturing), coal Chemicals mining (see Manufacturing)
Construction	57.9	60	General, street-highway, other heavy construction *
Manufacturing	303.1	49	Telephone equipment (98% *: Western Electric) Motor vehicles (85%: GM, Ford, Chrysler) Computers (85%: IBM) Heavy electrical equipment (100%: GE, Westinghouse) Drugs (90%*: American Home Products, Merck, Pfizer, Lilly) Photographic film (100%: Kodak, Polaroid) Copying equipment (95%: Xerox, IBM) Industrial chemicals (80%: DuPont, Union Carbide, Dow, Monsanto) Soaps and detergents (95%: Procter & Gamble, Colgate, Lever) Aircraft engines (100%: GE, United Aircraft) Aircraft (100%: Boeing, McDonnell-Douglas, General Dynamics) Iron and steel (70%*: U.S. Steel, Bethlehem, Armco, Republic) Petroleum refining (70%*: Exxon, Texaco, Gulf, Mobil) Cereals (95%: General Mills, Kellogg) Locomotives and buses (100% each: GM each)

Table 2–7 (continued)

Industry	*National Income (billions)*	*Portion of National Income under Market Power* [a]	*Concentrated Major Markets* [b]
			Flat glass (96%: PPG Industries, Libby-Owens-Ford) Aluminum (90%: Alcoa, Kaiser, Reynolds) Copper (80%: Anaconda, Kennecott, Phelps-Dodge) Tires and tubes (71%: Goodyear, Firestone, Uniroyal, U.S. Rubber) Dairy products (60%: Borden, National Dairy, Carnation) Metal containers (90%: American Can, Continental Can) Soup (100%: Campbell alone has 80%) Other: Coca Cola, 50% of flavoring syrups; Polaroid, 60% of instant cameras; Gillette, 60% of razors; New York Times *, 75% of its market
Transportation and utilities	94.6	77	Railroads, taxis and related intercity buses, buses, water transport, airlines (United, PanAm, American, TWA); oil pipelines (see Refining), telephones (AT&T), telegraph (Western Union); broadcasting (80–90%: ABC, NBC, CBS); electricity; gas; water and sewage; all mostly 100%.
Trade wholesale	80.4	9	Drugs, dairy products, electrical supplies, alcoholic beverages
Trade retail	120.6	16	Lumber and building materials *, farm equipment *, motor vehicles *, sporting goods and bicycles *, fuel *
Finance (banking, insurance, real estate)	139.0 [c]	37	Commercial banking * (69% in largest 17 SMSAs) (96% in 100 small metropolitan areas *) Securities brokers *, insurance, investment companies *

Table 2–7 (continued)

Industry	*National Income (billions)*	*Portion of National Income under Market Power* [a]	*Concentrated Major Markets* [b]
Services	167.3	52	Hotels *, funeral services *, news syndicates, car rentals, movies, pro sports, medical *, legal *, accounting and related *
Total	$1,024.0	42	

Note: Asterisked markets indicate regional or product submarket shares.
[a] The figures for construction and for manufacturing are estimates.
[b] Refers to the percentage controlled by the largest four firms in the industry; selected leading firms are named.
[c] Includes a large sum for imputed rent for owner-occupied houses.
Source: Personal communication from William G. Shepherd. See also Shepherd, *The Economics of Industrial Organization* (Englewood Cliffs, N.J.: Prentice-Hall, 1978).

the whole American private economy, first for corporations and then for unions. They reveal that about 35 to 45 percent of economic activity seems to occur in controlled markets.

This control varies considerably among regions and product lines. Table 2–7 highlights the large, dominant corporations. It shows that agriculture, despite the growth of corporate farming, has no measurable market power. Mining, on the other hand, has considerable concentration and is linked vertically to similarly concentrated manufacturing lines. Construction is somewhat concentrated in terms of regions.

Manufacturing is concentrated nationwide, and the concentration is growing. In 1941 the one thousand largest corporations controlled two-thirds of all manufacturing assets. In 1971 just two hundred firms controlled two-thirds of a much larger quantity of manufacturing assets. In 1954 industrial sales of the largest five hundred firms was about half of total sales; by 1974 it was two-thirds of total sales. In 1954 these firms earned two-thirds of total profits; in 1974 they earned three-quarters.[27] Half of U.S. manufactur-

Table 2–8 Market Power of Unions, 1974

Industry	*Thousands Non-supervisory Employees*	*% under Minimum Wage Law*	*% Unionized*	*Leading Unions*
Agriculture	1,373	43	3	United Farm Workers, Teamsters
Mining	612	99	54	United Mine Workers
Construction	3,771	99	73	17 building trades, including bricklayers, carpenters, operating engineers, plumbers, painters, iron workers, laborers (IUNA), sheet metal workers, electricians (IBEW)
Manufacturing	17,980	97	50	Many unions, including auto (UAW); electrical (UE, IUE), steelworkers, boilermakers, rubber workers, machinists, garment workers, clothing workers, graphic arts, typographical, meat cutters, paper workers, oil and chemical workers, bakers, printing pressmen, woodworkers
Transportation and utilities	4,185	98	77	Truckers (Teamsters), maritime, seafarers, longshoremen (ILA, ILWA), united transportation, machinists (airlines, IAM), transport workers, railway and steamship clerks, transit union, railway carmen, airline pilots, communications workers (CWA), postal workers, letter carriers
Trade wholesale	3,679	80	8	Retail clerks (RCIA), retail, wholesale, and department store workers
Trade retail	11,594	69		
Finance	3,576	76	1	

Table 2–8 (continued)

Industry	*Thousands Non-supervisory Employees*	*% under Minimum Wage Law*	*% Unionized*	*Leading Unions*
Services	10,223	73	16	Service employees (SEIU); hotel, restaurant, and bartenders; hospital (part of another union or SEIU); professional associations (not counted as unions); musicians
Private households	1,830	73		
Governmental	8,965	100	27	State, county, and municipal employees (AFSCME), government employees (AFGE, federal), police (FOP, other unions), teachers (AFT, NEA, UPC), firefighters government (NAGE), Teamsters
Total	67,788	86	30.7	

Note: Percentage unionized based on 1972. In 1972 there were 21 million union members, 79 percent of them in unions federated with the AFL-CIO. There were some 113 unions affiliated with the AFL-CIO and 62 independents. Major independents and their percentage of total union membership were the Teamsters (9 percent), United Auto Workers (UAW, 7 percent), United Mine Workers (UMW, 1 percent), United Electrical (UE, 0.8 perent), and a governmental union, NAGE (0.5 percent), leaving less than 3 percent in small, unaffiliated unions. Teamsters and UAW work in a number of industries. Some businesses have one industry-wide union; others are split up into a number of craft unions.
Sources: *Statistical Abstract of the United States, 1975*, pp. 369, 371, 372; Wilfred Sheed and Judith Ramsay, *Atlantic Monthly*, July 1973, pp. 42–69.

ing takes place in markets with four-firm concentration ratios over 70 percent.[28] Size does not necessarily mean market power, but there is a correlation.

Transportation and utilities are highly concentrated, partly because utilities are natural monopolies. Trade, like agriculture, is mostly competitive. Finance is not concentrated nationally because laws limit banks to accepting deposits in one state only. It is concentrated regionally by state, however. Services are very diverse; some are concentrated and others are not.

Concentration also comes from the union side, especially in mining, construction, manufacturing, and transportation. Less than a third of non-supervisory personnel are unionized. In 1974 there were 175 labor unions with 22 million members in a total labor force of 93 million, showing just 23 percent of the whole labor force in unions, concentrated in the urban North and West. In construction and trucking, unions are especially important because there is much less concentration on the employer side. Unions can increase concentration in industries like mining and manufacturing, as has occurred in the coal and beer industries.

It should be clear that most economic activity is in relatively competitive markets and most workers are not organized. The problem of economic analysis is to figure out how, and how much, the organized firms and workers can take advantage of unorganized businesses, consumers, and workers.

Not only is the analysis difficult, but firms have resisted revealing the information necessary to make it. In spite of the huge volume of information flowing from business to government, there has been no adequate system for line-of-business reporting. Yet lines of business, or markets, are what we have to know about. In their reporting, conglomerates mix together the accounting information on all of their lines. For example, all major car rental agencies are owned by larger firms, so we have no way of knowing if concentration is producing excess profits. The Federal Trade Commission in 1979, after years of litigation, finally succeeded in getting line-of-business reports from the conglomerates. They do not like to give up information, which they fear competitors will use. Even presidents had helped them block the FTC.[29] They correctly fear that if others know how well they are doing, they will get more competition. Their fear is the consumers' hope. Information is an important tool against market power.

How Market Power Works

Firms and unions with market power try to increase their prices and wages or keep them up when others have to lower theirs. They can force the costs of fighting inflation onto the unorganized. In a stable money supply situation, the unorganized would be forced by unemployment and bankruptcy to lower their prices of goods and labor. Since we have tended to increase the money supply and have inflation, the unorganized find themselves unable to increase their prices and wages as fast as the organized can.

Corporations with market power will absorb a severe decline in sales before considering a price decrease. Unions with power will absorb prolonged unemployment, sometimes helped by food stamps, unemployment compensation, and other tax-supported benefits, before taking a cut in pay.[30] Table 2–9 shows the ability of firms with market power to resist downward pressure on prices caused by economic contraction. Most recently, while competitive firms were raising prices 1.8 percent, dominant firms were raising theirs by 27 percent. (During expansions, competitive firms raise prices faster than do dominant firms.) Inflation has coincided with a decline in productivity since 1965, with corporations being able to pass along higher labor costs to the consumer.[31]

Among the organized are many linkages. Once established, unions avoid jurisdictional disputes with each other. Unions and corporations tacitly cooperate behind a facade of conflict and recrimination to pass on their costly settlements to customers. Firms are organized across industrial boundaries by traditional relations—between banks and manufacturers and by interlocking boards of directors, for example. The largest 123 corporations control over $1 trillion in assets, about one-fourth of all corporate assets. On average, each corporation connects with half the others through 530 direct and 12,193 indirect interlocks. In a *direct interlock,* a director of company A serves also on the board of B; in an *indirect interlock,* a director of A and a director of B meet as directors of company C. The bigger the corporation, the more it is interlocked with others. A few institutional investors, especially banks, may hold controlling interests in many corporations, but information of this sort is scanty. Ownership can be hidden. For example, seven banks used fifty-three misleading "street names" to hide their power over major electric utilities.[32] Big corporations have their own financial reserves and special lines of credit; they have a huge debt with its nearly autonomous role in the money supply.

Reformers sympathize more with unions generally because individually the income of the worker is so much lower than that of the executives and owners of businesses. Many unions in declining industries, faced with competition from abroad, new technology, or changes in consumer preferences find they do not get much advantage from their apparent power. Members of other unions may succeed in earning middle-class incomes, and the average union member is better off than the general population.[33] Often high hourly wages do not translate into high median annual incomes, however, because of chronic layoff, seasonal, and weather problems, which shorten the number of hours worked in a year, especially in construction.[34] Unions in the South and among farm workers are still struggling to organize.

Nevertheless, in particular local situations and industries, abuses of union power are occurring. Also, the relatively small increase in workers' wages may have much more economic impact than a sizable increase for executives because workers are so much more numerous. Restrictive work rules, violence, featherbedding, licensing restrictions, seniority rules, race

Table 2–9 Market Power in Manufacturing

		Changes in Prices	
Peak of Cycle after Business Expansion	*Trough of Cycle after Business Contraction*	*In Competitive Markets*	*In Monopolized Markets*
November 1948	October 1949	−7.8%	− 1.9%
July 1953	August 1954	−1.5	+ 1.9
July 1957	April 1958	−0.3	+ 0.5
May 1960	February 1961	−4.0	+ 0.1
November 1969	November 1970	−3.0	+ 5.9
December 1973	May 1975	+1.8	+27.0

Source: Howard J. Sherman, *Stagflation* (New York: Harper and Row, 1976) p. 165. Competitive markets were defined as those where eight firms controlled 50 percent of sales or less. Monopolized markets were defined as those where eight firms controlled 50 percent of sales or more.

and sex discrimination, and limited apprenticeship programs have negative economic impacts. In a broader context, professional associations (doctors, for example), can act in the same way as unions, restricting supply to increase the price of their labor by as much as 20 to 30 percent.

Reformers tend to be more critical of corporations, some advocating socialistic solutions and others focusing more narrowly on ad hoc regulation of specific markets. The great irony of our system of free competition is that its greatest defenders, the dominant corporations, practice it the least and have done the most to destroy it. Business is honest in saying that it seeks to maximize profits but less so in calling the system competitive. Competition, especially price competition, tends to cut profits, so big business tends to advertise all aspects of a product but its price. The ability to raise a price above competitive levels to get more profit is the most obvious aspect of market power. Monopolies may charge quite a premium, while oligopolies (the market is controlled by a few firms) may charge only a few cents above a competitive price. In both cases, though, the extra amount represents pure profit. In a typical case, a 10 to 30 percent price increase can double profits over the competitive level of about 6 to 8 percent. Less obvious aspects of market power are more inefficiency and waste, less production, less innovation, loss of productivity, and resistance to new technologies. An actual conspiracy among similar firms may not be necessary; price administration may follow unspoken agreements. The biggest firm in a concentrated market tends to benefit most of all.[35] Leading dominant firms include Exxon, General Motors, General Electric, IBM, Kodak, Xerox, Procter and Gamble, Coca Cola, Polaroid, Gillette, Kellogg, and U.S. Steel. Their power has been stable. Of the five hundred largest industrial firms in 1954, only fifty-six were not still in the largest five hundred twenty years later in 1974. The expansion of large business has meant the contraction of small business, whose influence with local elites does not extend to national elites. The cost of restricted market competition is difficult to estimate; it probably ranges from 3 to 9 percent of GNP.[36] In 1980 we can estimate the cost between $75 billion and $226 billion.

How to Get Market Power

Historically, there have been many different ways for firms to get market power. Around the turn of the century, again in the 1920s, and during the conglomerate movements of the late 1960s and 1970s, there were waves of mergers. The earlier ones tried to establish *trusts,* or cooperation among major firms in a market to squeeze out the others and boost prices. The gradual response was regulation, which now tries to prevent mergers in restraint of trade and to police numerous other unfair business practices. The current basis for market power also varies. In some industries, the high capital costs of getting started are a barrier to entry by potential competitors. The petroleum industry is an example. Psychological or image-oriented advertising can also produce monopoly, a strange one because it is based on the willing cooperation of the victim, the consumers. Patents are a legal monopoly, providing the incentive for invention, but in some cases the incentive may be too high. For example, drug prices are allowed to be high, making drug companies among the highest in return on the stockholders' equity. The government pays for 65 percent of drug research but does not share in the profits. Advertising also plays a role here to encourage physicians to prescribe specific brands of drugs. The government plays a role in market power when industry captures excessive influence in rate regulation. The federal government is also the enforcer of the laws supporting unions, including the Davis-Bacon and Walsh Healy acts, which require high union scale on federal contracts.

Examples of market power abound, but we will look at only one illustration: oil refining. The oil business is the biggest industry in the nation. Nine firms—Exxon, Texaco, Mobil, Standard Oil of California, Gulf, Standard Oil of Indiana, Shell, Continental, and Atlantic Richfield—are in the top twenty largest firms on the Fortune 500, and by far the largest industry group in the top twenty. There are ten more "small" oil companies in the next eighty and thirteen more after that, making thirty-one oil companies in the top five hundred altogether. They alone made over one-third of all earnings of the Fortune 500. The largest eight control 58 percent of national refining capacity, which on the surface seems to be a low market share. For many reasons, however, oil firms have market power. Oil markets—for example, gasoline—are regional rather than national, and regional sales are more concentrated. The companies swap crude oil and gasoline back and forth as needed. They form joint ventures and partnerships to bid on oil leases, to explore, to buy oil from the Mideast, and to ship oil through pipelines. Their strong vertical integration (from exploration to gas pump) makes it difficult for anyone to compete in just one operation. They use their control over gas stations to influence what tires, batteries, and accessories will be sold. They are expanding into other forms of energy and diversifying to other lines. They keep crude oil prices artificially high to take advantage of tax breaks. At the same time they can squeeze firms that operate only in refining or marketing. These factors produce a tight oligopoly in spite of the large number of firms.

Policies for Market Power

Political Climate. Each case of market power has its own remedy, but the first general step is to change the political climate. Market power has political roots, making the government itself one of the major causes of noncompetitive private practices. The regulatory agencies that set rates are perhaps the worst offenders, especially the Civil Aeronautics Board (CAB) and the Interstate Commerce Commission (ICC). Historically, the CAB has upheld artificially high rates, not only by inflating airline profits and overcharging consumers but also allowing wasteful flying of empty seats. Their rationale was to maintain service to low-volume airports and avoid chaotic, cutthroat competition. The fuel crisis, continued exposure, a new law, and some new CAB commissioners have begun to change the situation. In 1977, for example, the CAB approved cheaper fares to Europe, fares that it had rejected in 1974. In 1978 competition was relatively free, and the airlines carried 18 percent more passengers, increased profits 76 percent, and cut fares.[37]

The ICC regulates truck and rail rates in a way that requires trucks to travel empty on many return trips, that prevents efficient and innovative development of shipping among the different modes of sea, rail, air, and highway, and that has prevented innovation in railroading. The cost is estimated as high as $2.8 billion just in misallocation of freight between truck and rail.[38] CAB, ICC, and Federal Maritime Commission restraints on trade may cost as much as $23 billion per year.[39]

Although truck, rail, and water transportation have potential for competition, electrical power utilities and local telephones are inherent monopolies and require rate regulation or public ownership. Both approaches can be successful if properly managed. Private ownership tends toward political influence by the utility over the regulator. The regulators are the Federal Power Commission for interstate sales of energy, the Federal Communications Commission for telephones, and state public utilities commissions for intrastate power and telephones. Public ownership has less incentive to be efficient, but this does not seem to prevent it from being about as efficient as private industry.[40] Rate regulation has worked fairly well, but the regulatory agencies tend to be chronically understaffed and occasionally dominated by proindustry commissioners. The Federal Communications Commission, for example, has never held a full hearing on AT&T expenses, which have to be established (along with asset values) so that rates can be set. The FCC lacks the staff and the political will. FCC commissioners claim that they can be effective in regulating AT&T, the world's largest corporation, by talking with AT&T executives.[41]

There are many other regulatory and procurement agencies at the state and national level, each tending to be highly specialized and having missions other than the promotion of competition. These characteristics produce the invisibility that allows the effective functioning of the intensity problem. The industry that is intensely affected lobbies and campaigns for its vested interest, while the public generally is unaware of even the existence of the agencies.[42] One promising remedy is a consumer protection agency to advocate a public interest in the proceedings of the regulatory agencies, reducing the domination of vested interests. Such advocacy would parallel that of the courts.

International Trade. Turning to the general private economy, we find that a major force promoting competition has been international trade, a result of the policy of low trade barriers (such as low tariffs). Many Americans have lost their jobs because products manufactured by low-wage foreign workers are less costly. American investors have accelerated this process by building plants outside U.S. borders, but even they have not managed to outcompete the Japanese, West Germans, and others. In many product lines, there no longer is very much American production. What may seem unfair to some workers has countervailing benefits, however. Because foreigners have more of our money, they import more of our exports, providing new jobs for Americans. The Japanese may export quality cameras, but they import cheap ones (along with soybeans, logs, high technology goods, and so on). Our exports are especially strong in primary products, machinery, and weapons. The imports also benefit consumers by providing lower prices.

Europe and Japan have been so successful selling to us that they have increased their own incomes so much that they are no longer so competitive. They are starting to invest in the United States, creating jobs here to take advantage of cheap American labor. The world is increasingly interdependent. We need to make the competition fairer, however, by diplomatically seeking to lower barriers to our exports, to stop governmental subsidies to foreign imports, to develop foreign trade unions, and to increase foreign investment in environmental protection.

Antitrust Policy. Another general policy directed at maintaining competition is called *antitrust,* managed by the offices of the attorneys general of the states, at the federal level in the Anti-Trust Division of the Justice Department, and in the Federal Trade Commission (FTC). These agencies and private lawyers spurred by the prospect of triple damages have proven generally adept at controlling price fixing.

In May 1979, for example, twenty-two corrugated box manufacturers agreed to pay $298.1 million in settlements in a class-action civil suit against price fixing.[43]

The agencies also police an incredible variety of unfair business practices and have occasionally prevented mergers that would lessen competition. But they have been totally ineffective since the 1920s in breaking up the larger firms, and many other mergers have gone through. Consent decrees have given away power that should have been used to foster competition. (*Consent decrees* are agreements between a regulator and a firm, usually negotiated behind closed doors.) Major antitrust suits are too long, complex, and costly. Successful antitrust actions in the 1910s made the oil and tobacco industries much more competitive today than they would otherwise be. Yet the oil business has grown so much that the pieces of the Standard Oil trust today are bigger than the original company. Popular sentiment makes the oil companies an easy target, yet they are probably not the worst offenders of market power. Antitrust laws need strengthening, but there is little public support for the idea. The benefits of creating more competition are indirect, and they are hard to measure.

Wage and Price Control. There is much more popular support for wage and price control, although this is usually framed in terms of controlling inflation. In World War II, control worked fairly successfully. But when it was used again from August 1971 to January 1973, it did not. The disagreement is over whether control failed because it cannot work, as conservatives say, or because it was poorly administered, as liberals say. The two criticisms are related. The problem was that the controls imposed during the Nixon administration attempted to do too much with too little bureaucratic manpower and in the absence of legislation that would regulate conflict. It seems likely that any system attempting to control the whole economy cannot work because the bureaucracy required would be too big and expensive and thus self-defeating. The practical realities forced themselves on the Nixon control system, and more and more the competitive parts of the economy were exempted. To focus as needed on the monopolistic companies would require a change in the rationale of the program from controlling inflation to controlling one of its causes, market power. Also, a far bigger bureaucracy would have been needed, and since the problem is permanent, the bureaucracy would have to be permanent also. Instead the controls were ended prematurely, and inflation resumed.

One approach worth trying compromises the liberal and conservative positions and aims at market power. A wage-price monitoring agency, possibly the FTC, could monitor markets and assess their competitiveness. Serious problems would be more closely monitored, and existing antitrust and regulatory tools would be vigorously applied. The worst offenders would be subject to wage-price controls similar to those of utilities, on the principle that noncompetitive firms do not run much risk and deserve only the profits of the low-risk utilities. The controls would be implemented by a bureaucracy large enough to do the job, which would not be too expensive because only one or two major markets would be intervened. There would be no need to prove a conspiracy; the lack of competition would justify intervention, thus avoiding one of the major problems of existing law. The companies being controlled would be given an option of restructuring the industry to make it more competitive. If a restructuring plan were acceptable to the government, the controls would be removed and the industry broken up according to the plan.

There is little chance that this reform will occur because no one is demanding it. The best that can be said is that a new generation of economists is laying the theoretical and empirical groundwork that may eventually change the climate of opinion regarding the causes of inflation. Then politicians, the media, public-interest groups, and active citizens may move it higher on their agendas, overcoming the intensity problem and producing some action.

Consumer Protection and Advertising. Another aspect of market power is consumer information about the goods and services they buy. This has been one of the constant themes of the consumer protection movement. Other major thrusts have been the meeting of standards and protection of health and safety by regulation. The consumer protection movement involves many more activists at many levels than attempts at reforming market power. One reason is that the informational, health, and safety aspects are more easily conceptualized, rousing more concern. The complexity of most other market power issues impedes participation.

An example of consumer information reform is to require more information about the products and services we buy. Food packages have weight, contents in descending order by weight, and nutritional value printed on the label as a result of reforms. But they could also have more specificity regarding contents, proportions of the major ingredients, and shelf life. An example of the meeting of standards would be the repair of technically complex products like electrical appliances and vehicles. Consumers themselves cannot police repair services. The government can require some knowledge through licensing requirements and can check on honesty by posing as a customer and requesting repair of a rigged television or car. Such programs have worked well, increasing consumer confidence and benefiting legitimate businesses at low public cost. However, much remains to be done. Research by the U.S. Department of Transportation using three test situations in sixty-two auto repair shops found that fifty-three cents of each repair dollar was wasted.[44]

Advertising is another aspect of market power, which creates brand-name monopolies. The primary positive function of most advertising is to improve consumer information and thus the efficiency of consumer decisions. This in turn creates confidence, increases sales volumes of the more attractive goods and services, and lowers prices. Much advertising, perhaps most, fulfills this function. On the other hand, advertising also creates psychological satisfactions and brand-name identification. A large part of the price of detergents, cosmetics, tobacco, alcohol, fast food, toys, toothpaste, aspirin, cold remedies, and other items is caused by the cost of advertising, especially on television. This advertising appeals to personal insecurities, hypochondria, self-indulgence, nicotine and alcohol addiction, and children. Most claims are undocumented and are even too vague to be documented. Government tries to stop false advertising, but it does not present very much useful consumer information on television. As a result, much of our culture consists of commercialism and the bland, biased, and violent programming it sponsors.

The other side of the problem is nonadvertising. Bans on advertising reflecting consumer interests (such as the ban on cigarette commercials on television) are relatively rare. Far more frequent are the bans on advertising of professional services and certain products, especially prescription drugs. Lawyers, for example, find it very difficult to establish a practice because they cannot announce their fees or even their presence in a community. The result is less choice and higher prices.

There is in all of this an important question about how much the government should defend us and how much we should defend ourselves. Government must do much, but a large responsibility falls to us. Few publications are more useful for this than *Consumer Reports*. And few things would jolt the economy into greater efficiency than consumers paying more thoughtful attention to their spending.

The power of elites is manifest economically in tax loopholes, subsidies, inflation, unemployment, market power, consumer information, and advertising. The intensity problem and cooption make it difficult to reform the system. For example, tax reform requires horizontal equity, vertical equity, and greater simplicity. The case study showed the importance of procedural reform, and the citizen profile reminds us of the importance of state and local tax reform. To control inflation, we need tax reform, restraint on social and military spending, and the resulting balanced or surplus budget to hold down money supply. We cannot use fiscal-monetary policy to stimulate employment but should pay attention directly to hard-core unemployment, especially to create public-service jobs. Dominant corporations and a few unions exercise market power at the expense of small business, unorganized workers, and consumers. We need to strengthen a number of policies fostering competition, such as deregulation. Consumers must also do more to protect themselves.

Notes

1. *San Francisco Chronicle,* March 16, 1975, from the *Toronto Globe and Mail.*
2. The standard deviation is 0.7 for the eight figures. Chance accounts for some variation.
3. *Statistical Abstract of the United States, 1978,* pp. 288, 290.
4. Malcolm Sawyer, "Income Distribution in the OECD Countries," in *OECD Economic Outlook: Occasional Studies* (Paris: OECD, 1976).
5. Joseph Pechman and Benjamin Okner, *Who Bears the Tax Burden?* (Washington, D.C.: Brookings Institution, 1974), p. 62.
6. "State and Local Bonds," *Public Interest Economics,* March–April 1978, p. 3.
7. *People and Taxes,* June 1975, pp. 6–10, published by Tax Reform Research Group.
8. *Statistical Abstract, 1978,* pp. 275, 570.
9. Ronnie Dugger, "Oil and Politics," *Atlantic Monthly,* September 1969, p. 73.
10. James Smith, "The Concentration of Personal Wealth in America, 1969," *Review of Income and Wealth,* June 1974, pp. 145–149.
11. Philip Stern, *Rape of the Taxpayer* (New York: Random House, 1973); *Special Analysis Budget of the United States Government, Fiscal Year 1980,* Executive Office of the President, Office of Management and Budget (U.S. Government Printing Office: Washington, D.C.) p. 208.
12. *Congressional Weekly,* February 24, 1979, pp. 341–342.
13. Money market certificates, an innovation allowing savings and loan banks to offer returns comparable to Treasury bonds, seemed to work in 1978 to avoid loss of money for the construction industry.
14. *Special Analyses Budget, 1980,* p. 108.
15. Friends Committee on Legislation of California, *Newsletter* (March 1975).
16. *Special Analyses Budget, 1980,* pp. 109–110.
17. U.S. Bureau of Labor Statistics, *Employment and Earnings* (July 1977).
18. Ibid.
19. American Enterprise Institute, *Minimum Wage Legislation* (Washington, D.C., June 1977).

20. Ibid.
21. American Enterprise Institute, *Proposals to Prohibit Employment of Illegal Aliens* (Washington, D.C., October 1975).
22. *San Francisco Chronicle,* September 11, 1977.
23. *Budget, 1980,* pp. 211, 219.
24. *Special Analysis Budget, 1977.*
25. Ibid., p. 187; *Budget, 1980,* pp. 211, 219–230.
26. Congressional Budget Office, *Temporary Measures to Stimulate Employment* (September 2, 1975); *Defense Monitor* (September–October 1977).
27. Linda Grant Martin, "The 500: A Report on Two Decades," *Fortune,* May 1975, pp. 238–241.
28. Charles Mueller, "Monopoly," *Washington Monthly,* April 1971. See also Mueller, "Monopoly Power as the Cause of Inflation," pp. 81–98; Jerry Pohlman, "Wages, Unions, and Inflation: The Concept of Market Power," pp. 9–36; and Mayo Thompson, "Inflation and the Labor Unions," pp. 37–46, in *Wage-Price Law and Economics Review* 1:1 (1975).
29. *San Francisco Chronicle,* November 19, 1973, p. 58, from the *New York Times.*
30. Committee for Economic Development, *High Employment Without Inflation* (New York, 1972), p. 75.
31. *San Francisco Chronicle,* June 26, 1978, p. 55, from a *New York Times* article based on the Ph.D dissertation by B. Y. Hong for Columbia University in 1978.
32. Ibid., January 7, 1974, from the *Washington Post;* U.S. Senate, Committee on Governmental Affairs, *Interlocking Directorates Among the Major U.S. Corporations* (January 1978), p. 280.
33. *Hayward* (Calif.) *Daily Review,* October 5, 1975, from United Press, based on an AFL-CIO survey released in October 1975.
34. *Statistical Abstract, 1976,* pp. 368–377 (compare median annual earnings with hourly earnings). See also the 1978 *Abstract,* pp. 414–416, 428.
35. William G. Shepherd, "Elements of Market Structure," *Review of Economics and Statistics* (February 1972), and his *Market Power and Economic Welfare* (New York: Random House, 1970), pp. 186–194. See also Mueller, "Monopoly," and Ralph Nader and Mark Green, eds., *Corporate Power in America* (New York: Grossman, 1973); Federal Trade Commission, Bureau of Economics, *Staff Report on Market Shares, Concentration, and Competition in Manufacturing Industries* (Washington, D.C., September 1978), and its *Staff Report on Competition and Market Share Instability* (Washington, D.C., August 1978).
36. U.S. House, Subcommittee on Antitrust, *Future of Small Business in America,* Report 95-1810 (Washington, D.C.: Government Printing Office, 1978), p. 31.
37. "Where 'Deregulation' Works," *Consumer Reports,* May 1979, p. 284.
38. George Hilton, *The Northeast Railroad Problem* (Washington, D.C.: American Enterprise Institute, 1975).
39. American Enterprise Institute, *The Competition Policy Proposal* (Washington, D.C., September 1976).
40. Claire Wilcox and William G. Shepherd, *Public Policies Toward Business* (Homewood, Ill.: Irwin, 1975), chaps. 14, 15, and pt. 5, esp. pp. 555, 563, 599.
41. Nicholas Johnson, "Why Ma Bell Believes in Santa Claus," *Saturday Review,* March 11, 1972.
42. U.S. Senate, Committee on Governmental Affairs, *Study on Federal Regulation* (July 1977–December 1978).
43. *San Francisco Chronicle,* May 3, 1979.
44. Ibid., May 8, 1979, p. 3, from the *New York Times.*

3

Environment and Living Standards

The problems of economic reform that we have already discussed concern relations among human beings. Now we turn to the relations between humans and the environment, a complex equation of many variables and unknowns. We will discuss first the crucial balance between food and population and then turn to equally important questions of environmental quality, living standards, living styles, and technology. What balance of environmental quality and living standards do we want? How much are we willing to change technology and styles of life to get a better balance?

Population and Food

The fundamental truth has been hammered home by massive media coverage in recent years, based on extensive research and common sense: an increasing population compounds all of our environmental problems. Only a stable population is compatible with a healthy environment.

Populations have been booming in the last century and a half. Modern medicine has doubled life expectancies, and modern agriculture has greatly increased food production. In less-developed countries, excess population means too little food; in developed countries, it means destruction of environmental quality by modern technologies. An American consumes about twenty-five times the resources of a person in a less-developed country.

It is impossible to predict how many people world agriculture can feed. Optimists tend to focus on part of the problem, solving each part by increasing the application of resources from the other parts. Environmentalists (our reformers) tend to be more pessimistic, recognizing how all of the parts are related. They also are aware of how much destruction has already occurred. Several civilizations have destroyed their ecological basis through deforestation, overgrazing, overfishing, and salinization of irrigated land. American history can point to many cases of destroyed wilderness, polluted cities, and depleted resources. Environmentalists are also aware of our ability to shield ourselves from perceiving these problems and our ability to rationalize what we do see. Food and population dramatically illustrate the problem.

The current major limit on population is food supply, including the related problems of severe maldistribution of food surpluses in favor of the affluent. While the world's poor die of starvation, the affluent eat plenty of meat, overeat, waste food, and feed pets. Historically, and even today, starvation is the major method of controlling and reducing excess population. About 15 percent of all people have too little food. Starvation deaths as such are concentrated usually in drought areas. Starvation-related deaths are more commonplace: malnutrition weakens the body to diseases such as tuberculosis, pneumonia, intestinal ills, and diseases of infancy.

Limits on Food Production

Much of the food produced by modern agriculture takes advantage of fossil fuels, putting in more fuel energy than is produced in energy in the form of food. The great increase in productivity of modern agriculture is measured in terms of money, not energy. Thus, the United States produces three times as much food per acre as India but uses ten times the input of energy.[1] Many proposals to increase food supply also require an increase in energy inputs. We have doubled output, but only by increasing the energy input by ten times.[2] This energy subsidy is the essence of the Green Revolution and takes the form of equipment, irrigation investments, pesticides, and fertilizer, without which the new miracle strains of crops produce less than native strains. One ton of nitrogenous fertilizer requires one ton of steel and five tons of coal.[3] The Green Revolution buys time, delaying the day of reckoning, but we have not been taking advantage of it to control population and reform agriculture.

Good agricultural land is fixed and limited. In the United States, for example, the best 50 percent of the agricultural land supplies over 80 percent of food. Since 1935 about 100 million acres have been so eroded they can no longer be farmed. Also, the long-term productivity of prime land is being destroyed by chemical fertilizers. The most uncleared land is in the tropics, where slash and burn techniques allow four to five years of good crops before the soil is depleted. Under certain conditions, the rain may leach out the nutrients, and the sun may bake the clay soil too hard to plow. Without plants to hold and slow the flow of water, there can be erosion and flooding. Without the gradual release of water through transpiration of plants, the atmosphere becomes drier, and the area can turn to desert. The problem of desertification is a worldwide one increasing in urgency. Land can be irrigated by dams and irrigation projects but with risks and problems: energy costs, the spread of bilharzia (or schistosomiasis, a debilitating parasitic disease), waterlogging, and salinization. Land is also being destroyed by overgrazing, deforestation, and urbanization. Just when we need more land, it is being destroyed by ignorance and overpopulation.

Water is also essential, yet rainfall is limited. Groundwater is being pumped out faster than natural recharge, risking land sinking and salt water intrusion into underground aquifers. Even with drip irrigation and other conservation techniques, the amount of land and water is limited. Water systems have to be maintained against water weeds, which slow water flow and increase evaporation. Desalinization is expensive, uses much energy, and produces hot brines, a pollutant.

We can hope for more food from the sea, but it is mostly a biological desert. There must be nutrients for life, which come from continental runoff and upwelling ocean currents. Estuaries, coastal marsh, and the top layer of nourished water are the most important for life, yet they are also being polluted and destroyed at a rapid rate. Whales are nearly extinct, and the decline of other seafood indicates overfishing and overharvesting of shellfish.

Instability of climate and of monocultures is another major problem. We do not experience statistically average weather; real weather has great variations, reducing food supply. Even minor drought can cut production 30 to 40 percent. Our own activities can adversely affect the weather. Pollution, for example, blocks sunlight and slows plant growth. Regional monoculture means the use of the same crop (such as wheat or corn) in a large area and, increasingly in tropical areas, the strains of the Green Revolution. Plant diseases can spread extremely rapidly. Monoculture also reduces the genetic diversity needed to discover new strains to resist new diseases. Thus the real food production falls well below the possible ideal, and living too close to the ideal is very risky.

Food is further limited when the pollution produced by food production interferes with the main purpose. Fertilizers are especially dangerous, for excess nitrates cause groundwater pollution, loss of humus, and eutrofication. Pollution in general has already lowered our food production potential.

Food production will be limited also because of competition of the factors of production. The effects of producing meat are serious; the feeding of one cow eliminates food in the form of cereals for five to ten people. We also need cotton, wood, and other nonfood products from land that could produce food. Water, land, and energy are needed for mining, manufacturing, cities, and transportation. In the United States, millions of acres of prime farmland have been destroyed by housing and streets and only partially made up in newly irrigated land of lower quality and higher cost of production. About 1.25 million acres of farmland are being taken out of production each year.

High technology holds little promise for productivity breakthroughs. Natural engineering over eons of experimentation has produced systems of great miniaturization, survivability, diversity, and energy efficiency. Human engineering tends to be bulky, hard to maintain, and energy inefficient.

With perfect food distribution today, we would all be a little undernourished. Yet the demographic momentum (a young age distribution producing many children) of world population growth dictates that we will grow from our current (1977) 4 billion to over 6 billion by 2000. The Japanese, the world's most efficient farmers, have not found ways to improve their productivity very much over the last forty years. All of these problems suggest perhaps a sustainable population of about 5 billion people—a billion less than projected for 2000—if we can sustain the high energy inputs.[5]

Future Agricultural Systems

The long-term problem is not so much how we can feed a growing population but how we can sustain even the population we have now. If there are any grounds for optimism, it is in the combination of going forward with scientific research and going backward to more labor-intensive and nature-imitating forms of food production. Science can improve strains—by getting plants, for example, to fix their own nitrogen. The old techniques can get a high energy efficiency of fifteen of food for one of input and may be able to get fifty from one.[6] Highly polluting pesticides can be replaced by integrated pest management, especially biological controls. Under exacting conditions of water purity and location, farming the sea can be highly productive; fish ponds and rice paddies, for example, imitate natural systems but require much labor. Pollution may be turned around and used; water weeds and algae can be harvested for fuel, fertilizer, and possibly food. Reclaimed waste water and household gray water systems can supply water that is now wasted. Native tropical gardening and food crops from tropical trees show promise.

Ecological farming can use composted animal, crop, and sewage wastes for fertilizer. Such farming is economically competitive with high energy approaches and still uses labor-saving machinery.[7] Such farms are likely to be compartmentalized, mixing forestry, pasturage, crops, ponds and wetland, and intensive gardens, avoiding the instabilities of monoculture. They may be a useful compromise between the drudgery of farm labor and the energy waste of modern systems.

Scientific gardening, by contrast, is labor intensive, but a few hours per week of work can be enough to supply a whole family and can provide a welcome change from a sedentary occupation. Such gardening uses raised beds of loose, aerated soil; a variety of plants to replenish nutrients in the soil, to control pests, and to stimulate each other; triple or even quadruple cropping; natural fertilizers; dense planting to produce a greenhouse effect; and intense weeding. About fifteen square yards can produce enough food for a family of four; on half an acre, a full-time worker could produce enough crops to earn $8,000 a year. This system uses much more labor, no pesticides, no chemical fertilizers, less water by half, less waste, 1 percent the energy, and no fossil fuels, and it produces a yield per acre four times higher than does modern agriculture.[8]

Where populations are dense and poor, high-yield peasant agriculture may dominate; China, Taiwan, Ceylon, and Egypt are close to this already.[9] Where population is sparse, some agricultural production could go into methane or methanol fuel from agricultural waste and from algae farms, allowing some labor-saving machinery to be used and a larger area to be farmed. But the problem remains to ensure limited, stable population. Our soil bank is gone; high energy systems predominate; demand is at all-time high; buffer stocks are low. The world already lives on a thin margin.

Zero Population Growth

The other side of the food-people equation is that of pushing population down, or at least stabilizing it. We need to improve our scientific understandings of the *holding capacities* for the long term of each part of the earth's surface. The holding capacity is the number of a species in a given area compatible with biological diversity, stability and durability. We need to understand better the trade-offs between quantity and quality of life. In the developed parts of the world, affluence and education have lowered fertility rates dramatically, indicating that where choice is possible, population can stabilize using voluntary methods. A few countries in Europe have achieved zero growth.

Voluntary birth control methods are growing in importance in poor countries too. China has an outstanding program based on delayed marriages, services provided to women in isolated areas, authoritarian puritanism, and production-oriented patriotism. Recently, China increased economic incentives to individuals to reduce births. Several smaller countries have made good progress too.

By and large, however, growing recognition of the problem in underdeveloped countries has not yet produced much action. Cultural resistance and insurance births (extra children to be sure some survive) are major problems in rural areas, but more important is the resistance of governments and their unwillingness to push family planning services desired by many of their citizens. An estimated one-fifth of babies are not wanted. The youthful age distributions of Africa, Latin America, and Asia imply high birthrates in the future. The problem is relevant for the United States. We are the major food supplier to the excess population, and the surplus poor of Mexico, through illegal immigration, are a major factor in our continued population growth.

U.S. population growth, though slowing, may still add about 40 million people to our 1977 population by the year 2000. The general willingness to have small families and the continuing expansion of family planning services are contributing to stabilization and have produced a growth rate of 0.75 percent.

Much of our progress, and even world progress, is the result of the tremendous efforts of one major public-interest group, Planned Parenthood and World Population. It has clinics in 350 American cities, programs in 74 poor countries, and an annual budget of $110 million (1976), much supplied by contributions.

Of the many areas of interest, we will discuss two that are major issues: abortion and teenage pregnancy.

Abortion. Japan, the Soviet Union, and other countries use abortion almost routinely. Without it, their population growth could be 50 percent higher. However, their experience indicates that abortion declines as other methods of birth control are developed.

A sense of the sacredness of life is violated by abortion. The discrete event of a fertilized egg growing in the womb is one meaningful way of defining new life. For those who consider the fertilized egg as a life, termination by abortion is murder. Most of us have a strong parenting instinct; it may be stronger in women, particularly women who have cared for infants and children. Some activists proclaim a right to life for the fetus and seek political support for the abortion-as-murder point of view.

The position of reformers is less simplistic and has a greater sense of tragedy. They believe that life begins when the fetus is able to survive outside the mother's body, about the twenty-eighth week of pregnancy. Prior to that, the fetus is not a separate life; it is totally dependent upon the mother's body. Medically, abortion in the first three months of pregnancy can be performed in much greater safety than bearing a child. Morally, then, the issue is one to be decided by the mother in the first trimester. Abortion involves not life taking but the right of women to regulate their own reproductive processes.

Abortion also presents social questions. Is it worse for an unwanted child to be born or for the mother to have an abortion? How can we balance between life defined quantitatively or biologically, and life defined qualitatively, in which abundant nurturance is as important as birth itself? Abortions and unwanted children may be equally undesirable as a result of the failure to prevent conception in the first place.

Most reformers probably feel uneasy about saying they favor abortion because it is such an undesirable form of birth control compared with other methods, yet they support it. Before the abortion reforms of the early 1970s, women who wanted abortions frequently tried to abort themselves or had it done illegally, and they frequently died. Concern for these women became another reason for Planned Parenthood and many public-health professionals to seek reform. The politics of reform did not spring from the women who needed abortions, who were generally nonpolitical, concerned only with their specific problem, undesirous of publicity, and only temporarily in trouble.

In January 1973, the Supreme Court swept away the mosaic of laws on abortion and tied its decision to the constitutional right of personal liberty guaranteed by the Fourteenth Amendment. Abortion clinics sprang up to provide the service, the number of abortions boomed, and the number of maternal deaths dropped to almost zero. Although the Catholic church is particularly outspoken against abortion many of its members have followed the general public in a massive change of opinion toward tolerance.

So-called prolife (antiabortion) forces persist nevertheless and have succeeded in stopping federal funding for abortions for low-income women. Medicaid abortions in 1974 cost $180 each versus $2,200 for the costs of pregnancy and delivery. It would be hard to find a political group weaker than low-income women, except, perhaps, poor children. Most of the congressmen who voted for the cutoff were the same who have voted against benefit programs for these poor women and their children.[10] The same Congress continues to support abortion benefits for all federal employees, however, and has failed to promote positive alternatives, such as sex education.

Teenage Pregnancy. About 11 million teenagers are sexually active, and about 1 million teenage girls get pregnant every year; 30,000 are under the age of fifteen. About 40 percent of the pregnancies are aborted, linking this problem to the one just discussed.[11] But for the rest who have their babies, the problems are severe. The younger the mother, the poorer her family. Teenage mothers cannot get jobs; they go on welfare and get divorced at very high rates. Many are not married. Their pregnancies are part of a larger problem of adult neglect of teenagers, sometimes by families, often by educational and other social institutions.

Many American teenagers are caught up in a philosophy of naive romantic spontaneity. They are likely to get into situations where "it" can happen but they "didn't plan it," which makes "it" all right. American rates of teenage pregnancy are much higher than for European countries, possibly reflecting the American embarrassment of older people talking to younger people about sex. Young people are inundated by mass media emphasis on romantic love. Social pressures for sex are often much greater than those against it. In times past, social and economic sanctions against women having babies out of wedlock were extreme, not to say inhumane. Now we seem to have gone too far in the other direction, with no effective sanctions at all. The cost of the baby is paid by welfare programs, and thus by society as a whole, subsidizing the irresponsibility of immature parent-children.

We have spent hundreds of millions dealing with the consequences; now we are beginning to promote prevention. Some school systems and a few community centers for teenagers have good programs of education and counseling. In January 1978, the Carter administration proposed increased federal support for such efforts. All too often, however, controversy over sex education has paralyzed school systems, and many parents have not explained sex to their children. Reform will probably come one community at a time as a result of intensive efforts by a few active parents and teachers.

The longer-term questions regarding population growth remain. Is stabilization at a higher level enough? Or will we have to lower our numbers? Will we do it humanely and voluntarily? Will we have to use coercion? Or will nature do it to us?

Conservation and Extraction

Food versus population illustrates the larger problems of quality of life, living standards and styles, and technology. Population stabilization alone will solve only some of the problem of "standard of living" versus "quality of life." *Standard of living* is defined conventionally in America as having a job, having a decent place to live, having a car, and having some money. *Quality of life* concerns the overall environment within which the standard is enjoyed and the impact of the standard on the environment; it includes issues of pollution, conservation, the urban environment, and public spaces in general. Standard of living may mean having a camper; quality of life means having a place worth taking it to.

Most people are concerned about the environment and want to protect it, but only as long as existing standards of living are not jeopardized. Most people, unfortunately, have not thought very deeply about the conflicts between our current styles and technology and the quality of the environment.

In extracting huge quantities of resources from the earth (see table 3–1) and applying high energy technologies, we disrupt natural balances, destroy

Table 3–1 Resource Use per Capita in the United States

Nonrenewable Resources (1972)	*Pounds per Capita*	*Renewable Resources (1974)*	*Pounds per Capita*
Sand and gravel	9,000	Meats (carcass weight)	187.5
Stone	8,500	Fish (edible weight)	12.5
Cement	800	Eggs (number)	287
Clays	600	Poultry	50.6
Salt	450	Dairy products	345.2
Other nonmetals	1,200	Fats and oils	53.9
Iron and steel	1,200	Fruits	130.2
Aluminum	50	Vegetables (including	
Copper	25	potatoes)	294.0
Zinc	15	Beans, melons, peanuts	38.5
Lead	15	Sugar (refined)	101.9
Other metals	35	Grains	170.3
		Coffee and cocoa beans, tea	18.0
		Cotton (est.)	17.0
		Lumber, plywood, veneer (cu. ft.)	34.1
		Pulp products (cu. ft.)	23.1
		Wood, fuel, misc.	4.5

Note: We import over 90 percent of our platinum, chromium, aluminum, manganese, and cobalt; 50 to 90 percent of our titanium, tin, asbestos, nickel, zinc, and mercury; and 15 to 20 percent of our gypsum, iron, lead, and copper.

Source: *Statistical Abstract of the United States, 1975,* pp. 92, 639, 657; Council on Environmental Quality, *Environmental Quality, Fifth Annual Report,* (Washington, D.C.: Government Printing Office, December 1974).

the quality of life, and ultimately threaten life itself. The solutions require more protection of wilderness and resources, changes in our technologies, and, most difficult, changes in our material style of life within the same general standard of living. We need to reduce our resource needs, especially for energy, reduce pollution, reduce and recycle waste, deemphasize automobiles, and revitalize cities.

The elites and coopted middle-class groups profit from the existing system, downplay environmental degradation, assume their style of life will not change, strive to increase resource extraction, exaggerate the cost of transition, and pit environmentalists against those seeking conventional standards. They promote a generalized "growth is good" mentality characterized by exaggerated private property rights.

Wilderness

As one species among many, adaptable but only within limits, we need to understand nature. We study it to ensure our survival, to avoid becoming an endangered species ourselves. Our research may also discover less costly ways of doing things, reducing our need for resources. It may discover that preserving wilderness is cost-efficient and effective in ensuring survival. Studying nature is fascinating and satisfying; we can explore its ever-constant, ever-changing variety. Wilderness should be preserved for its beauty. It should be preserved for its health-giving recreational values: walking, picnicking, camping, water play, and other nonsitting, nonmotorized activities.

Including these reasons but transcending them, the reason most profoundly motivating for environmentalists, is spiritual. In a way neither logical nor illogical, the experience of wilderness transforms some people. "In wilderness is the preservation of the world" is the motto of a leading environmentalist public-interest group, the Sierra Club. The statement may be scientifically true, but its appeal is to our souls. We seek in wilderness deeper meanings, a special renewal, an expanded awareness, a fuller sense of being, and a closeness to the divine.

The protection of wilderness means protection of all kinds of habitat—not just the mountain with a lake in the foreground or a particularly windswept bit of beach. It includes oceans, continental shelves, tidal estuaries and coast, wild rivers and valleys, lakes and lakeshores, sand dunes, islands, hills, mountains, swamps, jungles, woodlands, thickets, chapparal, grasslands, plains, and deserts and their plant and animal species. It means protection against all kinds of extractive threats: mining, logging, grazing, power plants and power lines, erosion, dams, dredging, draining, filling, other water projects, recreational developments, urbanization by industry, shopping centers, subdivisions, and airports, and even against too many people walking on a path.

Resources

Very similar to wilderness preservation is the protection of productive resources, which have the additional justification of an obvious direct relation with the standard of living. These resources are of two types, renewable and nonrenewable. A further distinction can be made between physical and energy resources. Renewable physical resources include foods, fibers, and wood—the fish and crustaceans, grazing animals, grains, fruits, vegetables, legumes, other crops, cotton, other fibers, timber—and they include air and water. Nonrenewable physical resources include the metal and mineral ores, chemical ores, precious stones, sand and clay, construction aggregates (like gravel), coal and oil when used for products, and, in a sense, land. Renewable energy resources include hydroelectric power, geothermal power, tidal and wave action, wood, manure, vegetable waste, solar panels, windmills, draft animals, human energy, photoelectric cells, ocean thermal differences, and other forms of solar power. Nonrenewable energy resources include gas, oil, coal, coal shale, and uranium.

Conservation versus extraction poses clear-cut issues: to fell a tree or let it stand; to dam a river or let it run free; to fill for an airport or have a swamp; to build a pipeline or have a wilderness. For centuries, we had to be thoughtful about development because we had so little power at our disposal, and by the same token we encroached only gradually upon nature. Living in rural areas, hunting, fishing, and farming, we were so immersed in nature that we could hardly appreciate it. Its beauty was taken for granted, its bounty to be won by hard labor, its harshness to be feared and conquered. As the technological revolution began early in the nineteenth century in agriculture, industry, and urban life, nature became more bountiful and less harsh without a great threat being posed to wilderness and its resources. For the poor, the cities were as harsh as nature, and generally our economic relations with each other consumed our energies.

Even then a few conservationist issues were being posed and some political actions took place: Yosemite Valley saved in 1864, the marvels of Yellowstone in 1872. The national forests were established in 1891 and the National Park Service in 1916. The Sierra Club formed in 1892, the Audubon Society in 1905.

Such efforts saved pieces, but now the juggernaut of development, unprecedented in world historical terms, threatens much wilderness and resources it has not already destroyed. Our economy dwarfs all others in the world and has done so for decades. Although a few countries have recently surpassed our monetary average income, our living standards still surpass all others. Sweden is seven-eighths our level; Switzerland, four-fifths; France and Germany, three-quarters; Japan, two-thirds; Great Britain, three-fifths.[12] Never have so many people had so much money for so long. With 5 percent of the world's population we have 27 percent of the world GNP and consume from 35 to 50 percent of its resources.

Most of us are so used to our wealth that we do not even think of ourselves as wealthy. Yet we are the most developed country, gazed upon by others in amazement, wonder, and envy.

The whole world is striving to achieve our level of development, half-blind to the costs and straining world resources. World recognition of these problems is growing nevertheless. In Sweden in 1972, a U.N. conference produced the U.N. Environmental Program. Some progress has been made for a Law of the Sea, and much progress on preservation of species. But extensive and often irreparable damage has already been done. We do not have to predict environmental disasters; we have but to open our eyes to what has already happened.

Easily exploited resources have been used up; extraction must travel further, use more energy, itself in short supply, and destroy more wilderness. Foreign investments in energy and mining makes us dependent on poor people of some countries, where we may support exploitive regimes and adventurous military policies. Computers project mass starvation, or death by pollution, or disastrous climatic change, or exhaustion of energy or other resources if we do not change our ways. The assumptions the computers use can be questioned, but should our policy assume more traditional growth will be tolerated by nature? Or should we opt for prudence and leave a greater margin for error? Environmentalists choose prudence.

Conservation Politics

Conventional elite thinking is rooted in notions of GNP, development, property, and jobs. Theoretically GNP is value neutral, but in practice the choices based on GNP analysis are not. Increasing the GNP seems to require lower resource costs at just a time when environmental protection requires that they be more costly. Wilderness to save our souls clashes with resources to save our GNP.

Fortunately, protective activities also generate GNP, and a redirected economy can still have GNP growth, but of a different kind: energy conservation, solar energy, pollution control, recycling, urban revitalization, resource protection and enhancement, and better urban transportation systems.

Property rights are most asserted by those with the most property, who are often effective because of their economic power. Freedoms that meant opportunity for the common person a century ago now protect elite prerogatives. Some, with near-religious fervor, elevate an exaggeration of property rights to the level of the civil rights in the Constitution. They claim that public controls over property are immoral, illegal, and socialistic. However, events on one property affect others and the general public; hence government has a right to regulate.

When land is developed, there are side effects: traffic, congestion, air pollution, need for more street capacity, parking problems, viewshed degradation, noise, landslide and siltation off the property, sewage, storm runoff, fire and police needs, degradation of the habitat of which the property is part, energy consumption, school needs, other service needs, and weather alteration. Private development is a public problem and can therefore be regulated by the public through government. But there is a historic lag as the "right to develop" of elite power is gradually displaced by planning and zoning in the public interest. Such controls are still not very comprehensive functionally or geographically, and they still take existing life-styles for granted. Elites coopt the middle by translating threats to big property as threats to small also. Rarely is private property effectively controlled.

Environmentalists question the meaningfulness as a goal of "standard of living," GNP model simplifications, exaggerated property rights, and conventional thinking on jobs. How much happier are people for each increment of income they earn? When do diminishing returns set in?

Elections pose these questions in terms of candidate differences (a point that also applies to economic issues). In campaigns from 1970 to 1976, Environmental Action, an environmental protection group, identified twelve representatives with the worst environmental records and with a chance of being defeated. It called them "the dirty dozen" and campaigned against them. Of forty-one named, twenty-seven are no longer in Congress, a remarkable record for a low-budget public-interest group.[13] With the progressive members of the elites willing to act and with media attention stimulating voters, the conditions exist for reformers to cause upsets. They give the voters the information they need to vote in their own interest. As in the antiwar campaigns, voters are not interested enough to seek out information, but they will act on information given them.

Environmentalists have won much legislation. Taxes now support about a billion dollars of environmental research per year. In 1963 the Clean Air Act passed; in 1964, the Wilderness Act and the Land and Water Conservation Act; in 1968, the Wild and Scenic Rivers Act and the National Trails System Act; in 1969, the Endangered Species Act. Also in 1969, the National Environmental Policy Act (NEPA) was passed, a very important law that created the Council on Environmental Quality. In 1970 the air act was strengthened, and the Environmental Protection Agency was created. In 1972, the Coastal Zone Management Act, including the protection of marine mammals, was passed, along with a strengthening of the Water Pollution Control Act of 1948. In 1976 toxic chemicals were controlled, and in 1977 strip mines were regulated. The legislative record here is outstanding and is unmatched by any other area of reform in recent times.

NEPA mandated environmental impact statements (EIS), which require developers to provide information on environmental costs and to design ways to mitigate them. Environmentalists got the informational ammunition they could not otherwise afford. (Most people know time is money, but the elites know that time is money is information is power.) Vested interests, unwilling to oppose quality, let a significant reform slide through without all the usual debilitating compromise. After 1974 arguments against environmentalists—focusing on GNP, jobs, cost, and balancing of values—combined with the severe recession to set back environmentalist momentum. Battles now are more evenly contested; compromises are shaved in favor of existing systems.

Environmentalists have an ambiguous ally, science and technology, major forces that created the problems in the first place. Yet science and technology serve social masters and can serve the environment well, shifting production systems from standard-of-living emphasis to quality-of-life conerns. There is little need, desire, or possibility of returning to pretechnical standards, which can be romanticized but which most people avoid in practice. Technology is unlikely to help us have more, but it can help us do more with less.

A Pair of Case Studies:

New Melones Dam and the Kaiser Wilderness

Both of these cases involve grass-roots movements, one a failure and the other a success. The New Melones Dam on the Stanislaus River was part of the California water plan, which called for the destruction by dam of every wild river in the state and has almost succeeded. A drop in the projected population for the state eliminated the original justification for the dam made by proponents and will cost $400 million in taxes. In 1974 the State Water Resources Department said the dam was not needed and there was currently an excess of water. Congressman John McFall represented the district of the dam, was associated with the dam interests, and had seniority on the Public Works Appropriations Subcommittee, the heart of pork barrel water projects. He pushed for the dam. Yet from another point of view, the dam was inadequate; all of its water would not be enough to restore groundwater levels in the San Joaquin Valley below it. But none of these issues caused controversy.

The problem was that the dam would flood a great stretch of white water river rafting, ironically made enjoyable year round by an existing dam upstream and its steady release of water. Enthusiasts circulated "Deliver the River" petitions statewide and succeeded in getting the issue put on the ballot for a vote. In November 1974 less than half of the eligible voters came to the polls. Of these, 2.5 million (47 percent) voted for the river and 2.8 million for the dam. Public opinion polls before and after the election, which usually correlate very closely wtih actual election results, showed that 60 percent of voters favored the river. Why did it lose? The answer seems to be another illustration of the intensity problem: about 13 percent of those who voted were confused. They were not careful in reading the literature sent out with sample ballots. To a small extent, there was a problem because they had to vote "yes" in order to be against the dam; "no" was not against the dam but against the proposition to save it. To a greater extent, confusion was created by propaganda financed by pro-dam interests overwhelming the much more limited, underfinanced efforts of environmentalists. Dam interests had billboards throughout the state proclaiming "Stop pollution; vote no on Prop. 17" and "Wild river hoax." Television spot advertising featured pictures of dead fish. These interests spent half a million dollars; Friends of the River spent one-fourth as much. Most of the pro-dam money was contributed by prearrangement after reporting deadlines to hide the interests' identities. Thousands of other examples could be used, demonstrating important if bitter lessons in the exercise of elite power.

In the same election, voters elected Jerry Brown as governor. He supported the river but did not use the full weight of his office to stop the dam, which was built under federal authority. Neither was court action able to get state control over the project. New concern over drought overwhelmed the opposition to the New Melones Dam, but Friends of the River has become a sophisticated lobby on behalf of all wild rivers in the state. It continues to try to save the Stanislaus.

The Kaiser Wilderness is not too far from the Stanislaus River, but it happened to be in a different congressional district, a critical factor. Congressman John Krebs was elected in 1974, the same election that sealed the fate of the Stanislaus, and about the same time that the Forest Service was ready to log the forest of virgin fir above Huntington Lake. Forest Service plans were opposed by several summer cabin lessees and recreation interests, who had begun to realize in the late 1960s that Forest Service policy had changed. Under timber industry and presidential pressure, it became essentially a tree-cutting agency, convicted in court more than once of not following its own multiple-use-sustained-yield laws. Clear-cutting had turned a favorite hike into a moonscape, and opened up new roads destructive of natural values. They took an airplane ride over the forest, which revealed that vast areas had been clear-cut, which they had not seen before because of the screen of trees left along the highways. Above 8,000 feet, in the Sierra National Forest, rainfall is slight and winters are harsh, favoring slow-growing fir, but the Forest Service had planted the more profitable pines as if the area were like the wetter Northwest. Concern heightened in 1972 with the proposed logging near the cabins within a heavily used wilderness. Local activists and the Sierra Club required the Forest Service to develop an environmental impact statement, which it did, but it gave short shrift to wilderness values.

In 1975 Congressman Krebs and Senator Alan Cranston, also from California, introduced bills to have Kaiser studied for possible designation as wilderness. From that time until the president signed the bill on October 20, 1976, the Save Kaiser Ridge Committee mobilized thousands of supporters, including campers passing through the area who would otherwise have had no idea what was about to happen. As a result, congressmen from all over the nation received letters from their own constituents about an otherwise obscure issue. When Ridge Committee activists arrived to testify at Senate and House committee hearings, they were told time and again by the legislative staffs how important these letters were. The letters were particularly important because the writers had some idea of what they were urging and had a personal touch, which was obviously not part of an artificial pressure campaign.

Conservation lobbyists, at first fearful that controversy over Kaiser could slow down other efforts, discovered that the momentum of Kaiser was actually helping them. Krebs and Cranston's work was reinforced by their staff, who had flown out to look around and became committed to the cause. Partway through the process, a critical compromise occurred. Supporters of wilderness gave up on a large area of commerically valuable pine on the far side of Kaiser Ridge, and key opponents of the wilderness agreed to make the remainder, about 22,000 acres, a wilderness, thus avoiding the study process and another legislative battle. (The fir was worth $13 per thousand board feet; the pine, $82 per thousand board feet.)

The work of the Save Kaiser Ridge Committee included lobbying to get the necessary hearing held and giving testimony. The Senate's work came through first, and once the subcommittee hearing had been published, the bill passed the Senate with surprising speed. The issue was held up in the House for months, and then much of the hearing time was filibustered away by an opponent. Kaiser was the first wilderness Congress had ever considered that had marketable timber, adding to the opposition. By late summer 1976, Congress wanted to adjourn so members could campaign for reelection. Two days before the end of the session, Congressman Krebs moved to amend a popular omnibus parks bill by adding the compromise Kaiser bill. Congressmen, who had not expected the bill to reach the floor but had promised to vote for it if it did, supported the amendment by 370 to 7. The amended bill passed on a voice vote unanimously. Under the rules, one negative vote could have killed it, but opponents did not want to incur the enmity of their colleagues and stayed silent. The Senate quickly concurred, and the legislation went to President Ford's desk. Ford's ties were to the timber industry, but he also knew parks were popular and signed the bill. The Ridge Committee had spent about $12,000 in its campaign, far less than Friends of the River had, but against less powerful opponents. Before the campaign, the Kaiser committee members had not been particularly politically active and did not think of themselves as people who could get a law through Congress. By the end of their campaign, they had done so.

Numerous other examples could be developed of conflicts between conservation and extraction. Perhaps more than any other policy area, this one has attracted citizen activists and fostered many environmental groups. The leader is the Sierra Club. Conservation issues offer opportunities for participation at all levels of government greater than the economic issues we have discussed so far. The problems have included restoring strip-mined land; protecting species and their habitats; expanding the Redwood National Forest; reforestation; protecting the Siskiyous and the Tongass; dividing up the Alaskan lands; the pipeline issues; native American land claim settlements; local open space protection; saving wild rivers, marshes, estuaries, islands, lakes, shores, beaches and coasts; protecting farmland from urbanization; protecting wilderness from overuse, off-road vehicles, summer homes, and roads; and managing range land against overgrazing.

Our culture, acting socially, economically, and politically over a long historical period, has disrupted all purely natural balances and made us, along with nature, a manager of the earth. Can we live with less water? Less red meat? Less aluminum? Of all these renewable and nonrenewable resource problems, the most important is clearly energy.

Citizen Profile:

Protection of Wilderness

There is no spot so dear to my heart as Huntington Lake, California. I have noted in myself and in many others who come there each vacation season a possessive loyalty that makes them want to keep the area in an unchanged, uncrowded, and unspoiled state. This feeling produced the support and effort necessary to create the Kaiser Wilderness Area.

The proposal to log the north slope of Huntington Lake descended like a threatening storm upon all of us who had become so emotionally attached to the place. The timber sales of the last ten years had marched up nearly to the lake from the south and then to the east in the Potter Creek sale and the Butte sale. It was the Black Point Timber sale in the area of Mushroom Rock, however, that really moved the people into action. This sale, across a long-established scenic hiking trail to a wonderful vista point, was a visual disaster. Massive clear cuts of forty to sixty acres, selective cutting that left only seed trees, and a very poor trash and slash cleanup made this sale among the worst ever carried out in the Huntington Lake area. This sale generated an enormous amount of concern among the summer visitors and the summer home permittees. Protests were lodged to the Forest Service to stop the sales for the North Slope, but the momentum for the sales moved relentlessly forward. At last the only way to save the area seemed to be to ask Congress for a wilderness study.

I was asked by Mrs. Francis Hogan, a permittee in the Home Creek tract, to be chairman of a committee to help save Kaiser Ridge. I had never worked in any sort of political effort before and am one to avoid any confrontation possible. She insisted, however, and said that since I was not a permittee my leadership would carry more credibility than anyone else. With reluctance and trepidation I become the chairman of the Save Kaiser Ridge Committee.

I feel that one of my most effective bits of action was in getting the word of our political action group out to the campers. As the evening recreation director at the Lakeshore Resort, I had an audience to whom I could appeal. This had to be done with some discretion, however, because the resort owners feared a negative reaction if I spoke out too often or too strongly. To promote the recreation programs I have always used tear boards. These are just pieces of plywood with the programs nailed to the board with a sign inviting campers to tear off a program and take it back to camp. I kept each of the many boards round the lake supplied with our Save Kaiser Ridge flyers. This went on for two summers and proved to be very effective. Proof of this was found in our trips to Washington, D.C., to lobby the Congress and to attend the hearings for the Kaiser Wilderness bills. Many congressional staff members told us that they were impressed with the continuous flow of letters and their intelligence. Many of these letters were from our many campers who felt moved to write their own congressmen when they returned home from their summer vacation at the lake.

Much credit for the flyers and their content must go to Osmond and Peggy Molarsky of our Save Kaiser Ridge Committee and to George Whitmore and Hal Thomas of the Sierra Club. I would like to credit Paul Deauville of our Save Kaiser Ridge Committee as one of the most effective people. We agreed to work as co-chairmen of the committee shortly after we got organized, and Paul was the main power behind the whole movement.

Our greatest reason for success was our support from our new Congressman John Krebs of the Seventeenth District, California. He introduced our bill in the House of Representatives, organized the co-sponsors, and prodded the House and Senate to hold hearings on the bills. The last cliff-hanging days of the 1976 session of the Congress will never be forgotten by any of us. It came right down to the last minutes of the last days of the session before it was passed. I'm sure our cause would never have had much of a chance without the dedicated support of Congressman John Krebs.

One of the peak emotional moments of my life came in the spring of 1977 when Paul Deauville and I climbed to Black Point to see the new Kaiser Wilderness signs in place. We looked out over the expanse of green fir trees extending from 7,000-foot Huntington Lake to our right, up to 10,000-foot Kaiser Peak to our left, and to the rocky points and vistas around us. It was a thrill to realize that the new sign proclaiming the boundary of the Kaiser Wilderness Area beside us was there partly because of our efforts and that the view here would be the same when our grandchildren and their grandchildren made this same hike to this vista point in the future.

Charles Hull
Fresno, California

Energy

The energy problem is so deep that it can be considered the touchstone of the whole environmental crisis. Many people believe that energy has become expensive, but it is more accurate to think that energy is still cheap, encouraging waste. Historically, extremely cheap petroleum and natural gas have displaced other sources of energy. Even with the 400 percent price increase of 1970, oil is still cheap. Because our purchasing power has risen, effective energy costs as a percentage of income have not actually gone up since the early 1950s. Even at eighty cents a gallon, gasoline would take up the same share of median family income in 1974 as it did in 1955.[14] The large price increase of 1973–1974 has to be understood in this longer history. We have largely absorbed it, and most people have lost interest in the energy crisis. By contrast, the average price at 1975 exchange rates for gasoline in Europe and Japan was $1.35 a gallon. Since the incomes in these countries are lower, they are in effect paying about $3.00 a gallon; consequently their conservation efforts are greater. They use fewer and smaller cars, for shorter distances, less frequently. They live in insulated apartments close to work and use transit. Their industry is more energy efficient.

Natural gas has similarly been cheap, greatly benefiting consumers in a way few have appreciated, because of government-controlled prices.

Cheap gas and oil encourage consumption and waste. We have increased both our energy consumption and our dependency on natural gas and oil, which in 1972 supplied 78 percent of our energy. From 1972 to 1978 the U.S. increased its gasoline consumption by 16 percent. (See table 3–2.)

There are two major problems with oil supplies: our dependency on foreign suppliers and limits on what we can discover and extract from the

Table 3–2 *Energy Sources*

	Trillions of Btu			*% of Total,*
	1950	*1972*	*1985* [d]	*1972*
Coal	12,913	12,495	19,667	17.3
Oil	13,489	32,966	33,507	45.7
Natural gas	6,150	23,125	23,677	32.1
Nuclear energy [a]	0	576	12,509	0.8
Hydroelectricity [b]	1,440	2,946	4,797	4.1
Total gross energy	33,858	72,107	94,156	100.0
after utility use	32,831	66,658	69,647	
Per-capita energy [e]	232	345	387	

[a] In 1975, fifty-five reactors produced 7 percent of commercial electricity.

[b] The 1985 figure includes some solar energy.

[c] These figures are in millions.

[d] The 1985 figures are based on "business as usual, mild conservation, $11 oil."

Sources: U.S. Department of the Interior, *Energy Perspectives* (Washington, D.C.: Government Printing Office, 1975), p. 42; Federal Energy Administration, *Project Independence Report* (Washington, D.C.: Government Printing Office, 1974), appendix pp. 9, 16, 46.

earth. Dependency on OPEC makes us vulnerable to short-term cutoffs of supply, as occurred in 1973–1974 and because of Iran in 1979. We have not been self-sufficient in oil since 1950. We now import (1978) about half of our oil, making us much more dependent than we were in 1973. We must export more than ever to pay for it, but have not exported enough to prevent large imbalances in our international payments and erosion of the value of the dollar in relation to yen and marks. Our policy, virtually controlled by big oil until recently, has been to deplete our own oil first to avoid dependency. As a result, we are now more dependent than ever. Alaskan oil will just make up for loss of other domestic production, and this is also likely for any new offshore oil discovered. Canada and Venezuela are supplying less, making us more dependent on the Arabs. Military intervention to secure supplies is generally considered unfeasible, not to mention undesirable.

A longer-term problem is posed by the limits of economically extractable oil in the ground. The world had 5,573 quads (quadrillion Btu's) of measured energy reserves in oil and gas in 1973. The world is consuming 20.7 billion barrels of oil per year and 55 trillion cubic feet of gas.[15] If these figures stay constant, we will run out of these supplies in 2008. The figures are changing, of course. More reserves are being discovered and proven, but consumption is increasing, especially in the United States. Energy experts generally agree we must end dependence on oil before 2000. The public seems generally split between those who support the moderate steps proposed by the Carter administration and those who do not think that a crisis really exists.

There are two main thrusts of proposals to manage the energy crisis: develop more energy and waste less of what we have. There are also two major ways of analyzing alternatives: economic and energetic. The economic approach emphasized by energy elites looks at energy investments in terms of dollars. This emphasis seems to justify large investments in nuclear fission electrical power, in coal, and in other capital-intensive, high-technology, centralized power systems. The industry generally thinks that enough economic incentive will produce energy; in fact, it is important enough to have a large governmental development program to develop new technologies, which private industry can then use.

The energetic approach emphasized by environmentalists looks at energy in terms of energy: how much energy do we put in to getting energy, and how much usable energy do we get out? What is the most efficient way to get necessary work done? This approach emphasizes completely different policies: strong conservation to avoid waste, solar energy, and smaller, decentralized systems.

One of the reasons why the results are so different between the two approaches is that the dollar accounting system undervalues fossil fuels. Nature has supplied us with a vast storehouse of these fuels, a kind of energy capital so abundant that we can live off it a long time, but once gone, it is gone forever. At present rates of consumption, it will last only a short time more, and we will discover in practice how difficult it is to get energy. Even our vast coal reserves cannot long sustain exponential growth of consumption. Underpricing results in high consumption and waste, leading to premature exhaustion and possible collapse of the system.

Both energy elites and environmentalists advocate price increases, but in different ways and for different reasons. Elites favor higher prices to make more production profitable. They want to deregulate oil and natural gas. Environmentalists agree to some extent but fear windfall gains to big interests, which would use the money for private gain, to acquire more control over other energy sources, and to diversify into other businesses, which in fact has been happening. They also fear that we are bumping up against natural and economic limits far more powerful than incentives can overcome. In the continental United States, we have probably discovered about all the oil that can be found. In energetic terms, the energy industry is already the major user of energy.

Environmentalists favor higher prices through taxes on oil and gas to discourage consumption. This approach risks slowing the economy and is generally unpopular, but it has worked in Europe. Rebates to the poor can avoid a regressive impact, and other taxes can be adjusted to avoid taking too much money out of the economy. Another rationale for the tax is to consider it a charge for the pollution produced by burning fossil fuels. For many reasons, a price increase is fairer, more simply administered, and more effective across the board than coupon rationing, which has a superficial appeal but is an administrative nightmare. The tax would encourage conservation and make alternative fuels more attractive.

Electricity. Electricity plays a special role in the energy crisis. Table 3–2 does not show how much energy is wasted (waste is the difference between the energy value of the fuel going in and the value of the useful work coming out). Heat-based electrical generation is extremely wasteful, mainly because most of the heat is dissipated into the atmosphere or into a water coolant. A fossil fuel plant wastes about 65 percent of the energy value; a nuclear plant, about 80 percent, with some variation for the type of plant and how it is managed. Other systems also have waste, but largely because of heat-based electricity, about half of our energy inputs are wasted. Hydroelectricity is more efficient but is only about 15 percent of installed capacity, most high potential sites have been dammed, and those few remaining have value as free-flowing rivers.

Largely because fossil fuels are so cheap, electricity is cheap, and demand for it is growing faster than for other forms of energy. Because of waste, this demand is far more draining of resources than other forms. But after decades of unquestioned growth, the electrical utilities are facing a number of problems. Nuclear power is not working out. Utilities are being forced to switch to coal to avoid dependence on oil and are being required by law to install expensive stack gas scrubbers to remove sulphur, preventing air pollution. Demand for electricity peaks at certain times of the day, for which installed capacity must be adequate even though it goes unused the rest of the day. The peaking power tends to be more expensive, but consumers pay the same regardless of time. Therefore utilities are calling for time-of-day pricing for major users, for whom timing devices and special billing are justified. Declining bloc rates (which charge less as more energy is consumed) are also being criticized. Utilities are faced with such high investment costs that they are seeking ways to get consumers to finance expansion. Increasingly, utilities across the country will face these problems. They cannot meet predicted demand at existing prices but might not be able to sell their new supplies at a price based on true cost.

Why not find a way to use the wasted heat? The common-sense answer works in practice. Two major innovations are whole energy systems and cogeneration. A *whole energy system* uses the heat from an electrical plant to heat nearby buildings and for other moderate heat needs (such as hot water, air conditioning, and clothes driers), which are 87 percent of housing need and 84 percent of commercial need. In many places, especially Europe, such systems are in operation. One source of burnable energy for such plants can be solid waste, which is conveniently produced by the houses and commerce that need the heat. *Cogeneration* is the same idea applied to industry: a plant needing industrial-process heat can often find a way to get electricity from the heat at the same time. Utilities have underpriced their energy to industry until recently in order to keep a lucrative market, but the energy crisis is beginning to make this unsuitable.

Nuclear Power. Leading environmentalists have strongly attacked industry's solution to the energy problem: nuclear energy. Nuclear plants may well fail in terms of energetics: enormous amounts of energy are needed to build the plants and mine and process the ores. Construction takes about ten years, the plant works about forty years, and then it must be decommissioned because of excessive buildup of radioactivity. The radioactive wastes last hundreds of more years. The costs of decommissioning, storage of wastes, and guarding them are difficult to calculate. In dollar terms, nuclear energy is increasingly questionable. If the costs of tax loopholes, governmental development, and full liability insurance are considered, it is uneconomic. Utilities are subsidized for these costs but they face other problems: large increases in uranium costs, regulatory delays, construction delays and costs, unexpected excessive downtime, and expensive requirements for earthquake safety. Cancellations of plans for nuclear plants are outpacing new orders.

Safety considerations are extremely important. The same kind of deception of the people that occurred concerning Indochina from 1964 to 1975 has occurred in nuclear energy. The old Atomic Energy Commission (AEC) suppressed information critical of nuclear energy and promoted an industry that it was supposed to regulate. As incriminating information gradually leaked out, a profound mistrust of the AEC developed among environmentalists and some scientists, which has continued despite the reorganization of the commission into two new bureaucracies. Many eminent scientists, as well as many activists with strong feelings, are on both sides of the nuclear debate. In the last few years, the critics of nuclear energy have been winning. The risks of plutonium and breeder reactors and of related nuclear weapons proliferation have impressed President Carter and are becoming better known in the Congress and in Europe because of scientific and popular pressure.

Nuclear plants have safety and other operational problems. Generally excellent design has been defeated by the unpredictable human element. Promoters point with pride to the nuclear safety record; so far it is better than the fossil fuel energy industries. Environmentalists view with alarm the several near-misses. The accident at the Three Mile Island nuclear plant near Harrisburg, Pennsylvania, in spring 1979 was the worst in the history of the industry, and media coverage expanded public awareness. The accident released measurable but small amounts of radioactive krypton, radon, xenon, iodine, and carbon. We lack knowledge about the exact health effects of low-level radiation, some of which we are exposed to constantly in the form of background radiation. Generally, increasing exposure means increasing health risks, and estimates of risk have been rising.

The accident seems to have been caused partly by workers leaving backup cooling system valves closed but marking them as being open on a checklist. When the reactor started to malfunction, it was not clear what should be done because of ambiguity about reactor fluid level from gauges in the control room. Control personnel made several mistakes, disbelieving their temperature gauges, overlooking indicators, not turning on pumps for cooling, and the like. Workers and the Nuclear Regulatory Commission (NRC) inspectors did not immediately grasp the significance of a pressure spike recorded by a tracing needle showing pressure in the reactor. Two days later, its meaning was realized. Efforts to cool the reactor initially failed, perhaps due to an unexpected gas bubble, and some temperature readings went off the scale, over 700 degrees fahrenheit. Other problems included a stuck valve, a false gauge reading, and turned-off pumps. There was an outside chance of explosion, but another malfunction, a valve leak, let the gas escape. After cooling the reactor the company owning Three Mile Island faced problems of heavily damaged fuel rods, hundreds of thousands of gallons of radioactive water, years of decontamination and overhaul, tens of millions of dollars in expenses, and possible bankruptcy. Meanwhile, control panels and pressure relief valves of similarly designed plants are being improved.

Even before the accident, the NRC had withdrawn its backing of the Rasmussen Report on nuclear power plant safety, which had clearly underestimated the chances of accident. The worst accident to date occurred in

Chelyabinsk, Russia, where nuclear wastes exploded, were blown over hundreds of square kilometers, and killed probably several hundred people.

Other problems of nuclear power include transporting radioactive materials and guarding the whole system from terrorists. The most difficult immediate dilemma is nuclear waste. It may eventually be stored in underground saltbeds in New Mexico, about as geologically stable and water free an area as possible (though the problem of guarding it for several hundred or thousand years would remain). Other experts say saltbeds will not work. When companies cannot handle the burden of managing toxic wastes (Getty Oil, West Valley, New York) or a nuclear plant (Clinton, Tennessee), state and federal agencies must take them over at great public expense. The most feasible way to decommission a plant may be to let it cool down for 70 to 110 years before dismantling it, a long time to post a guard. Millions of gallons of radioactive wastes are now in eighty known temporary storage facilities scattered around the country, with more being added every day.[16]

Besides pollution by radioactivity, thermal pollution can be caused by the huge volumes of warmed water produced by the plants. There are also problems of where plants can be located—not too near cities (but near enough to supply energy to them), on stable land, near large amounts of water for cooling. Elite interests once hoped that about 950 nuclear plants would be in operation by 1990, but many increasingly recognize these projections as undesirable and even impossible. Now the political questions are over a much smaller number. Environmentalists believe that development of coal and solar sources and conservation makes nuclear energy unnecessary.

As of May 1979 seventy-two nuclear reactors were in existence, and another 126 were under construction or on order. The number of new orders has fallen dramatically, and the number of cancellations increased. While some would phase nuclear power out altogether, many cities depend on it, making shutdowns politically difficult. Stabilization of nuclear power would make the storage problem more manageable and stretch out uranium fuel supplies.

Coal, Solar Energy, and Conservation. Coal interests have tended to favor exploitation of coal wherever it can be found and with minimum regulation. Environmentalists tend to oppose strip-mining of western coal because of the difficulty, even impossibility, of restoring the land, of distance from markets, and of relatively low energy value of the coal. They tend to support gradual stripping of eastern coal with adequate requirements for restoration of land. Hundreds of square miles are being stripped every year, but many are not being adequately restored. Pollution from tailings and unstable overburdens menace Appalachian homes. Hopefully, a law passed in 1977 will improve the situation. Environmentalists favor eastern deep-mined coal with improved protections for coal workers.

Coal booms have already hit parts of the West in Wyoming, Montana, and Arizona. Traditional Navajos have lost out to coal interests in the four corners area of Arizona: their air is being polluted, their water table lowered, and the water polluted.

Environmentalists are enthusiastic about solar energy for many reasons, but many energy interests play it down. Solar energy is not just technically different; in most applications it is also socially different. It cannot be dominated by large companies. Most solar systems are inherently small scale, with single-building installations the most common. Many companies are likely to compete in supplying solar hardware.

The greatest drawback to solar energy is its high initial capital cost, often far above conventional counterparts. Much of this problem, however, is in how we think about buying things; generally we consider just the capital cost rather than also figuring in the operational costs. When these "life-cycle" costs are figured, combining capital and operational costs, solar is now cheaper than electricity for those moderate heating needs that are 87 percent of our total home use. Solar energy is cheaper than oil in many places and cheaper than gas and coal in some places, especially in colder climates. Solar works well in the North because it is in use more of the year, while fossil fuels run up a bigger bill. Solar definitely outcompetes fossil fuels when pollution costs are considered.

Solar takes many forms. Some are proven, like solar panels and windmills, and others are being researched and developed, like photovoltaic cells and methanol and methane from plants or organic waste. Hydroelectricity, a kind of solar power, is fully proven and almost fully developed. A key idea is to match energy production to end use needs, avoiding electricity. Space and water heating and cooling are 35 percent of all end uses. Heat over the boiling point is needed for cooking, clothes drying, and especially industrial process heat and constitutes 23 percent of end uses. Transportation is 31 percent and pipelines use 3 percent. The end use needs that most require electricity are the 4 percent for industrial electric drive and 4 percent for all lighting, electronics, telecommunications, industrial use, some mass transit, and home appliances. Solar power can replace electrical for most heat needs, especially moderate heat, with great energy savings. Small-scale, relatively simple-technology decentralized systems constitute a "soft energy path" as compared to the "hard path" with its huge, centralized, high-technology plants that cost so much to finance, require expensive labor, and take a long time to come into production.[17]

Some solar ideas involve high costs and high technology and are generally opposed by environmentalists. For example, ocean thermal energy conversion systems, fields of mirrors focused on a boiler, huge contraptions in space to beam back microwave energy where it is converted into electricity, and huge windmill projects are being studied. Fusion power has been portrayed to the public as free of radioactivity, yet actual experimentation involves processes as radioactive as fission power. Research on these kinds of systems and on breeder nuclear reactors has been favored by energy elites at the expense of research on small scale solar approaches.

As in the population-food problem, we can worry less about supply if we can lower demand by conservation. Both business elites and environmentalists now support conservation, but environmentalists are much more enthusiastic and far-reaching in their proposals. Reduced hot water and room temperatures, better appliances, less lighting, more heat pumps, elimination of pilot lights, more insulation, less frequent use of cars, more efficient cars, and more use of transit could greatly reduce energy needs. More use of bicycles and walking, living closer to work, and living in apartments would also help. Commerce, industry, and transportation have many ways to save energy. Much research has shown that saving energy costs 10 to 15 percent less than producing it. Zero energy growth is feasible with technical developments, elementary conservation, and minor life-style changes. The effort required is both personal and political. If it fails, our standard of living could be severely and abruptly lowered.

Progressive elites and academic analysts are beginning to realize the importance of solar energy, nonelectrical approaches, and conservation. The projection for 1985 of table 3–2 of 94 quadrillion Btus (quads) was the lowest of all the projections made in 1974 in the *Project Independence Report*, and this figure was lower than a Department of Interior projection made in 1972. Other projections by the Ford Foundation in 1974, by Oak Ridge in 1976, by the Joint Economic Committee in 1977, and by the National Academy of Sciences in 1978 produced steadily lower projections. The 1978 study forecast that by the year 2010 energy consumption could be reduced to 63 quads, below the 1978 level of 78 quads, even though population would be up 35 percent and the GNP doubled. Jobs would increase because soft-path jobs would cost less to create than the jobs of the hard path. Sweden uses about 60 percent as much energy as the United States does yet attains an equally high standard of living, and Switzerland does even better.[18]

Pollution

Pollution and solid-waste problems begin at the moment of extraction of resources from nature and are intimately tied to problems of conservation. Pollution and solid waste are side-effects of our technologies and style of life. For centuries, the environment has been used as a cheap dumping ground. How much are we willing to pay to clean up?

Pollution has human costs, such as loss of health, lower growth rates for food and trees, and the loss of space and ugliness of dumps. However, there can be no complete cleanup, for as we approach perfection, the costs become exorbitant. Environmental reformers are willing to go further than traditional elites. Most people want to clean up but not pay for it and not change their life-style.

A key concept of reform is to regulate firms and municipalities, requiring them to internalize the costs they previously externalized into the environment—that is, require them to clean up or pay for pollution they had previously forced the environment and others to pay for or suffer from. Usually firms and municipalities will reform only if forced to by a higher level of government. Pressure from people downwind and downstream can also help. Voters who are antireform in a local context can be proreform in the national context. In the local context, the costs are more obvious; in the national context, they are vaguer, and we assume that others will have to pay. In general, a mildly proreform national government is forcing the worst antireform firms and municipalities to clean up. This pressure is producing technological innovation, lowered costs, more jobs, a higher quality of life, and the discovery of new uses for former pollutants. Environmental protection is an infant growth industry, spurred by regulation.

Air Pollution

Air pollution has many causes and is of many types (not all are shown in table 3–3). The most important kinds relate to oil: refineries, vehicles, and power plants. Motor vehicles account for most carbon monoxide, half the hydrocarbons, much nitrogen oxides, and for most lead, ethylene, and asbestos pollution. Table 3–3 does not show photochemical oxidants, resulting when NO_x and HC are transformed by sunlight into smog.

Based on extensive research and hearings, the federal government has set standards for the six major types of air pollution. The standards are of two types, one based on human health and the other based on property damage, the killing or slowing of plant growth, and how clear the air looks. Federal standards have not been set for hydrogen sulfide, ethylene, asbestos, and other air pollutants. Air pollution is expensive for health. It causes millions of people to suffer more from respiratory ailments and to die younger. After smoking, air pollution is the major cause of a disease that was unimportant seventy-five years ago—lung cancer. Carbon monoxide in hemoglobin of the bloodstream robs blood of its ability to carry oxygen. It can cause lowered alertness, headaches, sleepiness, and death. Cab drivers and others exposed to traffic are hard hit.

Air pollution corrodes surfaces, requiring more frequent painting. Italy has lost much of its priceless heritage of stone sculpture from pollution dam-

Table 3–3 Air Pollution

Type of Pollution	Millions of Tons 1970	Millions of Tons 1976	% of Total by Source, 1976 Transportation	% of Total by Source, 1976 Fuel Combustion [a]	% of Total by Source, 1976 Industry [b]
Hydrocarbons (HC)	32.7	30.7	38.7	5.0	33.7
Nitrogen oxides (NO_x)	22.5	25.3	43.9	51.3	3.0
Carbon monoxide (CO)	110.0	96.1	80.0	1.4	8.9
Particulates (TSP) [c]	24.9	14.8	9.0	34.3	47.0
Sulfur oxides (SO_2)	32.1	29.6	3.0	81.4	15.2

[a] Stationary installations, mainly utilities.

[b] Excludes waste disposal and miscellaneous others.

[c] Suspended particles up to 1/250 inch, including smoke, dust, fumes, and droplets of viscous liquid.

Sources: *Statistical Abstract of the United States, 1978,* p. 215. The figures were supplied by the Environmental Protection Agency, *National Air Quality and Emission Trends Report* (1976).

age. Pollution slows plant growth and kills certain species. Farmers in the central valley of California have had declining crop yields because of pollution. The pollution drifts eastward to cause "smog disease" in vast acreages of mountain pines. Many people are concerned about dramatic, visible, high levels of pollution of short duration, but they are unaware of the costs of less visible, lower-level, long-term pollution. Smoke is easily stopped, but invisible pollutants can be even worse, resulting in such things as acid rain. Air pollution becomes water pollution, which kills fish and even makes farmland acidic. Sulfur oxides are initially invisible and difficult to remove from power plant chimney stacks. Visible secondary pollutants form from sulphur oxides. Fluorocarbons in aerosol cans threaten the ozone layer above the earth. Better instruments lead researchers to new discoveries about pollution. We now know, for example, that haze is composed of minute particles of carbon, ammonium, amines, amides, and sulphides, with unknown health effects.

Good progress is being made cleaning up the air, except for nitrogen oxides. Outdoor burning is largely banned; electrostatic condensers are widely used by industry to reduce particulates; automobiles have more control devices. Air-quality control districts in each air basin are making progress despite heavy industry influence and resistance. Nevertheless, pollution levels are still too high to meet the standards. In 1977, 159 of 247 regions had air that was too dirty. Too often progress is slowed by industry influence on air-quality control districts, regional planning agencies, state governments, and the federal government. American auto makers persuaded Congress to postpone 1975 standards to 1978 and then in 1977 got them lowered and put off again to 1980 and 1981, even though certain imports were already exceeding the standards.

Air pollution controls divide broadly between moving and nonmoving sources. Gas price increases in 1974 and 1979 showed that Americans could reduce gas consumption and reduce pollution at the same time. We bought smaller cars and drove them less and more slowly. From 1974 to 1975 the mileage of the average car jumped almost 15 percent, from fourteen to sixteen miles per gallon. Mandatory annual vehicle inspections are now generally needed to keep people from sabotaging control devices, insure proper tuning of motors, improve efficiency, and decrease air pollution.

Stationary sources are responsible for half of the controllable hydrocarbons, over half of the nitrogen oxides, and almost all of the particulates and sulfur oxides. The major stationary source problems are energy and transportation related. Most sulfur oxides come from burning fossil fuels in electric power plants. Utilities have been given the difficult choice between paying a premium price for low-sulfur fuels or investing in expensive stack gas scrubbers. The costs, passed on to consumers, play a role in encouraging energy conservation and nonelectrical sources. Oil refineries are the worst polluters of industry as well as supplying the worst moving source pollution. In 1977 the cost of controlling all pollutants from stationary sources was $6.7 billion, but the health benefit alone was over $8 billion. A 60 percent reduction of particulates from stationary sources would meet national standards and would produce benefits worth $41 billion to $52 billion. Benefits include more time on the job, increased productivity from workers with pollution-related diseases, decreased mortality, lower health costs, and increased real estate values from clear air. Impaired visibility, in fact, may account for 22 to 55 percent of the damages of smog.[19] Controls must be implemented nationally, even internationally. A weakly regulated factory can undersell a strictly regulated one, and most localities feel they cannot afford to lose industry.

Water Pollution

Water pollution is an equally serious problem with similar complexities, unanswered scientific and technological questions, need for stronger regulation, and costs of cleaning up. The role of the car is not as important overall here, yet still it is a major factor. Oil spills from drilling, shipping, and storm-damaged wells and sediment from port development are serious. Off Santa Barbara and Louisiana, extensive fouling of beaches has resulted in the death of large numbers of wildlife. The federal government suffers from the usual industry influence plus a conflict of interest. Since 1974, it has gotten over $5.5 billion per year from oil and gas royalties and bonuses from outer continental shelf leases. Even then, our government charges less for the oil than most foreign governments dealing with the same companies. Offshore production, now about 5 percent of the U.S. total, will increase greatly in coming years. As rigs go out deeper than 200 meters and waves get over 100 feet high, costs and risks go up significantly. Oil companies have paid for clean-ups after spills but have rarely been fined. Supertankers in recent years, starting with the *Torrey Canyon* in 1967, have been a major source of spills. As tankers get bigger and more profitable, they become structurally weaker and more difficult to maneuver. In 1976–1977, 11.5 million barrels of oil spilled into U.S. ocean waters from fifteen major spills, mostly because of lax regulation.[20] Thousands of smaller spills each year add a few million more barrels of oil.

Additional car pollutants get into rain water runoff. As municipal sewerage and industry decrease their pollution, the importance of pollution from storm water runoff increases. Sedimentation is caused by construction oriented to serving the automobile: paved areas, extensive suburbs, shopping centers, and suburban industry. Paved areas increase dirty runoff, cause larger flood volumes, prevent absorption of rain into the ground for plants and the water table, and hinder water conservation.

About 76,299 miles of streams and rivers are polluted; 95 percent of the 246 drainage basins in the United States are affected.[21] The EPA researched eighty-eight pollutants from 1963 to 1972 on thirty-five streams of roughly comparable importance. EPA found improvements over that period, especially for bacteria and dissolved oxygen, major targets of enforcement efforts. Some of the improvements were not enough, however, to reach standards needed to protect human and aquatic health; 84 percent of the streams exceeded phosphate standards and 74 percent increased their nitrate levels. About one-fourth of the streams exceeded nitrate standards.[22] Phenols (which affect the taste of fish and tap water), suspended solids (which endanger valued aquatic life), heavy metals (like cadmium, lead, mercury, iron, and manganese), and nine pesticides exceeded standards in at least one sample from over half of the streams in most cases. About 10 million tons of hazardous chemical and biological products, 90 percent in liquid form, were produced in 1970, and the volume grows at 5 to 10 percent per year.[23] Much better controls are needed, but they are costly.

Policies for Water Pollution. Several things can be done about water pollution: prevent the pollutant from getting into the water in the first place (point source control), reduce the volume of water needing treatment, treatment itself, and reuse of clean but not pure wastewater. Each approach has its costs and benefits, its life-style and technological changes.

Point source control is usually the cheapest approach. A good example is laws limiting the amount of phosphates that can be sold in household detergents. Data from Indiana and Erie County, New York, indicate dramatic reductions in pollution as a result. More use of soap instead of detergent would also help. Garbage disposals add enormously to the waste stream; in addition, the garbage could be used more directly to refertilize the land. Human fecal matter now polluting huge amounts of water could go into clivus multrum or other dry toilets, which compost the waste and produce useful fertilizer with no energy cost.

Point source control is especially important for industrial wastes and can be encouraged by special charges by municipal systems for treatment. Most sewage can be fairly easily processed in sewage plants and by nature; it is pollution mainly because of its concentration. Many modern chemicals, however, such as pesticides, kepone, polyvinyl chloride, and heavy metals are dangerous even in small quantities: they can accumulate in the food cycle, and they are expensive to remove. They can be regulated by point source control and possibly banned. Toxic pollutants are now the most important water pollution problem.

In this process, some old plants and outmoded systems are likely to be bankrupted or otherwise forced to close down. Loss of jobs and capacity, however, can usually be made up by new investments in new technologies. Pulp and paper mills, for example, historically among the most polluting of industries, have been required to clean up. The cost of controls is so small that it has no discernible impact on the amount of paper sold. The newer plants are both more profitable and less polluting. Similarly, severe restrictions on use of pesticides would reduce pollution and promote use of more effective techniques of pest control.

Reduction of volume, or water conservation, has much potential. Americans consume far more gallons of water per day than they need. Easy steps include toilet water tank devices that reduce volume per flush, turning off water while brushing teeth, and water-saving shower heads. Other feasible steps include the use of sink, shower, and kitchen wastewater (gray water) for yard and garden watering. Usually the price of water, like that of energy, is not high enough to encourage conservation. Water prices could be used for municipal revenue. In effect, charges could be viewed as a water tax to encourage conservation and to replace other more regressive taxes to some extent. A more common approach in drought areas is rationing, with penalties for overuse.

Some water will still need treatment by municipal plants. Use of septic tanks to avoid the expense of such treatment is feasible only in certain soils at low densities. The tanks eventually get clogged and pollute groundwater. They have to be carefully maintained, and regulation in most places is lax or nonexistent. With any concentration of population, a sewer system and treatment plant are necessary. Treatment has three levels: primary, secondary, and tertiary. *Primary* removes suspended solids and is fairly easily accomplished with screens, filters, and settling ponds. It produces a clear effluent. *Secondary* treatment can reach several levels up to removal of 85 percent of the biochemical oxygen demand (a major measure of pollution). Secondary treatment also chlorinates the effluent to kill bacteria. If the volume of effluent is small enough and the body of water receiving the effluent large enough or has enough circulation, the treated sewage may be discharged with much of its load of dissolved chemicals. *Tertiary* treatment includes producing drinkable water, commonly obtained by filtering treated effluent through beds of activated carbon.

Secondary treatment is fairly common, tertiary less so. Towns along the Mississippi River must treat river water to tertiary levels to get needed drinking water. They then dump their own polluted water into the river. It does not take much imagination to think of a better way and get a clean river as a bonus. But the game seems to be to impose a little more pollution on other people than they impose on you.

Cleaning up works. Seattle and San Diego have had outstanding success, and citizen action was a critical part of it, in spite of the fact that people do not want increased taxes. The pattern of reform was to study the problem, make projections and plans, and lobby through institutional changes setting up a regional sewage authority and eliminating or modifying local agencies and tax rates. In such a process, technical information is converted into plain English about costs and benefits, and a plan is taken to the people in the form of a vote on a bond issue or on a reorganization plan. Once the basic political commitment has been made and the new authority started, it takes about a year to make even more specific plans. Then it takes several more years to build the new plants, lay the sewage collector pipes, and put the facilities into operation. This whole process took Seattle and San Diego more than ten years, but the environmental payoff came faster than expected. Within two years of completion, fish and birds returned to the waterways and began to multiply in number and diversity. Recreational use, including swimming, became possible. Some fifty water bodies have been greatly improved since the 1960s. In other places, like Lake Erie, San Francisco, and New York, weak implementation of adequate laws has slowed the cleanup.

Once water is treated, it can be reused for groundwater recharge, pasturage, irrigation, golf course watering, recreational streams and lakes, and so on. Experiments so far have been very promising, but there are unanswered questions about the buildup over a long time of minute amounts of pollutants. Reducing salt compounds is a persistent technical problem. There is also a problem of balancing values: purifying water may be more expensive than it is worth, while clean but impure water may help save and enhance open space and agricultural production. Reuse is more feasible if source point control can keep difficult pollutants out of the water.

The Ocean. The ocean is our biggest water pollution problem. Historically it is the world's biggest dump and the one in longest use. Pesticides (mainly DDT), plastic, and crude oil are found through the oceans. In 1968 the United States alone dumped almost 10 million tons of industrial waste, sewage sludge, and construction and demolition debris into the Atlantic and Pacific oceans and the Gulf of Mexico. In 1973 the figure was almost 12 million tons.[24] The ocean provides 1 percent of our food and is our major source of atmospheric oxygen. We depend on phytoplankton (or plankton algae) more than on trees and grass to use sunlight to convert carbon dioxide into oxygen. Yet this photosynthesis is already slowed by DDT.[25] If the ocean becomes too polluted, from pesticides or other causes, we of the dangerous species will become an endangered species.

Scattered over the bottom of the ocean are nodules of copper, nickel, manganese, and cobalt, enough to last for the foreseeable future, but it will be hard to remove them without stirring up huge volumes of sediment. Already deep-sea mining techniques produce "plumes" of red clay discard, which cover many square miles of surface. It takes five years, because of wind, tide currents, and waves, for the tiny particles to sink through the hundred yards of euphotic zone, which receives sunlight and where most marine life lives. The wetlands and shallow ocean off the coasts are especially abundant with life, yet they are the most threatened by overfishing, river pollution from industrial urban areas, and filling for houses and industry. Life in the ocean seems to be declining. Only international cooperation can ensure the ocean's survival and probably our own. Yet each country is reluctant to give up powers to an international body. It is not just the fault of governments; their policies reflect popular feelings.

Industries resist controls as much as nations do. The five industries in the United States that cause the most water pollution are oil, iron and steel, paper, electric power, and chemical. Their lobbying associations spend about $54 million a year and employ over a thousand people, much of it to lobby against controls. These industries have 353 major plants not in compliance with 1977 EPA standards, about 63 percent of the total plants not in compliance.[26]

Other Pollutions

Other pollution-related problems are the greenhouse effect, turbidity, thermal water pollution, radiation, and noise. Deforestation and excess carbon dioxide (produced mainly by burning huge quantities of fossil fuels) cause the atmosphere to retain heat. CO_2 increased about 5 percent from 1958 to 1977. On the other hand, atmospheric turbidity (the amount of particulates and water in the air) has been increasing, possibly reflecting more of the light of the sun back out into space, reducing the heat reaching the earth. We do not yet understand the impact on climate of our activities.

Thermal water pollution is associated with nuclear plants, which need 234 gallons of water per million Btu compared with 146 for fossil fuel plants. Water temperature is one determinant of aquatic species. A large volume of warmed water radically changes the habitat around the point of discharge.

Noise pollution comes in loud and soft forms. We impose some on ourselves—by electric shavers, vacuum cleaners, power mowers, radio, loudspeakers, motorcycles—while some is imposed on us—the same sources and by trucks and airplanes. Reform is at an early stage. Acceptable limits have been worked out in sones and decibels, but monitoring equipment is not widely disseminated, and there are few effective abatement ordinances. Growing concern, however, is producing stronger regulations. Soft noise—from refrigerators, forced air systems and fans, electric typewriters, fluorescent light hum and whine, distant traffic, incessant background music—can add up to ever higher levels of background noise. Loud or soft, noise threatens hearing and lowers the quality of life.

Radiation pollution through X rays and fallout has been well recognized. Nuclear test bans have stopped fallout (except from China), and fairly rigorous controls over X rays have limited their threat. One real concern is that nuclear power plants, through accident or terrorism, may spread radioactivity in a large downwind area. Fear of such radiation is another important reason so many are fearful of proliferation of these plants. Radiation, however, relates to an immense spectrum of wave lengths, including all broadcasting and microwaves. As our use increases, we need more careful research on the whole range of radiation.

Solid Waste

Solid waste is an unwanted by-product of our style of life and standard of living. Solid waste includes agricultural, mining, and industrial waste, but we will focus on household waste—our own wastebaskets and garbage cans. From 1971 to 1976 we increased our waste per person per day from 24.6 pounds per week to 25.8, producing 144.7 million tons nationally. The national garbage can contained about 31 percent paper, 10 percent glass, 9 percent metal, 4 percent plastics, 17 percent food waste, 20 percent yard waste, and 9 percent rubber, leather, wood, textiles, and miscellaneous.

Old-fashioned dumping has long been considered undesirable; dumps stink, pollute the air when burning, breed vermin, are dangerous, and look bad. New-fashioned sanitary landfill consists essentially of digging a hole and burying the waste. Landfill is less and less workable as available dump sites fill up, and new ones are too far away.

There are four major solutions to the problem: source reduction, reuse, recycling, and burning for electricity and heat. Since the late 1950s there has been about a 50 percent increase in the use of plastics, aluminum, and paper for packaging previously unpacked items, such as fresh fruits and vegetables, takeout foods, and hardware. One estimate is that a return to 1958 levels of packaging would save 550,000 barrels of oil per day (energy equivalent), equal to 30 percent of the volume of oil flowing through the Alaskan pipeline. Source reduction would not only reduce solid waste but would also save energy and reduce pollution. But people are willing to pay more for convenience and cleanliness.

Other source reduction includes the repair and longer use of clothing, furniture, appliances, and cars, to name just a few, and the use of cloth instead of paper napkins and towels. At some point, everything needs to be thrown away, but in general we throw away too much too soon. The automobile increases the problem because it makes it easier to carry waste, and it is difficult to enforce rules against littering from cars (and of cars).

Reuse primarily refers to bottles but has application to other containers. Smashing bottles into cullet and remanufacturing into glass is far more costly in energy and pollution than transporting back to the factory and washing. Bottles can also substitute for cans. We are able to reuse glass milk bottles, wine bottles, and soda bottles. Oregon has led the nation with its "bottle bill," which requires deposits on all cans and bottles. The law has led to the near disappearance of throwaways in the state. In one year, bottle and can litter was cut by two-thirds. Enough energy was saved to heat 11,000 homes. Bottles and cans in trash collection was cut by 88 percent. Beer and soft-drink manufacturers also saved money, reusing each bottle an average of twenty-four times. Soft drink sales decreased by $1.7 million, but their costs decreased by $4.4 million, for a $2.7 million profit. Distributors and retailers had higher costs in handling the returned bottles but nevertheless came out ahead. The throwaway bottle and can industry collapsed, throwing 350 people out of work, and reducing bottle and can industry profits. However, 715 new jobs were created in handling bottles. Ninety-one percent of the Oregon public were in favor of the law. The Oregon experience gives reformers the information they need to try to overcome the intensity problem: intense bottle maker resistance and public apathy.[27]

We can imagine a further step: a bottle economy of standardized shapes and sizes and round-tripping for many products now bottled and canned. This change would allow standard-sized boxes, which could also be made for reuse, reducing cardboard waste, and the same applies to shopping bags and boxes. With a slight change of life-style, we could save money, energy, and resources, and reduce pollution.

Recycling involves remanufacturing an item—for example, melting bottles and cans to make new ones. This practice is more efficient than dumping them. In glass making, it reduces energy requirements and pollution. Aluminum is increasingly recycled. In 1977 about 20 percent of the total manufactured was from scrap. Rags, newspaper, cardboard, computer cards and printouts, and other clean paper are being recycled. Food waste and yard cuttings can be used for compost or pig feed on an industrial basis. About 6 percent of household waste is currently recycled.[28] Recycling supplies about 1 percent of our material resources. Recycling centers, popular a few years ago, are less used now, patronized by a relatively few committed people. New initiatives are needed. Industry is proposing expensive capital-intensive, centralized sorting and processing systems, but experimentation with home-segregated waste promises to be the most economic approach. The problem is to give people an incentive to sort, which can be supplied by a higher collection rate for unsegregated garbage and a lower rate for segregated. Our concept of "wastebasket" may have to change to more specialized "paper-basket," "wet garbage pail," and "bottle box," a simple sorting easily performed by most people. Garbage trucks also need separate compartments and can deliver presorted waste to a recycling plant. Again, a simple life-style change can be economical, conserve resources, and reduce pollution. Office paper recycling, a little easier than household, has caught on in many places.

Burning for electricity, the fourth major solution, ties in with total energy systems using otherwise waste heat for space heating and reducing transmission losses. It also greatly reduces the volume of solid waste to be disposed of. Many European cities have such plants; so do a few American cities (one is Ames, Iowa), while other cities (St. Louis and Baltimore) have had problems. A study in 1973 showed that heat from oil at $7 a barrel costs $1.35 per million Btu, while heat from solid waste ranges from about $.80 on down. Several technologies have established feasibility, including pollution control techniques. By 1980 waste in forty-eight urban areas could produce 1,259 billion Btu's and substitute for 616 thousand barrels of oil per day.[29]

Pollution control and solid waste reforms are growing in economic importance and could become an important industry with proper regulatory incentives. The economics are already favorable in many markets. The problem is to pull together a number of innovations to make them all the more efficient working together. Governmental leadership and cooperation from industry are needed, but without citizen involvement, government will be slow, and industry will promote self-serving approaches. Regulation to discourage externalizing costs to the environment is needed more than costly tax incentives or subsidies and puts the burden where it belongs—on the consumer and not the taxpayer. With regulation-created market incentives, private investment would come in with the diversity, competition, and efficiency needed to make environmental reform work. Once established, pollution and solid waste industries could place more vested interest behind reform. The results of solid waste reform can be less energy needs, lowered material resource needs, conservation of trees and wilderness, reclamation of dumps, and less pollution.

Prices are important. Aluminum, for examples, takes twenty times as much electricity to process from ore than from scrap, so electrical rates affect recycling. Success in recycling has been stimulated by paying people—$.23 a pound in 1979—for their waste aluminum. Wilderness protection reduces raw material availability, increases its cost, and improves incentives for solid waste reform. In 1973 scrap metal prices rose, providing the incentive to pull old wrecks out of ditches, yards, and pastures. A record of over 80 million tons of scrap iron and steel was consumed that year. Copper and lead price increases have similarly encouraged better use. Paper is especially sensitive to price changes. More expensive pulpwood would greatly increase recycling. In 1974, the energy crisis increased the processing costs of raw resources, again helping the economy move toward reform. Just as it is becoming more expensive to pull things out of nature, it is also getting more expensive to push things back into it; higher costs for garbage disposal help reform. Reform requires a detailed understanding of economics and technologies to find where small regulatory leverage can produce big results. It requires political action to overcome the intensity problem and get government to use those levers.

The Urban System

The car, including vans and pickups, is our major means of transportation and is sometimes an end in itself for power, styling, and fashion. It has transformed world society, giving people unprecedented speed and mobility, and in the process it has radically altered human settlement patterns and related social systems. As recently as 150 years ago, most people lived in rural areas or small towns. Even the largest of old cities had fewer than half a million people, and they had constant problems of illness from poor sanitation and poor diet. They depended upon the puny surplus of a vast hinterland. Transportation was by foot and animals and the vehicles they could pull. The result was a very compact city, both horizontally and vertically. The only residents needing a place to park a personal vehicle were the members of the small elites. Public and elite places were often beautiful and spacious, but for the most part, cities were overcrowded, unhealthy, and unsafe. Nevertheless, this premodern city had vitality. It was far more interesting than outlying areas; it was the center of politics, intellect, culture, and economics, the producer of a heritage we take for granted.

The sweeping changes of modernization changed the city, as it did everything else. Manufacturing came to concentrate there. Progress in public health and agriculture made huge agglomerations of people possible. Literacy, education, religion, science, law, business, and so on developed a social base for the urbanization.

Transportation inventions spread the city upward and outward. Steel girders and motors allowed the invention of the elevator, a vertical mass transit system, and the construction of the buildings they serve. These same developments led to the invention of the railroad, whose power of social transformation has been exceeded only by the car. The railroad in the city was the trolley and later the subway, along which a new kind of city, the early modern city, could spread outward. The populations of these early modern cities boomed up over the million mark, but their use of land was still compact and their densities high.

In the early twentieth century, the automobile was invented as a commercial product, and by the 1920s yet a third type of city began to develop—the automobile city. By this time in the United States, more people were living in cities than in the town and country, but the impact of the car was just beginning. The standard of aspiration became an urban job, a car, and a single-family home, the goal most have attained today.

In 1900 the car was an elite toy, and fewer than five thousand a year were produced. By 1915 it had functionally replaced the carriage. By 1920, there were 9.2 million cars registered (among 24 million households), and almost 2 million a year were being produced. Just ten years later in 1930, 2.8 million a year were being produced and 23 million were registered (among 30 million households), but public transportation was still strong. During the 1930s and 1940s, the early modern city hung on in its competition with the automobile city, helped by buses, which were more flexible than trolleys, and by the limited purchasing power brought on by the depression and World War II. In the late 1940s, 1950s, and 1960s, mass transit systems went bankrupt, were allowed to disintegrate, or became heavily subsidized. Rights of way became freeways, and parking lots proliferated in the old cities and in the newly emerging automobile city, the suburb. In the late 1960s and 1970s, more than 10 million vehicles were being manufactured almost every year. In 1977 there were 114 million cars registered (among a national total of 74 million households). We thus went from 0.3 cars per family in 1920 to 1.5 cars per family in 1977.[30] We drive cars farther and for more purposes than we did in the 1920s, and we have fewer alternative forms of transportation.

We have a natural tendency to assume the continuation of things as we know them, yet any long-range view of history should teach us to think of what we have as transient and temporary. Our reliance—really, dependency—on the automobile is not carved in granite. We use the automobile because in our personal calculations it makes life better for us. These calculations are made within a setting that favors the car. The cheap gas and cheap land system, the aspiration for a car and a house, the suburb-freeway-parking lot architecture, and the extensive land-use ethic that results have produced the highest mass standard of living ever. The benefits are obvious; what we usually fail to calculate are the costs. Changes in conditions may change our calculations.

Environmentalists are challenging this urban system, which we will discuss in three ways: transit, intensification, and density with quality.

Transit

Reformers have tended to support the development of rail transit systems but are beginning to move away from a heavy emphasis on them for several reasons. One important reason is their high cost compared with the number and kind of people served. They are cost-efficient if densities are relatively high, as in New York City (26,300 people per square mile) and Chicago (15,100), and are less feasible where densities are low, as in Atlanta (3,800) and Los Angeles (6,100). Modern fixed-rail transit systems have had large cost overruns, but modernizing old trolley systems has been fairly cost-effective. But even when the number served is high, mass transit systems can be questioned because of the users they serve. Too often, the major beneficiaries are white, affluent suburbanites who get a subsidized ride through central city problems on their way to the central business district. Nevertheless, despite these and other problems, mass transit systems are desirable and efficient in dense cities. In those cases, the systems should be attractive enough to maximize their ridership. There is a world of difference between the noisy, dirty, ugly, jerky system of New York City and the smooth, quiet elegance of San Francisco's BART.

Generally, bus systems are proving more efficient than fixed rail. A major problem is to give buses preference over cars, especially those with only one or two passengers. The government has to be willing to regulate use of the public way to achieve the greatest efficiency. Several techniques are being experimented with to give buses preference. A lane of a freeway can be reserved for bus and car pool use. Important access ramps can be expanded with two lanes, one for buses and car pools with a green light and the other for other vehicles, which get a green light only when they can get on the freeway without causing congestion. Preferential toll gates and free tolls can be used for buses and car pools. Car pools can also be encouraged by special information services, putting people in touch with each other and by reserved close-in parking spaces at the place of work.

These devices can slow down inefficient traffic and speed up the efficient. We have learned from experience that usually cars whiz by buses. It is important to reverse this learning process on congested corridors, so that drivers see buses go whizzing past them and realize the advantages of transit. Bus and car pool systems are likely to be much less costly than fixed rail systems. Minneapolis, for example, discovered it got mass transit results from buses and special ramps for 3 percent of the cost of transit.

Paratransit refers to systems not based on fixed routes, fixed schedules, fares, and full-time drivers. Car pools are one example, and there are many others, which can supplement transit and reduce the need for cars. Van systems are growing in popularity. A company lets an employee use a company-owned van personally at a subsidized rate. In return, the employee agrees to carry a certain number of other employees to work. The employee-riders have a door-to-door service at a cost much lower than a personal vehicle.

Monopolistic bus and taxi interests have generally made the jitney illegal. A jitney is a car or bus that picks people up wherever it can find them, usually along a bus route, and takes them to a destination area where it can drop them off at or near the door. Jitneys can be driven by part-time drivers; they can proliferate as needed and disappear when not. Fares and general routes can be advertised or known by custom. The jitney survives illegally in Pittsburgh, where it connects a black residential area with downtown. But taxi companies resist jitneys, fare splitting, easier licensing, and other changes, which would allow free enterprise to operate.[31] Since most people do not care too much about jitneys, the intensive interest prevails.

A couple of other methods, though a bit slow, are nonpolluting, very efficient, healthy, technically proven, and solar powered: bicycling and walking. Bicycling is the most efficient form of locomotion. Efficiency can be measured in terms of calories per gram of weight per kilometer. A person on a bike uses 0.15 calories; a salmon, 0.4; horses, cows, dogs, some birds, jet transports, cars, light planes, and jet fighters, all in the 0.5 to 1.5 range; fruitflies and mice, in the 15 to 80 range.[32] Outside the United States, bicycles are usually far more important than cars. In poor countries, bicycle carts are often used for freight. In the United States, flat college campuses enjoy the most bicycle traffic because they exclude vehicles from the main grounds, have populations most able to ride, and develop rules and privileges for riders, making the system work. Elsewhere easy rentals, buses that can easily accommodate bicycles, safe parking, segregated bike paths, and other encouragement can help bicycles. Both bicyclists and walkers need more protection from cars.

In a very few places, the sacredness of the car has been challenged. To encourage noncar movement and to protect neighborhood quality, traffic barricades have been put up to stop through traffic, streets have been narrowed to reduce traffic, streets have been closed, and parking has been reduced. Such schemes have to be extremely well planned and may have some costs, such as congesting arterials and slowing emergency vehicles and buses. Large-scale restrictions have to be carefully integrated with land-use planning.

Land Use and Urban Efficiency

Land-use reformers seek to increase urban densities and avoid more suburbanization and its costs. Yet intensification is usually associated in the public mind with a decline in the standard of living. Central cities are associated with congestion, pollution, crime, poor schools, decay, and racial problems. Environmental reform also requires an attack on our social problems.

The current trend is leapfrogging housing subdivisions based on freeway extensions. Development interests at the state and federal level, which control transportation spending, have succeeded in building a huge freeway system. While major highway building has slowed down considerably, the implications for land use are still being worked out. Development interests at the local level bring effective pressure to bear on local governments for suburbanization. Over the last twenty-five years, suburbs have doubled in population while central city, town, and country areas have grown at less than 1 percent per year. Suburbs have well over a third of the population; central cities and town-and-country have less than a third each. Recently some town and country areas have started growing, suburban growth is tapering off, and several central cities are declining.

Meanwhile, trends in household composition are changing in a way that will make intensification easier. (See table 3–4.) The suburban house is ideal for families with children and bigger families, both of which are on the decline as the birthrate drops and the number of older people increases. Over 97 percent of the population lives in "households." (The remaining 2.8 percent lives in "group quarters," such as detention facilities, mental hospitals, college dormitories, and rooming houses.) There are about 74 million households in the nation (1977). About 18 million of these are "unrelated individuals"—people who do not live with someone they are related to by blood or marriage. Most of them live alone. About 26 million families (people who are so related) have no children. Thus 59 percent of all households have no children. The average household size dropped from 3.37 in 1950 to 2.86 in 1977, a drop of about 15 percent, and the trend to smaller, childless households is expected to continue.

Although household changes might lean toward intensification, affluence tends toward suburbanization. In 1976, the United States had about 81 mil-

Table 3–4 Distribution of Population by Place

Place	Population [a]		Average Annual % Change			% Total Population	
	1950	1973	1950–1960	1960–1970	1970–1973	1950	1970
Central city [b]	53.7	63.6	1.1	0.6	−0.3	35.5	30.3
Suburbs [b]	40.9	79.3	3.3	2.4	1.6	27.0	37.8
Town and country	56.7	66.9	0.5	0.7	1.5	37.5	31.9
Total	151.3	209.8	1.7	1.3	1.0		

[a] The figures are in millions.
[b] As defined in 1971 in the 243 Standard Metropolitan Statistical Areas.
Source: *Statistical Abstract of the United States, 1975,* p. 17.

lion residences, of which about 72 percent were single-family homes and mobile homes. Our housing stock has generally improved in quality and quantity since World War II. Reform seems to require discouraging extensive land use and favoring multiple units and intensive use. However, much depends on circumstances. The first problem is to protect peripheral open space and stop the leapfrogging by confining development to the fringe. Better yet is to stop it even on the fringe and allow building only on vacant lots and previously overlooked areas that fall within existing urban service area. Circumstances favor multiple housing near mass transit stops. Confining development and increasing multiples will tend to increase densities, making auto-based systems less workable and mass transit systems more feasible.

Land-use reforms by local government, however, have not been motivated so much by the desirability of intensification as by the undesirability of continued sprawl. More and more communities are trying to stop growth or at least control it. They are worried about increasing air pollution, congestion, loss of open space, and other changes, which produce an even more profound fear of loss of neighborhood and community. Those who advocate controlling growth are often charged with wanting to leave the disadvantaged stranded in central cities. The response is that continued suburbanization is no guarantee or even a real promise for the disadvantaged. Also, communities, like ships, have limited capacities, and to let everyone on is to ensure that everyone drowns. The challenge is to revitalize the cities, not destroy the suburbs too.

Planning in Suburb and Central City

Another theme in addition to intensification and controlled growth is planning. Land-use planning suggests a kind of reasonableness and efficiency that hides its real variability. It is as much planning to plan sprawl as it is a more intense form of urbanization. Planning only means a relatively thorough consideration of the facts, not necessarily an environmentally progressive solution. In practice, intensification, growth control, and planning are all usually associated with each other. Research on specific examples indicates that a planned dense community has measurable advantages over an unplanned sprawl. The planned approach can save half of any area as open space; sprawl, on the other hand, covers all of it and has no developed park area. The planned development costs 44 percent less to build and has somewhat lower operating costs. It has 45 percent less air pollution, less storm water runoff, less sedimentation during construction, less traffic, and less noise, though what there is is concentrated in the occupied area. The planned approach uses 44 percent less energy and 35 percent less water.[33]

Many Americans do not want to live in apartments; our middle-affluent culture is oriented to single-family houses. Much of the dislike springs from the fact that apartments are associated with noise, overcrowding, and central city problems. It is hard to separate these social conditions from the architectural form. Condominiums generally have attractive social conditions, and the owners have to be middle class to afford them. Condominium development, initially slowed by overpromotion and unworkable forms of self-governance, is recovering and likely to increase in popularity. Condominiums and better apartments house a small but important segment of the population because they are showing that higher densities do not necessarily detract from our quality of life or standard of living. Every big city has middle-to-high-income neighborhoods that flourish despite surrounding and even penetrating urban problems.

Federal, state, and regional efforts to plan controlled growth have been minimal. Most power is in the hands of local governments, which are usually controlled by development interests. Controls like land-use plans and zoning ordinances often protect existing organized neighborhoods but have not dealt with larger issues. In a few cases, like the California coast, San Francisco Bay/Suisun Marsh, and New York's Adirondack Park, large-scale citizen movements have been able to push for laws with strong controls over private development. When the California legislature failed to pass a coastal bill, the initiative process was used successfully, allowing the voters to make law. By and large, increased controls have been upheld by the courts. Control-oriented local governments require costs of major services, especially sewers and wastewater treatment plants, to be paid by developers. Federal funding of sewage projects has attempted to make sure that increased capacity does not lead to more suburbs, leading to more air pollution. How effective it is remains to be seen.

Many people realize the costs of lack of planning too late. San Jose, California, lost its vast orchards, open space, clean air, waterways, and low tax rate before it realized that all these losses were a result of uncontrolled growth. San Jose elected a mayor in 1974 who advocated slow growth. That same year, Petaluma, California, learning from the experience of others, adopted a strong control plan, which may help it to avoid San Jose's problems. As islands of control spread and more and more land is unavailable for urbanization, the question arises as to where the extra people will go. The answer seems to be to build and rebuild on land within urban service limits. Enough land is probably available for ten to thirty years of growth of this sort.

There are corresponding trends in the central city. In suburbia the questions are about new building and open space; in the city they are about rehabilitation and rebuilding. The trend has been away from the high public costs and low social benefits of rebuilding (as in urban renewal) and toward cheaper, socially beneficial rehabilitation. Few people realize how large the "rehab" and remodeling market is. In 1974, for example, remodeling added the equivalent of 700,000 new six-room houses, as compared with 870,000 new single houses. About 600,000 housing units are destroyed each year, many unnecessarily. Increasingly unable to find a cheap house farther out or unwilling to drive farther to work, people are improving the places they have or are moving into closer-in, less desirable houses and fixing them up. The Department of Housing and Urban Development (HUD) had to foreclose on about 175,000 houses across the country because of the recession and corruption and mismanagement of certain programs. Since 1976 HUD has turned these into assets by offering them cheaply to people who will live in them and upgrade them. Yet there are continuing problems. HUD was slow in foreclosing, leaving many houses empty too long and open to vandals. Cities have failed to maintain services. Private lenders see values declining and are fearful of lending in certain areas (this practice is called *redlining*). The situation is ambiguous. Some central city areas are healthy and growing; others decay and are abandoned.

An Alternative to the Car-Suburb System

The car-suburb system can be compared with a radical alternative. Our discussion here will pull together a number of problems discussed previously as they pertain to major alternatives of urban systems. The car-suburb system typically ranges from about one house per acre to fifteen per acre for town-

Figure 3–1 Density with Quality in the Modern City

Drawing by Bob Newey, Hayward, California.

house style developments; about four per acre is an average. The system is designed for fluidity of movement for cars. Most of us are familiar with it.

The alternative would also average about four units per acre but in a radically different way that would combine density with quality. See figure 3–1. Large areas of open space would be left untouched, concentrating housing on less land at about thirty to sixty units to the acre—about one-tenth the space needed in suburbs. High-rise structures are not necessary; such densities can be achieved with buildings averaging three stories high. (In fact, high rises have wind, safety, and energy problems; they have high construction costs; and they are less acceptable than low rises are to many Americans.) We can include two-story town houses in the outer area and higher structures in the most central area. The interior space of the apartments would have to equal that found in typical suburbs. Such space, sound insulation and other amenities to achieve comparability, and higher land costs would add to the cost of the apartments. On the other hand, apartments cost less than houses to build, and the new system radically reduces transportation and energy costs. Such density does not allow much land for large parks in the urbanized area, but it has much room for mini parks, trees, and greenery in all public areas. Above all, there is no space for personal vehicles. People within the area have to walk, ride bicycles, and use public transportation. They would have access to personal vehicles at the edge of the area, where it meets the car system.

Exclusion of cars may seem like a radical step, but it is not a new idea. Typically campuses, shopping malls, parks, amusement or theme parks, and large buildings exclude cars while accommodating large numbers of people in large spaces. Certain parts of many downtowns or central city areas have the densities needed but still accommodate the car, greatly reducing their quality. Some of these areas have the kind of low-rise, middle-class character of combining density and quality, and they show levels of car ownership of only 20 percent of households. Decaying areas around mass transit stops become prime candidates for implementation of a denser system; much can be done through rehabilitation.

The denser system essentially converts much pavement to direct social uses of housing, commerce, employment, schools, and visual amenity. Most streets could be sidewalks one lane wide; major arterials need be mostly only two lanes.

Apartments are appropriate for the shift in household composition away from large families.

How do the costs and benefits of the car-suburb system compare with those of density with quality?

Wilderness is saved and becomes an amenity adjacent to the city under the dense plan. If we extend the general idea to include use of buses and trains to achieve access to more distant wilderness, more wilderness is saved. The car system has been immensely destructive of wilderness, building suburbs over it and extending pavement into it.

Resources are saved by the dense system, which requires far less minerals, farmland, and renewable resources than does the car system. Road construction and car manufacturing consume huge quantities of resources; suburbs cover prime crop and grazing land.

Energy conservation is radically improved by the denser system, which uses far less energy for home heating (the units insulate each other) and transportation. There are savings in both the creation of the system and its operation. The car system is the most energy-expensive style of life ever practiced on a mass scale.

Energy production is more efficient for the denser system because it lends itself to whole energy systems, burning solid waste, and to district solar heating, in which sunny-side units help the shady side in heating, and vice-versa for cooling. Buildings would have solar panels for space and water heat. The car system is less efficient in using solar or whole energy systems, relying heavily on fossil fuels.

Air pollution is radically reduced in the denser system. The major cause of air pollution now is the car-suburb system, especially cars and refineries.

Water pollution is substantially reduced because of less sedimentation from construction, reduction of oil spills, radical reduction of concrete and asphalt areas that are subject to storm runoff, and a cleaner impervious area than in the car system.

Water conservation benefits from a compact approach because of the naturally retentive capacities of open space. Less impervious surface allows greater penetration of rainwater and natural filtering and maintenance of groundwater. Outside water use is radically reduced through the elimination of most yards and lawns in the intensive system, though public landscaping and community gardens would need water.

Noise pollution would be greatly reduced by the elimination of cars and motorbikes, which cause about half of the noise of urban areas. However, other types of noise like radios and hi-fis could be more of a problem in the dense area without stricter regulation because people are closer together.

Solid waste reforms need to be built into the denser system, adding to its clear advantage respecting the closeness of pick-up points. Source reduction, a bottle deposit law, and home separation of trash and garbage would tie into burning waste for electricity and space heat in the whole energy plant. Litter would also be reduced, but, like noise pollution, what there is would be more objectionable, requiring some regulation. The car system lends itself to litter and long pick-up and disposal distances, as well as auto junk.

Land waste is the hallmark of the auto system, dedicating about 35 percent of the urban area to transportation purposes, which cannot be used for direct social purposes. It is difficult to say how much would be needed for an intensive system—perhaps about 15 percent for vehicles still needed for commercial, public safety, and transit purposes.

Time waste is a frequent problem of the car system during rush hours on major arterials. Congestion also aggravates pollution, energy, and health problems. Such delays waste time the way pavement wastes space. Congestion is unlikely in the dense setting, which will also have far better transit. However, residents will move about more slowly and may perceive a disadvantage. What is important, though, is not speed but the time it takes to achieve the objective. Averaging thirty miles an hour, it might take us twenty minutes to drive home from work, moving over a long distance in the car system. However, even averaging five miles an hour in the dense system, it might also take us only twenty minutes to get home because the distance is so much shorter. We must also consider the time it takes to make money to pay for either system. Again, it is hard to say which system is better respecting time of travel, and the two may be very difficult to compare.

Visual amenity will characterize the intensive system if properly executed in a way difficult to imagine knowing our central cities of today. Urban ugliness is created mainly by pavement but also by litter, utility lines, advertising, and lack of trees. The private and commercial spaces and parks of suburbia tend to be attractive; the public streets, ugly; the industrial and institutional spaces, mixed. Achieving the advantage of density depends on execution. It is not how dense you build it but how you build it dense.

Safety is a major problem of the car system. The car is the most dangerous form of transportation ever used on a mass scale. Car accidents are the leading cause of death measured as years of life lost against a life expectancy of seventy. Cars kill more children than other mishap or disease.[34] Every year millions are injured, tens of thousands killed, thousands disabled. Density with quality would cut this toll to a minute fraction. Children could play in most places without fear of traffic and could walk to school.

Health is also a major problem of the car system, to some extent because of its air pollution, but also because it results in a sedentary way of life. The pollution produces death from respiratory diseases; the sedentation, from heart disease. Walking is an excellent conditioner. Many people might consider it a burden of the intensive system, but walking (and bicycling) will help them live healthier and, possibly, longer. The car system on the other hand, discourages those who would walk and makes cars a necessity.

Mobility is radically different between the two systems. The car system works well for nonrush hour trips, trips to areas with large parking lots, and nonroutine trips over a wide geographic area. The dense system will provide adequate to excellent mobility along major traffic corridors and can better serve some areas (such as central business districts) without parking. Having accustomed ourselves to certain kinds of mobility, we will perceive some loss in an intensive setting, and it will take some time to realize the potentials of the new system.

Transit is feasible in an intensive setting. The increase in volume and decrease in distances will make it pay its own way. Transit is necessarily feeble in a car system. We have been slow to recognize the incompatibility between the two systems.

Pedestrians of the car system—the old, young, the disabled, the poor—are disadvantaged by the great distances, poor transit, inadequate sidewalks, and life-threatening vehicles wrought by the car system. A dense setting ends this discrimination against the politically weak.

Central city neighborhoods have often been adversely affected by their own increased use of cars, by freeways coming through them to connect suburb and central business districts, and by the loss of affluent population and jobs to suburbs. The quality of an urban residential street goes up as traffic goes down and is reflected in more social interaction, more social ties, and more stability of residents on such streets.[35] A dense approach could turn around much of the decline of central neighborhoods now adversely affected by traffic. Implementation should involve the understanding and participation of the affected people. Making the transaction to density with quality is complex, and there may be many satisfactory halfway stations.

Central business districts (CBDs) are indirectly involved in the comparison. They would not have dense residential systems but would limit cars. Now CBDs are served by cars, causing serious traffic, parking, pollution, noise, safety, and health problems because their streets are not usually designed for cars. Freedom for the car has meant loss of mobility for transit and a lowering of the efficiency of CBDs. Under the intensive system, access would be by mass transit, with consequent greater fluidity of movement. There would be more patronage for mass transit in the CBD.[36]

The sense of community is likely to be higher in a dense setting than in suburbia. Instead of moving about in socially isolated vehicles (the CB radio revolution notwithstanding) to places outside the community, we are more likely to move as pedestrians to places within the community. We will get to know each other more, possibly developing the community spirit that can make us less dependent on government and reduce loneliness and anomie. All too frequently, suburbanites yearn for community while fearing their neighbors. The dense system risks loss of some privacy, but the privacy of suburbia can be exaggerated.

Crime will probably be reduced in the dense setting, if only because we will know our neighbors better, a major factor in crime control. In addition, those who commit crimes will find that they have no escape vehicles, no traffic to disappear into, and no cars to steal. Heavy stolen objects will be harder to transport. Residential streets could be mostly cul de sacs, which are safer. The correlation between population density and crime is peculiarly American, and the dense setting removes some of those causes.

Private costs and public costs help sum up an important dimension of the differences between the two systems. Private costs of owning a car are about $3,000 a year, with additional costs of property damage from pollution and private costs of accidents and disease related to cars. Parking and street costs affect rent or the price of a house, the price of goods and services we buy, and our salaries. Suburban housing costs are also higher compared with apartments and the shorter utility lines needed by a dense system.

Public costs to a great extent are covered by taxes on gasoline and car registration fees, but there are other costs. Police and health services, for example, are generally covered by regular taxes, and most local street repair is paid by local taxes. It is difficult to say what the costs of the dense system would be, but they seem likely to be less than for cars.

This discussion is by no means conclusive. Study and experimentation are needed to test the concepts. Preference for one system over the other depends on balancing many values; neither is perfect. The density with quality system seems attractive enough to be worth some major experiments. It attempts to save the quality of life while maintaining the general standard of living by making radical changes in our style of life.

What would happen to the car and oil industries if we move in a major way toward density with quality? They would decline slowly. But the money we spend on our car does not disappear with the car. Some will go to mass transit and car rentals. The rest we are free to spend in new ways, stimulating those industries to grow.

Another concern is what happens to existing suburbia. American values are likely to emphasize the freestanding dwelling for some time, and the massive stock of such houses will meet demand for a long time to come. A result of density with quality could be, though, to stop further suburbanization and save open space. Demonstration of the attractiveness of density is essential to changing popular values and the long-term success of the idea.

We may be forced as well as attracted to the idea by rapidly rising fuel prices, and the less we conserve, the sooner higher densities may be necessary. If we are forced by scarcity to convert quickly, the results may not be as appealing as a gradual, carefully planned transition.

The density with quality system does not need to appeal to everyone; it need appeal only to enough people to make it economically viable. Many people already do not own cars, and others try to minimize their use. They and other people interested in environmentally sound living could be attracted to dense areas. In fact, many already live in such areas, but without the advantages of less traffic and more transit. The more who want such a neighborhood, the more open space can be saved. A will to make the cities livable needs to replace the desire to escape them. An intensive ethic needs to replace the extensive ethic of the car-suburb system.

The density with quality system is the ultimate in the general densification policies being sought by environmentalists. They provide a positive goal to fight for, getting away from just fighting proposed antienvironmental developments. There will be many beneficiaries, but the effective political pressure will come from environmentalists. They will not make money at it, so it is necessary for knowledge of the environmental crisis as a whole to motivate action, overcoming the intensity problem.

Most of us have become deadened to the real costs of the car-suburb system. Changing the system seems so impossible to us that we fail to realize that we could take effective action collectively through democratic government. Only when we add up all the costs and think about the future of gasoline can we experience the mind change needed for support for new kinds of leaders. Rationalizing each of the individual costs, we continue to hide the crisis, helped along by a huge complex of economic interests heavily committed to the car-suburb system.

Jobs and Environmental Reform

Environmentalists seem to oppose jobs in general when they oppose destructive projects, but their positive proposals actually create as many or more jobs. The major problem is to make the transition from the antienvironmental jobs that we have a clear stake in to the proenvironmental jobs being created, which we have no specific stake in. Defensive businesses and unions sometimes take an inconsistent attitude, emphasizing the jobs of antienvironmental projects and the costs of proenvironmental projects. Obviously the costs of reform create jobs. We can pay for it in small increases in the prices of products to cover regulation, or we can pay taxes to cover public projects. Such reform may mean that fewer people can afford the products, affecting their standard of living but buying a higher quality of life. We have money. What do we want to buy? What kind of jobs do we want to create? Fortunately, once an environmental reform is in place, it usually develops its own vesting of interests, ensuring its defense.

Consider energy. A zero energy growth policy was tested on an econometric model, which discovered that the GNP could increase 100 percent over 1975 by the year 2000 and would have more jobs.[37]

The federal government spends about $11.6 billion a year on the environment, especially on pollution control. Water treatment facilities construction over the last few years has been one of the biggest public-works projects in American history. Regulation is calling forth additional state and local spending and private spending. About 34.7 billion was spent in 1974 on air and water pollution and solid waste abatement.[38] By 1975 an estimated 1 million jobs had been created, and less than 10 percent of requirements had been met in pollution, solid waste, and strip-mine reclamation. Bottle deposit laws, waste resource recovery, and whole energy plants will create more jobs. We are committing about 2 percent of our GNP to pollution and control. Price increases during the inflationary year of 1974 were only 3 percent due to pollution controls. Most workers dismissed because of plant closings based on inability to meet pollution controls found jobs in environmentally cleaner plants, which expanded production to compensate for the closed plants. Far more jobs are being created than lost. For urban revitalization, one rough estimate of rebuilding and rehabilitating housing of typical central cities is 1.2 million jobs per year for five years.[39] New energy industries, especially in the solar area, are already starting to grow. Environmentalists are surprisingly progrowth, but the growth they advocate is of a different kind.

Stabilization of population is essential for protecting natural areas against destructive exploitation and for reducing starvation and malnutrition. Modern farming is running into limits on its productivity and is even reducing the earth's carrying capacity. Traditional techniques can also be destructive, leading to deforestation, overgrazing, salinization, desertification, and related problems. Within limits, organic and scientific farming and gardening can reduce fertilizer, pesticide, water, and other resource needs to produce food and can make traditional agriculture more productive. The world is struggling with limited success to control its population, but Americans also have problems, among them abortion and teenage pregnancy. Similar conflicts exist between protection of wilderness and renewable resources and continued exploitation and consumption of resources by destructive technologies and life-styles. Energy is particularly important. Hard paths need to be displaced by the soft paths of solar energy, conservation, and life-style changes.

Pollution threatens us in many forms—in air, water, climate, heat, radiation, and noise. Cleaning up is expensive but affordable, and progress is being made against certain kinds of pollutants. Much more needs to be done against industrial and often popular resistance. Our activities now threaten the global climate and the oceans. Overreliance on the automobile is a cause of many problems, especially in cities. Reform requires transit, planned intensification of land use within urban service limits, and possibly development of density with quality. Environmental reform requires a redirection of the economy to new kinds of growth.

Notes

1. William Ophuls, *Ecology and the Politics of Scarcity* (San Francisco: William Freeman, 1977), pp. 42–43.
2. Ibid., p. 53. In developing nations, one calorie of energy yields up to sixteen of food, but in the United States, one energy calorie yields less than a calorie of food.
3. Ibid., pp. 53–54.
4. Ibid., p. 50. Council on Environmental Quality, *Environmental Quality* (Washington, D.C.: U.S. Government Printing Office, 1978), pp. 274–275.
5. Ophuls, *Ecology*, p. 57.
6. Ibid., pp. 42–43.
7. Mary Lou Seaver, review of *The Poverty of Power* by Barry Commoner, in *Not Man Apart*, August 1976, p. 13. Commoner cites William Lockeretz of the Center for the Biology of Natural Systems. The conventional farms studied produced $179 of crops per acre with operating costs of $47 and 18,400 Btus of energy per net dollar earned. Similar but organic farms produced $165 of crops per acre with costs of $31 and 6,800 Btus per net dollar.
8. *San Francisco Chronicle*, March 14, 1976; Harold Gilliam, "The Organic Wonderland at Stanford," *San Francisco Chronicle*, September 8, 1974; John Jeavons, *How to Grow More Vegetables* (Palo Alto: Ecology Action, 1974), uses Alan Chadwick's "biodynamic-French intensive" techniques.
9. Ophuls, *Ecology*, p. 61.
10. *San Francisco Chronicle*, October 10, 1977. One hundred seventy-six Congressmen voted against half of the thirty-two major social welfare bills between 1973 and 1977.
11. *San Francisco Chronicle*, January 24, 1978, from *New York Times*.
12. Paul Samuelson, "U.S. Still the Richest?" *Newsweek*, August 18, 1975.
13. Environmental Action, *Annual Report* (Washington, D.C.: 1976).
14. *San Francisco Chronicle*, December 20, 1974, from United Press.

15. U.S. Department of the Interior, *Energy Perspectives* (Washington, D.C.: Government Printing Office, 1975), pp. 2–21.
16. TRB, "Aslosh in Waste," *New Republic,* September 24, 1977.
17. Amory Lovins, *Soft Energy Paths* (San Francisco: Friends of the Earth, 1977), pp. 80–81 and passim. This is an excellent summary of the reform position on energy.
18. Council on Environmental Quality, *The Good News About Energy* (Washington, D.C.: Government Printing Office, 1979), pp. 3, 7.
19. *San Francisco Chronicle,* May 7, 1979, based on a study done for the Environmental Protection Agency.
20. *Statistical Abstract of the United States, 1978,* p. 216.
21. *Statistical Abstract, 1975,* p. 183; Council on Environmental Quality, *Environmental Quality* (Washington, D.C.: Government Printing Office, 1978), pp. 90–98.
22. Council on Environmental Quality, *Environmental Quality, Fifth Annual Report* (Washington, D.C.: Government Printing Office, December 1974), pp. 284–285.
23. Ibid., pp. 139, 286–287.
24. *Statistical Abstract, 1975,* p. 182.
25. C. F. Wurster, "DDT Reduces Photosynthesis in Marine Phytoplankton," *Science* 159 (1968):1474–1475; D. W. Menzel et al., "Marine Phytoplankton Vary in Their Response to Chlorinated Hydrocarbons," *Science* 167 (1970):1724–1726; C. F. Wurster, "Aldrin and Dieldrin," *Environment* 13 (1971):33–45.
26. "The Filthy Five," *Environmental Action,* September 10, 1977, pp. 6–9.
27. Mike Bowker, "The Oregon Solution," *Yodeler,* June 1976, p. 7. *Yodeler* is published by the Bay Chapter of the Sierra Club.
28. *Statistical Abstract, 1978,* p. 214.
29. Council on Environmental Quality, *Environmental Quality, Fifth Annual Report,* pp. 131–137.
30. *Statistical Abstract, 1977,* pp. 43, 649.
31. "Trouble in Mass Transit," *Consumer Reports,* March 1975, pp. 190–195; "Paratransit," *Consumer Reports,* April 1975, pp. 261–264.
32. S. S. Wilson, "Bicycle Technology," *Scientific American,* March 1973, p. 90.
33. Real Estate Research Corporation, *The Costs of Sprawl* (Washington, D.C.: Government Printing Office, 1974). For a critique, see Alan Altschuler, "The Costs of Sprawl," *Journal of the American Institute of Planners* (April 1977):207–209. For a more positive view, see Warren Johnson, "The Case Against Mid-Century Spread," *Sierra Club Bulletin,* June 1974, pp. 14–16, 38.
34. *San Francisco Chronicle,* January 29, 1978; Marc Lalonde, *A New Perspective on the Health of Canadians* (Ottawa: Information Canada, 1975), p. 15.
35. Donald Appleyard, *The Street Livability Study* (San Francisco: Planning Department, 1970). For a lengthy international study, see Donald Appleyard, *Livable Urban Streets* (Washington, D.C.: U.S. Department of Transportation, 1976).
36. Limitations on vehicles are advanced in central business districts of other developed countries. See Organization for Economic Cooperation and Development, *Streets for People* (Paris: OECD, 1974).
37. Ford Foundation, *A Time to Choose* (Cambridge, Mass.: Ballinger, 1974).
38. *Statistical Abstract, 1978,* p. 213.
39. Pat Heffernan, "Jobs and the Environment," *Sierra Club Bulletin,* April 1975, pp. 25–29.

4

EQUAL RIGHTS FOR ALL WOMEN
U.A.W. E.R.A.
YES
SUPPORTS E.R.A.
U.A.W.
E.R.A.
REGION 4
U.A.W. SUPPORTS E.R.A.
E.R.A. NOW
ROBERT JOHNSON
DIRECTOR
ONE YEAR
TO RATIFY
COMMITEE FOR

Social Justice: The Pervasive Problems

Social justice seeks to achieve several goals: equality of opportunity; help for those unable to support themselves; nondiscrimination respecting race, sex, or other attribute not related to work, ability, or luck; and the somewhat conflicting idea of making up for the adverse results of past discrimination. The Constitution guarantees certain personal and political rights. Social justice means making it possible to enjoy those rights. It requires such services as protection from crime and health care. Social justice means giving all children the education and other services they need to have a fair chance to get jobs and compete in the economy, a goal especially difficult for the disadvantaged. Social justice includes an idea already discussed: affording a minimal opportunity to work to all poor employable people. These goals are expensive. They compete with some other reforms, and they are helped by security reform and tax reform.

We fall too far short of these goals, for many reasons. Primarily, economic elites place a higher value on other goals and are reluctant to divert more wealth and power toward social justice. There are many other reasons, though, including the apathy and occasional hostility of the dominant popular culture toward the disadvantaged and the unwillingness of some of the needy to help themselves. Also very important are our lack of understanding and insight into the problems and the inertia of bureaucracies in implementing flawed solutions.

Poverty

We usually think of poverty as one of the most important problems we face. If we define American poverty simply as some people having less than others, then it is a major problem. But if we define it as a living standard that falls below a measurable level and dehumanizes its victims, then poverty is not a major social and economic problem but a relatively minor political problem; hence it is much easier to solve. The idea that dehumanizing poverty is widespread in America is a popular misconception. In fact, economic trends and social policies have greatly reduced the number who are poor under the second definition and have reduced the amount of money needed to move them above the poverty line. Simply getting more money for poverty programs has declined greatly in importance in recent years, while the problem of the inadequate functioning of the programs themselves has increased.

Historically, most people who have risen above poverty have done so by hard work. Then and now, many who persist in poverty are not just poor in income but poor in spirit or are disabled, ill, mentally handicapped, or too old or too young to work.

The simplest way to define poverty is in terms of income, called *income poverty*. The poverty threshold is three times an "economy food plan" determined by the federal government. It varies with household composition. It is the best definition for statistical purposes, but like any other definition has weaknesses. People just one dollar above the poverty line are classified as not poor, for example, although they may suffer more deprivation than many below the line. Some people are voluntarily poor, seeking harmony with themselves and nature or living communally at a subsistence level. Most native Americans are poor by middle-class standards yet may have a standard of living that is adequate in physical terms and have a rich cultural heritage and a beautiful landscape. Neither does income poverty measure ignorance and despair. Statistics on deprivation are much less available and less extensive than on income poverty. Income poverty, despite definitional shortcomings, is highly related to poor housing, hunger, poor clothing, victimization by crime, lack of education, and poor health care. For example, in 1970 an estimated 15 million Americans went hungry, a number smaller than those falling below the poverty line, and for all practical purposes contained below the line.[1]

Our perception of poverty should be rooted in history. Poverty has been a constant condition of the human race. For over a century, the best escape from European poverty was immigration to America, and the best escape from American poverty was migration westward and to cities. For millions, the dream came true, a major reason why so many are now so loyal to the system. People do not form social loyalties on the basis of purely intellectual analysis but from personal experiences. Historically, the family was the major welfare institution, with charity picking up some of the slack.

For some people, however, the dream never came true, and they got no help. They suffered long and died young. The 1930s pushed millions back into poverty for several years. Since World War II, automation and imports have caused poverty for some. New coal-mining machinery spelled much higher pay for some coal workers, but it also created a large number of unemployed. Cotton-picking machinery ended the sesonal drudgery of thousands of southern poor, but it did not give them anything better. New farm machinery increased the acreage farmers could plant, and smaller farmers could not compete. Some farmers were blown away by drought, wind, and dust in the 1930s. Many of the losers from the fields and mines came to the cities of the North and West. Urban poverty has a rural origin. Yet even today, rural areas have more poverty, especially in the South, and higher mortality and disease rates than the cities have. The cities handled much of this implosion of the poor but could not handle all of it. Along with the degraded urban environment are found related social problems: high unemployment, family disorganization, high crime rates, racial tensions, safety and health hazards, high death and disease rates, and weak educational and health services.

Except for some farm labor and housekeeping, modern American poverty does not result from the rich exploiting the poor, because the poor do not generally perform labor needed by elites or the economy as a whole. The poor are mostly irrelevant and forgotten.

Before and during the superficial prosperity of the 1920s, no national programs dealt with poverty. Franklin Roosevelt's New Deal of the 1930s laid the foundation for most of our current programs: social security, employment services, collective bargaining, minimum wage, welfare, unemployment insurance, public housing, jobs programs, and policies for general economic recovery. Some of our problems with the functioning of policy today stem from a failure to adjust the programs created then. World War II and prosperity afterward reduced interest in poverty; employment was high.

Then in 1964, Michael Harrington published *The Other America,* which pulled together existing facts, presented them in an interesting way, and expressed effective moral outrage about the problem of poverty. Support from President Johnson enabled reformers to push through a number of new programs. The War on Poverty was the first initiative in this area since the 1930s. Head Start programs and legal services for the poor have been a lasting legacy, but for the most part the programs did not work. There was too much mismanagement. Too many people tried to do too much too fast, and too many of them were incompetent or dishonest. Too much money went to poverty workers instead of the poor. Attempts at political organization of the poor could not work on a short-term basis and roused opposition from local elites unwilling to raise their taxes to pay for their share of the programs. The poor can and will participate effectively in making policies that affect them, but it takes time and patience the antipoverty elite did not know it had to have. It was easier to blame the poor for their incompetence than to develop the competence.

The war in Indochina eventually reduced the funds available for the War on Poverty, but more important to its demise was a shift in philosophy toward transferring income to the poor, a view that became dominant during the Nixon administration. Social security, food stamps, and Medicaid increased so much that they dwarfed the War on Poverty. They have increased more than defense spending or anything else and they have solved much of the problem. The effects of the recession of 1974–1975 were less damaging to many people because they could take advantage of the several programs.

Statistics

In 1947 30 percent of Americans were poor. That figure was reduced to 11.6 percent by 1977, a remarkable accomplishment. Even this 1977 figure is too high because of the way in which the Census Bureau figures income. It does not include food stamps, housing subsidies, Medicaid, Medicare, day care services, home-grown food, and miscellaneous unreported income. The best research so far indicates that 6.5 percent of the population in 1976 was poor.[2] The poverty line constantly rises with inflation and varies by type and location of family. From about $2,000 in 1950, the poverty line for a nonfarm family of four rose to $6,191 in 1977.

Table 4–1 provides data on poor persons by age and by the race and sex of the head of their household. The largest group—about 37 percent—is the 9.2 million persons in households headed by white males. The table also shows the rate of poverty (the percentage poor of all people in that kind of group). The number of people in white, male-headed households of all incomes is quite large, so the poor persons turn out to be a small portion of the group total, 5.9 percent. The highest rate of poverty is for one of the smaller groups: 65.1 percent of children in black, female-headed households.

Children form 41 percent of all poor persons. Our system denies equal opportunity to many children because of the poverty of their parents. Large families are correlated with poverty: 35 percent of low-income families but only 10 percent of nonpoor families have three or more children. Single adults with dependents, usually mothers with children, are especially likely to be poor. Almost one-fourth of the poor fourteen years and older work as full-time housekeepers, and almost a third can work only part of the year or part time because of home responsibilities.

Table 4–1 Poverty by Age and Head of Household, 1977

	Age of Person			
	Under 18	*18–64*	*65 and Older*	*Total*
Percent of Total Poor, by Head of Person's Household				
White male	13.2%	20.0 %	4.0%	37.2%
Black male	4.5	5.7	1.5	11.7
White female	10.9	12.5	5.8	29.2
Black female	12.0	8.3	1.6	21.9
Total	40.6	46.5	12.9	100.0
Poverty rate				
White male	7.1	4.5 (15.7) [a]	7.3	5.9
Black male	18.8	12.0 (28.8) [a]	27.5	15.8
White female	40.3	17.7 (23.7) [a]	21.3	25.5
Black female	65.1	42.8 (43.8) [a]	46.6	52.9
Total	16.0	7.4 (22.6)	14.1	11.6

Notes: The total number poor was 24,720,000. The head of the household was considered male if an adult male was present. (This practice is changing.) "Black male" includes a small number of other nonwhite races.

[a] The rate for all persons eighteen and over living in families appears first; the rate for all persons eighteen and over not living in families (unrelated individuals) appears in parentheses.

Source: Compiled from data in U.S. Bureau of the Census, *Current Population Reports,* Series P-60, No. 116 (1978), pp. 21–23.

The poverty rate for preschool children in female-headed households is extremely high: 68 percent. About a million and a half children are affected. The first five years of life are the most important for the development of a healthy personality, which in turn is the basis for successful learning and working. Child poverty is correlated with poor health care, poor nutrition, stunted growth, low intelligence, poor education, unemployment, and crime. Poor families produce an estimated three-fourths of the mentally retarded in the United States.

Child poverty, female-headed households, and teenage pregnancy are intimately linked with each other and are growing more serious. The increase in female-headed households has been correlated with an increase in divorce, separation, absent fathers, unwed mothers keeping children, more jobs for women, and more welfare. Male-headed households, meanwhile, have decreased dramatically in their poverty—from 70 percent of the poor in 1959 to 49 percent of a much smaller poor population in 1977.

Teenage mothers are typically immature: they find it difficult to raise a baby on welfare, to get an education, to get job training, to find a job, and to circulate socially. The fathers usually cannot (or will not) support the family and are not willing to take sole responsibility for the child. Many desert their families, often to make it easier for the mother to qualify for welfare. Until recently, agencies made little effort to enforce laws requiring child support from absent fathers. But during twenty months from 1975 to 1977, the HEW Child Enforcement Program spent $320 million to collect over a billion dollars in child support.[3] In California nine out of ten single-parent families with the head under twenty-five years old are on welfare; virtually all are women, and most of them have little education, little training, and little work experience. Over 80 percent of single-parent families with preschool children are on welfare, regardless of the age of the head. Welfare pays better than most jobs they could hold.[4] In the industrial states, taxpayers have mostly taken over the economic role of supporting families.

Even with welfare and a program to force child support, 14 percent of all mother-child families (those without a father in residence) are poor; in 1976, these amounted to about 2,660,000 people.[5] The amount of money needed to overcome poverty for children, especially young children, is pitifully small compared with the size of the economy. Child poverty is part of a larger failure of our society to invest in children. Other aspects include juvenile delinquency, drug and alcohol abuse, crime, lack of jobs and training opportunities, poor education and lack of alternatives for teenagers unable to meet academic demands, lack of adequate parental and school discipline and counseling, and lack of sex education. We later blame the adults who result from these failures and pay a high price ourselves in welfare, crime, and lost work. This country can afford some minimal level of decency for children.

We do much better with the old, reducing their poverty to 4.6 percent of all old people.[6] Aged poor are especially likely to be living alone; their poverty rate is over triple the rate for aged poor living in families. The old are about 13 percent of the total number of poor. The old plus children are 54 percent of all poor.

Both sexism and racism are related to poverty. There are over twice as many poor people in households headed by white females than in those headed by black males, and the rate of poverty is higher (26 percent versus 16 percent). Half of the poor live in female-headed households, yet such households are only 11 percent of the total population.

Racism is also important. Sixteen percent of white females (including those in male-headed households) are poor, while 28 percent of all black males are poor. Among blacks, female-headed households are more common: thirty-nine percent (compared with 12 percent of white families). The poverty rate of black female families is extremely high, 51 percent.

History and racism have produced a geographically concentrated black population and similarly concentrated poverty in the rural South and in ghetto census tracts of big cities. Whites, by contrast, are more spread out. For example, in 1978 65 percent of poor blacks living in central cities were found in low-income census tracts, as compared with 28 percent of poor whites in central cities. Similarly, 78 percent of poor blacks living in non-metropolitan areas resided in poverty census tracts as compared with 44 percent of poor whites.

Poverty statistics are less extensive on other aspects of poverty; figures for Spanish speaking are not available. Data on those of Spanish origin show a poverty rate of 22 percent, double the national average (1977 figures). Those of Mexican origin are concentrated in the Southwest, Puerto Ricans in New York City, and Cubans in Miami. Most impoverished of minorities are native Americans, numbering about 793,000 in 1970 and growing. Their median income may be about $1,500 per year.[7]

The disabled and ill have three times the poverty rate of the general population, and those of working age are especially poor. Their rate in 1977 was 46 percent, one of the highest of all working-age groups.[8]

Education is the most important background factor contributing to poverty. Almost two-thirds of all poor families have a head with less than a high school education. Their rate of poverty is over double that of families with heads with a high school education or more. (See table 4–2.)

Poverty is usually temporary in the lives of those who experience it. Families continually fall into poverty and rise out of it, often because of events that seem to have little relation to underlying causes. A study of about 5,000 families representative of the national population from 1968 to 1973 discovered that only about 3 percent stayed below the poverty line all six years. Short-term causes were most easily identified: having a child increased poverty; their leaving home when grown reduced it. Divorce formed poor female-headed households; remarriage ended it and its poverty. A nonworking spouse's finding a job would end poverty, but disability or retirement would create it. Altogether 25 percent of the families studied experienced poverty at least one year.[9] Other data show that the average welfare family stays on the rolls two and a half years and has 2.4 children; 81 percent are headed by women.[10]

In sum, poverty primarily affects persons in female-headed households and minorities, some of the old (especially those living alone), the ill and

Table 4–2 Education, Income, and Poverty, 1977

Level of Education of Head of Household	*Family Median Income*	*Number of Family Units (Millions)*	*Poverty Rate* [a] *(%)*	*% of Total Poor*
Elementary	9,606	10.2	17.7	39.8
Some high school	13,030	7.7	13.6	23.1
High school graduate	17,110	18.1	6.5	25.7
Some college	19,033	7.7		
College graduate	23,409	5.2	3.0	11.4
Graduate school	26,042	4.3		
Total or average	16,574	53.4	8.5	100.0

[a] The total number of poor families was 4.6 million.

Source: Compiled from U.S. Bureau of the Census, *Current Population Reports,* Series P–60, no. 116 (1978), pp. 7, 26.

disabled (especially of working age), the institutional population, and the uneducated. It affects most people temporarily, for reasons over which they have little or no control.

Policies for Poverty

We will assume that children, the aged, the sick, the physically and mentally disabled, and the primary parent (usually the mother) of children under six who do not have high-quality day care available should not be expected to work. In some cases they should be encouraged to work and given opportunities, but they should not suffer poverty if they do not work. About 70 percent of the poor fall into these categories, leaving 30 percent who can be expected to work, and mostly they do. Work provides most of the income for poor families and historically has been the major way out of poverty. People are constantly moving into higher-paying occupations and industries and into economically growing regions. For those who can be expected to work, the opportunity to rise above poverty should be available through policies like job training, employment services, and public-service jobs. The constant movement of people into and out of poverty indicates that most would hold public-service jobs as a temporary expedient and to get work experience. Such jobs would not only end the poverty of the worker but much of the poverty of their families. Those able but unwilling to work would be denied most kinds of assistance. Such denials would deal with a major objection most people have to welfare—that it gives to the undeserving. The number of recipients of welfare able to work is a small fraction of the total receiving aid, but the principle is important.

The remaining 70 percent of the poor should be given the resources needed to end their poverty. The four major ways now used to help the poor are food stamps, Medicaid, housing aid, and monetary welfare payments. All are based on need.

Food Stamps. Food stamps are increasingly important. About $6.9 billion was budgeted for 1980 to reach 17.4 million beneficiaries.[11] Any program as huge as food stamps will have many problems of administration and equity, but on the whole the program has been very successful. Numerous adjustments have been made over recent years to keep the undeserving from receiving stamps, to prevent fraud, to simplify the paperwork, and to make sure that the needy get stamps. Sometimes the offices are still too far away or the paperwork too much of a hassle, but field research has discovered that most of the severe malnutrition that plagued certain rural areas has disappeared. This major social reform did not occur as one big event but grew through a series of significant events. Liberals battled to create it and extend it; conservatives struggled to improve its management and effectiveness. The public has been generally supportive, probably because of a feeling that food is less subject to abuse than money aid and because of sympathy for such an obvious human need.

There are fifteen other federal food programs providing $4.3 billion for 1980. They include school lunch and breakfast programs, a summer food program, a day-care food program, and a special supplemental food program for women, infants, and children (WIC), which has reduced infant mortality and the incidence of low birth-weight babies.

Food stamps were an important innovation for a little-known reason unrelated to food. Previously any earned income was deducted fully from a welfare grant, removing any incentive to work. Food stamps, however, are not lost that way. They decline more slowly as income goes up, preserving the incentive to work. Food stamps thus established the principle of preservation of incentive to work. An earlier attempt, President Nixon's Family Assistance Plan, failed because of an unlikely alliance of conservatives (who thought it too generous) and liberals (who thought it not generous enough). Nixon's plan was a cash system and therefore was more easily denigrated as welfare while food stamps had a more positive image of combatting hunger. Also, the FAP was a big program, while food stamps started small and grew. Food stamp policy is typical of reform in America: half a loaf today, half of the remaining half next year, and so on. Now food stamps are as big as Nixon's plan was budgeted to be.

Housing. Housing assistance is a second way to provide needed resources to the poor, giving about $5.3 billion to about 3.2 million families in 1980.[12] There are about 1.3 million low-rent, public-housing units, of which 84 percent were built as public housing by or for a local housing authority, 3.5 percent were purchased by such an authority (not originally built as public housing), and 12.5 percent were leased by the authority for subleasing to others.[13]

Public housing has less popular support than food aid, probably because it is more associated with central city problems like crime, poor schools, and decreasing property values. The recipients are more easily identified and stigmatized, and it is harder to adjust the benefit as income changes. Some public-housing projects produced areas of high service needs and then failed to provide the services. One very large project in St. Louis was even torn down because it had so much crime and was so heavily vandalized.

Housing programs have suffered from large, abrupt shifts of policy in the 1970s. In 1973 the four major programs were suspended (although old commitments continue). These programs have had a very mixed record. Some housing authorities are well managed, but others have been riddled with corruption, have had excessively high costs, or have been undermined by adverse economic trends. Home ownership assistance programs were affected by all of these negative factors, leading to large-scale legal prosecutions of public and private housing officials, abandonments of houses, and foreclosures. This program by 1977 was gradually being rescued by allowing sales to "homesteaders," who could buy a house for one dollar. Recipients had to live in the home and make certain repairs within a few years. The housing programs in general were plagued by having too many different ways to qualify for them, too little money to be effective, and too many rule changes. In many ways the housing aid effort has shown reformism at its worst, unfortunately overshadowing several fine local housing authorities.

In 1975, a new program was started under section 8 of the Housing and Community Development Act of 1974: the lower-income housing assistance program. Unlike the old programs, which attempted to provide housing for the poor by building, leasing, or renovating by special agencies, that then rented to the poor, section 8 tries to provide the poor sufficient buying power to find their own housing. An eligible low-income family is required to allocate a certain percentage (usually 25 percent) of their income to rent. A local agency using federal funds supplements this amount as needed to rent minimally adequate housing in its area. Under the existing housing subprogram of section 8, the family then searches for the housing that is best for it. The family can take into account various factors and weigh them far more effectively than can a bureaucracy, and it is in a better position to request maintenance from a landlord because it is paying a market rent and can leave if it has to. The section 8 program enables many more poor to be benefited with less money per recipient and a much simpler, smaller bureaucratic structure. The system is also less paternalistic, and it allows dispersion of the poor throughout moderate-income areas. The subsidy can easily be adjusted with changes in income and city. The free market can respond to demand, probably by rehabilitating marginal structures, which is cheaper than building new ones. The 1980 federal budget put about $2.1 billion each into public housing and section 8. The section 8 program is not yet very pervasive—too little funds and too few housing units are available—but it keeps growing.

Health. A third way to help the poor is health care. In 1966 despite fierce resistance by conservative elites, especially the American Medical Association, a major reform, Medicaid, was made. Like food stamps, Medicaid can be used to help the near poor, not just the poor, thus preserving the incentive to work. For 1980 about 24 million people were budgeted for about $19 billion in Medicaid and other federal health aid, more than the amount for food stamps and housing combined.[14] Unfortunately much of the potential advantage for health care of increased purchasing power has been lost. The supply of health services was not flexible enough to respond quickly to an increase in demand, so prices went up. Paperwork hassles meant that many health providers were not reimbursed on time. Poor patients frequently could not recognize good care and often were cheated by corrupt health practitioners. Sometimes the poor abused the system. Complaints by the poor were largely unprocessed by overworked, understaffed, often incompetent state agencies, which were deferential to the providers. Reimbursement rates were often too low, but corrupt doctors and hospitals found ways to increase the rate of claims for services fraudulently. Quality varied considerably among states and even counties. There were glaring cases of abuse and ineffectual to nonexistent administration. In this case it becomes necessary to reform the reform.

Public sympathy is high for health aid, and the reasons are obvious. Like food, health is essential to equality of opportunity and, even more basic, survival. The poor suffer the worst health and the worst health care, and those with catastrophic illness are likely to become poor.

Monetary Payments. A fourth way to help the poor is extremely efficient in ending income poverty but is also less popular with the public: giving money to the poor. This practice solves the poverty problem by definition, but we are uneasy about how the poor will spend the funds. Will they loaf and avoid work? Gamble? Drink? Buy a Cadillac? Some of them will. The poor are like everybody else except for income. And like most other people, most of them would spend the money wisely, as demonstrated in a project involving 1,357 families in New Jersey in the mid-1970s. The experimental group was given some cash even if they did not work, but the incentive to work was maintained by giving them more money if they did work. For example, one subgroup was guaranteed a poverty line income, but for each dollar earned, they lost only fifty cents in benefits. They worked about as hard as the control group. They improved their houses, paid debts, trained themselves for better paid work, and looked for better jobs. Older recipients took it easier; younger ones stayed in school longer. One of the most interesting results of the experiment was how little difference there was between the control and experimental groups.

A closer analysis of the New Jersey experiment and the results of a test in Seattle and Denver, however, have indicated that the poor may work less if they get automatic income maintenance. The Seattle-Denver study found that male heads of households worked about 5 percent less; wives, about 22 percent less; and female heads, about 11 percent less. Divorces were higher among those getting benefits than among the control group, evidently because spouses could get along economically as well apart as together. But looking even closer for qualitative data may show greater benefits than costs; the money enabled parents to use the time to pay more attention to children and to complete educations.[15] Marriages held together by economic necessity may have higher rates of domestic violence and tension.

A large income maintenance program is unlikely to be implemented soon because of its cost. There are, however, a number of other cash programs that go most of the way to eliminating income poverty. The *earned income tax credit,* budgeted for $2.2 billion in 1980, reduces the income tax for low-wage workers or makes a payment to them in a way that preserves the incentive to work.

The two largest federal cash welfare programs for the nonworking needy are supplementary security income and aid to families with dependent children. Supplementary Security Income (SSI) benefits the aged, blind, or disabled. In 1980 4.2 million recipients were budgeted to receive $6.3 billion. Aid to Families with Dependent Children (AFDC) for the same year was budgeted for $6.7 billion to reach about 11 million recipients in about 3.6 million families. State and local governments add several billion dollars of their own to the federal budget figure. About 8 million of the recipients are children, over two-thirds of whom are under the age of twelve. Less than 4 percent of the families have unemployed fathers present. Some states provide a modest supplement for SSI recipients; it is mainly a federal program established in 1974. The SSI program replaced one that involved federal, state, and local administration and tax revenues. After many months of difficult transition, the SSI program is proving itself more efficient than the previous system. The current AFDC program continues to involve federal, state, and local administration, an inherently complex approach in which each level of government makes up some of the rules and provides some of the money.

The contrast between SSI and AFDC is interesting in other respects. There is more public sympathy for the aged and disabled who get SSI, the benefit levels are higher, and SSI is less demeaning to its recipients. SSI is a relatively simple federally administered program, whereas AFDC is administered by counties and is under pressure to cut costs while providing for the needy. There has been a proliferation of rules varying from county to county and subject to different interpretations by different welfare workers. Generally, the eligibility technicians and social workers have too big a case load and too few resources, making it difficult to check for fraud and to provide help quickly when needed. Though welfare is temporary for most people, public attitudes have developed about "welfare types" based partly on fact. Some people have a hard time coping and take advantage of the system. They tend to abuse themselves with drugs and alcohol and their children with violence and neglect. They do not pay the rent. They lie, cheat, and steal. They do not try to improve themselves and blame others for their problems. They can be noisy and disrespectful. It is hard enough for most people to tolerate such behavior in anyone, and to have to pay taxes to support such "losers" is aggravating and gives the whole welfare system a bad name. The welfare system needs to be tougher on those who abuse it, but it must respond in some way to the real needs of even unlikeable people.

Another problem with AFDC is its disincentive to work. In some places both parents may work full time at the minimum wage and receive $2,158 less per year than if the father were to desert the family and the mother were to quit work and go on welfare.[16] Welfare benefits vary greatly from place to place also. In 1975 Mississippi averaged about $60 a month in AFDC benefits per family, while New York City paid $411 per month.[17] Earnings are usually deducted almost in full from welfare benefits, and there are serious delays in qualifying for benefits. Therefore, there is a great temptation to cheat by not reporting earned income until one is secure about the future. Demeaning treatment by the bureaucracy alienates recipients, making cheating all the more likely. Minor cheating is widespread and not too important, but obviously the AFDC system needs reforming.

Other important cash welfare programs are certain veterans' pensions benefits, costing about $4.2 billion in 1980, and general assistance, which is financed by states and counties, fills in the gaps left by federal programs, and cost about $3 billion in 1980.[18] Small programs reach native Americans, refugees, and other categories. The cash transfer programs combined added up to about $22 to $23 billion, combining earned income credit, SSI, AFDC, veterans' pensions, and general assistance. Adding in the benefits of food stamps, other nutrition programs, housing aid, and Medicaid—all called *in kind transfers*—the total of benefits based on need comes to about $58 billion.

As large as those expenditures seem, they are about one-third of the total spent by the federal government to assure security of income. The other major programs include social security (composed of old age pensions, survivors' benefits, and disability benefits), Medicare (composed of hospital benefits and supplementary medical benefits and technically part of social security), unemployment compensation, workers' compensation (for job-related accidents and diseases), military, civil service, and other retirement, veterans' benefits, railroad retirement, and benefits for disabled coal miners. In 1977 these benefits combined with the need-based benefits totaled $180 billion.[19] State and local government spent about $53 billion on similar programs. Combined they come to over 12 percent of the gross national product, as compared with about 5 percent in 1950.[20] These programs reach about 16 million families and about 9 million unrelated individuals.

Results of Poverty Programs. The poverty programs, based on need, and the other income security programs, generally based on an insurance concept, have an uneven impact on the poverty-prone groups. The overall impact is that the cash programs reduce poverty from 21 percent of the population to 11 percent, and the in-kind programs reduce it further to about 7 percent. But the aged benefit the most, starting off 54 percent poor and ending at 5 percent poor. Mothers and their children start off 58 percent poor and after transfer programs are 14 percent poor. Similarly, nonwhites start 41 percent poor and are reduced by the programs to 13 percent poor. Least benefited are single persons (people living alone or in households without other family members) who start 48 percent poor and wind up 17 percent poor after transfers.[21]

We have gone most of the way toward eliminating poverty. The poverty gap is the amount of money needed to lift all those below the poverty threshold above it. The Census Bureau estimated that the gap between actual income of the poor and the poverty income threshold totaled about $10.5 billion in 1977.[22] Since the bureau leaves out food stamps, other food programs, housing aid, and health aid (the in-kind benefits), which total $35.5 billion, the real poverty gap no longer exists statistically. The major problem now is to improve the functioning of the programs.

Improvement is not simply a question of easy administrative adjustments. The statistics presented above oversimplify very complex administrative programs, and the poverty threshold itself is not useful as a guide to benefits. The main job is to unify and simplify the programs, but some increases in expenditures may be necessary. The high-benefit states do not want to see benefits for their citizens lowered even though current programs may put their poor well above the official poverty line. The poverty thresholds themselves may arguably be 60 percent too low, which would increase the number poor by over 125 percent. The census also undercounts the poor more than any other income category. Health and housing dollar values include more waste than if the poor were able to buy with cash. These considerations probably outweigh the underreporting of transfer income. Measurement of poverty is inherently not objective; there is room for disagreement over what is poverty and who is poor.

Simplifying the Programs. Simplification can be achieved in many ways. Reformers tend to favor a federal program, eliminating the complicating role of two autonomous levels of government (the states and localities). As a smaller step, we could at least move toward more uniform national rules. Similarly, within the federal government, the needs-tested programs for those unable to work could be concentrated in one agency, rather than spread out as they are now. Special cases could be left to counties' general assistance much as they are now for the relatively few needy not covered by federal rules.

How far above the poverty line to raise income depends on whether the program includes an incentive to work or a requirement to do so. One incentive approach is to deduct only fifty cents in benefits for each dollar earned. Alternatively, it is argued that such an incentive is not needed because the great majority of poor cannot work and that incentive would expensively increase the number eligible for aid. Rather than an incentive to work, those able to work might be required to do so at a public-service job, with additional benefits provided, if necessary, to raise household income above the poverty line.

President Carter's proposed reform incorporates most of the ideas presented here; it distinguishes between those who can and cannot work, creates jobs, requires work from those able, and has a work incentive. The reform would cost $431 billion, only $6 billion more than the system currently does. It would, however, move to an all-cash system, which has the advantage of simplicity but also the problem of getting public support. The work incentive, also, would add substantially to welfare rolls.[23] Public attitudes are contradictory; one poll showed 58 percent against welfare but 81 percent approving of aid to single-parent families, of food stamps, and of Medicare.[24]

Services for the Poor

Although the major part of the poverty problem is a lack of jobs and transfer payments, some aspects require special services. For example, the old who are unable to cook for themselves can be helped by "meals on wheels" programs. Other examples include activity centers, police protection, transit services, and nursing home regulations. Senior citizen centers and other services may not be essential to end income poverty, but they can make life more worth living.

Mental health programs are needed because the poor have a much higher incidence of mental problems, like drug abuse, alcoholism, mental retardation and deficiency, depression, and schizophrenia. Mental disability is a cause of poverty, which itself aggravates the distress. A number of problems fall between clear health and clear disability. The poor tend to be fatalistic about their situation and fearful of trying something new. They have a hard time sizing people up, do not know whom to trust, and too often get hurt when they do trust. Poverty involves ignorance about what to do about poverty and an inability to use words to get help from others. Educational services are urgently needed since lack of education is the characteristic most highly associated with poverty. The poor need education about simple matters like how to spend money wisely, because low-income people are often poor shoppers. They have, for example, little understanding of what interest is and borrow too much at high interest. The way such help is provided is equally important; a program can be defeated by paternalism or incompetence.

The poor need legal services because too often poverty means a deprivation of legal rights. Early in the War on Poverty, a legal services program was started experimentally. It proved to be an outstanding success and used class action suits against all levels of government to force them to carry out the law. It was so successful, in fact, that local elites protested the increased tax costs, and the Nixon administration replaced it with the tamer (but still useful) Legal Services Corporation.[25] Legal services can help with abusive debt collection practices, family relations, and individual dealings with government.

Some additional services for the poor are aimed at specialized populations like native Americans, non-English speakers, refugees, prisoners, and juveniles. Welfare programs like AFDC, SSI, and county general assistance use social workers, who could be far more effective if their case loads were reduced. Reforms to create jobs and adequate welfare would help to reduce and simplify case loads.

Most of these programs, both transfers and services, are designed to correct defects in unhealthy economic systems. Poverty may also result from the failure of economies in whole communities or regions, leaving most people poor. Policy for these areas is complex because it needs to deal with a whole social system and integrate a number of policies into a coherent development program. Community development often bases itself on improving production to sell to other areas: a dairy farm, a greenhouse project, an irrigation project, a strawberry project, a cucumber project, or other labor-intensive industries. The surplus is used for youth camps, health services, education, and other services. Such projects have tremendous appeal because they can solve economic, environmental, and social problems at the same time. Based mainly on self-help, they use few outside resources. The Graham Farm in North Carolina, for example, teaches poor blacks, Chicanos, and whites about organic farming techniques, which they can implement with little money and are highly productive, mainly of vegetables. The poor find a path upward, the environment is protected or enhanced, and the economy improves. Construction skills, welding, cooperatives, and bookkeeping are also taught. This project is not supported by government (the USDA is committed to big agribusiness approaches). Graham Farm is supported by a public-interest group, the National Sharecroppers Fund. Another example is the black government of Fayette, Mississippi, aided by the Medgar Evers fund, which has attracted industry and improved services in a deep poverty area.

Citizen Profile:

Urban Community Organizing

I became interested in politics in high school in my home town of Soquel, California. Ed Borovatz, then a high school teacher, had a lot of influence on me and my friends. We became involved in a local "growth control" movement. I also developed other political interests in high school and college, such as nursing homes. After college, I taught eight hours a week about national and world affairs and took oral histories from the folks in local nursing homes. To improve teaching I had a class of the teachers themselves, and also helped the Citizens Committee for Better Nursing Home Care.

I was also a ranch hand, a house painter, a washer and waxer of mobile homes, and tutor for two elementary school kids. It was a great life. I used my bicycle most of the time. The area was a hothouse of ideas for social and ecological reform. But I also had a growing feeling that there wasn't much future or security in my life and that the ministry might be a better way to serve. I was influenced by conversations with Paul Pfotenhauer, a Lutheran pastor. I had developed an interest in scriptures and theology, and I saw a way to get into community organizing and survive. Ministers, seen as discreet and trustworthy, have an occupation that opens doors better than any other. They can counsel without being paid, make referrals, and tap the resources of their congregations to solve problems.

I was accepted at San Francisco Theological Seminary in San Anselmo and worked for churches in Michigan, California, and Nevada. Through my studies and experiences I came to value and feel more comfortable with the church itself while retaining my interest in community work. For my third year internship, I went to the South Hayward Parish in Hayward, California. The parish is supported by four churches of different denominations and engages in local community organizing to deal with poverty and other social problems. I have been working thirty hours a week (often more). Sometimes I help individuals, like the guy who'd been stabbed and lost his job but whose disability check hadn't come and he wasn't qualified for food stamps. I gave him some food, called around to the various agencies, and explained the system to him—you almost need a college degree to understand it. I also help organize people. We had local people needing job training but who had no transportation; we were able to petition to get some courses in a local school. We helped a rent relief initiative get qualified for the ballot. People on fixed income were really hurt by rent increases coming after proposition 13 had led them to believe rents would be lowered.

The frustration of this job is that there is no end to it. It's a complicated, ambiguous process, with no clear good guys and bad guys. The specific goals—emergency food, job training, rent control, tree planting, community gardens—are not so important as getting people involved. I circulated hundreds of fliers and talked with dozens of people in the Tyrell area, where there are some real problems they need to work on, trying to get them to a community meeting. There was community bloc grant money potentially available if people could decide what they wanted. Only ten people showed up—the people who were already involved.

Yet the job is also satisfying. The ten who showed up, for example, have come a long way since Tom McCoy, the Methodist minister of the parish, started working with them. The church can help people develop their power in a way government cannot. Empowerment seems to come from a fascinating interaction between individuals and their immediate group. There is a real art to getting people to come together. They develop a motivation to work on problems that affect them, a group spirit, and individual commitments to work for their fellows. One woman during the rent relief campaign overcame her helplessness; she was thirty-seven years old, had kids, and had not worked for four or five years. She hit the roof when her rent was raised. She talked to her neighbors, got into the campaign, and did much of the bookkeeping. She made new friends, one of whom offered her a bookkeeping job. She's employed now, with a decent income, a social life. People can give of themselves when dealing with a problem they can do something about. I get excited when people catch on to taking power over their own lives.

Jim Burklo
Hayward, California

Sexism

Many forms of discrimination pervade our society; the most important are sexism and racism. Discrimination generally means that a dominant group limits the opportunities of others for reasons not based on the ability or worth of the victims. Other discrimination exists against the aged, homosexuals, the disabled, and the young. Less obviously, some white males are systematically disadvantaged by low-income, low-education backgrounds.

Historically, most groups in American history have felt the sting of Anglo-Saxon male discrimination. The earliest settlers came with a full suitcase of prejudices, even against other English speakers because of their economic status, dialect, social class, religion, or region of origin. The affluent looked down on the poor; the aristocracy down on the low born; the Puritans down on other religions; the English down on the Scots; the Irish, the Welsh, and the Cornish. As an American consciousness developed, "Americans" looked down on Europeans, Asians, native Americans, and blacks. We have always been blissfully unaware of how much the Chinese looked down on us.

Discrimination against women runs deep in our culture and in many others. Women have derived most of their wealth, power, and status from their fathers, husbands, and sons, but nexer have participated as fully as the men. The situation is more complex because for most of history, male and female roles have been so well defined and strong that challenging them seemed unthinkable. As with other forms of discrimination, the victims accept it to some extent. Many women have enjoyed and placed a high value on performing the woman's traditional role of homemaking. Had men placed as high a value on homemaking as their own work, sex roles might continue distinct and with much less discriminatory deprivation. More likely, if men placed a high value on it, they would do much more of it themselves.

More and more American women, however, have not found the homemaker role attractive enough, and many find it intrinsically boring. They have the ability and desire to do other kinds of work, often more highly rewarded by society. Other women are pressured into working by financial need.

Child Care

Discrimination makes child care a woman's issue. Men generally impose a child care burden on women; women are less willing to abandon their children. Real damage is done if children receive inadequate parenting. Children should not have to pay the price of ending sex discrimination, but ending it depends on reducing the uncompensated time women spend on child care. Child care is the expensive intersection between family and work. Since most men in the short run are unwilling to put in enough time of their own, it is reasonable to have them pay for quality care. In the long run, men should learn child care and do it more as fathers and day-care workers.

High-quality day care is the means to reconcile much of the conflict between parenting and working. There are four distinct child-age groups, each with its own requirements: infants and toddlers (to about three years), preschoolers (to about six years), grade schoolers, and teenagers.

High-quality care for the youngest group is especially important and exacting. They require a lot of attention for their physical needs and for sustained bursts of conversation with an adult. Older toddlers can also play by themselves, with an adult available on demand. They thus require high-quality intermittent attention from one or two adults over a long period of time. Usually this is provided by parents and grandparents. Parents can work if they can find the quality of care needed. Some have jobs where some of the work can be done at home, and some have spouses or relatives who will commit their time.

Others must turn to professional day care. An experiment in Boston for babies and toddlers who came to day care at about four months and left at two years five months indicated no difference in development from similar children raised at home. The day care was like home. One experienced day-care worker worked with only three children. Unlike most babies, who experience anxiety when separated from their mothers, the experimental babies did not experience this anxiety; they already knew their day-care parent.[26]

Good day care for the preschool group can help development and learning during these critical years. The child can be examined for visual, hearing, speech, dental, and other health problems, which, if caught early, can usually be compensated for with no serious loss of development. If nutrition is a problem, a day-care center can supply good meals. High-quality day care can often provide more good toys and playmates in safer surroundings and with better supervision than at home. An enriched verbal environment can stimulate language skills. It can help develop notions of discipline, fairness, and how to get along with others. Parents can be involved through night meetings and conferences with teachers about their children and how they can be helped. Many parents with low-education backgrounds want to help their children and welcome cautious advice; others need to be encouraged to take more interest. In a time of family disintegration, child care can strengthen the family and help break the cycle of poverty.

After-school day care for grade school students and activities for teenagers are much less expensive because adult-child ratios can be larger and the amount of time per day is less.

Although day care is expanding, too much of it is of inferior quality. For example, a ratio of one adult to five children for the preschool group is a standard based on extensive experience of child development professionals. Further, the caring adults must be qualified by temperament and experience. They should not have high turnover because it is difficult for children to adjust to new adult personalities. Yet many day-care centers do not meet these standards.

In some ways adequate day care should not be difficult. As school enrollments drop, former teachers become available to head day-care centers, and classrooms become available for these purposes. An adequate public-service job program could pay persons otherwise on welfare to work under supervision, freeing parents to pursue training, look for work, or hold a job. Unfortunately, too many centers are physically inadequate and understaffed or poorly staffed. Inspection to protect child welfare is inadequate to cover the proliferation of services in recent years.

An estimated 18,000 "latch-key" children under six years old are being left alone during the day so mothers can work. Many others are virtually alone because the day parent is sleeping after a night shift.[27] Important federal legislation to fund child care has been vetoed as "undermining the family," part of the sexist attitudes still characterizing mostly male legislative bodies. It is expensive to pay attention to children; caring cannot be mass produced. Making quality child care available to low-income parents is essential to reconcile children's needs with expanding equality of opportunity for women.

Sex-role Stereotyping

Most people subscribe in theory to the fundamental equality of all people, regardless of sex, yet a large number live and feel more comfortable with notions about essential social differences between the sexes. The notions themselves are a problem, as well as the way they are imposed on people who do not share them. One goal of reform is to make all roles more freely chosen, an idea that includes more parity at home and at work. Sexism can be defined as anything that prevents humans of either sex from reaching their full potential because of sex-related discrimination.

Both sexes are profoundly influenced by the way they were brought up and by the role models they can observe. We learn attitudes about ourselves and the roles we should play, including a sexual dimension, very early, before we realize we are learning anything. They become deeply ingrained before we have a chance to do anything about them. Formal education in later years can expose us to all kinds of possibilities, but our most profound learning experiences often involve discovering who we already are. Mothers primarily (and fathers secondarily) influence these learning experiences, each generation reproducing not just biologically but culturally. The ultimate liberation of women may depend not on abandoning the parenting role but on performing it differently. Many, perhaps most, women still accept some systematic inequality and help perpetuate it.

A big problem for the feminist movement is not the few women who glory in their stereotyped female roles but the many who are only partially aware that they are doing so. Equality is still something to some extent learned by most feminists. They have to examine the sexism within themselves and realize their essential equality with men. Many women find homemaking unsatisfying and a kind of symbol of their exploitation. When they have attacked it, they sometimes alienated other women who find value and satisfaction in the role. Most women do not want to rebel against their femaleness in the quest for equality. They wish only to affirm their own definition and to resist having it defined from a purely male-serving point of view. Many reject labeling themselves "women libbers," probably because the media have identified the term with the most radical behavior, with its antimale overtone. They prefer the terms *womens' movement* or *feminism,* which affirm femaleness and equality at the same time.

Exaggerated publicity of the more extreme aspects of the women's movement has led to popular misunderstanding. Many women disassociate themselves from the movement though say they support equality. However, many who say they believe in equality do not practice it. Equality is not just a promise; it is also a threat, just as abandoning male stereotypes feels unsettling to men. All of us fear freedom at least a little. If there is too much choice, we discover we do not know who we are, which is disturbing. Embracing any role, and particularly roles that are subservient and dependent, protects against that anxiety. It makes life easier, because such roles are relatively easy to perform, avoiding the embarrassment and agony of failure. (Even so, many fail and suffer, unable to break through to an unstereotyped self-acceptance.) If women are to achieve full equality, they will have to do something most men are also reluctant to do: participate as citizens in society. Deference and subordination avoid the risks of full awareness and responsibility for both sexes.

Male stereotypes are deeply ingrained, also. Western culture does not subordinate women as much as Hindu, Moslem, and Latin cultures do, but there are still pervasive denials of opportunity to women regardless of their ability. Many men do not think of themselves as sexist, so it has to be discovered by having it pointed out in specific behavior. Men are slightly more liberal than women on abortion but much less likely to take the children in a divorce. Their defense is that they have to earn a living and cannot take care of the children. To accomplish equality for women, men have to accept new roles and responsibilities. Men may also need a "movement" to enable them to spend more time with their children, to not have to succeed except at being themselves, to not have to dominate, and to view women as equals.

Schools and Media

These basic philosophical attitudes are reflected in the way we raise children. Feminists are concerned with how they can change their child-rearing patterns for equality, something over which, ironically, they have much control. They have far less control over the schools, however. Many school texts teach inequality in a subtle way. Generally males are portrayed performing traditional male activities, and vice versa for female. Sex-integrated activities are not often displayed, nor are women who are athletic, who were independent and ambitious makers of history, leaders in politics, business, and the professions. Stories about women low-wage workers, single people, older women, and single-parent families are rare. A breakthrough in portraying blacks and other minorities has finally occurred; the sex revolution has just begun. We can hope to see female surgeons instructing male nurses and stories about the Founding Mothers.

Higher education, especially graduate schools, continues the pattern, producing too few women doctorates, lawyers, doctors, MBAs, and engineers.

Indeed, by graduate school age, many women have subordinated their careers to their families or have limited their expectations.

The mass media, especially television, also socialize children. Most television programming mirrors conventional middle-American cultural values and sex-role stereotyping. Sexism, built into the language and imagery through traditional cultural patterns, helps teach little girls to limit their expectations and to be attractive, passive, and dependent. Theoretically, talk of "man" and use of "he" officially includes both sexes, but women may not feel included. Hence, there is an effort to desex language, using *firefighters* for *firemen, he and she* phraseology, structuring sentences to avoid the problem, and so on.

Economic Aspects

The impact of sexism on income, occupations, and politics is still severe despite some progress. The income data presented above, showing the relation of sexism to poverty, is repeated for every income level. The male-female comparison of year-round full-time workers is interesting. In 1977 men with an eighth-grade education earned a median income of $12,083; women with four years of college earned $11,605.[28] Almost two-thirds of the adult poor are women; over two-thirds on welfare are women. Unemployment is higher among women, and it may influence women to turn to crime, typically shoplifting and prostitution, to earn a living. In all earnings information—occupation, industry, education, overall—white men are at the top, black men below them, white women a little below them, and black women clearly at the bottom.[29]

Women increasingly have been leaving the home to work. In 1940, 15 percent of married women worked; in 1978, 50 percent. In about one-fourth of these families, the wife contributed 40 percent or more of family income. (Unmarried women are even more often employed than married ones.) Women hold about 40 percent of all positions, but stereotyping is quite evident; very few occupations are within 10 or even 20 percentage points of the participation rate. Women are 60 percent or more of librarians and related occupations, nurses, dietitians, therapists, health technologists, social and recreation workers, preschool and elementary teachers, office managers of certain kinds, hucksters and peddlers (the designation is from the Bureau of Labor Statistics), retail sales and most other clerks, tellers, bookkeepers, cashiers, clerical supervisors, office machine operators, secretaries and related work, telephone operators, dressmakers and seamstresses outside factories, laundry and dry cleaning operatives, packers and wrappers, sewers and stitchers, textile operatives, unpaid family farm labor, food service workers, health service workers, child-care workers, hairdressers and cosmetologists, and maids and servants. In many of these occupations, women are over 90 percent of the number employed. About thirty occupations fall in the range of 30 to 60 percent women, notably personnel and labor relations workers, college and university teachers, secondary teachers, vocational and educational counselors, editors and reporters, athletes and kindred workers, entertainers and artists, research workers, buyers, health administrators, building managers, restaurant and bar managers, school administrators, real estate work, assemblers, manufacturing inspectors, machine operatives, bus drivers, and janitors.

Women are underrepresented in most professions, such as accounting, engineering, law, science, medicine, and religion. They are underrepresented in politics, public administration, corporate management, most technical work, the more highly paid kinds of sales work, nearly every skilled craftwork occupation, mining, truck driving, heavy equipment operating, construction labor, freight handling, groundskeeping, and farm labor.

Starting salaries are lower for women than for men, and more women are employed below their educational level. Only one-fourth of grade school principals are women, with fewer still at junior high and senior high levels, despite high percentages of women at the teacher level.

We fail to take economic advantage of women's talents. About three-fourths of job training slots go to men. Ironically, training is needed to meet the growing demand for paid work using homemaking skills. We are having to create paid positions in cleaning, cooking, shopping, chauffering, and routine care of the elderly, disabled, and children, and hence need to train people for this kind of work. A housewife with small children could reasonably demand $12,000 a year for her services; she would make that doing the same thing for others, probably working fewer hours.[30]

Affirmative Action

Affirmative action refers to compensatory programs to make up for the results of past discrimination. Most of it is noncontroversial, but certain aspects are extremely controversial. Making up for the past for some may mean lessening present opportunity for others; helping blacks and women may mean hurting able white males, for example.

Most Americans believe that ability should take precedence over affirmative action. The problem, however, is to determine ability. Do the tests really measure it? Poor schooling may fail to develop the real ability of a person, especially as measured by tests. Many graduate schools for several years have had special admissions students who do not meet entrance requirements but come from disadvantaged backgrounds and show academic promise. These students generally have difficulty in their first year or two in the program, but they generally prove themselves about as able as regular admission students. They can excell at serving needy clients that able white males may pass over on their way to lucrative professional specializations. Similar success occurs with affirmative action in employment.

Reformers generally support affirmative action as the only realistic way promises of equality of opportunity can be accomplished. If a driver hits a pedestrian, it is not enough to say that we are sorry and promise not to do it again (stop discriminating). We have to take the victim to the hospital at some inconvenience to ourselves to make up in part for our mistake (affirmative action).

The American system is riddled with similar deviations from test-based measures of ability, deviations that have generally been upheld in the courts. Teachers, for example, are given tenure, which shields them from competition based on merit but protects them when they take controversial positions. Seniority rights are a nonmerit discrimination benefiting first-hired and older workers; compulsory retirement discriminates in favor of younger workers. A union shop to protect workers from arbitrary employer abuse also hinders decisions based on merit. Colleges seek geographic diversity and favor children of their faculty and graduates and of wealthy or influential people. The elites that proclaim merit are sometimes unlikely to use it; at least, they tend to find it in people peculiarly like themselves. Executive promotions depend as much on networks of personal contacts as on objective measures of ability. Our system of taxing wealth gives immense wealth to a few with no test of merit at all. Justice for women and minorities is at least as worthy as other time-honored deviations from merit.

Reform requires a balancing of values, so a word is needed in relation to white males. It is unjust to deny opportunity to those with real ability and folly to benefit blacks and women with poor ability. There is little evidence this has happened, but it may. The tendency of many personnel officers to use affirmative action as an excuse to deny employment, or to implement it in an unthinking way has created some impression of arbitrary benefits to the disadvantaged. Such conflict should be minimized by special efforts to improve test scores by the disadvantaged, to make tests relevant for the job, to make qualifications depend on more than just a test, and to recruit from the disadvantaged. Such actions make it much easier to meet the targets of affirmative action plans. Also, as the Supreme Court made clear in its 1978 *Bakke* decision, targets cannot be achieved by simplistic quotas which discriminate in reverse. Affirmative action requires a difficult balance.

The Politics of Gradual Change

Elite and popular attitudes are mildly favorable to equality for women, but the progress that has been made has been the work of a relatively small number of activists who support public-interest groups. The Civil Rights Act of 1964, the Equal Employment Opportunity Act of 1972, the Equal Pay Act of 1963, the Equal Credit Act, similar legislation at the state level, executive orders, administrative actions, and court decisions have resulted from pressure and have produced much, perhaps most, of the legal change that would be required by the equal rights amendment. Occupations of all kinds are opening, especially at the first step: tokenism. Women can more easily establish an independent credit rating, qualify for a mortgage, and do business. A number of discriminations respecting family relations have ended, and more are likely to end. Women are now completing college at about the same rate as men, and graduate education is opening up.

So far we have looked at the low value placed on women's traditional roles, the notion of equality of the sexes, socialization, education, economics, affirmative action, and child care. Many more aspects could be covered. Social security and state family laws still discriminate. In delivering health services, male doctors often fail to respect women as social equals. In criminal justice, the crime of rape until recently has received low enforcement priority and has tended to treat women in a degrading way. Deeply rooted in culture, sexism crops up everywhere.

The League of Women Voters is one of the best ways for women to become generally involved in reform. The league has about 140,000 members, who are mostly educated and affluent. It takes positions on a wide range of issues after careful study, is nonpartisan, and is not connected with vested interests. Although relatively moderate and perhaps too cautious, the league is important politically because of its thoughtfulness and persistence.

The modern revitalization of feminism, however, came mainly from more radical voices willing to question the entire system. Women's groups have proliferated on campuses and in cities and have been active politically for the causes discussed here and others—including market power, consumer protection (women do 85 percent of spending), population, and poverty. They have helped the peace movement and with security reform and have campaigned against nuclear power.

Ms. magazine, radical local groups, the National Women's Political Caucus, and the National Organization for Women (NOW) have played a leading role in the resurgence of feminism. NOW has moved from relatively philosophical concerns to practical politics. In 1974, there were 69.2 million men of voting age and 75.5 million women. The women's movement is trying to move politics toward women's issues (such as child care, the equal rights amendment, and abortion), female candidates, and female voting majorities. The movement is generally reformist, yet women who succeed in getting elected have much the same spread of views as male politicians. Will more equality for women make a better system, or just a different one?

Racism

White Americans have historically discriminated against native Americans, blacks, Mexicans, Chinese, Japanese, Filipinos, Puerto Ricans, and even racially white groups of low income and special cultures. We will look at the first three, who, like women, have been almost totally excluded from top political and economic positions.

Each of these groups has greatly increased its political activism and economic self-reliance. But what the group can be expected to do for itself in spite of a discriminatory system must be balanced with what changes the system must make to allow opportunity to the group. Overemphasis on one or the other is common. It is easy to blame racial minorities for their problems and ignore the role of institutional racism. Most whites discriminate not consciously but by indirection through a world view whose political results are inadequate resources for equality of opportunity. It is also easy to blame the system, when one of the clearest lessons of history is that no one person or group can "liberate" another person or group. Social theories that blame "systems" overlook a fundamental truth of common sense: when we do well at our work, our family life, or community involvement, the credit goes to us. Too many women, blacks, and others have triumphed over difficult odds; too many have risen above their original condition for us to say that the system stops all progress. Ironically, some who have done the most to help themselves also have an ideology blaming the system—a view contradicted by their success. If the system was as bad as, for example, the Black Muslims said (prior to 1975), then it is hard to explain how it was possible for them to do so much. Life is too complicated for simple theories. Reform requires both that minorities change themselves and that the system change to give them the same opportunities given whites.

Native Americans

No chapters of American history are more tragic than white devastation of native Americans. In 1877 near the Canadian border Chief Joseph of the Nez Pierce ended his flight from the U.S. calvary saying, "Our chiefs are killed. The little children are freezing to death. My people have no blankets, no food. My heart is sick and sad. . . . I will fight no more." Indians were settled on the most worthless land white men could find for them at the time. Reeducation attempts similar to totalitarian techniques tried to change Indian culture. The Bureau of Indian Affairs (BIA) mismanaged the reservations with paternalistic heavy-handednesss. Concerned whites and Indians have done much to save knowledge about what over 300 native cultures were like, but from the ending of the Indian wars in 1877, native

Americans have faced recurrent crises of demoralization and repression. The ravaging of the Indians has proceeded hand in glove with the ravaging of the environment and the extinction of species, and the three seem inseparable, destroying cultures, landscapes, and species in the name of progress. The Bureau of Indian Affairs, even in recent years, has sold mineral rights cheaply on large acreages of reservations and failed to collect millions of dollars in rentals and royalties. Indian timber, lands, and water rights have also been violated, and their civil rights are often ignored. More strip mining, power plants, and pollution are in the offing.

Books by Vine Deloria, Jr., and others have awakened greater awareness of Indian problems, and Indians have become more militant, following the examples of blacks. In 1972, a group of militants in Washington, D.C., occupied the BIA building there, and stole its files, which documented extensive abuses. Reformers are still seeking abolition of the BIA and creation of a new agency outside the resource-oriented Department of Interior. A congressionally established review commission has so recommended after a year of research, but Congress moves slowly, if at all, on Indian affairs.[31]

Meanwhile public-interest groups like the Association on American Indian Affairs, the Center for Constitutional Rights, the National Indian Youth Council, and numerous tribal organizations are implementing their own fund-raising, community development, health, and education projects, and they are using lawyers to assert long-ignored rights. This militance has created strains within tribes and is not itself fully defined. On the decline are the passive reservation Indians of the lower class and a tiny Indian elite manipulated by whites but economically better off than others. On the rise are Indian entrepreneurs who use every pragmatic tool of legal, political, and economic power to rise economically. Also on the rise are traditionalists who seek to preserve their whole culture, including its primitive but environmentally sound and socially satisfying technologies.

Dozens of cultures and millions of Indians have been decimated since Europeans discovered the New World, but finally in the United States, today there is a new vitality and excitement for native Americans, which should yield a higher measure of equality of opportunity. Non-Indians can help by paying attention, lending lobby support, and giving money to reform efforts.

Mexican Americans

In the 1840s, the United States seized about a third of the territory of Mexico, which covered an area from present-day Texas to California. Many Mexicans migrated north after the conquest, especially during the turbulent years of the Mexican Revolution (1910–1920). They continue to come, mostly illegally, pushed out of Mexico by extreme poverty, overpopulation, and lack of jobs and pulled by low-paid jobs in the United States.

The Immigration and Naturalization Service (INS) and its Border Patrol are too understaffed to keep out illegal aliens, and the sanctions against an illegal are so mild that they are not discouraged. A false alien registration card, entitling the holder to social benefits, can be purchased for about eighty dollars. An estimated $13 billion a year is paid out to illegals for food stamps, Medicaid, uncollected income tax, and money sent out of the country. (Perhaps even more is collected in income tax and social security.) Many Americans lose jobs to illegals. There is no penalty for employing illegals, and many, especially in agribusiness, do so knowingly. In 1971 Congress passed a law against such hiring, but it is still being tested in the courts. Yet it is difficult to penalize employers without discriminating against all people of Mexican descent, and some sympathize with the plight of the poor Mexicans. Persons of Mexican appearance with poor English are automatically under suspicion of being illegal.

Mexican Americans, like native Americans, have followed the blacks in an ethnic awakening. All three major minorities have language differences from standard English, but only Spanish is recognized as an official second language. Activists have campaigned to increase the use of Spanish in the media, government offices, schools, and documents. In a few places, Mexican Americans have a potential majority of votes, which can be mobilized by reform activists.

Another kind of struggle for Chicanos relates to migrant farm workers, who have long been excluded from coverage by the laws that allow most workers to unionize. Other laws designed to protect these workers have been only weakly enforced by the states, the Environmental Protection Agency, the Department of Labor, and others. For years César Chavez has led the United Farm Workers (UFW) in California. The UFW has had support from the AFL-CIO, many Catholics, and other activists. They persuaded sympathizers around the nation to boycott table grapes, lettuce, and Gallo wines (officially ended in January 1978). At first, these efforts succeeded, and many contracts were signed in California. But then the Teamsters intervened, conniving with employers and presenting the workers with a take-it-or-leave-it contract; workers could take work under the contract or not at all. Politically powerful growers resisted the farm workers on every front. In 1975 Jerry Brown won the California governorship with help from farm workers, and he was committed to their cause. Once in office, he negotiated a compromise farm labor law, the first to regularize farm unions. Implementation of the law was resisted by growers and political leaders, but after the UFW again mobilized its supporters in 1976, both sides seemed willing to make the compromise work. UFW prospects brightened when the Teamsters largely withdrew from the fields. Some small growers were caught in the middle between the large-scale growers and the UFW, but the UFW story generally was a classic case of confrontation between money, power, and property rights against poor minorities and reformers. Upon this success, the struggle for many other farm workers, in other states and in other crops, is beginning.

Blacks

Of these three minorities, blacks have generally ascended the highest on the socioeconomic ladder, achieving an average income about equal to people in Great Britain and Italy, though it is still low for the United States. In 1977 the median black household income was $8,422, about 60 percent of the white level.[32] Most of us are familiar with the history of the enslavement of Africans, their transport to this country, their role in the agricultural development of the South, and their migration to northern and western cities, especially during the world wars. What we are less familiar with is the Jim Crow system, which was as bad as slavery and which was implemented by violence after northern troops left the South at the end of Reconstruction in 1877. The hopes of the Reconstruction era were destroyed and did not rise again until virtually the 1950s. The southern white elite successfully coopted poor whites, dividing the power of the lower- and moderate-income class. Remnants of the Jim Crow system still persist in most of the South today.

The main black response to white racism falls along a spectrum from radical to reformist. The radical element can be characterized as black nationalism and is evident in the thinking of W. E. B. Du Bois, Marcus Garvey, Elijah Muhammed, and Malcolm X, in the back-to-Africa movement, the Black Muslims, and the Black Panthers. The radical element has spoken most clearly to the black lower class, which, though diminishing in size, still benefits little and suffers much from the system.

At the other end of the spectrum has been a more middle-class style, based on black Protestant churches North and South, which can be characterized as integrationism. It is evident in the thinking of Booker T. Washington and Martin Luther King, Jr., in organizations like the National Association for the Advancement of Colored People (NAACP), which has the most recognition and support of any black political organization; in colleges like Tuskegee, Howard, and Meharry; and in magazines like *Ebony* and *Jet*. Most blacks support the integrationist position because, realistically and pragmatically, it promises more results. The integrationists have used official white values to attack actual white practices. For a long time, the major arena was the courts, used to require elites to obey their laws, always a chronic reform problem. Blacks have generally worked as interest groups within the system with significant support from friendly whites. Integrationists have always risked loss of a black identity in the quest for improvement, however. The genius of the civil rights revolution has been to affirm blackness while pursuing economic integration. The affirmation, in fact, inspires the self-confidence needed to pursue the long and difficult struggle.

The Civil Rights Movement. The civil rights revolution of the early 1960s built on earlier steps made after World War II: the integration of the military, ordered by President Truman; the integration of professional sports, inaugurated by Jackie Robinson; the 1954 Supreme Court decision to integrate the schools; the presidential decision to use the National Guard to back the Court; the general prosperity of the country; the Montgomery bus boycott; and the election of a liberal president in 1960. Young reformers discovered dramatic ways to publicize long-festering realities: lunch counter sit-ins, freedom rides, marches, demonstrations, challenges to presidential nominating convention delegates, wade-ins, and voter registration attempts. The new movement started perhaps in 1955 in Montgomery, Alabama, when Rosie Parks, a black woman, was too tired to move to the back of the bus, as required by law. Black protest cohered under the leadership of Martin Luther King, Jr., who went on to national leadership, speaking as effectively to whites as to blacks. Legislative accomplishments finally came in 1964, 1965, and 1968.

The radical white response—"segregation forever"—was largely a middle- and lower-class phenomenon. The elites were generally willing to accommodate once they recognized the strength of the movement and the cost of stopping it. They could accommodate a lot because so much that needed to be done cost very little money. The radical white response received heavy media coverage. The brutality of police suppression, of burnings of crosses and houses, of bombing churches in which children died, and of murdering civil rights workers was well publicized. Victims can get justice if the media accurately report their plight; the fashion of the times made for more coverage. With some accommodating elites and an awakened citizenry paying attention, reformers were able to exert leverage for several significant reforms.

This movement bears some similarities to the antiwar, the women's, the environmental and other movements in America. Movements are cyclical, rising and falling over a period (usually of years) and shifting the consensus within which policy is made. Events, conditions, and attitudes coincide to increase concern and the number of people involved, overcoming the intensity problem. The media disseminate enough information to generate interest, and decision makers know that their actions will be closely scrutinized by many people. Public-interest groups play a key organizational role, made stronger by the surge of interest. Often groups are created as part of a movement. New leaders rise to prominence. For many, perhaps most, the movement is something they see in the news with only a distant connection perceived to their personal lives; it may have some impact on how they vote when reformers can help them make the connection.

Just as movements are hard to predict in advance, it is hard to explain why they fade. The racial movement achieved many of its legal objectives and made real progress but still has far to go. The peace movement ended the war but did not reform security policy. The environmental movement, which may still be going on in some ways, has made major accomplishments but has stalled in some ways because of the 1974–1975 recession. Politics concerning a problem goes on after the movement declines and the front-page headlines fade. The stronger organizations play a long-term role, becoming part of an enduring system of politics. In civil rights, the NAACP, which was caught unaware by the early movement, caught up with it and is now once again the major group for blacks. The movement groups have collapsed, shrunk, or declined, and media attention has drifted elsewhere. Progress thus depends on solid organizational strength and enduring citizen commitment to get marginal but important decisions.

Leadership at the presidential level for racial integration, so evident during the Johnson years, came to a standstill during the Nixon and Ford administrations. Nixon appointees to the departments of Justice and of Health, Education and Welfare were indifferent to black rights, undermining community action, legal services, and school desegregation.[33] Southern racists were nominated for the Supreme Court, but they were not approved by the Senate after long and difficult battles by reformers. Few prominent blacks worked for either administration. Open housing became a dead letter.[34] Proposals to undermine black voting were pressed upon Congress but were not approved. If progress were not being made, at least the consensus was holding against complete decay.

Federal agencies developed huge backlogs of unprocessed civil rights complaints between 1969 and 1976. Year after year, the Civil Rights Commission reported these abuses in detail and denounced them in uncompromising language; other reports confirmed the stalemate and the dangers. But no meaningful action was taken. A program for black capitalism and another for integrating unions hardly got off the ground. Some emergency funds for school integration were held back.[35] State and city affirmative action plans, dozens of them, were not monitored or adequately enforced.[36] Revenue sharing and other funds to states were inadequately monitored.[37] Regulatory agencies acting in the name of the consumer protected industries from black competition.[38] All this tied together as a "southern strategy" to win Republican voters among white southerners.

Racial Progress. There has been some progress within this dismal picture, however, even at the federal level. Nixon and Congress substantially increased social spending through social security, Medicare-Medicaid, and food stamps, programs that disproportionately helped blacks. Civil rights enforcement spending, $346 million in 1975, helped keep some pressure on regarding federal affirmative action, enforcement of private affirmative action, rights, and public accommodation. Despite public hostility to school integration, the Republican administration presided over a decline in all-black schools (under pressure of court orders). (Carter's 1980 budget for civil rights enforcement was $592 million.)

The statistics show steady progress within the federal government. Once exciting and hopeful, affirmative action has become boring, legalistic, and bureaucratic, but it is working. For example, women and minorities at higher federal levels have increased steadily. Even more money, about $2.6 billion, was spent for minority assistance programs, such as Indian programs, minority business aid, special help for desegregating schools, and aid to black colleges.

Education and employment are improving gradually, under the slow prodding of federal enforcement efforts from above and blacks from below. Exposure and publicity by public-interest groups and the Civil Rights Commission continue to play key roles, and they lean heavily on research. When the Civil Rights Commission discovered that the Department of Defense (DOD) was violating clear legal requirements that prime contractors have affirmative action plans, it publicized its report. DOD then began holding up funding until the plans were made and approved, an effective enforcement technique requiring little staff time. But these plans soon bumped up against a shortage of qualified minorities. When McDonnell Douglas Corp. wanted to hire thirty-five black engineers, it discovered that only three hundred black engineers were being produced each year in all fields of engineering, and some of them were Africans, who were returning home.[39]

Overall, however, tremendous progress has been made. Public accommodations have been desegregated. Voter registration of blacks increased in eleven southern states from 2,164,000 in 1964 to 4,149,000 in 1976, largely because of the Voting Rights Act of 1965. By 1976, over 7 million black voters nationwide had elected or helped elect 3,979 black officials at the federal, state, and local levels. By 1978, 4,503 blacks had been elected.[40] Half a dozen major cities now have black mayors. Several southern states have or have had moderate governors, one of whom was Jimmy Carter. Racial tensions in southern cities have largely eased. Blacks are important as voting blocs in many districts. The black caucus of the House of Representatives has grown in sophistication and strength. Two statewide officers in California, the lieutenant-governor and the superintendent of public instruction, have probably been elected with more white votes than any other blacks in history have received. Public opinion polls show substantial declines in racial prejudice.[41]

The educational level of blacks have been increasing at a significant rate. Most are graduating from high school, and with 10 percent of all college students, they almost equal their share on a population basis. This great progress seems likely to produce solid, long-range economic improvements. The income gap has been narrowing gradually. Forty-four percent of blacks own their own homes, much lower than the white level, but the gap is still closing because they are increasing their rate of home ownership much faster than whites are.[42] Almost 70 percent of blacks are above the poverty line. While disproportionately poor, blacks are still mostly middle class and lower middle class. Blacks have steadily improved their jobs, increasing in both white-collar and union categories. In 1979 the National Center for Health Statistics reported that the gap in life expectancy between whites and blacks narrowed from seven years to five in the past decade.[43]

Case Study:

Actions Against Employment Discrimination

Both blacks and women still find employment discrimination a pervasive problem. It is one of a number of different kinds of discrimination that persist despite being illegal. Progress would be faster with more governmental commitment. Much of the thrust for reform still comes from underfunded public-interest groups which depend on citizen contributions, public-interest lawyers, and employees willing to come forward with complaints.

One of the first concerns of the National Organization for Women was to lobby through a law giving the Equal Employment Opportunity Commission (EEOC) power to take sex-discrimination cases to court. The EEOC, created in 1964 to serve race rights, was given responsibility for sex discrimination in 1972. NOW lobbied the EEOC, presidents, and Congress to take action and provide funding to combat unfair job practices, and by 1975 the EEOC had investigated over 40,000 cases for women. When an Ohio woman took over her deceased husband's service station in 1975, the oil company at first denied her a franchise. She complained to NOW, which picketed the local company headquarters, lobbied the national headquarters, and found a senator to question an oil executive at a congressional hearing. In two weeks she got her franchise back.

Major EEOC cases such as those involving AT&T and General Motors, have set new standards for moving toward equal rights. AT&T, for example, had 1,800 sex and race complaints against it when it asked the Federal Communications Commission for a rate hike in 1971. NOW, the NAACP, and the EEOC sued to have the FCC deny the increase. After three years of litigation, AT&T agreed to pay thousands of women and blacks $38 million in back pay and raises and $22 million in another suit in 1974. Individual cases are also taken to court to the extent that funds and evidence allow. One woman, for example, with help from NOW, was able to get a better job plus $30,000 in back pay, overtime, and interest. The Equal Pay Act of 1963 has won additional millions for women. Minimum wage protections have been extended to two categories largely filled with women—domestic service and retail clerks. Advertisements for employment used to be divided into categories for men and women. A NOW lawsuit persuaded the Supreme Court that there was no right to advertise something illegal like sex discrimination any more than illegal drugs.

The use of lawsuits for equal rights was pioneered by the NAACP for blacks and is now carried out principally by a separate organization, the NAACP Legal Defense Fund, dependent as NOW on contributions. In 1977 in Louisiana, it won a suit against Cities Service Oil Co., which agreed to pay $1.75 million to 374 blacks, to establish an apprenticeship program to train blacks in proportion to their number in the local parish (county) population, to train and promote workers previously held down, to use only EEOC validated tests, and to advertise for workers in sources accessible to blacks. Additional money went to the Legal Defense Fund for legal fees. This kind of settlement greatly strengthens public interest law.

There is now a mosaic of precedents generally favorable to the cause of equal employment opportunity. Blacks and women would advance faster were it not for the failure of the government to enforce more aggressively fair employment laws. In 1974, for example, the EEOC had 85,000 unsettled cases, and the average complaint took twenty-six months to settle. By 1980

the Carter administration budgeted $124 million to process 93,000 charges of discrimination and to make 125,000 investigations. It will take several years to see if this significant commitment is effective.

Poor Ghetto Blacks. The great problem of race was analyzed in detail and summarized starkly by the Kerner Commission in 1968. It concluded that we were moving toward separate and unequal societies—one white, the other black—and it condemned the fundamental cause, white racism. Now, over a decade later, it may be time to revise that dire prediction and focus more clearly on the black lower class in the cities. This group, far smaller than the black population as a whole, has suffered a deterioration so complete that it is a serious threat to itself, to other blacks, and to society as a whole. Its members, especially the young men, commit crimes all out of proportion to their numbers, even considering their poverty. Ghetto blacks are just as often the victims. Young blacks suffer extremely high rates of unemployment, drug addiction, alcoholism, teenage pregnancies, broken families, and juvenile delinquency. Welfare dependency is high, and schools in these areas are terrible generally. Ghetto blacks lack education and skills. Aliens and women take entry-level jobs once held by black men, and the jobs are moving to suburbia. On the streets blacks learn survival in an underground, often illegal, economy. The seventy-six major civil disturbances from 1968 to 1972 all occurred in black ghettos—among them, Watts, Detroit, and Newark. Unlike white violence directed at blacks, which helped the movement, the rioting evoked no significant commitment of resources for ghetto problems, and the devastated neighborhoods have been slow to recover, if at all.

Some children and adults with determination develop skills and leave the ghetto. Some neighborhoods can organize and get improvements. The chances, however, are against most ghetto blacks. In Columbia Point, a large, low-income housing project in Boston, 53 percent of 443 children under the age of six had one or more of these conditions at home for one or both parents: serious drug addiction, serious alcoholism, documented psychosis, significant mental retardation, more than two criminal convictions, only one parent with five children under the age of six, or a mother who had two children before she was eighteen. A program for physical health was not improving educational performance because the children were too sleepy, too hungry, and too traumatized by events in the home. Family fights kept them up most or all night and exposed them to violence. They also saw violence on their way to and from school, had drugs urged on them by pushers, and were robbed of their change. Some ate no breakfast. Crime was so rife that a modern shopping center set up to help the area closed because of shoplifting, muggings, and purse snatching. A day-care center was able to reach some women, but others saw its advice as hostile to their life-style. They consistently and completely avoided any self-criticism, a survival mechanism in their hostile environment but not one that really helped them. They blamed the establishment, which, as if to fulfill a prophecy, cut funds for Columbia Point day care.[44]

Each extreme of the conflict between rich white and poor black has focused on the faults of the other and rationalized its own behavior. It is not fashionable to blame blacks for part of their problems, but it is clear that many have not absorbed the positive black identity that has fueled the reformist movement. Too many are destroying themselves and their children when they should be bringing effective pressure to bear on white society and taking advantage of educational opportunities. Recently some black leaders have developed this theme.

Political Action. The NAACP is the major organization for political action for blacks, but two other groups illustrate effective action despite the ending of the civil rights movement. The Voter Education Project has helped register millions of black voters in the South, but 3 million are still unregistered and the registered are sometimes harassed.

The Southern Poverty Law Center, headed by Julian Bond, has been successful in recent years in finding dramatic cases and making fund appeals to citizens. One example is Johnny Ross, arrested on suspicion of rape in Louisiana and put in a lineup. The victim did not identify him nor did he match the description of the rapist. But the police beat him into signing a confession. He had only a few minutes with his lawyer before trial, and at the trial conflicting testimony was presented. He was found guilty and, at the age of sixteen, sentenced to die in the electric chair. He was put in a tiny cell with one bed, which he shared with three adult convicts. Letters from Law Center supporters led the prison system to put him in a juvenile camp. The Supreme Court struck down Louisiana's death penalty for rape, changing his sentence to twenty years. As of 1978, the Southern Poverty Law Center was seeking a new trial.[45] Many cases are equally dramatic; others are more technical, attacking the routine injustices of the massive discrimination still tolerated by our system. With media and public apathy of the late 1970s, legal case work by public-interest groups becomes once again a major tool against racism. It would be easier to celebrate the great progress the nation has made if it did not have so far to go.

The pervasive problems of social justice—poverty, sexism, and racism—are intimately related to each other. Female-headed households and minorities are disproportionately poor, the result of discrimination that affects all women and minorities. The United States has made great progress dealing with the three problems but has a long way to go. The expansion of the economy, hard work, and transfer programs for welfare and income security have all but eliminated poverty as defined by the government. Yet the problems of low-income people are serious. The solutions seem to lie in reforming the reforms—that is, in federalizing and centralizing welfare programs related to income, which have developed piecemeal over the years. Then those able to work could be required to take public-service jobs; others, the majority of children, the old, and the disabled, would get food stamps, housing aid, Medicaid, and money as needed to end poverty. Legal services, services for the old, and community development are also needed. Sexism and racism affect the whole society. Reform involves expansion of high-quality day care, reduction of sex-role stereotyping, nondiscrimination in employment, affirmative action, and continuing political action by women, native Americans, Mexican Americans, and blacks. Ending discrimination is a complex process requiring both a new consciousness among the oppressed and an active commitment by society.

Notes

1. Nick Kotz, *Let Them Eat Promises* (Garden City, N.Y.: Doubleday, 1971).
2. Congressional Budget Office, *Poverty Status of Families under Alternative Definitions of Income*, Background Paper 17 (June 1977), cited by *Focus*, Fall 1977, p. 5. *Focus* is published by the Institute for Research on Poverty, University of Wisconsin, Madison.
3. *San Francisco Chronicle*, February 12, 1979.
4. Ibid., April 27, 1977; *Hayward* (Calif.) *Daily Review*, April 26, 1977.
5. *Focus*, Fall 1977, p. 5.
6. Ibid.
7. American Indian Fund, "How About Equal Rights for This American, Too?" (April 1979).
8. Computed from U.S. Bureau of the Census, *Current Population Reports*, Series P-60, no. 115 (July 1978), table 14.
9. Survey Research Center, *The Changing Economic Status of 5000 American Families* (Ann Arbor: University of Michigan, 1974).
10. *San Francisco Chronicle*, April 16, 1977.
11. *The Budget of the United States Government, Fiscal Year 1980*, Executive Office of the President, Office of Management and Budget, (U.S. Government Printing Office: Washington, D.C.), p. 260.
12. Ibid., p. 261.
13. *Statistical Abstract of the United States, 1978*, p. 797.

14. *Budget, 1980*, pp. 235, 242.
15. *Focus*, Fall 1977, pp. 1–2, 12–13; ibid., Fall 1978, pp. 3–4, 9. See also Stanley Masters and Irwin Garfinkel, *Estimating the Labor Supply Effects of Income Maintenance Alternatives* (New York: Academic Press, 1978); *San Francisco Chronicle*, February 28, 1979; and "A Difference of Opinion," *Fortune*, December 4, 1978, pp. 145–146, 148.
16. TRB, "Alice in Welfareland," *New Republic*, October 4, 1975, p. 1.
17. Ibid.
18. *Budget, 1980*, pp. 258–260, 268–269; *Statistical Abstract 1978*, p. 288. "Other public assistance" was basis for 1980 general assistance estimate. See also the *Abstract*, Sections 10 and 11 for other statistics.
19. *Statistical Abstract, 1978*, pp. 333.
20. Estimated from ibid., pp. 327–333, 440.
21. *Focus*, Fall 1977, p. 5.
22. Bureau of the Census, *Current Population Reports*, Series P-60, no. 116, p. 28.
23. *San Francisco Chronicle*, September 13, 1977.
24. Ibid., August 8, 1977.
25. Charles Peters and Taylor Branch, "Inside OEO," in their *Blowing the Whistle* (New York: Praeger, 1972), pp. 77–100.
26. *San Francisco Chronicle*, January 3, 1976, based on research by Dr. Jerome Kagan et al. of Tufts Medical Center.
27. *In the Public Interest* (July 1977). It is published by the Fund for Peace.
28. Bureau of the Census, *Current Population Reports*, Series P-60, No. 116, pp. 13–14.
29. See *Employment and Earnings*, published monthly by the Bureau of Labor Statistics, any issue.
30. *San Francisco Chronicle*, September 6, 1975, based on Social Security Administration studies, and updated to 1980.
31. *Hayward* (Calif.) *Daily Review*, July 20, 1976, column by Jack Anderson.
32. *Statistical Abstract, 1978*, p. 462.
33. Peters and Branch, *Blowing the Whistle*, chaps. 5, 10, 11.
34. U.S. Commission on Civil Rights, report of August 1974.
35. *San Francisco Chronicle*, March 2, 1973.
36. U.S. Commission on Civil Rights, *The Federal Civil Rights Enforcement Effort* (Washington, D.C.: Government Printing Office, October 1970) is just one example.
37. U.S. Commission on Civil Rights, *The Federal Civil Rights Effort* (November 1975).
38. U.S. Commission on Civil Rights, *Federal Civil Rights* (October 1970), vol. 1, no. 36.
39. U.S. Commission on Civil Rights, *The "System" Can Work* (1971).
40. *Statistical Abstract, 1978*, pp. 519–520; John Dean, *The Making of a Black Mayor* (Washington, D.C.: Joint Center for Political Studies, 1973).
41. *San Francisco Chronicle*, October 13, 1975, based on a Gallup Poll.
42. *Newsweek*, October 4, 1976; *Hayward* (Calif.) *Daily Review*, May 19, 1979.
43. Ibid., *Daily Review*.
44. Doris Bennett, "Five Years. . . ," *Radcliffe Alumnae Quarterly*, Fall 1976. See also Lee Rainwater, *Behind Ghetto Walls* (Chicago: Aldine, 1970).
45. Southern Poverty Law Center, *Poverty Law Report* 6 (Spring 1978):4 and (June–July 1978):4.

5

Social Justice: The Major Institutions

Institutions for criminal justice, health, and education are important both for dealing with poverty and discrimination and for the social quality of life of the whole society. Crime, for example, is now a far more important problem for most people than the set of values with which it competes, the civil liberties of suspects and criminals. We are better protected from the government than we are from each other. Less crime need not require less liberty, but it may require more citizen attention. Health and education, on the other hand, have been better managed and are less salient in opinion polls as problems, but that does not mean that they have been well managed. The costs of poor policy for all three institutions are highest for the disadvantaged.

What are the best policies for these institutions? How much are we willing to pay for what are often indirect and future benefits? How can popular support and understanding be generated? And, similarly, how can discipline be brought to bear on intensive institutional interests in need of reform? The answers determine how much social justice we will have.

Crime

Some Statistics

Some level of crime is inevitable in human societies, but the United States suffers from a crime rate far higher than that of other developed democracies

Table 5–1 Homicide Victimization Rate, 1974

Country	*Crude Rate per 100,000 Population*
United States	10.2
Canada	2.5
Australia	1.8
Japan	1.3
West Germany	1.2
Sweden	1.1
Italy	1.1
England and Wales	1.0
France	0.9
Non-U.S. average	1.4

Source: *Statistical Abstract of the United States, 1977,* p. 174.

(table 5–1). Within the United States, the crime problem is disproportionately concentrated in big cities (table 5–2).

Among social groups, the primary victims are low-income and minority people. Except for rape, men are much more likely to be victims than women. Black men have the highest victimization rates. White men are about seven

Table 5–2 Crime Rates and Urbanization, 1977

	Violent Crime	*Property Crime*
250,000 and up (59 cities)	1,070	6,749
100,000–249,999 (110 cities)	600	6,563
50,000–99,999 (265 cities)	444	5,562
25,000–49,999 (604 cities)	342	4,927
10,000–24,999 (1,398 cities)	264	4,161
Under 10,000 (4,925 cities)	230	3,676
Rural areas (1,910 agencies)	176	1,909

[a] Offenses known to police per 100,000 population.
Source: *Statistical Abstract of the United States, 1978*, p. 179.

times more likely to be murdered in the United States than in other developed democracies; blacks, about fifty times. (See table 5–3).

Arrest rates indicate probable characteristics of those who commit crime. They are mostly young, mostly male, and disproportionately black. Of over 7 million people arrested in 1976, 72 percent were white, 25 percent were black, and 3 percent were "other." Men were 84 percent of the total, and 23 percent of them were under eighteen years old. Among women arrested, 34 percent were under eighteen. The eighteen- to twenty-four-year-old age group comprised 32 percent, making youths 57 percent of all arrests. Women are most likely to be arrested for shoplifting, prostitution, and drug- and liquor-related offenses. Men are more likely to be arrested for crimes of violence and other crimes of property, with younger men committing the more serious crimes of murder, rape, robbery, assault, arson, and vandalism.[1] Older men tend to commit gambling and liquor-related offenses, again indicating the young male nature of serious crime.

Crime rates have been rising since World War II, a period of abnormally low crime. Crime rates in the 1930s were very high, but prohibition and the depression were powerful causes. In the late 1970s, crime began to stabilize and taper off, mainly because of a reduction in the number of people in high-crime age groups. Crime rates are still about double what they were in the mid-1960s, however.

Table 5–3 Victimization Rates, FBI Index Crimes, 1975

	White		*Black*		
	Male	*Female*	*Male*	*Female*	*Total*
1. Homicide [a]	12.2	3.8	93.9	19.7	13.4
2. Rape [b]		2		2	
3. Robbery [b]	9	3	22	8	7
4. Aggravated assault [b]	14	5	19	11	10
5. Burglary [c]	87		129		92
6. Larceny [c]	126		114		125
7. Auto theft [c]	19		27		19

Note: The seven crimes listed in the table are used by the FBI to compile indexes of crime, violent crime, and property crime, based on police reports.

[a] Rate per 100,000 population fifteen years of age and over.

[b] Rate per 1,000 population twelve years of age and over.

[c] Rate per 1,000 households.

Source: *Statistical Abstract of the United States, 1977*, pp. 171–173.

Crime also includes self-victimizing crime (sometimes called victimless crime) and "polite" or "upper-class" crimes, broadly divided into organized crime and corporate crime.

Social Reform and Crime

The worst crime areas are the black ghettos of the big cities; the worst real unemployment rates for young men are in the black ghettos of these cities. The crisis of the ghetto and lower-class blacks referred to earlier manifests itself with deadly clarity here. Reforms of the criminal justice system will help, but they cannot affect the fundamental social causes of crime. The employment and welfare reforms already discussed are essential for reducing crime.

Suburbanization has done more than cause grave and increasing environmental problems; it is also linked with a private escape available to the more affluent. Low-income people are left in the central city, where they are five times more likely to be robbed than anyone above the median income. Alcoholics, drug addicts, the old, the disabled, and females are heavily victimized—and also politically weak. Many people are afraid that crime will touch them, and they change their habits to try to escape it. Although their symbolic concern is high, the affluent and political elites suffer relatively little from crime. Thus they are not motivated strongly enough to deal with it, either in terms of the conservative theme of more punishment or in terms of the liberal theme of more rehabilitation. Both themes are expensive to implement.

Most crime oriented to getting money is like a business or occupation that has to be learned and has calculated risks and rewards. Children learn crime hanging out with older youths, who pick it up from still others; television and movies keep the pot boiling by glamorizing crime. A typical forty-five-second robbery nets about $10 to $20; it beats working. Of 113 adult robbers in Oakland, California, 75 percent were unemployed, and over half were not looking for work. About a fourth were addicts and alcoholics, who were often high when committing their crimes. About half did not plan their robberies and did not think about getting caught. They worked familiar downtown streets, ganging up on solitary weak victims. Men were victimized at night near bars and brothels, and women were robbed any time on the streets and near shopping centers. Thirty percent of those caught were released without being charged, and 20 percent of those charged were not convicted.[2]

Elites and lower classes seem unable or unwilling to deal with crime. It is ironic that in many cities, crime is considered the primary problem, but residents do not organize their neighborhoods, seek to control guns, seek to decriminalize and regulate self-victimizing crimes, report crimes to police, monitor sentencing, and know where elected officials stand on relevant issues.

Neighborhood Alert. Some actions to combat crime can be taken individually—for example, locking the doors, using throw bolts, marking goods with identification codes, and so on. Yet many people are burglarized before they take these precautions. Next, we need to know our neighbors so we will be able to identify strangers. The high mobility of our society cuts off contacts with neighbors, but these can be reestablished with only a little social assertiveness. The police can help with neighborhood alert programs. Neighbors can meet at a local home, where they can exchange names and telephone numbers. When suspicious behavior is noticed, a neighbor can be called to increase the number of witnesses, improving evidence for court purposes and lessening chance of retaliation by the criminal. Many high-crime neighborhoods have succeeded in reducing crime dramatically using these methods. Are we more afraid of meeting our neighbors than of crime?

Gun Control. The uncontrolled proliferation of deadly weapons has made them so available that they have become themselves a causative factor in crime. Motivation is not the only cause of crime; opportunity is important also. About two-thirds of murders are committed with guns, largely because shooting is so easy compared with stabbing, strangulating, hitting with a blunt object, drowning, poisoning, or blowing up a victim. Most murders are crimes of momentary passion, which would not occur if it were harder to kill. Also about 100 law officers are killed each year. Unless we make spectacular assumptions about American culture being extremely violent, there is little other than the availability of guns to explain why our murder rate is so much higher than in other countries. Those countries have strict controls over guns, drastically lower gun murder rates, and correspondingly low overall homicide rates. They also have much lower rates of gun crime and fewer accidental shootings. In America, guns are used in about one-fourth of assaults and over 40 percent of robberies. About 2,000 to 2,500 people a year die in gun accidents, often from the gun that is supposed to protect the family from criminals. Guns are used in about 14,000 suicides a year and cause about 100,000 injuries.[3] Unless a gun owner is well trained and practiced in gun use, the gun may be more of a threat than the criminal.

Guns are available to the mentally disturbed, ex-convicts, the mentally deficient, and juveniles. The media popularize gun crime techniques. Americans own about 135 million small guns, as compared with the U.S. Army's 5 million. About 2 million more handguns are made each year, and 400,000 are imported.[4] Many of them are of cheap metal and of no use except to kill and maim.

The vast majority of Americans has supported gun control ever since opinion polls were begun in 1937. When John and Robert Kennedy and Martin Luther King, Jr., were assassinated, Congress was flooded with letters asking for gun controls. Five presidential commissions since 1967 have recommended them, but no effective action has been taken. Why? Few examples illustrate the intensity problem better than gun control. The momentary intense feeling ebbed, so that by the following election, hardly anyone knew where their representatives stood on the issue. The intense interests in favor of gun control include law enforcement agencies because law officers are frequently killed by guns. A couple of small public-interest groups are also struggling to be effective. The intense interests against gun control are the gun makers and sellers, organized as the National Rifle Association. This elite has coopted gun enthusiasts with propaganda against gun control, some of it alleging that control is a communist conspiracy to disarm Americans. The campaign has been so successful that many people think the right to bear arms is constitutionally guaranteed. The reality is that this right exists in the Fourth Amendment to the U.S. Constitution only in the context of a well-regulated militia, which is, in a modern sense, just what gun control could establish.

There are many different control proposals. Banning handguns is a relatively extreme approach compared with more moderate and politically feasible, if still difficult, approaches. Banning the cheap metal handguns is feasible. A more moderate approach would treat guns as being about as dangerous as automobiles. Automobiles are registered and their drivers licensed, a system that is so accepted that it does not occur to us to eliminate it out of fear the government might take our cars away. Registering guns would be similar to registering cars and would allow better crime detection. Licensing owners could involve giving a written test on gun laws and safety and the equivalent of a driver's test; those applying might be required to show that they can take apart a gun, reassemble it, and load, fire, unload, and store it.

Because so many people own weapons, it would take time for the law to become effective. Probably reform will have to be implemented state by state to get experience with effective and acceptable systems. Radical proposals have lost at the polls, so moderate approaches should be attempted. Citizen-based public-interest groups could be especially important. The strong Japanese gun control law, incidentally, was not a product of its history or culture. It was imposed by American occupation forces after World War II. Sometimes Americans baffle the Japanese.

Self-Victimizing Crimes. Certain illnesses and immorality as defined by the dominant culture have long been treated as crimes. Police, courts, detention facilities, and rehabilitation waste time handling such problems. Abortion used to be an example of such a crime; changing the law lowered the crime rate. Much enforcement effort goes into drugs, drinking, gambling, and sex offenses, which involve voluntary participation or, in the case of alcoholism and some drug addiction, pathological dependency on a drug. Such activities do not have to be condoned or left unregulated, but they can probably be better managed by decriminalization. Legislated morality has never worked very well.

Prostitution is a special problem where economic pressures push women into it. Improvement in education and public-service jobs are essential to reduce such pressure. Another aspect of the problem is uneven enforcement, which falls heavily on lower-class streetwalkers and lightly on more affluent call girls. Also, vice crimes are the only category of felonies for which female arrests outnumber arrests of males, yet obviously males are equal participants. In some places, pressure from feminists has led to more equal enforcement and arrests. Prostitutes, being outside the law, find it difficult to use the law when crimes are committed against them, and pimps often brutalize them. Some legislation and regulation of prostitution could make it easier to control the criminal aspects and enforce public health measures. Equally important is an outreach program to help prostitutes find better ways to make a living. In a large, complex, urban society, where a lot of money can be quickly and easily made, there will be some prostitution. We now manage it in a counterproductive, hypocritical way.

The System of Criminal Justice

Now we can turn to the system of criminal justice, each component of which has special problems limiting its effectiveness.

The Police. The police too often have been criticized for problems largely beyond their control, such as social forces, the courts, and detention facilities. Few people realize how relatively few police there are. In 1974 there were 450,000 local police, or 23 per 10,000 people.[5] Considering that these police are spread over three shifts while people live twenty-four-hour days and that many police are committed to administrative and noncriminal duties, there are very few police on duty against crime. Further, police work is increasingly professionalized, mostly for the better, but with some growing problems of loss of discretion, which do not make common sense.

The net result is that citizens must become important in the enforcement process. Yet citizen cooperation is lacking in the central cities where the crime rates are highest. Central city police forces often have problems of white racism, where mostly white police work mostly black areas. The problem is especially severe in lower-income and high crime areas of central cities, where the police are so overwhelmed that they, too, often become part of the problem, alienating local people and themselves engaging in crime. Police may become a self-protective gang, lying, planting evidence, verbally and physically abusing people, and using cover charges, such as loitering or resisting arrest, to hide their actions. Once such corruption becomes established, it can worsen and spread, becoming all the more difficult to eradicate when finally discovered. Increased killings of policemen lead to a defensive, suspicious, and paranoid attitude of good and bad cops alike, part of the difficult situation they work in. Black police officers have an especially difficult time on many big city forces, getting too little support within their departments and on the streets.

Rates of solving crime are extremely low. Only about 25 percent of property crimes are solved, although the perpetrators may be identified with other crimes. Most stolen property is never recovered, a result of the mobility, size, and impersonality of our cities.

Most departments now have a quasi-military system, rigid hierarchy, a highly defined police role, and a division between detectives and patrolmen. Periodic rotation of duties and use of cars inhibit policemen on the beat from knowing people. Yet the typical patrolling system may be irrelevant for crime. Kansas City, for example, tripled patrol cars in one area, kept the normal number in another, and had no cars in a third. All three areas had the same crime rates, the same level of citizen reporting, and the same citizen perceptions of protection.

Other techniques have shown much more promise. Police-run fencing operations (seventy-one in forty-one cities from 1974 to 1978) have recovered $163 million in loot and led to the arrest of over 6,500 suspects.[6] Other examples include patrolling high crime areas at times that crimes are likely to be committed, police acting as decoys by imitating typical robbery victims, as undercover agents, psychiatric screening and counseling for cops, and programs to talk with citizens and merchants. Talking can lead to better self-protection by citizens and better police awareness of citizen needs. Having police teach in junior high schools can open up communications with alienated youth, helping them understand what police are allowed to do and what rights they have.

The victimization data leave out one important type, on whom we have no statistics and against whom the crimes involve small amounts of money or simple assaults. This type, perhaps the most submerged of all victims, is the boy growing up in a high crime area. He is intimidated and shaken down by older youths, and he lacks defenses. He does not know to turn to the police, who are very unlikely to believe him and lack the manpower to provide protection. The boy comes to believe that might makes right and falls into the same criminal pattern as he grows up. Community organizations and youth programs in which police take part can help, but most are too small compared with the size of the problem.

Beyond these specific opportunities lies a more profound challenge: humanizing the police role without losing professionalism. Police need to be taught more social science and to learn psychological techniques that work better than force and legalism. Patrolmen need broader discretion and responsibilities, blurring the patrolman-detective distinction. Social services that build or destroy trust between people and police form about 80 percent of policework. Lost children, drunks, burglary prevention, noise complaints, family fights, parking, and so on can be handled in ways that pay off for citizen cooperation against serious crime. The most dangerous aspect of police work, in fact, is intervening in family fights. Police programs can be linked to family counseling. For example, on a first call the police can calm the parties involved and bring in a trained family counselor, who also meets later with the couple. If a second call has to be made, it goes to the counselor. Similarly, youths with first offenses can be diverted before trial to intensive training and counseling programs.

This new kind of professionalism deemphasizes arrest and citation statistics; it emphasizes a social-problem-solving attitude and working with other agencies. One suburban city using these techniques cut its burglary rate 8 percent over three years while the rate in cities of similar size went up 39 percent.[7]

The Courts. The courts are failing at swiftness of decision and certainty of punishment for grave offenses, especially in those large urban jurisdictions where crime rates are so high. Prosecution is managed by district attorneys and their staffs. In many places, their work load is too great to push cases against defendants who have aggressive legal defense. Quite apart from the merits of the case, they are forced to negotiate pleas. Lawyers on both sides may prefer negotiation to keep the cases under their control. Judges are so swamped that they are almost always willing to accede to the lawyers' agreements. Typically, the charges are reduced in exchange for a plea of guilty, called plea copping. Reduced charges means reduced punishment and the problem of misdemeanor punishment for felony crimes. Rarely do first offenders go to prison. For each 1,000 serious crimes, 20 people are arrested and 6 are eventually found guilty.[8]

Judges in the local district courts are in a difficult situation. The Supreme Court has sought procedural perfection, resulting in an elaboration of rules often beyond the capacity of even professionalized institutions to administer. Any deviation from the rules may mean a new trial; at worst, obviously guilty people go free because of minor procedural mistakes.

Judges must also choose between equally unsatisfactory kinds of sentences. They can send the culprit to state or federal prison, where he (almost all of the seven index crimes are committed by men) is likely to mature into a hardened criminal, or they can put him on probation, where he will receive so little real help that he is likely to commit another crime. The prison option is very expensive for taxpayers; the probation option is expensive for victims. Similar problems exist for jails (detention for a year or less, run by local governments) and parole (like probation, only it comes after serving some time in prison).

Judges and prison authorities have also tried to make the punishment fit the criminal rather than the crime. A person judged contrite and responsive to rehabilitation might be sentenced lightly; a person judged to be hardened receives a long term. Although this approach makes some sense, it has the problem that middle-class people more often receive light sentences than lower-class people do. Similar problems exist where punishment is lowered for diminished capacity (temporary craziness) and insanity. The affluent can also afford delay, better lawyers, and bail, and for these and many other reasons, the system is biased against the less articulate, the poor, and the minorities. More and more recognition is being given to the public's right to a swift trial and to fixed punishments, regardless of who committed the crime.

Many of the improved procedures result in improved justice, but the increasing case loads mean that we should consider greatly expanding our courts, making them more efficient, and reducing their case loads. Expansion and management reforms are gradually being made by the system. Citizen pressure, however, seems necessary to reduce case loads by legislative actions. The courts handle many unnecessary areas (self-victimizing crimes, for example). There are many examples from civil law that could better be handled administratively: auto accidents, landlord-tenant disputes, bill collections, judicial ratifications to make settlements free of taxes, divorce, child custody, adoptions, mental illness and senility problems, conservatorships, execution of wills, medical malpractice, bankruptcy, and so on. Administrative decisions could be appealed to the courts. Workmen's compensation, for example, is handled administratively and does not overburden the courts. When California adopted no-fault divorce and Massachusetts adopted no-fault auto insurance, the burden on their courts decreased. Arbitration systems need to be developed for many more kinds of civil disputes. More people can get swifter, less expensive justice in these ways.

Some reforms for managerial efficiency are sufficiently controversial and important that citizens should become involved. Judges, like other professionals in public employ, tend not to have their performance reviewed. There is often less review of their qualifications than for a teacher when an appointment is made, yet the judge gets a kind of instant tenure. The inevitable judicial incompetence, laziness, and bias is thus harder to root out. Judicial appointments are made as political favors in many areas. In others, progress has been made by using commissions on judicial qualifications. We also need ways to measure performance. Does a backlog result from too many cases or a poor judge? Procedures nominally allowing such review are dominated by the judges they are supposed to regulate.

Other reforms include reducing the use of juries in civil cases, making more efficient use of jurors' time, and speeding up jury selection. Jury duty too often wastes jurors' time.

Delay in the courts has probably done more to keep innocent people in jail than mistaken convictions. A census in 1972 of 4,000 city and county jails revealed that 57 percent of prisoners being held had not been convicted of the crime for which they were detained. Over a third were awaiting trial and the rest were awaiting arraignment or transfer to other authorities.[9] In a few cases, the nature of the crime or the prisoner warrants detention, but usually people are kept because they cannot afford bail. For many minor offenses, when the person finally comes to trial, they are sentenced to time served and released; thus they are punished first and judged second. Accused persons can be released without bail on their own recognizance—that is, their own word that they will show up for trial. One program interviews prisoners to see if they have community ties and are considered reliable. Prisoners released in this way showed up 96 percent of the time for trial, a better record than for those posting bail, and hundreds of thousands of dollars of jail costs were saved.

Overloaded criminal calendars and jails are not universal. They tend to be more common in big cities and on nights and weekends. To some extent, bringing in extra judges on a temporary basis can work down a backlog of cases, a managerial issue easy to implement. More difficult to implement politically is night and weekend courts, since judges largely control their working hours. Many jails are like freeways, where the rush hour is Friday night to Monday morning. Current calendars (no backlog of cases) can reduce the size of jails that are needed, as well as increase justice.

Procedural Reform. Reducing the burden on the courts will also require a change of judicial philosophy at the highest levels. Few societies have gone as far as ours to try to make all decisions by rules, eliminating human judgment (or arbitrariness). But our values seem to have become unbalanced toward procedural perfection at the cost of substantive justice considering all aspects of a problem. For example, challenges to the procedures implementing a California law to get drunk drivers off the road have prevented its implementation, costing perhaps a thousand lives a year. Meanwhile, certain European countries have implemented far tougher laws and saved thousands of lives. How much is the freedom to loiter near public toilets worth to us in relation to reducing deaths from drug addiction? Suppose we decide that felony defendants should be given an attorney if they cannot afford one. Should we then make this decision retroactive? A limited retroactivity would merely be expensive, but the actual decision applied to Florida in 1963 led to over 6,000 post-conviction motions to overthrow convictions that were constitutional when they were made and for which retrial was difficult or impossible because of cold evidence. A large part of the court burden is reconsideration of cases long decided. The Supreme Court itself cannot guarantee infallibility, only a limited finality.

Similar congestion is generated when federal courts consider the same cases as state courts in order to ensure due process and equal protection required by the Fourteenth Amendment. Overuse of this "collateral attack" on a state court judgment has generated thousands of federal cases and lowered the importance of the state court systems. Moreover, errors can be made by a higher court. In *Miller* v. *Pate* (1967), the Supreme Court clearly misunderstood the evidence that convicted the rape-murderer of a child eleven years earlier, resulting in his release.

The quest for perfect procedure has resulted in congestion, delay, and injustice. Accused persons can go to federal courts concerning any part of a state trial any time, delaying or stopping state action in the name of getting injunctive relief, declaratory relief, civil rights protection, and removal to federal courts. If the prosecution or judge makes a mistake, the trial may be aborted because of the protection of defendants against double jeopardy, but a mistake by the defense can lead to as many as five trials. Every trial has several issues, each one of which may be reviewed many times, once at each stage of a single court proceeding. Convicts with talent or money can become indefatigable litigants clogging the system. Trials are diverted to side issues or each phase of the main proceeding is slowed as much as possible. Jury selections become filibusters taking many weeks, while in England the most difficult cases take a few minutes. Esparza, a burglar caught in the act in December 1968, was not sentenced until March 1970, fourteen months for a simple case when two is supposed to be the maximum. Prosecutors, defenders, judges, and even court reporters and clerks procrastinate.[10] But the primary responsibility falls to the judge.

One typical reason for attack on a judgment is competency of counsel or mistakes in self-representation. In some cases, the reason may be valid, but the trend is to argue it regardless of the substance of the rest of the trial. Instead of denying frivolous appeals by the affluent, judges have tended to allow them to the poor. Situations can develop in which a defendant may refuse to cooperate with his defense attorney because he wants to defend himself, but self-defense may lead to reversal of the decision because the defendant was incompetent to act as his own attorney. Noncooperation with the attorney leads to lack of defense, also grounds for possible reversal. Multiple defendants can conflict among each other, some demand separate trials, others, joint trials. Alleged defects in jury instruction are another grounds for appeal, and there are many others.[11]

Of all the grounds for attacking decisions, one that seems to offend popular common sense the most is the suppression of evidence because of technical mistakes by police or prosecution. Undeniable evidence of guilt may be thrown out for such reasons, sometimes allowing the guilty to go free. In these cases, guilt becomes irrelevant. The loss of substantive justice is greatly out of proportion to the nature of the mistake in many cases, but judges have not been given any other tool to discourage misconduct. They need a way to sanction the police for their mistakes proportionate to the mistake, without ignoring the evidence of crime. Rules for suppression are now so complex that they are difficult to administer and provide ample means for lawyers who are seeking reversals.[12] The English system works far better; it allows trial judges to suppress questionable evidence only if they think the police acted unfairly. Appellate judges avoid second guessing the trial court.

The dilemma for the citizen is that there is no public-interest group for reforming criminal justice comparable to the American Civil Liberties Union. The ACLU, in pursuing full implementation of the Bill of Rights, fulfills a public interest, but the balancing of values requires protection of the public from crime, probably better pursued by a group organized for that purpose. Most law-and-order groups, however, take too simplistic an approach. The trend of law that has produced court congestion came one decision at a time by intelligent people, and reversing the trend will be a similar process. Without reform, disrespect for the courts and fear of crime could sweep away valuable protections of our basic procedures.

Sentencing and Punishment. Convicted persons are often not punished for their crimes, and punishments vary from judge to judge and place to place. In one large California suburb, burglary rates were soaring; two-thirds of them were attributable to heroin addicts. The police chief asked the local judges to send convicted addicts to jail, which they started to do, and burglaries declined by half in five months. (Neighborhood alert contributed also.) [13] In 1977 a borderline mental defective with a long record of felonies shot and killed a police officer. He had escaped from a low-security jail because the system did not supply the report needed to place him in a high-security prison. He had been sent to jail for a burglary committed while on probation for another crime and after his escape had killed a ninety-three-year-old man. He had been sent to state prison for this crime but was released in 1976 because prison authorities had not received any information about his background.[14] The public image of an ineffective criminal justice is shaped by stories such as these, but the statistics on sentencing are just as frightening.

Over two-thirds of felony arrests are dropped without trial because of insufficient evidence or uncooperative witnesses. Twenty-three percent of those charged with robbery in Los Angeles were out on bail, probation, or parole at the time. New Orleans keeps habitual offenders in jail longer and sets bail higher; its arrest rate of ex-convicts was only 7 percent. One-fifth of delayed trials in Los Angeles were due to fugitive defendants. When prosecutors make an effort to go to trial and avoid bargaining, they can increase felony convictions markedly; one city almost doubled the number sent to prison in one year. Meanwhile, in one major city 90 percent of burglars with a major prior record are not sent to prison.[15] Also, prosecutors and police cannot keep convicts in jail; it is up to judges and prison authorities, and premature release causes crime.

It is now fashionable to say that rehabilitation through parole and probation does not work. It would be more accurate to say that parole and probation officers have been too overworked, and that parole and probation have been granted too indiscriminately to violent persons. Nevertheless, it is true that the record of serious rehabilitation efforts is mixed, and we do now know how to cause rehabilitation.[16] We are beginning to realize that the commitment to live within the law is made primarily by the person. We also know that we can put people in detention, and, while detained, they do not commit crimes against the general public.

Because crime is not just a result of social conditions but also a learned and even rational behavior, punishment for crime is essential to stop it. Most crime is committed by repeaters. In one study of 10,000 adolescents of Philadelphia, 6 percent had committed five or more offenses by the time they were eighteen. This 6 percent committed two-thirds of all the violent crimes committed by the whole group. Another study indicated that crime could be cut to one-third the present level in New York City by keeping repeaters in detention. Deterrence and rehabilitation could produce even more gains.[17] England, to follow up on previous comparisons, sends many more of its burglars to prison, and has a much lower crime rate.

Rehabilitation. One appeal of rehabilitation is to save upward of $23,000 per prisoner per year of tax money and convert the convict into a taxpayer. Unfortunately, many programs seem to be based more on a desire to save money than to be effective. With recidivism rates approaching 80 percent, it may seem hopeless to try at all. Having stressed the importance of punishment, it may seem contradictory to stress the importance of rehabilitation. Yet the two are not necessarily contradictory, any more than discipline and acceptance are contradictory. Intensive rehabilitation for young first offenders is a very promising area.

Rehabilitation has a physical and a social aspect. Much of penal reform consists of improving physical prison conditions. Prisons (and jails) generally need to be smaller and have adequate food, space, medical care, and exercise space for the health of the prisoner. When released, the person needs some way to earn a living. The social aspect, however, is equally important. The prisoner-guard relationship tends to be dehumanizing for both. Prisoners are treated as powerless losers, reinforcing their unconscious self-images and identification with the criminal life. Rehabilitation will not work until social aspects of rehabilitation become as recognized as physical aspects. Generally physical conditions range from inhumane to good; social conditions range from inhumane to poor. The most important category for rehabilitation is nonviolent prisoners from lower-class backgrounds. Middle-class prisoners tend to rehabilitate themselves, and prisoners with records of repeated violence tend to be extremely difficult to reach.

Of about 220,000 persons in prisons and about 140,000 in jails, about 96 percent are men.[18] Many (and in some categories, most) jails lack educational, recreational, medical, and visiting facilities. Perhaps 5 percent of expenditures in prisons goes into health, education, job training, and other rehabilitation; the rest is spent on custody. Yet this custody does not prevent the development of gangs among prisoners that dominate the social environment as prisoners mix among themselves. Prison environments are often more lawless than free society; deaths, suicides, maiming, torture, homosexual rapes, and beatings are all too common, especially where prisoners are kept in large dormitory rooms without guards inside all night.

Prisoners can make life impossible for a guard who tries to control their rackets and smuggling from the outside. They may cause disturbances when the guard is on duty to give him a bad reputation. Such a guard may get dismissed because "he cannot handle the prisoners." Because of overcrowding, mattresses may be placed on the floor next to urinals, and juveniles may be mixed with hardened criminals and the mentally ill. In some states, prisoners are made "trusties" and are given guns to guard the other prisoners. Prisoners do all of the menial work of running a prison, which reduces costs, but there is not enough rehabilitative work to keep them busy and to teach them needed skills. Prisoner complaints about cruel and unusual punishment are systematically ignored by the courts. Sometimes special efforts with support of outside groups can get action. In 1976 a judge ruled the whole Alabama state prison system unconstitutional as cruel and unusual punishment.

Successful rehabilitation programs avoid the authoritarian and distant relationships with prisoners that seem to characterize the unsuccessful programs. Tom Murton's effort in Arkansas demonstrated some possibilities. As warden he improved the physical conditions by ending mismanagement and allowed prisoners to elect their own leaders for deciding work assignments and discipline. He was able to eliminate most criminal activities—the rackets and victimizing of weak prisoners—within prisons. Murton also discovered a burying ground for murdered prisoners, implicating previous wardens. They were well connected politically, and Murton was dismissed. The cases were not prosecuted, and conditions reverted to roughly their previous level. In 1970 a federal judge threatened to close the whole system if improvements were not made.

Rehabilitation also includes helping released prisoners. In some cases, release can be gradual, allowing a person to go out to work, go to school, get medical help, or visit their family. Getting jobs is especially important and difficult because most employers are rightfully suspicious of employing ex-convicts. Special programs are needed here, including more training and public service jobs. Halfway houses can provide a place to live and to associate with law-abiding people while a job and another place to live are found. Possibly half the people going to prison have not committed violent crimes. Work furlough and restitution to the victim could work better than straight imprisonment. Rehabilitation is helped by a close social relationship with the ex-convict as a person, to discover and help in crucial areas of weakness. Rehabilitation does not work from formulas but from caring, an extra effort that evokes and reinforces a positive commitment.

There are many other aspects to reform of the criminal justice system. Citizens need to become involved both in volunteering direct assistance to juveniles, prisoners, and ex-convicts and in lobbying politically for effective punishment and rehabilitation. Some reforms—night and weekend courts, use of restitution and fines, arbitration and reconciliation services, decriminalization of self-victimizing crimes, intensive supervision and job assistance for first offenders of nonviolent crimes, and therapeutic living centers—will decrease prison populations. Other reforms—fixed sentences for repeat and violent offenders—will increase prison populations. Still others involve setting up profitable prison industries, giving prisoners skills and income and lowering prison costs. In or out of confinement, people would benefit from more considerate social treatment and adequate physical settings.

Upper-class Crime

Organized crime, corporate crime, and other types of crime are important but in different ways from the crimes discussed so far. Organized crime and corporate crime are characterized not by the commission of acts but rather conspiracy to have others commit acts. Yet such crime is also similar in many ways to other types of crime. For example, attitudes and techniques are learned in the home and on the job from associates and superiors. The same rationalizations are used to legitimize behavior and deny guilt. There is a similar code of feigned forgetfulness, ignorance, silence and the use of law and lawyers to avoid punishment. The difference is that affluent criminals face weaker laws, less enforcement effort, smaller chance of being caught, and even smaller probability of punishment. Further, they are better organized, plan better, and make more money.

Organized crime emphasizes gambling, loan sharking, and scamming businesses (bankrupting them or bleeding them illegally). It also includes labor racketeering, cigarette smuggling, hijacking, and consumer fraud. A couple of dozen "Mafia" families of largely Sicilian extraction have been identified, each dominating a city or region, but other ethnic groups and persons are active, especially in the volatile drug traffic. The level of this kind of criminal activity depends largely on the amount of enforcement effort by police and prosecutors. Organized crime typically seeks out corruption and pays off crooked officials. In a typical cycle, sooner or later, the activity becomes too big and visible, and media exposure occurs, leading to public concern and a special prosecution effort. Within a few years, however, the criminal activity picks up again, largely because the public is tolerant of such activities, actively seeks them out, or is too scared to inform police.

Enforcement has been made more difficult in recent years because organized crime has learned to hide its activities in a maze of corporations, financial transactions, and secret bank accounts. Such manipulation allows them to receive their money with the appearance that it was legally earned (called *dry cleaning*). These criminals pay their income taxes very carefully. Enforcement has been made more effective by improvements in the protection of witnesses, granting them immunity from prosecution and, at some expense, giving them new identities and jobs far from where they are known. Court-ordered eavesdropping and taps on telephones can also be very effective. Certain kinds of organized crime could best be reduced by changing laws—for example, legalizing certain forms of gambling and even using it to raise public money, as certain states have done. Changes in drug laws—decriminalizing marijuana, for example—could take some of the profit out of drug abuse. These two examples are closely related to the self-victimizing crime problem and are reminiscent of an earlier crusade, prohibition. Cigarette smuggling might be eliminated with a uniform nationwide cigarette tax with proceeds redistributed to states. Such a tax could also discourage smoking and be a source of tax revenues.

Corporate crime is probably best defined by the kinds of laws that generally respectable companies are prone to break, laws that have little or no criminal sanctions and that are too often vague in describing just what is illegal. These laws are tax laws (problems of incredible length and complexity), product safety laws, labor bargaining laws, warranty and guarantee laws, antitrust laws (price collusion, unfair practices), worker safety laws, equal employment and equal pay laws, building codes, laws against advertising deception, and pollution laws. Large corporate legal costs are deductible as a business expense, and no systematic crime records are kept on corporations. Standard Oil of California, for example, left off a required valve on offshore wells in Louisiana. A storm broke the pipes, leading to oil pollution of ocean and coast and their wildlife. Standard fought the number of violations down from 900 to 400, pleaded no contest to the remaining ones, and paid a $1 million fine, equivalent to a $10 ticket for a person making $25,000 a year.[19] The criminal records of individuals stay with them for life, but there are no similar records indicating that Standard is at least a 400-time loser. Some companies try to place a stigma of unreasonableness on the law enforcement agencies. Some laws and enforcement may indeed be unreasonable, but the intensity problem gives the companies excessive influence.

Recent important cases include insurance fraud (Equity Funding), violations of oil price controls by major companies, numerous price fixing and pollution cases (such as the automobile industry's conspiracy to delay smog devices or U.S. Steel's long legal war against the EPA), Medicaid frauds, grain company export frauds, self-dealing by having a bank lend to companies all owned by the same person, illegal contributions to politicians, infected intravenous solutions, and increasing business tax frauds.

Unevenness of sentencing is a problem. The man who pulled off "one of the largest systematic lootings of a public company ever recorded in the history of this country" (C. Arnholt Smith) did not go to prison. In 1974, about 1,100 persons were convicted of income tax fraud, of whom about 400 went to prison, mostly for less than six months. Also in 1974 about 1,600 persons were convicted of stealing cars, of whom about 1,100 went to prison with an average sentence of over three years.[20] Systematic data on sentencing are not readily available although there are some examples of stiff penalties for upper-class criminals. The lack of data reflects the lack of public and elite interests as compared with lower-class crimes. Many people seem to feel that it is much worse to rob directly than indirectly, with a gun rather than with a pen. Yet the sums involved in corporate and organized crime are substantial and are definitely comparable with other sorts of crime. Unlike many other areas of policy, there is no effective national public-interest group concerned in a sophisticated way with these issues, making it difficult for citizens to be effective.

Our passivity in the face of crime parallels that of many other problems. Reasonable and specific solutions worth trying are not being implemented—in fact, are not being popularized to get support. Americans tolerate crime rates much higher than in most other places and which drastically lower the quality of life. The primary level of government in this area is the state, which would have to implement most of the reforms outlined. Reform evidently requires a significant increase of state-oriented public-interest groups for criminal justice reform.

Health

Americans have made many advances in health and enjoy generally high levels of health. Life expectancy has steadily been growing longer, and infant and maternal mortality have gradually declined. Many causes of death have declined in importance, and many communicable diseases have been all but eliminated. More than 90 percent of Americans have health insurance or are eligible for public programs. Most Americans are happy with the quality of care that they receive, and most receive the world's highest level of care. The United States has a surplus of hospital beds, has an adequate supply of health professionals, and leads the world in health research.

To obtain this generally high level of health, we spent $163 billion in 1977 ($700 per person) and expected to spend about $200 billion in 1979. Our GNP commitment rose from 4.5 percent in 1950 to 8.8 percent of a much larger GNP in 1977. Did we get our money's worth? Health reformers would say definitely not. Our life expectancies rank from eighth to twenty-second place, depending on what tables are used. Sweden, which spends about as much of its GNP on health as we do, ranks first, with male life expectancy about five years greater and female life expectancy about two and a half years greater than ours. Other countries spend much less than we do but get results as good or better.

The two major areas of failing in American health policy are in prevention and in care for the needy. Both areas have a common cause in the excessive influence of profit-making systems in government. Companies that sell unhealthy products resist reforms that would reduce use of those products. Companies with unhealthy work places resist regulation to make them safer. Doctors and hospitals resist effective regulation and socialization of the health system. The media seem quick to criticize some aspects of foreign public health services without recognizing their success in relation to the resources used. Sweden ranks first in public expenditure; we rank thirteenth. Our fear of "socialized medicine" may be dangerous for our health. Yet few realize how far we have moved to a public system of health finance. About 42 percent of health expenditures are paid directly by government, and another 4 percent is spent through tax loopholes that subsidize health care for high-income people.[21]

Health care costs are rising faster than the rate of inflation, especially for hospitals, without a corresponding increase in health. About one death in eight could be prevented with proper medical intervention. About one-fourth of women are not seeing a doctor during the first three months of pregnancy. Only 30 percent of sexually active teenagers are using contraceptives. Over one-third of the people over forty have never had an electrocardiogram to check their hearts. Half of all Americans did not see a dentist in 1977, and a fifth had not seen one for at least five years. About 5 percent have no insurance or public program protection, and another 15 percent lack protection against health catastrophes. About 9 percent of families have medical expenses out of pocket of more than 15 percent of their income.[22]

Blacks have a 70 percent higher rate of infant mortality and have five times the white level of maternal mortality. They are four times more likely to die of hypertensive heart disease and chronic kidney disease and five times more likely to die of tuberculosis.[23] Blacks have much higher rates of hypertension and liver disease. Migrant workers are even worse off, as are native Americans. The statistics fail to convey the real tragedy. In May 1977, Lorie Ann Cardosa, a four and a half year old, died near Tampa, Florida. She had been playing around a migrant labor camp, where she had locked herself in an abandoned refrigerator and suffocated. She was revived partially, and the doctor sent her to a hospital with better facilities, but she was not admitted there, or to three other hospitals, because her family could not pay. After an hour and a half of traveling around in an ambulance, she suffered a severe heart seizure and died. The major reason for her death was that she was the child of migrant farm workers. Less dramatic but just as real are those who die by degrees, worn out by stoop labor. Agriculture is the third most dangerous occupation, and one-fourth of farm workers are children.[24]

The problems of physical health are well summarized in table 5–4, which uses a conventional approach to causes of death. The leading killer is heart disease, followed by cancer.

These statistics are incomplete in one major respect, involving a problem of perception by almost everyone. The most available and publicized American statistics focus on causes of death with no regard to age. Yet the most important deaths are the premature deaths, and the more years lost against normal life expectancy, the more important it is. Such deaths have a serious impact on longevity rates, yet the causes of such deaths are radically different from those of old age.

In table 5–4, accidents ranked fifth and sixth as causes of death; in table 5–5, they rank first and third, with motor vehicle accidents the most important cause of death in our society. Both tables leave out important causes of death that could be reduced by better public policy: diseases of early infancy (caused often by poor nutrition and sanitation), bronchitis, emphysema, and asthma (caused often by smoking and air pollution), and homicide (caused in part by a defective system of criminal justice and the lack of social reform). Similarly, diseases listed in table 5–4 are preventable, as well as the next four most common diseases of mumps and measles (prevented by innoculation), infectious hepatitis (prevented by good sanitation), and tuberculosis (prevented by good diet and public health controls).

The goal of reform is to prevent illness and accident and to provide basic health care for everyone. Health is necessary for the enjoyment of the freedoms guaranteed in the Constitution and for equality of opportunity. In discussing this area, we will look at prevention in terms of promoting health and of regulation; then we will examine the care delivery system and its problems of inflated costs, training and licensing, organization and finance, and mental health.

Table 5–4 Health Statistics

Major mortality indexes	*1950*	*1976*
Female life expectancy	71.1	76.7
Male life expectancy	65.6	69.0
Infant mortality (per 1,000 live births)	29.2	15.2
Maternal mortality (per 1,000 life births)	83.3	12.3
Leading causes of death (per 100,000) [a]		
1. Heart disease (mainly ischemic heart disease)	357	337
2. Cancer	140	176
3. Cerebrovascular diseases	104	88
4. Influenza and pneumonia	31	29
5. Accidents other than motor vehicle	38	25
6. Motor vehicle accidents	23	22
7. Diabetes mellitus	16	16
8. Cirrhosis of liver	9	15
9. Arteriosclerosis	20	14
10. Suicide	11	13
Temporary disability and disease		
Restricted activity days per person (includes bed-disability, work-loss, and school-loss days)	16.2 [b]	18.2
Acute injuries per 100 population	29.6 [c]	32.1
Leading reportable diseases in thousands of new cases per year		
Gonorrhea	287	1,002
Streptococcal sore throat, scarlet fever	65	395
Chicken pox	N.A.	184
Syphilis	218	72
Acute infestive, parasitic, respiratory, and digestive system conditions (millions)	291 [c]	325
Chronic disability		
Limited in major activity, all ages	9%	11%
Limited in major activity, 65 and over (leading causes are heart conditions, arthritis, and rheumatism)	37%	39%

[a] In 1976, heart disease caused 38 percent of all deaths and cancer 20 percent of all deaths.

[b] The figures are for 1960.

[c] The figures are for 1970.

Source: *Statistical Abstract of the United States, 1978,* pp. 69, 74, 75, 117, 120, 121; ibid., *1975,* p. 64.

Table 5–5 Most Important Causes of Death, 1971

Cause	*Years of Life Lost before 70*
Motor vehicle accidents	213,000
Ischemic heart disease (artery contracts cutting oxygen to heart muscle)	193,000
All other accidents	179,000
Respiratory diseases and lung cancer	140,000
Suicide	69,000

Note: Population is for Canadians; data exclude infant mortality. Comparable data for the United States are not available.

Source: Marc Lalonde, *A New Perspective on the Health of Canadians* (Ottawa: Information Canada, April 1974), pp. 14–15.

The most productive way to improve health is to prevent accident and disease. The human body, so incredibly complex, resilient, and vulnerable, is more easily maintained than repaired. Except for old age and certain mental and developmental disabilities, the need for treatment is a sign of the failure of prevention.

The leading cause of premature death, the motor vehicle, is in some ways imposed on us by our system, yet it also involves self-imposed risks and political, if unconscious, choices. Historically, the effort to reduce the slaughter on the highways has focused on the driver, the most obvious cause of most accidents. Hence, we developed an expensive system of driver training, licensing, and police regulation. Next, the roadway was recognized as a contributory cause, so freeways separated traffic flows and avoided intersections, and signal and road marking systems developed, as well as engineering standards and maintenance systems. Third, activist Ralph Nader exposed the vehicle itself as a contributory cause, and automobiles were made safer. All of these themes are important today, making our roads safer than they were. Perhaps the major weakness now is the lenient treatment of drunk driving. In the future, development of mass transit, bicycles, and walking can eliminate the need for cars for most routine trips, especially in the density with quality setting. Meanwhile, motorcycle, van, and truck deaths are soaring.

Health Promotion

The majority of people are not sick, but they are not as healthy as they could be. Their poor condition has to be explained in terms of a lack of insight and willpower. Popular health education for adults is virtually ignored in government policy. Health-related messages are delivered to everyone by the private sector, and they are nearly completely against health and in favor of alcohol, tobacco, sugary foods, useless self-prescribed medications, and cosmetic treatment of social and psychological problems. Over a billion dollars a year is spent by a gullible public on generally overpriced, useless, or dangerous medications like aspirin, cold remedies, vitamins and minerals, laxatives, and laetrile. We are urged to fulfill our personalities or to get the love we need by buying cars, cigarettes, liquor, or a certain brand of coffee. Prime-time television is loaded with slick appeals to our materialism and insecurity. Its assault is both on our pocketbooks and on our psyches, a threat to our physical and mental health, which continues because it works.

A man forty-five years old can add eleven years to his life, and a woman seven years to her life, by following seven simple rules, according to a large-scale research project: eat regularly and not between meals; eat breakfast; get about eight hours of sleep per night for men, seven for women; keep close to normal body weight; do not smoke; do not drink too much; and exercise regularly. Medical science cannot lengthen life as much as these simple rules can.[25]

Would people respond to educational efforts? Are we somehow susceptible to negative appeals and not to positive ones? A Stanford University experiment tried to find out if heart disease could be so prevented. In one town, information was distributed by local newspaper, radio, and television stations and by local physicians. Ninety families received personal instruction; others received pamphlets. One other town got less effort, and one town got none. Six hundred people statistically selected in each town were interviewed after a while and given physicals. Within two years, 44 percent of the sample from the first town had given up smoking. Their saturated fat consumption had decreased significantly. They demonstrated knowledge about how to prevent heart disease. Blood pressure and cholesterol decreased significantly. Weight reduction remained a problem but might have been tied into quitting smoking and lack of exercise emphasis. The second town had a slight improvement, and the third town none.[26] Many public health experts are thinking about an advocacy approach.

Elements of health education include diet, mental health, home and auto safety, emergency aid techniques such as cardiopulmonary resuscitation, self-monitoring and home monitoring of blood pressure and other conditions as appropriate for people at risk and the chronically ill, the hazards of self-medication, child health and safety, and venereal disease. We will look at four of these here.

Smoking. It is increasingly recognized that alcohol is a dangerous drug in our society, more dangerous than heroin, but the fact is that tobacco is far more deadly than alcohol and may involve a deeper addiction. Although there are about 5.5 million alcoholics in the country, there are about 50 million smokers. Classic alcoholic deaths from cirrhosis of the liver run in the tens of thousands; classic smoker deaths from lung cancer run around 200,000 per year.[27] Overwhelming scientific evidence shows that the more we smoke, the sicker we are and the sooner we die. After 500 pages of summarized statistical research, one report concluded: "No single known measure would lengthen the life or improve the health of the American population more than eliminating cigarette smoking." [28] Smoking cuts wind, increases the pulse rate, causes chest pains, raises blood pressure, incapacitates hemoglobin, and puts into the air such poisons as carbon monoxide, particulates, tar, nicotine, 3–4 benzpyrene, ammonia, and cadmium.

Smoking is the major cause of lung cancer, chronic bronchitis, and emphysema and a leading cause of heart disease and arteriosclerosis. Smoking is a major cause of accidents, especially fires. Smoking workers are less productive because of the distraction of smoking, sickness, and premature death. Sixty years ago, lung cancer was a rare disease; now it is the major form of cancer, and the rate is still growing, while most other forms have decreased as a cause of death. Lung cancer is deadly; 90 percent who get it are dead within five years. In emphysema, air sacs of the lung stiffen and rupture, the body is chronically short of oxygen, and there is shortness of breath, chronic cough, quick exhaustion, and, finally, death.

The number of smokers has been growing since 1950, spending $14 billion per year to do so in the face of clear warnings extensively reported. Nicotine clearly is addicting, far more powerfully so than is commonly realized or admitted. The effort to reach youth is inadequate. Smoking rates among teenage girls are on the rise, more than compensating for the declining number of older male smokers.

When tobacco advertisements were banned from television in 1971, expenditures for that purpose declined by $146 million, but the industry is still spending about $400 million (as compared with advertisements for all forms of alcohol at about $300 million).[29] Other dangerous drugs are prohibited from advertising to the general public. Tobacco advertising is 5.3 percent of all advertising sales, the highest of any major industry, and tobacco profits, measured as rate of return to investors, were higher than any other industry from 1964 to 1974.[30] The government subsidizes tobacco growers. Industry money swamps meager educational efforts by a ratio probably greater than sixteen to one. The message dominating our media is that smoking is associated with nature, youth, health, sex appeal, and prestige. The reality is that it is associated with bad breath, dirty, smelly surroundings, insecurity, wasted money, addiction, premature aging, poor health, disability, and death.

Smoke does not respect nonsmokers' air space, and much evidence indicates adverse effects of ambient smoke on nonsmokers. Under pressure from public-interest lawyers, notably John Bahnzaf of Action on Smoking and Health (ASH), and from newly organized groups of nonsmokers, smoking is increasingly being prohibited from public places. Second-hand smoke is particularly dangerous because it is not filtered by the tobacco or filters, and cigar and pipe smokes are worse than cigarettes. Nonsmokers affected include the young; even stillbirths and infant deaths are higher among smokers.

The American Cancer Society, the American Lung Association, ASH, and many other antismoking and prohealth groups have not been able to use the most effective medium for reaching people—television. They are limited to a few public-service spots and are unable to launch a well-financed campaign. Yet in 1970, some of the most powerful advertisements ever seen on television were required to be broadcast under the fairness doctrine, another Bahnzaf initiative. One particularly effective advertisement showed a well-known actor describing his impending death from lung cancer. The impact was increased when the man died, and the advertisement continued to be shown. Smoking began to slow. Unfortunately, when prosmoking advertising went off the air, the antismoking advertisements went off also, and the fairness doctrine does not apply to the print media. Smoking began to rise again. In 1978 a new federal effort against smoking was launched.

A high nationwide tax on tobacco could raise revenues to improve health. Because of inflation, the excise tax on cigarettes is less than half the value it used to be. The cost, probably over $12 billion in health care, welfare, and lost productivity, is paid by society as a whole. Antismoking advertising could be reinstituted, and school programs could be strengthened. Tobacco subsidies could be ended. Businesses could offer incentives, as a few have, to stop smoking, and health insurance rates should be lower for nonsmokers. The intensity problem operates with a vengeance to slow reform, yet new hopefulness is generated by groups of nonsmokers lobbying government for increased legislation.

The Swedes have led the way. Even though their consumption is one-third ours, cigarettes in Sweden cost $1.50 a pack, and they are banned from vending machines; sales are limited to tobacco shops. Prosmoking advertisements are banned; antismoking ones are extensive. Moreover, an extensive education program is conducted for children. Swedes are measurably healthier.

Exercise. If smoking is the hard "don't" for Americans, then exercise may be the hard "do." We have become a nation of sitters and riders. Many of us who think of ourselves as healthy are far below an optimum of fitness; we are ambiguously between sickness and real health. Exercise is intimately linked with smoking and weight control. About one-fourth of the population is fifteen or more pounds overweight, and many use the excuse that they smoke to avoid gaining weight.

Exercise reduces weight by burning up calories, but it takes a lot of exercise to burn off a pound, usually more than people are willing to do. Other benefits, however, occur in raising the level of blood sugar (depressing subjective appetite), and in perspiring, requiring a lot of drinking of water, which fills the stomach. The results of exercise can be physiologically measured by a slower resting heartbeat, stronger breathing systems, more blood supply, less cholesterol, more high-density lipoprotein, more muscle mass and tone, and better utilization of oxygen. The average woman who is in shape can run 1.65 miles or more in twelve minutes; the average conditioned man, 1.75 miles or more, even into old age.[31] The subjective benefits are also usually great: better digestion, better sleep, more energy and alertness, less tension and depression, and a greater subjective sense of health and well-being. Employers report greater productivity. Individuals report fewer colds, fewer headaches, less lower back pain, and so on. Exercise can overcome the effects of heart disease and help prevent it. Statistical research on the correlation of exercise with longevity is difficult to do. The best studies look at vigorous frequent exercisers in relation to the less active and in the absence of complicating other high-risk factors. Exercisers have less heart disease and fewer sudden deaths from heart attacks. One such study, for example, looked at 6,351 men over twenty-two years.[32]

Good exercise—running, bicycle riding, and swimming—gets us breathing hard, putting a steady demand on our muscles. Jogging and walking can be effective if done long enough. Frequency is important; the weekend athlete overstresses a weak body.

Government policy does not give a high priority to encouraging exercise and making it easier. Our car-accommodating system means that we do far less walking than Europeans, who by choice and necessity walk more and are somewhat healthier and more fit. Exercise is primarily a problem of adults, but most policy concern goes into schoolchildren. Related points have been made above when discussing the environmental reform of density with quality.

Diet. Diet education would deemphasize red meat, sugar, fat, and salt and emphasize nonmeat protein complementarity, fruits, and vegetables. Meat is expensive and reduces the amount of food available for export to needy nations; excess meat seems to be linked with digestive disorders over the long run. Protein from rice, beans, eggs, cheese, nuts, breads, pastas, milk, and so on may be healthier and is generally cheaper.[33] Some breakfast cereals with 40 percent or more sugar are essentially candies, appealing to the one genetic weakness of a human race that would otherwise eat a balanced diet.

Sugar robs appetite for healthy foods, causes fat and cavities, and contributes to diabetes. The dental crisis alone justifies a massive information campaign about sugar. Statistics indicate that blacks have especially poor diets, a major cause of some of their health problems. They drink too much coffee and soft drinks and too little milk and fruit juice. Excess salt causes high rates of hypertension.[34]

Mental Health. Education on mental health is especially difficult, yet progress is being made. Mental illness is often an extreme form of mental stress, and it is important to know when to go for help. In many cases, depression or schizophrenia will manifest itself quite clearly, but most people, though they know something is wrong, have little specific understanding of what to do. We tend to separate mental and physical health problems in our thinking, but our bodies do not make the same distinction. Smoking, for example, is a mental health problem too. We think of physical health as scientific, treatable, and socially acceptable, while mental illness seems mysterious. Yet more and more we are finding physical health bases for problems that we thought were emotional or social in nature. Similarly, we find our mental attitudes putting our physical health at risk.

The intensity problem makes it unlikely that public demand will produce more health advocacy, especially the television spot advertisements that would be most effective. It is more likely that a growing consensus among professionals, aided by relatively few concerned citizens, will gradually increase educational efforts.

Health Regulation

Consumers. Preventing accident and illness also requires regulation. We have already discussed pollution controls, an important kind of regulation aimed at improving health. Seventy to 80 percent of cancers are thought to be caused by diet, smoking, pollution, cars, and other environmental factors. Yet more funds have gone into treatment for individuals than prevention for whole populations.

Unlike health education, health regulation has been a major thrust of the consumer protection movement. Consumer pressure led to the establishment of the Consumer Product Safety Commission in 1972, which has been concerned with aerosol sprays, flammable fabrics, packaging of household poisons, safety devices for refrigerator doors, toys, and so on. The commission worked with activist shoppers, who became, in effect, unpaid inspectors supplementing the tiny commission staff. About six hundred hazardous toys are successfully being kept out of stores, saving lives and injuries.

In 1970, Ralph Nader's first campaign bore some fruit in the form of the

National Highway Traffic Safety Administration, which has imposed some design changes and safety devices on cars. Related deaths and injuries have declined.

Compulsory seat belt devices, however, bumped up against popular annoyance and resistance. Some people turn off the devices, and many do not use seat belts. How far should the government go in protecting us, even against ourselves? The debate between air bags and seat belts rages on, and a major consideration for air bags is that they, unlike belts, do not require human cooperation to work.

Possible reforms include annual vehicle inspections to reduce pollutants and have seat belts operational, required wearing of belts on arterials, and peremptory proceedings against drunk driving suspects. Countries with such laws have fewer traffic deaths. The Safety Administration has also been slow to act on stronger bumpers and safer gas tanks.[35] What progress was made resulted from pressure from citizen-supported public-interest groups, at least until 1977, when President Carter appointed a reform lobbyist to head the agency.

Unlike the two new agencies just mentioned, the Food and Drug Administration has been around long enough for vested interests to capture excessive influence over it and long enough for consumers to organize counterpressure. With stronger laws and more publicity, the FDA has been improving its performance. Stricter screening of drugs has reduced the number of new drug introductions and removed many harmful or ineffectual drugs from the market. Advertising has been restricted. Our drug law, now the toughest in the world because of reform, is perhaps even too tough, raising questions about the costs of not allowing new drugs on the market. Other countries introduce new drugs first, balancing risks and gains differently from us, perhaps benefiting sooner but also suffering from tests that fail. Everyone wants to protect health, but the balancing of values is complex and difficult. With so much disagreement among disinterested experts and with common sense limited in such a technical area, there is a real question of just what constitutes reform. For the citizen, the practical approach may be to be thankful that drug regulation has been so successful and to concentrate on a multitude of other problems until the experts are more in agreement.

Workers. Regulation for workers is politically a little different from that for consumers because workers have a more intense interest in their work places and often have unions, which can be effective advocates of reform. Possibly 100,000 workers are killed by their jobs each year, about 2.2 million are injured, and about 390,000 contract occupational diseases. These diseases include byssinosis (caused by cotton dust in textile mills), black lung (coal dust in mines), silicosis (sandy dust), arsenic poisoning, asbestosis (asbestos filaments), and poisonings by pesticides, heavy metals, and dangerous chemicals. About 1,680,000 workers in nineteen major noisy industries are likely to suffer hearing loss over their lifetime. Some health threats take time to materialize; not until 1974 did we discover high rates of liver cancer among vinyl chloride workers. Asbestos workers face not only asbestosis but higher death rates from lung cancer and tumors of the abdomen. Coal workers have not just black lung to worry about, but also cave-ins, explosions, and dangerous machinery. Ten times as many days of work are lost from occupational illness and accident as are lost from strikes. Particular industries and plants are very unsafe and have not improved much over the last fifteen years or more.[36]

The general safety of an industry can be measured in terms of lost workdays per hundred full-time employees. Of some fifty industries in 1976, security and commodity brokers seem to be the safest with 4.1 lost workdays. Water transportation workers ranked the worst, with 284 lost workdays. The rest of the most dangerous dozen are, in decreasing order, anthracite mining, lumber and wood products, trucking and warehousing, bituminous coal and lignite, oil and gas extraction, food and related products, primary metals, stone-clay-glass, rubber and plastics, fabricated metal products, and construction.[37]

There are two ways of conceptualizing the problem. One way emphasized by unions is penalties, inspections, and requirements for safety devices. Another way involves an economic analysis of risk. There is no such thing as perfect safety, and approaching it is more expensive than most people will think it is worth. It makes little sense to spend enormous sums for minor improvements in one area while another could improve with less effort. The biggest risks remain smoking cigarettes and driving cars. With limited resources, we have to concentrate on the most productive changes. A large part of accidents are caused by workers themselves. This approach emphasizes making employers pay for losses of health and higher wages for increased risk.

Both approaches have value. The first approach is embodied in a major reform, the Occupational Health and Safety Act of 1970 (OSHA), covering about 62 million workers in 5 million places of employment. The OSHA machinery has not worked well, partly because of inexperience and partly because of cumbersome procedures protective of industry. An independent review commission has an enormous backlog of cases. A major reduction of minor regulations in late 1977 may reduce the confusion and resistance encountered in its first six years, but better standards are needed, especially for health.[38] Continuing effectiveness will also depend on active participation by affected workers. All too often employers blame workers. For example, pliant doctors are used to label a worker allergic when he reacts to poisonous chemicals. Such rationalizations are used to avoid the cost of safety measures.

Health Care Services

The problems of providing health services include training, organization, costs, and financing of physical health and the special area of mental health.

Training Health Workers. Do we need to train many more doctors to meet a doctor shortage? Answering this question depends on assumptions about the whole system. For example, there is no problem of training more doctors if we were to utilize the doctors we have more efficiently. One major change would be to redistribute doctors geographically and socially, reducing availability to overserved cities and higher-income people and increasing doctors for the hinterland and lower-income people. Another major change would allow the development of a new kind of general practitioner to fill a major gap in the system—primary care. More use of assistants by doctors could also end the problem. Others see the shortage ending because medical schools are graduating more doctors.

These changes, however, are unlikely to occur or, if they do, to be sufficient to stop our importing of doctors from other countries. About one-fourth of doctors in practice have been foreign trained, and the number steadily increases. Most of them are foreign nationals whose services are desperately needed in their home countries, but we can offer them much higher personal income. This is one aspect of the "brain drain" by which poor countries aid the rich.

In 1970 the Carnegie Commission on Higher Education declared a massive crisis and recommended a 50 percent increase in medical school enrollments. There has been a significant 68 percent increase, from 8,059 graduates in 1969 to 13,500 in 1976.[39] Nevertheless, many able applicants are turned away from medical school, and the percentage of foreign doctors practicing in the United States is expected to increase. The government gives medical schools about half a billion dollars a year to train doctors, conditioned on their willingness to train in needed specialties, like family practice, and to improve geographic distribution. About 6 percent of the money is in the form of scholarships conditioned on willingness to serve in the Indian Health Service or the National Health Service Corps, which assigns graduates to needy areas in hopes they will locate there permanently.[40]

Much of the shortage is also a problem of poor use of doctors' time. Too much goes into catering to the hypochondria of the affluent. Too much is spent on giving shots, changing bandages, managing the chronically ill, delivering babies, taking histories, treating cuts and colds, and many other tasks better performed by assistants including nurses. Legal restrictions on nurses and medics keeps them from practicing the medicine they know. As doctors increasingly specialize, a vacuum has been created in primary family care. Progress has taken the form of new regulated professions; nurse practitioners and physicians' assistants work under a doctor's supervision but can handle primary care. Resistance to these new forms comes from patients and doctors alike. Doctors fear a loss of importance and money, but have been won over to some extent by letting them regulate the assistants and get part of their fees. Patients fear loss of quality while still paying the high fee. Reform seems to require the emergence of more assistants and political influence based on their intensive interest in upgrading their role.

The problem of skills extends past formal training. Periodic relicensing is needed to ensure that doctors remain aware of the latest knowledge. Surveys indicate extensive poor practice, a factor behind the malpractice crisis. Doctors have done a poor job of disciplining themselves. They tend to treat symptoms rather than make the diagnosis required by scientific medicine. They rely on salesmen to inform them about new drugs, overprescribe drugs, especially antibiotics, and carry out too much elective surgery. Much of the income of the American Medical Association comes from drug companies, and medical societies have generally taken little action to discipline themselves or drug companies. Possibly 5 percent of doctors are incompetent, some because of alcoholism, drug addiction, or mental illness. The malpractice crisis of 1974 led some states to upgrade their systems of discipline. The Academy of Family Practice has led the way in requiring extensive study and periodic recertification.

Organization and Finance. The way that health services are organized is intimately linked with the way that they are financed. The dominant system is fee for service, characterizing both doctors and hospitals. Historically, most reform has consisted of finding new ways to finance the fee demands of the established service providers. The system has an incentive to provide a service, whether needed or not, discourages those with little money from seeking preventive medicine, and denies service altogether to those with no money. Only the integrity of most providers has kept the system going.

Methods of finance include out of pocket; Blue Cross, Blue Shield, and other private insurance programs; governmental employee programs; Medicare; and Medicaid. None of the formal programs initially had any particular incentive to control costs; they were too easily passed on to the taxpayer, business, or premium payer, who in turn was in no position to judge if the increase should be paid. Service providers soon learned how to provide services to maximize their own income. Equally important, doctors had little incentive to cut costs. The result has been inflation, to some extent for physicians and, above all, for hospitals. The price index for semiprivate room rates, for example, went from 57.3 in 1960 to 326 in 1978 (as compared with all items going from 88.7 to 193.2). Drugs, dentists, certain routine operations, and eye examinations, however, did not inflate faster than all items;

some even failed to keep up.[41] Extensive Medicaid fraud has added to the problems of unneeded services and inflation.

On the other hand, the health system has been effective in some ways. The statistics, for example, show that our health is improving, and Medicaid-Medicare have helped the poor and the old. Hospital rates reflect the cost of higher technologies provided by modern hospitals, both for equipment and for people to run it. Also, hospital workers are finally getting adequate pay, long overdue for nurses, laboratory workers, and janitors. The statistics point to overuse of fee-for-service hospitals as the major problem.

There is potential for reform, but it involves marginal issues of great complexity. The federal government has instituted two new major organizational innovations, PSROs and HSAs, to control costs. The PSRO is the Professional Standards Review Organization and is a local panel of doctors who review patient files to see if their doctors measure up to professional standards. The danger is that PSROs may impose "cookbook medicine" over a doctor's sophisticated judgment, but this danger seems less than that of poor medical practice. Some doctors may fear a demystification of medicine. PSROs may be useful when they have a specific mission; in New Mexico, for example, they were used to control and reduce injections. Other techniques—for example, requirements for second opinion—may be better for controlling optional surgery.

HSAs are health service agencies set up in many regions around the nation. Unlike the PSROs, the HSAs allow broad participation, including by interested citizens. HSAs are supposed to do complex health planning for the long run, but their immediate mission is to prevent costly competition among hospitals in buying expensive equipment that would go underused.

These attempts to regulate details may not be as productive as efforts to change the incentive system, however. For example, if individuals could save on their health costs by not smoking, by exercising, by controlling their weight, and by showing knowledge of health precautions, they could be rewarded with money, part of what is saved by their reduced need for services. Also, instead of retrospective reimbursement based on costs to hospitals, they could announce prospective schedules of charges, allowing insurers to choose lower-cost hospitals or to reimburse based on lowest available charges, with patients to pick the extra cost if they want a high-cost hospital. Doctors' standard charges and specializations could be advertised. Some system is needed to allow the financing agencies to channel patients in nonemergency situations to the lower-cost services. In fee for service, the doctor is the main decision maker for all costs, and doctors have not had any particular incentive to be efficient. Incentive system changes can either restructure the doctors' decisions or reduce their power by involving the financing agencies more deeply in the decisions.

The major organizational and financial innovation in recent time is the health maintenance organization (HMO), a radical break from fee for service. An HMO is paid a monthly fee by its clients, and it gives them basic services without any other charge or with a very small one. The HMO can calculate what services most people will need routinely, so the fee is to some extent a payment for services, but it also covers serious unexpected needs and thus functions as insurance. The HMO has an incentive to keep its clients well, or it makes less money by having to provide them more costly services. Since fees and services are comparable and HMOs are large enough to have reputations, clients can shop around and even compare the HMO with insurance for fee for service. HMO fees are usually paid by payroll deduction, which is far more efficient and regular than billings by providers to insurers. Patients may be more likely to have small medical problems checked, curing them before they get serious, which is a key to preventive medicine. HMOs also have advantages from group practice, use of paraprofessionals, centralized administration, complete patient files for better diagnosis, many such files for analysis of health trends, and economies of scale. For years, the AMA fought HMOs and succeeded in making them illegal in several states and in slowing down federal support for them. Kaiser Foundation in California is one of the biggest and oldest; according to some studies it provides care equal to or superior to fee for service at 20 to 30 percent less cost. It has low hospitalization rates and does less surgery than most community hospitals.

Case Study:

Federal Health Money

Federal spending on health has increased rather steadily, and it took a big jump in 1966 with the implementation of Medicare-Medicaid. The growth has occurred despite strong opposition by the AMA to most governmental intervention in the field. The AMA appears to be the loser, an intensive interest gradually losing ground to reformers and public support for more equitable services. Also, the AMA has not preserved the mythic reality of the family doctor practicing alone, treating rich and poor in a scientific and personal way. Yet at a more important level, the AMA has largely succeeded in preserving the income and the power of doctors, and it has succeeded for the time being in slowing the movement toward national health insurance.

Federal programs started with those areas organized medicine could least object to, and each step was successful largely in proportion to the resources committed. Under the Hill-Burton program, for example, about $4.5 billion has been spent over the last thirty years to build hospitals, especially in poor and rural areas. General hospital beds are in good supply, even excess in places. Also, health insurance for federal employees has given the government extensive experience directly, and similar programs for state and local employees adds to that experience indirectly. Governments are major employers, so the amount spent has been large. The AMA has also found it difficult to object to government-sponsored research. Over the years, fifteen institutes of health and several additional agencies have been created and are now spending over $3 billion per year. This success has meant that hospital construction, insurance for civil servants, and research funding are not major citizen concerns. Lesser sums have gone into about a dozen grant-in-aid programs to the states and the National Health Service Corps. Indian health spending, long neglected, tripled in the 1970s; it cut infant mortality by 30 percent and tuberculosis by 32 percent.

European countries for some time have had successful governmental health programs, branded "socialized medicine" by the AMA. In 1949–1950, a major but unsuccessful attempt was made to enact national health insurance. Labor unions (excluding the AMA), reformist citizen groups, President Truman, and northern Democrats supported it, and the AMA, the Republicans, and the Dixiecrats did not. Meanwhile private insurance schemes were growing despite AMA opposition to them. During the 1950s, more modest schemes were developed, but, consistent with the Republican philosophy of minimizing the federal role, the Eisenhower administration did not support them. The election of President Kennedy revived hope, but the key committee, the House Ways and Means Committee, never let a significant bill reach the floor. In the Senate, however, bills to help the old were getting closer and closer to passage each year. The old were 10 percent of the population, but they had 25 percent of the health costs and generally lower incomes. More help to the poor was also getting support.

A key event, perhaps the key event, took place in November 1964. In the process of electing Johnson over Goldwater for president, the voters elected a liberal Democratic Congress committed to expanding established social programs. Johnson had "coattails"—people who ordinarily would not vote Democratic did so for both president and Congress. There is little evidence that many voters explicitly connected Medicare-Medicaid with their candidate preferences, but implicitly there was a general willingness to support that kind of action, and the Democrats took their victories as mandates for this reform.

The new composition of the House forced a change in the composition of the Ways and Means Committee. Year by year, the Democrats had been slipping proreform members onto the committee; now there was a big increase and a tipping of the balance of power on the health issue. Chairman Wilbur Mills, at the height of his power and all but unchallengeable in his domain, changed his mind and decided to support this kind of reform. A strong bill was immediately introduced, H. 1 (reflecting symbolically its priority among a multitude of bills that Congress was going to pass). Ordinarily a weaker bill would have been introduced and then weakened even more. The political system prefers smaller bites, as in all the previous case studies on the oil depletion, the dam and wilderness cases, and court cases on discrimination. However, at times the system becomes capable of more significant action.

During Ways and Means consideration, the AMA made a kind of lobbying error by proposing its version of a way to pay doctor bills. The Democrats leaped at the idea while ignoring the AMA scheme, and Medicare Part B was born. The bill came out of committee even stronger than it had gone in. It passed the House on a key vote of 236 to 191. Voting for the bill were 10 of 138 Republicans, 38 of 98 Dixiecrats, and 188 of 191 northern Democrats. The decisive margin was supplied by the newly elected freshmen Democrats. In July 1965, Johnson signed the bill in the presence of his mentor, President Truman, remembered from the 1949–1950 fight: for the same forces defeated then had at long last succeeded.

In October 1965, the AMA, having spent millions to defeat the bill, reversed its position. Doctors now could bill the government for their poor and old patients, and began to make more money than ever before. Medicare for the old and Medicaid for the poor have been growing at 18 percent per year in recent years and are the major reasons the federal government has moved up to paying directly for about 41 percent of health services. Out-of-pocket payments by consumers have declined from about 60 percent after World War II to less than 30 percent today. Private health insurance has increased like the government and now supports about 25 percent. Charity and foundations carry a small and declining part of the burden, now about 4 percent.[42]

National Health Insurance. The major proposal for equitable health care is national health insurance (NHI). Our experience with Medicare and especially Medicaid has been sufficiently negative—overuse, bureaucratic delays and paperwork, fraud, skyrocketing costs—that NHI is being delayed until these programs work better. Some of the Medicaid problems result from working through the states, creating an autonomous level of administration with its own rules. This problem has also plagued the welfare system, and yet both programs could have the simplicity of a federal transfer system like social security. Welfare reform is moving in the direction of reorganization and simplification, but health benefits seem likely to grow piecemeal for a few years more. We may, for example, improve Medicaid in the low benefit states and implement a new health insurance system nationwide to cover only catastrophic illness. The Carter administration proposal of March 1979 takes this approach. When federal and employer benefits, now covering 66 percent of care, pay for even more care, we may see the necessity for reforming the pluralistic patchwork into NHI. There are many schemes, and each steps on toes of vested interests. It may not be possible to rationalize the whole structure because of the intensity problem, but this is what Senator Kennedy's scheme would do, including vigorous cost controls. Both Carter and Kennedy's schemes combine employer, employee, and federal contributions.

One big challenge for national health insurance will be to create a system of finance that is flexible and provides an incentive to control costs. For example, many insurance schemes now do not require a second opinion on optional surgery. When one insurer required a second opinion, operations dropped off sharply, 60 percent for appendectomies and 75 percent for hysterectomies.[43] The insurer acted to protect the interests of the premium payers, which most insurers have been very slow to do. Could NHI be set up some way to reward the cost controllers? Could it be set up to finance without favoritism both HMOs and fee for service? Could it be set up to reward individuals for protecting their own health (by not smoking, for example)? If it could do these things, then it would probably not increase health costs, and many people not reached by existing programs would be covered. The interests that pushed for Medicaid-Medicare are still working for the broader program. Recent inflation has set back that hope, making NHI seem too expensive. Political pragmatism is now emphasizing cost controls through detailed regulation. Yet there are both conservative and liberal voices for a more sweeping approach. Conservatives like to engineer incentive systems that would create market-like mechanisms for efficiency and decentralization; liberals like extending adequate health care to those who now lack it. The organization-finance area is so complex that it almost defies citizen participation, yet it has a certain fascination, and the professionals seem unlikely to reform the system alone.

Mental Health

Mental health issues are somewhat separate from the physical health issues, and they are fragmented politically. The developmentally disabled include mental retardates and victims of cerebral palsy, infantile paralysis, and certain kinds of epilepsy. The mentally ill include those unable to function normally mainly from causes such as depression, manic-depression, schizophrenia, and senility. The developmentally disabled and the mentally ill are the two main areas of traditional concern. There are two kinds of substance abuse, alcoholism and drug abuse, each with its own issues and politics despite the similar basis. Problems of family mental health—such as spouse beating, child abuse and neglect, and juvenile delinquency—overlap with crime and have programs usually separate from each other. People generally have far less understanding of these issues than of physical health and often have misperceptions and anxieties, making the problems worse. Most people do not realize how many people are affected by mental illness, broadly defined. Almost one-third of all hospital beds, for example, are for psychiatric care. (See table 5–6.)

Mental health has made progress. Personnel per 200 residents of institutions for the developmentally disabled increased by 88 percent from 1960 to 1970, and expenditure per resident went up 181 percent.[44] Hospital expense per day for psychiatric care went up over 1,000 percent from 1960 to 1973; personnel per patient more than tripled. Commitment in many other areas is also increasing. Advances are being made in mental illness on two fronts, psychoactive drugs and scientific understanding of brain nerve chemistry. The drugs have been the most useful for those actually engaged in treatment, giving them a way to manage behavior and control symptoms. The drugs have enabled many more people to live outside mental hospitals and have helped a very large increase in the number of people served by various outpatient facilities. At the same time, the duration of contact per patient has decreased considerably. Scientific advances have produced some treatments useful for practitioners, such as lithium carbonate for manic-depression, but for the most part applications lie in the future, pending better understanding.

Mental health treatment poses some of the most important and interesting questions in our society regarding individual freedom. On the one

Table 5–6 Mental Health Statistics

The Developmentally Disabled				*1975*	
Children (includes speech impaired, learning disabilities, mentally retarded, emotionally disturbed, deaf, hard of hearing, visually handicapped, crippled, and others), in millions				7.9	
Patients under treatment in public facilities for the mentally retarded, in thousands				180	
The Mentally Disabled	*1950*	*1955*	*1970*	*1975*	*1976*
Inmates in mental hospitals, in thousands			434		
Psychiatric admissions per 1,000	2.0		3.3		3.1
Days in psychiatric hospitals per 1,000	1,659		862		429
Inpatient care episodes per 100,000		795		847	
Outpatient care episodes (in mental health facilities) per 100,000		233		2,185	
Substance Abuse		*1970*	*1975*	*1977*	
Ever used heroin, age 18–25, in percent				3.6	
Number of arrests, drug laws, in thousands				569	
Alcoholics, in thousands		5,400	5,750		
Number of arrests, driving while intoxicated, in thousands				1,104	
Number of arrests, drunkenness, in thousands				1,209	

Table 5–6 continued

Family Mental Health	*1970*	*1972*	*1975*
In homes for dependent and neglected children and unwed mothers, in thousands	52		
In training schools for juvenile delinquents (includes detention homes), in thousands	77		74
Delinquency cases, age 10–17, in thousands	32		40
Jail inmates age 14–17, per thousand		5.2	

Note: The purpose of this table is to give an idea of orders of magnitude and kinds of measurements available. Some numbers, like the number of heroin addicts, are especially uncertain. Years are presented as available.

Source: *Statistical Abstract of the United States, 1978,* pp. 52, 110, 115, 187, 196, 200, 363. Estimate of heroin addicts is from National Institute on Drug Abuse, *National Survey on Drug Abuse* (Rockville, Md.: 1977), p. 73. (One-third have used heroin twenty times or more. Current use is under .5% for all age groups.)

hand, a strong case exists that many mentally ill have been denied decent treatment defined in terms widely accepted by specialists. But there is not much popular interest in providing such treatment; it is mainly a question of human decency and respect for personal freedom. On the other hand, a strong case exists that what passes for treatment—manipulation of people with abusive attitudes, shock therapy, and manipulation by drugs—is often a kind of psychiatric assault. Nontreatment and overtreatment have parallels in physical health, but the abuses are far worse in mental health.

Nontreatment persists despite the general advance. A large minority of the disabled and ill are, in effect, punished for their condition. Mental institutions are directly comparable to prisons. The worst have barred windows, locked doors, straitjackets, solitary confinement, and institutional coldness. Electroshock is being reduced, but forced drugging is common. Patients may have to work without pay and may be subjected to medical experiments. In one institution in Alabama, patients lived in barnlike structures with no privacy, not even in the bathroom, and with no personal possessions. Clothing was shoddy; there was overcrowding. Patients had to perform unpaid housekeeping chores and did not get any therapeutic work. Aides were undertrained and overworked, leading them to ignore most patients and to be cruel to some of them. Cockroaches and flies; broken toilets; heavy odors of filth, urine, and feces; use of cattle prods; solitary confinement in wooden cages; unsanitary food preparation; numerous fire hazards; and a dehumanizing attitude toward patients were found. A concerned lawyer was able to publicize these conditions and to pursue court action based on denial of constitutional rights. Many similar cases are being pushed by reformers, such as mental health workers, lawyers, and civil libertarians.[45]

The Alabama legislature doubled the funds to the institution when these conditions were dramatically exposed, despite Governor Wallace's warning there was no extra money available. The number of patients was reduced. Straitjackets and solitary confinement were eliminated. Money was found; the lobbyist showed how much was being spent on swine shows and beauty contests and suggested different priorities. At a critical time during the lobbying, each legislator received a picture of a girl in a straitjacket with flies on her mouth and face, symptomatic of the larger problem. Alabama is now toward the middle of the list of states in per-capita mental-health expenditures.[46] But what about those spending less? Some states spending more have similar problems through poor management. Similar punishment is often given to alcoholics thrown in jail, addicts detained without treatment, juveniles in homes that work like prisons, and children in abusive homes.

The failures of mental hospitals to live up to their potential, and their inherently institutional nature, has led to an increased use of board and care homes. These homes are found in most cities in moderate-income neighborhoods run by untrained but experienced people who receive income from the SSI payments for their residents. These places can provide homier surroundings and reduce confinement; most patients are not only nonviolent but more shy than average people. Day-care programs can provide therapeutic work, exercise, entertainment, and travel to make life more pleasant, and they can stimulate improved functioning. Such homes are useful for people not ill enough to institutionalize but not able to live on their own.

Unfortunately board and care homes may fail as badly as mental hospitals because of the chronic tendency of government to underfund services for the politically weak. Board and care has been sold in part as a way to save money, so too little money is provided, and regulation is weak. The dispersion of patients makes mistreatment harder to discover. Drugging continues in board and care, producing cheaply managed zombies who get to choose between watching television and walking the streets. The victimizing of the victims of mental health problems continues, and it includes many children. Yet dedicated reformers have shown that some progress can be made.

Overtreatment is a function of our very real ignorance about mental illness and our willingness to pretend that we know more than we do. There is a tendency among mental health workers to shield themselves from human relationships with patients using pseudoscientific jargon. Labels are used as substitutes for therapy, like *schizophrenia, maladaptive, negativism, inappropriate effect, pathological,* and *unsocialized,* which may be helpful as descriptive terms if used carefully but do not explain anything. The facade of expertise also occurs in physical health when doctors seem unable to explain the problem in simple terms to patients. Highly trained psychiatrists given a set of identical cases will agree among themselves only about 60 percent of the time on who is normal, who neurotic, and who psychotic.[47] Superficial diagnosis yields manipulative treatment: Tense? Have a tranquilizer. Can't sleep? Take a "barb." Can't stay awake? Have a diet pill. Want to talk with a therapist? Don't have time.

In one experiment normal people feigned an unusual symptom, were admitted to several mental hospitals, and were labeled schizophrenic. They were given pills, and their normal behavior was interpreted as insane. Taking notes was called "engaging in writing behavior," for example. They were eventually released as "in remission." The patients were more likely to catch on to the normality of these people than the staff who typically retreated to their offices. The pseudopatients also discovered that patients frequently threw away the pills they were supposed to take. When informed they had been duped by pseudopatients, the hospitals improved their screening, rejecting more applicants, and also discharged more patients.[48]

Adequate treatment is possible, but it takes a commitment of resources. At Bronx State Hospital, for example, a reform administration doubled the number of psychiatrists and increased the number of psychologists by more than six times and the number of social workers by five times. The median stay dropped from over fifteen months to less than two, and patients correspondingly increased their contact with real life.

Services can be upgraded in the community too. The Neinken Pavilion in Brooklyn exemplifies what can be done, emphasizing treatment of people in their locality to prevent institutionalization. The pavilion is informal, similar to a modern doctor's office, with staff dressed informally and informal movement of people. There are no locked doors or reception desk barricades. Patients drop in for group therapy or individual sessions with a variety of specialists. They come on their own or are sent by relatives, schools, churches, or police. Drugs are used very carefully. The pavilion has an outreach program: mental health workers meet with community groups to explain their services and educate on mental health. A storefront clinic serves clients far from the pavilion itself. Fieldworkers respond to crisis calls and can help families avoid more explosive conflict, which might produce psychosis in a member or destroy the family. Crisis interventions are followed up to the extent the family wishes. Fieldworkers can also act as ombudsmen, helping clients deal with policemen, welfare, health, and educational bureaucracies.[49] Lack of outreach is a major weakness of most community mental health centers.

The goal of treatment is not cure in most cases, because much mental illness is chronic. With help, many people can function fairly normally; families can be held together, situations restructured, jobs held. The challenge is to manage the illness rather than the patient. In fact, the best results are obtained with the active cooperation of the patient. As with rehabilitation of criminals, treatment will be unsuccessful if people are handled in an authoritarian way.

Community mental health programs are especially needed for families, alcoholism, drug abuse, and juvenile delinquency. The family is the primary cause of many mental health problems, especially child abuse, juvenile delinquency, and drug abuse. It can aggravate physiological weaknesses and magnify the worst aspects of our general culture and society. (There are types of mental illness that families do not cause, of course, such as schizophrenia and depression.) Abusive parents need reeducation in parenting and insight into their own upbringings; such parents usually love their children and vice versa. Juvenile delinquency can largely be predicted by the age of six, partly using two to five (depending on presence of the father) characteristics, such as discipline patterns and affection.[50] A three-year study of over two hundred young drug abusers showed in every case a family background of emotionally impoverished relationships.[51] Government cannot do the task alone. Many volunteers are needed for befriending children having problems in school, to work with juveniles, and to lobby for better programs.

The terrible cost of alcoholism alone justifies a greater commitment. As with other mental health problems, the unacceptable behavior is accepted and hushed up, so everyone suffers—the victim, the healthy people protecting him or her, and even society.

As with the other social topics discussed, the major problems affect those of lower socioeconomic status. Poverty aggravates mental illness, and the mental problems make it difficult to deal with poverty.[52] The affluent use their power to look the other way and buy private solutions. The income solutions discussed earlier for poverty are not enough. Much more citizen action is needed to understand and manage mental health problems.

Citizen Profile:

Mental Health

In 1969 I came to Hayward, California, with my husband and five children and soon became involved in the local League of Women Voters. I was introduced to mental health issues by Gail Steele, who was very active in this area. I was also teaching at junior colleges and active in PTA and family activities.

In mid-May 1972, my sixteen-year-old daughter became mentally ill, although at the time we had no idea what it was or meant. She had many friends, played basketball, went to parties, and was active in extracurricular activities. One day in class she started screaming and crying. She was taken to the Family Crisis Center at Juvenile Hall and then, on the advice of a social worker, to the then-new Emergency Shelter Program for women, where she stayed two days. On the third day she went "for a walk," winding up at the police station, where she claimed to have killed people. At first we hoped this behavior was simply a result of exhaustion, but it didn't go away. The family had therapy. I withdrew from other commitments that summer and for the next two years as my daughter's hospitalization became more permanent.

I was caught up in guilt, sometimes fostered by mental health workers who in turn were taught that mental illness is caused by the family, or perhaps only by bad mothers. I acceded to any demand to help my child, for example, taking a long trip to Napa, the state mental hospital, for what turned out to be a matter that could have been handled on the telephone. The professionals, I began to realize, simply did not understand the problem. For example, my daughter was initially misdiagnosed as schizophrenic and given inappropriate medication. Sometimes she was overdrugged to keep her comatose. My family was being abused as well by the attitudes and treatment of the mental health bureaucracy.

The revolving door treatment kept me busy. My daughter would be released, then go to a police station, to a security officer at a shopping center, or to a fire station—she spent much time in fire stations. She would go to some authority figure, threaten suicide, then be taken to a psychiatric emergency room, to a mental hospital, and then she would be turned out again. In the spring of 1974, I desperately needed a place for her to stay, but no one knew of anything. Gail Steele urged me to talk to the Eden District Mental Health Advisory Committee, which she had formed. There I expressed my frustration, discovered board and care homes, and was able to place my daughter in one. The

Mental Health Association needed a study of board and care homes, so I helped out. I was asked to be president of the county Mental Health Association and to serve on the boards of other mental health organizations.

California has a long history of reform efforts in mental health, one little part of which was a law to open citizen advisory committees to families of patients and to ex-patients. This apparently small change opened up the system to new concerns. I was appointed to the Napa Hospital Advisory Board for the Mentally Disabled. The board members have keys to the wards, and we used them to make unannounced inspections. We have held frequent meetings, pressed for the release of a report showing staff negligence in accidental deaths of patients, and we kept the pressure up.

By 1978 I was tired of working full time without pay. After years of volunteer advocacy, I wanted to manage a service agency myself. I applied to be executive director of the Emergency Shelter Program, was accepted, and have now been running it for several months.

My biggest frustration is that there are not enough beds anywhere. It's incredible—I knew of it before but did not really understand. We are turning away staggering numbers of women and children. We cannot accommodate people who are under the influence of alcohol or drugs or who are severely mentally ill, but even so more than a hundred women and children a month who are clearly eligible cannot get in. They are escaping dangerous husbands, or sleeping in cars, their kids sometimes literally starving. We can keep people only a few days; very quickly we have to find them welfare support and counseling. We can do the most for the battered women who are ready to change their lives. We lost fifteen beds in May 1978 when we lost some CETA allocations; we now have only twenty. The new regulations make CETA salaries so low that the competent are usually not willing and the willing are not often competent. Proposition 13 cuts have hurt also. We are getting involved in a complicated fight for "title twenty" money (from the Social Security Act) to build up from our existing revenue sharing base, but even revenue sharing is in political trouble. We were recently accepted as a United Way agency, which will help. Despite the constant struggle for funds, Alameda County deserves credit for putting half of its revenue sharing money into social programs; most counties put it all into tax relief.

My work is very rewarding—I feel needed every day I'm here. My office is in front, where I can hear the people who come in. When you give counseling, you are not often sure of the result, while the emergency shelter provides a real, immediate, important service to destitute and endangered women and children. We protect them from injury, exposure, and hunger. Some women begin to change, to build their self-esteem, and to get jobs; they begin to turn their lives around.

Arlette Merritt
Hayward, California

Education

Education, like health, is fundamental for equality of opportunity. Without it, children and young adults do not get skills they need for a job and are less likely to develop their intellectual abilities. Similar to other social problems, quality of education is closely correlated with socioeconomic status. The United States has done better in this area than in any of the others when compared with other developed systems. Our educational system provides a major route of upward mobility for able and motivated people. (See table 5–7.) The nation is especially outstanding in providing opportunity at the college level. Educational levels have been steadily and significantly increasing. Many problems of education stem from trying to reach social classes or cultures who were never reached before. These achievements reflect a historic commitment by the American middle class, elites, and reformers to large-scale public education as a primary means to personal development and equal opportunity.

Education as a social institution comes second only to the family. In 1978, it took 7 percent of GNP, or about $142 billion, and employed about 5 million teachers, administrators, and librarians. Closely related are producers of educational supplies, books, buildings, transportation, and so on. If that were all, it would be about as big as defense, or health, or certain industrial complexes. But education multiplies its social importance because it also involves the labor of about 60 million students, from nursery school through graduate school. Another 17 million participate in adult education.

A system so large and important naturally has problems. Fortunately, reforms in education, as in poverty and health, do not require much new

Table 5–7 Educational Attainment, 1950 and 1977

Level	*1950*	*1977*
Percent of population completing		
0–4 years	11.1	3.7
5–7 years	16.4	6.9
8 years	20.7	9.3
1–3 years high school	17.4	15.2
4 years high school	20.8	36.1
1–3 years college	7.4	13.4
4 years or more college	6.2	15.4
Total population over 25 years (millions)	85.0	120.9
Median school years completed	9.3	12.4

Sources: *Statistical Abstract of the United States, 1973* pp. 114, 117; *Statistical Abstract 1978,* p. 143.

funds. They do, however, require a fair system of raising funds and some increase of funds for underprivileged students. Equally important are organizational and curricular changes to improve the quality of education within the limits of current resources. In discussing these problems, we will look at the topics of basic education (primary and secondary) for children with low education parents, organizational and curricular changes in basic education, the goal of basic education, the goal of higher education, and the financing of higher education.

Basic Education

The greatest area of failure in American basic education is the education of children whose parents have low education themselves. Low education is highly correlated with lower socioeconomic status. The problem is evident in truancy and dropping out of school, in the low quality of performance needed for a high school diploma, and in the inability of 17 percent of the population aged eighteen and over to read above a fourth-grade level.[53] In 1973, 19 million Americans were functionally illiterate; they were unable to read a driver's test, a newspaper classified advertisement, or the directions on a bottle of medicine.[54]

The most motivated and able can make an upward ascent in spite of the system. The least able and most alienated would not be much helped by a better system. In between is a large number of fairly able children who will respond to adult leadership. If they fail to get a basic education, we must blame adults.

Research shows that the primary statistical correlation of educational attainment is the education of the parents. Parents have much more influence over children than schools do. They completely dominate the first few years of life. Even after schooling starts, children spend most of their time under a parent's supervision before and after school, on weekends, and during vacations. Educated parents tend to stimulate their children intellectually, conversing with them, providing for stimulating play, and acting as models by the reading and talking they do themselves. By contrast, in the worst cases among the poor, the child has parents with employment and mental health problems and grows up in an atmosphere of need, indiscipline, failure, dependency, defeat, and frustration (remember the Columbia Point example).

Parents are so important that schools, in the aggregate statistics, do not seem to make much difference. The Coleman report of 1966 discovered this from surveying 600,000 children, 60,000 teachers, and 4,000 schools. The researchers found that about the same school resources were dedicated regardless of social class, and what resource differences there were did not affect educational attainment.[55] Most of the subsequent research has backed up these findings in varying degrees. Common sense, however, tells us that good schools promote more learning than bad schools do and that more resources generally help make better schools. Common sense may be right: the aggregation of large amounts of data obscures the factors that make for quality in a school. The primary adults responsible for education may well be the parents, but the schools, in the reform view, have a sizable responsibility of their own. There is evidence that if adequate resources are committed and used correctly, lower-class children can catch up to grade level and perform as well as their middle-class peers. This idea is central to the idea of reform, but implementation is blocked by at least two major side issues, race and the quest for equal resources.

Race and Education. The problem of race has received far more attention than the more important problem with which it overlaps, educating lower-income children. The reasons seem to lie in the geographic concentration of blacks, the poor educational systems of the rural South, and the special crisis of poor ghetto blacks. Spanish-speaking Americans and native Americans face some similar problems. A child from one of these minorities does not usually speak the same language (or dialect) or have the same culture as the teacher does.

It is traumatic enough for a middle-class child to walk into that first classroom. The school systems need extra resources to have teachers and curricula geared to the child's language. Such commitment is usually lacking, resulting in inequality of educational opportunity from the first day of school.

(Another view, however, points out that in the past large classrooms with authoritarian teachers and non-English-speaking students worked fairly well and can today.)

Race has been a major issue because the quality of black schools has so obviously been way below that of white schools. The crisis of the black ghetto poor manifests itself in their schools. They have problems not faced by lower-class children of the past. The junior highs and high schools have disproportionate problems, preventing learning from being possible: false fire alarms, drugs, alcohol, constant or frequent fighting and yelling among students, extortion, knives and guns, robberies and muggings in parking lots, attacks on teachers, vandalism and break-ins, arson, and ethnic racial conflict. Many ghetto schools no longer educate; they function as a day prison, providing custodial care to keep youths off the streets and out of public trouble, imposing minimal discipline without purpose. Teenagers become alienated and drop out, get jobs, have kids of their own, bum around, or get into trouble with the law.

Most adults in these schools find ways of doing their jobs but without the emotional investment necessary to be effective. Teachers are demoralized by discipline problems, violence, and rules that make it impossible to get the problem children out of their classrooms. They are demoralized by the lack of adequate programs for the problem students, by the enormous demands for attention that many students make, by the general disinterest in learning, and by low performance. Many poor teachers hang on, pulling down a pay check. And the good teachers have too much work to do for too little recognition. They usually become cynical or burned out, or they quit; they go to suburban systems, which appreciate their talents and pay them adequately. Turnover in the ghetto schools disrupts continuity. Parents may be unaware, uncaring, or unable to exercise influence.

Aging and decrepit buildings may aggravate the problems, but the physical structure is secondary to the social. Ghetto schools are usually part of large city school systems, where the central bureaucracy has become too large and distant from the classroom. Legislatures, even further removed, leave school systems to work under self-defeating laws or impose innovations too frequently and with too little participation by teachers and parents.

As table 5–8 shows, school dropouts are a major problem for both races. Blacks have a more serious problem but have been moving toward white rates. The "not in labor force" category contains a large number of discouraged workers who are not counted in the unemployment rate. About half of dropouts are not employed, as compared with only one-fourth not employed among high school graduates.

In 1954 the Supreme Court ordered desegregation within each school attendance district, throwing out the old concept of separate but equal schools. It did not, however, require busing among school attendance districts.

Table 5–8 School Dropouts

	1965	*1977*
Dropouts aged 16–21		
Not in labor force (thousands)	1,123	1,154
Unemployed (thousands)	278	497
Not in labor force and unemployed as % of total dropouts	46.9	49.6
Unemployed whites (thousands)	203	344
Unemployed blacks (thousands)	75	145
Dropouts aged 14 to 24 [a]		
Total (thousands)	4,716	5,148
% of total population	13.6	11.7
% of total white population	12.4	11.1
% of total black population	22.8	15.9

[a] The data in the first column are for 1967.
Source: *Statistical Abstract of the United States, 1978,* p. 147.

For ten years, the integration order was ignored and resisted in the South where segregation existed by law. In 1964 the Civil Rights Act created two powerful federal tools: the Justice Department was empowered to get court orders to desegregate, taking over from the hopelessly underfunded NAACP, and the Department of Health, Education and Welfare was empowered to withhold aid from segregated districts. In 1960 federal aid was about 4 percent of total school expenditures, and it had grown to 8.5 percent in 1978. The aid goes to the most needy districts, where it is a much larger part of their funding, and many such districts are in the South. The South has made more progress than the rest of the nation (see table 5–9).

In the late 1960s, the courts moved against de facto school segregation (accomplished by practice). Neighborhood schools produced segregation, so the courts ordered busing for racial balance within whole school systems. For smaller systems, shorter distances, and mostly white districts, good results could be accomplished at relatively low cost, but busing flies in the face of popular notions, even among many blacks, of neighborhood schools. It has been an explosive issue in bigger districts. There are, nevertheless, many examples of success, where black children are performing better and whites are performing as well as they did in the past.[56]

White flight to suburbs and increasing black populations in central cities to some extent have resegregated previously integrated schools. The courts

Table 5–9 School Segregation

By Region	% Blacks in Schools under 50% Black	
	1968	1974
32 northern and western states	28	23
6 border states and Washington, D.C.	28	31
11 southern states	18	45

By Urbanization	Millions Aged 5–17 Enrolled Inside Central Cities		% Change
	1960	1977	
White	9.6	8.1	−16
Black	2.6	4.0	+54
Percent black	27	49	

Source: *Statistical Abstract, 1978,* pp. 151, 142; U.S. Office of Civil Rights, *The Directory of Public Elementary and Secondary Schools,* Fall 1970, and unpublished data.

are not willing to take the next step, which is to bus between school districts, even when it might mean shorter distances and greater results. The 100 largest school districts have become the most segregated. From 1968 to 1972, they lost 426,000 white pupils and gained 146,000 black pupils. Some northern whites have imitated southern whites and set up private white schools, reached by buses. Some busing is fraught with so much tension from outside the schools that education suffers, and black children there do worse than in segregated schools.

Racial balance is a small part of school busing in general. Busing for all purposes takes funds from direct use. In 1950 28 percent of students were bused at $31 per pupil; in 1972 46 percent were bused at $77 per pupil.[57] Busing now costs almost 4 percent of total educational expenses.

Busing can be worthwhile because it can help develop racial understanding, but sometimes other methods can be used more efficiently. Busing is only indirectly related to the crucial problem of equality of opportunity. Inequality also affects poor whites. Policy should deal with the real issue of social class. For example, white workers earn 50 percent more than black workers, but the top fifth of white workers makes 600 percent more than the lowest fifth. Differences within races are more important than those between races. Some statistics indicate that 15 to 20 percent more is spent on white schools than on black, but 100 percent more is spent on rich children than on poor. The *Brown* decision in 1954 looked at only a small part of the problem and did not attack the basic problem of discrimination against the less educated of both races. It is understandable that white lower classes in central cities see busing as just one more factor hurting them as the affluent grow more so in the suburbs. Judges, aware of the difficulties, seem to be easing up on busing. Yet black leaders have had little enough leverage with busing and generally view separation as the anathema of inequality.[58] Nevertheless, most blacks go to mostly black schools, even with much busing for racial balance.

Equal Resources versus Enrichment. A second side issue is the quest for equal resources. There is a profound crisis in support to the schools. Schools have historically depended on the property tax, which meant that low-wealth districts with large school populations could tax themselves more than high-wealth districts and still have less money per pupil than the wealthy districts. Many poor districts are claiming justifiably that they should be able to spend as much per pupil as the richer districts. Money into education has been increasing steadily. In constant 1976 dollars, per pupil expenditure has increased from $607 in 1950 to $1,699 in 1976.[59] Federal and state aid to poorer districts has improved but often without corresponding increases in pupil attainment. The Elementary and Secondary Education Act of 1965, a major reform, has helped but has not accomplished equality and has been spread out over such a large number of students that its impact is nearly lost. Federal spending has been criticized for this and for spending the money in ways that equally benefited middle-class students. Much money went to increase salaries and thus did not increase resources for children or was wasted on little-used or otherwise questionable equipment.[60]

Just as important, equal resources may not produce equal results, or, more realistically, may not bring lower-class students up to a minimal standard by graduation. Some evidence seems to indicate that more resources must be put into the education of lower-class children; a compensatory effort is needed to give them equal opportunity. Further, money must not be dissipated in ways that do not effectively reach children; there must be leadership from teachers, principals, and superintendents to put money, program, and caring all together.

Many parents can be productively enlisted to help their children, but with lower-class parents, teachers have to make greater efforts, and community aides are needed to make personal contact. It is slow work, and the parents are naturally sensitive about how they are treated and may have feelings of inferiority.

Research has yet to show that reducing class sizes is cost-effective, but common sense and the experience of teachers indicate that more individual attention can be given in smaller classes. Teachers in large classes have a dilemma: they can concentrate on those who seem interested and able, while the rest stagnate, or they can stop pushing and just try to keep everybody reasonably happy. If they give low grades to poor students, they may be accused of being poor teachers or racists. So the trend has been to kill kids with kindness and give diplomas to semiliterates, protecting their egos while failing their education.

Enrichment has worked in many cases, especially where administrative leadership prevents the dissipation of the additional resources. When teachers at one central city black junior high school diagnosed reading problems on an individual basis and encouraged pupils to work diligently on individually assigned work, the students gained four years and one month after one year of work, catching up to national norms. Special funding allowed small classes, and teachers were carefully selected. Test scores are up; vandalism and attacks on teachers are down. Once littered, the school is now kept clean, and the emphasis is on successful learning. Unfortunately tax cuts and seniority systems threaten continued progress. Many similar success stories show that the schools can overcome the disadvantages of the background of their students.[61]

Enrichment in black schools can use and has used a lot of black materials that would not be justified in a largely white classroom. The history of blacks, their struggles and accomplishments, their current problems, and so on can be much more heavily emphasized, developing a positive self-identity and awareness. Predominantly black districts also allow more black control over the schools. Jesse Jackson, a black preacher from Chicago and one of the most recognized leaders nationally among blacks, has been promoting Push for Excellence, a motivational program for black youth reaching three cities in 1978.

Sociological research on peer influence (showing that blacks perform better in a mostly white classroom) influenced the courts in favor of busing. Therefore, other research documenting the centrality of enrichment might also develop legal weight. If we simply turn away from busing, we turn our back on all lower-class children because one method did not work too well in all places. Conversely, establishing the value of enrichment would help all children of poor, low-education parents.

Reforming the Schools

Enrichment. Granted that we need enrichment, what is it? The field of education is a morass of conflicting theories, methods, goals, and measurements. It is an area of inquiry that has had outstanding intellects but suffers from an excess of generalities. As we have tried to develop more sophisticated goals, traditional, defined academic and vocational goals have declined in relation to rather vague objectives of general personal development.

It now seems clear that an emphasis on accepting children as they are has overbalanced challenging them to become what they can. It has been all too easy for teachers to take the pressure off, especially when administrators and parents go along with it. The pendulum is beginning to swing back toward more emphasis on performance. A major impulse for this is the decline in scores on academic achievement tests above the fourth-grade level.[62] The Scholastic Aptitude Test, designed in 1941 to measure basic thinking skills, is still an excellent predictor (after high school grades) of performance in college. From 1963 to 1977, SAT scores dropped slowly but steadily, by forty-nine points for verbal and thirty-two points for math on a six-hundred-point scale. Careful research on the reasons revealed that most of the decline from 1963 to 1970 was due to more disadvantaged students (low income, minority, women in math) taking the test to get into college and having average lower scores.[63]

From 1971 to 1977, however, most of the decline was attributed to national experiences (an unpopular war, assassinations, riots, Watergate), more single-parent families, the distraction of television, less motivation of students, and school factors (reduced academic requirements, easy electives, less time in school, excessive absenteeism, grade inflation, automatic promotion, less homework, and easier textbooks).[64] The resources are there to do better; teachers are better paid and better educated than ever before, and they have smaller classes. In addition to changing the above factors, we need to know when students fall below grade level, to give them after-school work or summer work, and to hold them back a grade as necessary. Schools that have continually insisted on standards have not had the drop in test scores. Insistence on performance worked fairly well in the past with a less humane system; it should be possible now to be both humane and demanding.

The innovative search for better methods and our reawakened concern for performance have combined to redefine high school graduation requirements to make them more relevant for situations young adults will have to deal with. To be eligible for graduation, students may be required to be able to read and explain a lead article in a newspaper; follow instructions for marking a ballot; fill out the short form of the income tax and a job application; write a personal letter about a typical situation; give instructions about a task; respond in a job interview; spell common words; do some checkbook calculations; show an awareness of how to look for a job, of good health habits, and of laws important for daily living; discuss a topic in the news and their opinion on it; and distinguish between statements of fact and fiction. These kinds of requirements are minimums; they are needed to jolt the system back toward some minimal level of accountability using relevant criteria. Such performance would be the minimum required of all graduates; most students would do more.

In sum, enrichment seems to require extra resources for disadvantaged children and a dedication to using them for clear academic and vocational goals. There is a seemingly endless list of organizational, architectural, and curricular innovations, each with its adherents and some measure of success. Perhaps the key is the general ability and commitment of the teacher, enhanced by training based on observation of the teacher in the classroom. Systematic research has been attempted. Project Follow Through is a special federal effort to help Head Start children through kindergarten and the first three grades. Research on 170 schools in the program around the nation indicated that, contrary to previous aggregate sociological research, teacher conduct is the biggest factor in student achievement.[65]

The most successful curriculum relied heavily on extra time for reading and math and on drill, practice, and praise. Some research may overlook the importance of teacher conduct because of the difficulty of measuring it. Lumping good teaching in with bad could show that teachers are not as important as parents. A more sophisticated approach reasserts the importance of good teaching.

By junior high and even more by high school, a few students have developed attitudes hostile to schools. At some point for some students, it is counterproductive for the system and the student to continue trying to relate to each other. Unrealistic legal requirements for attendance can negatively affect both youth and school, detracting from the education of the more committed. The rules do not work; some inner-city high schools have average daily attendance under 50 percent of official enrollment. It seems desirable to have schools that can require certain standards of attendance, being on time, and personal conduct so as to focus on learning as best the system can provide it. Attending such schools would be a privilege, not a right, but with standards acceptable to the large majority. For the alienated, teen centers would be available for counseling and nontraditional attempts to develop survival skills. Some centers have developed high morale and helped motivate adolescents who were previously uninterested in advancing themselves.

As we develop better information on the education of the disadvantaged, we may be able to define what resources are needed for equality of opportunity. Busing may not be the most productive investment. Some combination of enrichment, insistence on performance, tested curriculum, voluntarism, and teen centers could do better.

Parental Involvement, Parental Choice, and Teacher Professionalism. The classroom aspects of educational reform are closely linked with the larger decision-making process. Too often, decisions are imposed by legislative, judicial, and administrative fiat, with little parental, teacher, or student participation. There are fads in education as in everything else, much of it shallow sloganeering. Organizational innovations should put initiative and responsibility into the hands of parents and teachers. Students also can participate to the extent of their maturity.

Students' current lack of participation in high school decisions is a major socialization experience, teaching passivity and alienation from the political process as a whole. High school students learn that there is a "they" who have to be appeased with a lot of time and good behavior so they (the students) can do what they really want to later. This split is important to later work attitudes; people learn merely to go through the motions to get money and leisure time. Such attitudes may be more common to lower socioeconomic strata; upper strata more often like their work and feel they are participants in the larger society.

One promising organizational innovation is the modified voucher system. In the Alum Rock school district of San Jose, California, parents are given a voucher and a choice of fifty minischools, each having its own group of teachers and classrooms. Thus, parents have to be involved if only to decide where to send their children to school. Even their neighborhood school has several minischools within it. To help them make up their mind, a directory describes each minischool. Most parents choose the basic skills types of programs, followed by individualized. Other programs are bilingual/bicultural, careers, creative arts, fine arts, learn by doing, multicultural, and open. Another publication provides information about how well the students in each program have done on various tests and other quantitative information, including measures of student feelings and budgets. There is additional information about how to choose a minischool and how to make a school visit. If one type of school lacks demand, the teachers can shift to one more in demand. Parents have far more information, choice, and influence than in conventional school districts.

Teachers have more influence, too, because most of running a minischool is in their hands. They have more control over curriculum (each group of minischool teachers works as a team), and they have ample factual feedback on how well they are doing. Alum Rock teachers had to put in a lot of uncompensated time at the beginning to learn how to do all the administrative work—thinking through their program, showing parents around, preparing materials, handling the budget, and group discussions. The problem of schools, like most other institutions, is not primarily to weed out the incompetent but to inspire the competent.

Alum Rock has received $4.3 million in extra federal money for the program. First-year test results were inconclusive, but second-year results showed strong gains, though it is difficult to tell if this success resulted from the voucher program or the money. The Alum Rock experiment uses people from the community to help in the classroom and to work with parents, which is especially important in its low-income, high-turnover area. Parents can serve on advisory boards. If they do not like a minischool, they can move their children. As important as test scores is overwhelming student, parent, and teacher satisfaction with the project.[66]

The Politics of Basic Education. The politics of educational reform is increasingly difficult. Only about 44 percent of all households have children under eighteen, so support must come to some degree from people with grown children or no children. But the intensity problem means that the big push for reform must come from parents and teachers. The National Education Association has long lobbied for schools, and in recent years the more militant voice of the American Federation of Teachers has burst noisily on the scene. It is too easy to dismiss teacher unionism as just a way to get more money. Yes, teachers would like to get paid as much as, say, a craft construction worker. In 1974 craft construction workers had median annual earnings of $12,142 while basic education teachers made $10,493. (Teachers have summers off, but construction workers also have days off due to weather and unemployment, making the occupations somewhat comparable.) [67]

The reduction in school-age population has produced a surplus of teachers, tempting school districts to keep pay down despite the high qualifications of the average teacher. Over three-fourths of primary teachers have masters' degrees. Teachers in general average eight years of teaching experience. They are becoming better organized and effective as advocates, constantly working locally and through the AFT and NEA against the "cut costs—fire teachers" syndrome. Their efforts are not only to increase compensation but to improve the quality of education. Some teachers just put in their hours, but many work overtime and lobby politically for education. Parents are more difficult to organize, but there is a national network trying to reassert the importance of performance.

Higher Education

While a major goal of basic education must be to bring everyone up to a practical minimum, the major goal of higher education is to help the more motivated and able reach their highest personal and social level. Unlike advanced, professional, technical, or vocational education, higher education seeks to develop the whole person. Just as basic education suffers from the vagueness of its goals, so also does higher education, allowing faculty specialization to have an edge over the students' needs. The specialization is paralleled by a great decentralization of control to departments, and from departments to individual instructors, each classroom a fiefdom. As with doctors, police, executives, and other professionals, the system works as well as it does only because of the personal commitment of most college faculty. The machinery for accountability is weak at best. The edge given to specialization means that research and publication are more important than good teaching. Many institutions say that they emphasize teaching but do little to measure what is going on in the classroom, and thus they have little evidence on which to base a judgment of teaching quality.

Some campuses with required use of student evaluation forms are in a position to do better at judging quality. We need to experiment with tests at the beginning of a semester or quarter to compare with results at the end to see what students learn. We need more class observation by other teachers and by professional evaluators. We need to develop a body of scientific literature on college teaching as we have for basic education. Over time some measures of teaching quality can be developed.

Liberal Education. As we pay more attention to how well we are doing, we have to define the goals more clearly. Higher education should have two major components, the liberal arts and practical experience. The liberal arts component is generally defined as course requirements for a degree and should include a number of areas. *Philosophy* is one. It should be defined as a series of questions and possible answers to illuminate basic thinking processes: logic, epistemology, metaphysics, aesthetics, and ethics, and their interrelationships. *History,* independent of its superficial relevance but made relevant because it is human and fascinating, is another. Our sense of history should have awareness of the vast sweep of events, of a detailed reality of life at some very different time and place, and of the many dimensions of history: Western versus other regions; political; economic and technological; social, intellectual, and scientific; and religious.

Liberal arts should encompass *science,* taught not as knowledge but as a process of finding out. It should include the scientific method in a wide range of applications—physical, biological, and social. We need to understand the importance of paradigms, measuring devices, and their interaction. We need a sense of how social forces influence science and how science has shaped society. Liberal arts should do much better at teaching *religion,* making it relevant, like philosophy, to the students' active concerns. Some students are religiously active but lack perspective on how their concerns fit into history; others are uninterested in conventional religion and think they can ignore it. Liberal education should make students aware of the inevitability of expressing values in the way we live and help them formulate meaningful beliefs for themselves.

Liberal arts should break down our natural parochialism. History and awareness of a *foreign culture* are very valuable. Many colleges have a language requirement, but that alone is not enough and in fact becomes meaningful only if followed up by a chance to use the language in other courses, such as on the literature and arts, history, society, and politics of a country with the culture. Such education also helps shape informed opinion on our relations with that country. Liberal education should include *treatment of our current problems* and what citizens can do about them. Good citizenship does not pay off in money, status, or power. It takes an awareness of relatively distant realities to make the work of citizenship meaningful.

Other liberal arts requirements should include *proficiency in speech, listening, and writing*. Most of our ability to converse develops outside class. Colleges could systematically stimulate verbal expression. Listening skills are also not taught but are picked up as we go along taking notes in classes and from other experience. A little training might help. Writing is the most difficult and most emphasized form of expression, but often students who fear writing can avoid courses that require it and may not learn to write. A more systematic effort should be made to make sure students do some writing each term. A healthy body is also a liberal value, and education should encourage participation by all in athletics. Students need knowledge about how the body works and on mental health.

Many different people are students, and like any other role, it has its problems in practice. For some, the best course is to drop out; college is not for everybody. Many are better able to take advantage of college when they are older. Still, many campuses could provide a more supportive milieu for students and reduce their cold impersonality. The process should be basically enjoyable. A final goal of a liberal education should be to create a lifelong interest in learning by making the process itself interesting.

Jobs. Most liberal education is poorly integrated with the world of work. Too many courses emphasize lectures; too few allow expression from the students. Many want to do something active to contrast with studying. Learning experiences from outside the classroom are poorly integrated with formal requirements. Noncourse activities like campus newspaper work, summer jobs, parttime work, student clubs, and volunteer work with the needy do not convert easily into credit, regardless how much is learned. Internships in business or government can be very useful for learning about the real world and the kinds of work available and need to be much more extensively developed. Campaigning and lobbying can provide similar experiences oriented toward citizenship. Writing about such experiences could be a way to meet the writing requirement. In the junior year there is a special need for career counseling, which is generally available, and for special courses on jobs and graduate school, which are not so common.

There is no particular impetus in higher education to define the goals of the undergraduate degree and little impetus to improve attainment of the goals. The system is not so bad as to motivate enough people to reform it; it is doing a fair job in a haphazard way. Reform of higher education is also made difficult by the intensity problem of the major consumers, the students, who do not have the knowledge, the status, or the time to change the system.

Scholarships. A large number of students can benefit from higher education but are not so outstanding that they can get scholarships under the existing system. Many are forced to spend so much time earning a living that their education suffers. Room, board, and tuition charges for a year range from about $1,704 average (1978) at a public junior college up to about $5,231 for private universities. Yet these charges cover only about a fourth of actual costs; the rest comes from government, private endowments, and private contributions.[68]

Some money can be expected from parents according to their income, and students can be expected to earn some at summer and part-time jobs. Loans are more questionable because the indebtedness is so difficult for many to afford, and there have been a large number of defaults in the federal student loan guarantee program. College education has become as important as high school education used to be, indicating that it should also be as supported as high school from public funds. In fact, the strong trend has been toward increasing governmental support for state universities and junior colleges. There is, however, an alternative that could also put more power in the hands of students and strengthen the beleaguered private institutions: grants to qualified students, which they could take to whatever college they choose. (Grades would have to be kept up and institutions would have to be accredited.) The federal Basic Educational Opportunity Grants are a step in this direction.

Crime, health, and education pose problems requiring large and complex institutions supported by taxes. The affluent are the least needful of public services because of their ability to buy private solutions, but they also contribute to the problems in important ways, such as corporate crime, promotion of unhealthy products, unsafe work places, and profit-oriented health services. They resist the taxation and commitment of concern needed to deal effectively with the problems, although through gradual reform we are spending about enough in the areas of health and education. Reducing crime requires social reform, mainly effective education and job training and public-service jobs, neighborhood alert, gun control, decriminalizing self-victimizing crime, removing many routine matters from court, continued professionalization of police, a change in court philosophy toward substantive justice and effective punishment, physical and social reform of prisons to encourage rehabilitation, and more prosecution of organized and corporate crime. Improving health is best achieved through prevention by health advocacy and by regulation. Better incentive systems are needed to control costs, and better coverage is needed for low-income people, both of which can be accomplished by national health insurance of some kind. Relicensing of physicians would ensure maintenance of skills. Health maintenance organizations overcome certain disadvantages of fee for service. Mental health services are the weakest part of the health care system. Education of the disadvantaged requires not so much busing or equal resources as compensatory resources and leadership emphasizing performance. Modified voucher systems show promise of improving parental choice and teacher control. Higher education needs a more defined liberal arts, integration with the outside world, and more student grants.

Notes

1. *Statistical Abstract of the United States, 1977*, pp. 177, 178.
2. *San Francisco Chronicle*, May 5, 1975. The data came from a three-year study by the University of California, Davis.
3. *Statistical Abstract, 1978*, pp. 78, 182, 184, and *Statistical Abstract, 1976*, pp. 67, 158, 159.
4. Ibid., p. 160; *Newsweek*, January 24, 1968.
5. *Statistical Abstract, 1976*, p. 164.
6. *Hayward* (Calif.) *Daily Review*, September 29, 1974; May 2, 1979, based on information from the U.S. Law Enforcement Assistance Program.
7. Ibid., September 24, 1973; Patricia Lunden, "The Menlo Park Police," *Atlantic Monthly* (September 1973) :16–24.
8. *Statistical Abstract, 1977*, p. 176.
9. *Statistical Abstract, 1976*, p. 171.
10. Macklin Fleming, *The Price of Perfect Justice* (New York: Basic Books, 1974), pp. 7–8, 14–16, 31–35, chaps. 4–8.
11. Ibid., chaps. 9–10.
12. Ibid., chap. 14, pp. 122–124.
13. *Hayward* (Calif.) *Daily Review*, June 6, 1977.
14. *San Francisco Chronicle*, September 28, 1977.
15. Ibid., April 25, October 2, 1977; James Q. Wilson, "Lock 'Em Up," *New York Times Magazine*, March 9, 1975.
16. *San Francisco Chronicle*, October 1, 1974.
17. Wilson, "Lock 'Em Up."
18. *Statistical Abstract, 1976*, pp. 44, 171.
19. Sarah Carey, "America's Respectable Crime Problem," *Washington Monthly* (April 1971).
20. *San Francisco Chronicle*, September 6, 1975 (column by Milton Moskowitz), October 5, 1974.
21. *Statistical Abstract, 1976*, p. 871; Ruth Leger Sivard, *World Military and Social Expenditures 1978* (Leesburg, Va.: WMSE Publications, 1978), pp. 24–27, 73, 236, 393; *Statistical Abstract, 1978*, pp. 99–100; *The Budget of the United States Government, Fiscal Year 1977*, Executive Office of the President, Office of Management and Budget (U.S. Government Printing Office: Washington, D.C.), p. 131.

22. *San Francisco Chronicle,* March 21, 1979, based on Department of Health, Education, and Welfare, *Health—United States—1978* and Congressional Budget Office, *Profile of Health Care Coverage: the Haves and Have-Nots,* both released in 1979.
23. *San Francisco Chronicle,* November 19, 1977, based on a Congressional report on black health.
24. *Sojourners* (October 1977) : 18.
25. *San Francisco Chronicle,* September 22, 1975.
26. Ibid., October 3, 1975, report on Stanford University Heart Disease Prevention Program.
27. *Statistical Abstract, 1976,* pp. 65, 92, 93; U.S. Department of Health, Education, and Welfare, *If You Must Smoke,* Publication no. (HSM) 72-7520 (1970).
28. San Francisco Chronicle, January 19, 1976.
29. Statistical Abstract, 1976, pp. 818–820.
30. "The Fortune 500," *Fortune,* May 1975, p. 230.
31. Ken Cooper, *The New Aerobics* (New York: M. Evans, 1970).
32. "Exercise and Your Heart," *Consumer Reports,* May 1977, pp. 254–256.
33. Frances M. Lappe, *Diet for a Small Planet* (New York: Friends of the Earth/Ballantine, 1971); Ellen B. Ewald, *Recipes for a Small Planet* (New York: Ballantine, 1973).
34. *San Francisco Chronicle,* November 19, 1977.
35. Ibid., October 23, 1973, column by Jack Anderson.
36. *Congressional Quarterly Almanac* (1970), pp. 675–682; *Newsweek,* August 17, 1970. See also Rachel Scott, *Muscle and Blood* (New York: Dutton, 1974).
37. *Statistical Abstract, 1978,* p. 435.
38. Philip Harter, "In Search of OSHA," *Regulation* (September–October 1977) :33–39.
39. *Special Analysis Budget of the United States Government, Fiscal Year 1977,* Executive Office of the President, Office of Management and Budget (U.S. Government Printing Office: Washington, D.C.), p. 195.
40. *Budget, 1977,* pp. 132; *Special Analysis Budget, 1977,* pp. 195, 202–203.
41. *Statistical Abstract, 1978,* p. 491; *Statistical Abstract, 1976,* pp. 72, 440–441.
42. *Statistical Abstract, 1976,* pp. 72–73.
43. Dr. Frank G. Slaughter, "U.S. Medical Care: What's Wrong?" *Family Weekly,* September 30, 1973, pp. 4–6.
44. *Statistical Abstract, 1975,* pp. 44–83.
45. Walter Goodman, "The Constitution v. the Snakepit," *New York Times Magazine,* March 17, 1974, p. 21.
46. Ibid.
47. *San Francisco Chronicle,* February 1, 1974.
48. Ibid., January 18–19, 1973; D. L. Rosenhan, "On Being Sane in Insane Places," *Science,* January 19, 1973, pp. 250–258; *Science,* April 27, 1973, pp. 356–369.
49. Gertrude Samuels, "Street Psychiatry Comes to Brooklyn," *New York Times Magazine,* November 17, 1968, p. 57ff.
50. Sheldon Glueck and Eleanor Glueck, *Of Delinquency and Crime* (Springfield, Ill.: Charles C. Thomas, 1974).
51. *San Francisco Chronicle,* October 13, 1970.
52. Leo Srole et al., *Mental Health in the Metropolis: The Midtown Manhattan Study* (New York: McGraw-Hill, 1962).
53. U.S. Bureau of the Census, *Current Population Reports,* Series P-20, no. 279 (January 1975).
54. F. Armbruster, "The More We Spend, the Less Children Learn," *New York Times Magazine,* August 28, 1977.

55. James Coleman et al., *Equality of Educational Opportunity* (Washington, D.C.: U.S. Department of Health, Education, and Welfare, 1966).
56. Southern Regional Council, *Three Myths* (Atlanta, Ga.: S.R.C., September 1976).
57. *Statistical Abstract, 1975*, p. 132.
58. John Mathews, "Fooling with Busing," *New Republic*, October 11, 1975, pp. 5–6.
59. *Statistical Abstract, 1978*, p. 148.
60. *Changing Education*, September 1973. The magazine is published by the American Federation of Teachers.
61. *San Francisco Chronicle*, September 22, 1976, based on a report from the National Assessment of Education; May 7, 1979, on Ben Franklin Junior High School in San Francisco. See also U.S. Office of Education, *Education in Action: 50 Ideas That Work* (Washington, D.C.: Government Printing Office, 1978).
62. Armbruster, "The More We Spend."
63. Willard Wirtz et al., *On Further Examination* (Princeton, N.J.: College Entrance Examination Board, 1977).
64. Ibid.
65. Jane A. Stallings and David Kaskowitz, *Follow Through Classroom Observation Evaluations 1972–1973* (Menlo Park: Stanford Research Institute, August 1974); Jane A. Stallings, "What Teachers Do Does Make a Difference" (paper, available from SRI International, Menlo Park, Calif., September 8, 1976).
66. Joel Levin, "Alum Rock," *Phi Delta Kappan*, November 1974; Personal communication with Alum Rock School District.
67. *Statistical Abstract, 1976*, pp. 129, 383.
68. Ibid., pp. 144–145.

6

The Political Machinery

Democracy and efficiency are in tension with each other, and they are difficult to balance. Democracy requires much flow of information to affected parties, much time for them to participate in decisions, and, consequently, slow decisions. Efficiency requires making decisions speedily and carrying them out. Too much emphasis on democracy tends to produce stagnation, benefits to established interests, and radicalism by those frozen out because intense minority interests use procedures to slow, delay, and stop decisions. Too much emphasis on efficiency tends to produce simplistic decisions that unnecessarily cause problems and decisions that are unrefined by debate over the balancing of values. Good government requires both, and we lack enough of either.

Procedures all too often slow reform and impede participation. As in the oil depletion case study, procedural changes are needed before we can get substantive reform. Typically, citizens start off with one small policy they want to change, only to discover by persistently asking questions that procedures stand in the way. To some extent, better policy depends on better machinery to produce it.

What is better? In addition to procedural goals of democracy and efficiency, reformers have substantive goals, so "better" procedure often means that which is more likely to get the substance. They tend to prefer federal to state and local power; a federal decision has national impact. They often prefer executive to legislative decision making; one executive is easier to reach than many legislators and is also a key to legislation. Many prefer the Supreme Court; if a constitutional angle can be found, a decision can be implemented quickly nationwide with little effort. These preferences vary from issue to issue, however, and reformers are quick to defend states' rights when they prefer state decisions. They are about as consistent as vested elites. We all find it difficult to embrace systems that make decisions we do not like. There are many equally valid ways to define democracy, making it as difficult to resolve issues of procedure as those of substance.

Civil Liberties

The central concern of this section is civil liberties and, within that, the procedures that give citizens the information they need to control government. Civil liberties are a bulwark of individual and group freedom, against which neither state nor private parties may trespass in a democracy. The protection of such freedom is an essential function of democratic government, a reason for its being. We will look at secrecy problems, illegal dissent, the international human rights issue, and two important public-interest groups, Amnesty International and the ACLU. (Major problems of civil liberties also occur in social issues such as racism, sexism, crime, and mental health.)

Civil liberties include the rule of law, with concepts of due process, equal protection, and an independent court system. Liberty includes the personal freedoms of the First Amendment—speech, press, assembly, and religion—as well as privacy and many property rights. The Bill of Rights also enumerates many freedoms relating to criminal justice, limiting the coercive power of the state. Civil liberties include political rights, mainly to register and vote, to run for office, and to petition for redress, but also by implication and necessity the right to know what the government is doing. These rights are further amplified and secured by legislation, by court decisions, and, above all, by a general commitment to make them work.

In the overall political system, the weakest support for civil liberties comes from the people and the strongest from the elites, which is the opposite pattern from most of the issues previously discussed. The people strongly support civil liberties in principle, when vague and isolated from other issues, but in specific cases, other values lead to suppression of the liberties. Free speech sounds fine until you hear someone say something you strongly disagree with. How much freedom for Nazis and Communists? For sexual deviants and pornographers? For religious zealots seemingly brainwashed by strange new cults? For scientists supporting racial inferiority doctrines? These issues sometimes pose difficult issues for sophisticated judges, but generally those who are educated have a more detailed understanding of how rights work in practice and a more tolerant attitude.

When elites' commitment to civil liberties is weakened, as it was during the McCarthy and Watergate periods, the only way toward restoration is reassertion by most of the elites and by reformers, isolating the most anti-libertarian elite. Congressional red-baiters, led by Senator Joseph McCarthy, were weakened by declining support after the army hearings in 1954; the Watergate episode ended with the resignation of President Nixon in 1974. We may now be enjoying in the late 1970s a high point of civil liberties.

The problem, however, is permanent, because the greatest threat to civil liberties is complacency. We can set up a state to protect our liberties, but who will protect us against the state? Who will police the policemen? The price of liberty is eternal vigilance.

Secrecy

There are close links among liberty, information, and citizen influence over government. In practice, given the diversity among elites and the participation of reformers, secrecy issues usually take the form of one elite's—usually the presidential elite of loyal appointees, bureaucrats and members of Congress—keeping secrets from other elites—the dissenting bureaucrats, congressmen, and other reformers. The governing elites have many legitimate secrets to keep in national security, personnel, criminal investigations, and trade secrets of business. Except for national security, the limits of legitimacy are fairly well defined under Freedom of Information acts. Government keeps secrets officially for the best of purposes (such as national defense) and expects others to believe assertions that the concealed information is indeed protecting our security. Such secrecy is backed up by lying, refusing to answer questions, falsely involving security classifications and Freedom of Information Act protections, distortions and misleading statements, closed hearings and meetings, and so on.[1]

In the last few years, an unusual number of secrets have been revealed. But in no important instance so far has the information had any measurable adverse impact on national security or other values. If anything, the national security has been undermined by an extensive loss of confidence in the believability of government. For the most part, the information has revealed policies the people needed to know to make government accountable and included information about conscious efforts to mislead the people. The real reasons for secrecy seem largely to have been contempt for dissenters; a belief that the perpetrators were above the usual democratic process; a desire to cover up mismanagement; convictions about their own sincerity, purpose, and ultimate trustworthiness; and a preference for the convenience of not having to explain or justify decisions.

Most secret revealers are not radicals. Their major characteristic is a sense of right and wrong. They simply tell an outsider—perhaps an auditor, a reporter, a lawyer, a politician, a friend, a grand jury—what they know.

Leaks. Successful leakers (those who reveal secret information) need to be careful. They need reporters they can trust not to reveal the source, such as Jack Anderson, who, with his staff, exposed President Nixon's misrepresentations about the Vietnam War, the India-Pakistan conflict, the ITT-Nixon connections, Chile, CIA assassination attempts, the secret $100,000 Hughes donation to Nixon from Bebe Rebozo, and so on. To fight leaks, elites set up counterintelligence activities. Nixon, for example, set up the Plumbers to find leaks to Anderson. Leaks from Deep Throat to the *Washington Post* were important in blowing the lid off the connections between the Watergate burglars and the Committee to Reelect the President. A 1975 House report on the CIA was leaked to Daniel Schorr, then a CBS reporter, who gave it to a New York newspaper. If the identity of the leaker is discovered, he or she is usually fired or transferred to a less sensitive position.

Since an elite is often unable to find the leak, it may attack whoever reports it. The Nixon administration launched a major attack on the broadcast media, for example, with implied threats to use the FCC to refuse renewal of licenses. In another case, columnist Anderson published Senator Paul Fanin's drunk driving record, which contrasted with Fanin's tough "law-and-order" image. Fanin was able to influence the FBI to investigate Anderson's long-distance-call record with the telephone company in an attempt to trace the source of the leak. The FBI used an unlisted number from the call record in its investigation.[2] On another occasion the FBI arrested an Anderson associate on false charges and used them to get a court order opening up telephone company records. The FBI used its subpoena to get far more records than it needed to investigate the charges, evidently looking into leaks on B-52 flight patterns over North Vietnam, Watergate stories, drug smuggling reports, and leaks from the FBI's own secret files.[3] At one point a bunch of suspicious characters tailed Anderson, whose family then spied back on them.[4] Fortunately, most attempts to force newsmen to reveal sources of political information have failed.

Whistles. Secrets are also undermined by "whistle blowers," people who reveal previously secret information without particularly hiding their identity. Whistle blowers, if they have not already left their employment that gave them the information, are usually fired or harassed by their superiors. These firings dampen the revelations needed for accountability. A decision in April 1974 by the Supreme Court reinforced this chilling effect; it decided the government could dismiss an employee even when the charges made by the employee were in good faith.[5] The protections are weak.

A. E. Fitzgerald, the official who revealed the waste in the Lockheed C5-A case, had to spend almost four years before he was able to get the civil service to order the air force to rehire him and give him back pay. He still does not have his old job. In 1974 John Holt was fired for revealing information to Congress about a government computer network and for "defaming" his fellow workers. Perhaps equally important, Holt's revelations about the solicitation of funds for Nixon by top officials of his (Holt's) agency had led to their suspension.[6]

The problem of blowing the whistle was documented in a Senate study of seventy cases of federal employees, plus additional statements from those afraid to speak out. The federal code of ethics requires employees to expose corruption but also forbids them releasing data from government files. In theory, witnesses to Congress are protected; in practice, the Justice Department does not go after high officials who abuse whistle blowers.[7] Free speech is denied not by police and prison but by economic reprisals against careers, which works about as well.

Investigations. Secrets are also found out by investigative reporting, strengthened in recent years by the Freedom of Information acts. President Ford in 1974 vetoed an improvement of the acts (FIFA) but was overridden by Congress.[8] Reporters and public-interest group researchers can use FIFA requests to get information previously denied them, and bureaucrats can defend themselves by pointing out that they have to release the information under FIFA rules. Other rule changes in recent years have been opening up the system to those who take the trouble to look.

Investigative reporting sometimes is revealing without getting secrets. Reporters can use information from the public record to show patterns that undercut elite statements. The government is so big that one part cannot keep track of what the other parts are saying. In other cases, secrecy can be undermined by simply calling attention to it.

Whistle blowing and investigative reporting are combined when an insider resigns, tries to get additional information, and writes about a problem. Victor Marchetti, a former CIA employee, is an example. When he tried to publish an account of his CIA work, the CIA sued him, demanding 339 deletions in his book. In 1974 the judge reduced the deletions to 15, saying generally that the CIA had exceeded its authority and failed to prove a need for classification.[9] Usually it is extremely difficult to get courts to review classified information, which results in great overclassification. Another court review occurred in the Daniel Ellsberg Pentagon Papers case and found no damage to national security. (The case is complicated by the fact that it was thrown out of court because of withholding of information by the government.)

Whistle-blowing congressmen are relatively hard to stop because of congressional reluctance to discipline one of their own and because of sympathy for the whistle blower. For example, Congressman Michael Harrington released classified testimony on the CIA role in Chile, which contradicted public statements by Secretary of State Henry Kissinger and other public officials. From a reform point of view, Harrington's action gave people information they need to judge their own government, which was secretly spending millions of tax dollars to overthrow a democratically elected regime in a foreign country. But from the elite perspective, Harrington was breaking the rules and giving aid to the enemy. He was removed from the investigation of the CIA but was not censured because of a technicality revealing that the testimony was not given in an official hearing.

The whole security classification system rests on executive orders, not laws passed by Congress. Congress has never made it a lawful function of the executive to withhold information from the public, nor has it made revealing classified information a crime. It is illegal to give information to a communist country and to reveal intentionally information injurious to the United States, but the injury and the intention have to be shown in court. The collapse of the Ellsberg case, the lack of statutes for official secrets, and the thrust of FIFA discourage excessive secrecy and help leaks, whistles, and investigations. But it is a seesaw struggle because the government keeps its classifications, overextends legitimate protections, investigates dissenters, and fires employees who reveal the truth. Sometimes the government is right and its critics wrong, or the matter is too complicated to tell who is right. Reformers feel the balance is too much for the government, but they are holding their own. They beat back an attempt in 1975–1976 to make most of the revelations of official misconduct of recent years a criminal offense in the future.

Invasions of Privacy

A second major governmental threat to civil liberties is illegal activity (bugs, taps, searches), which invades privacy in the name of national security or fighting crime. No one disputes the need to pursue these goals; the problem is one of excesses, which undercut other, equally fundamental values. Violations of privacy by the CIA, the army, the FBI, and other agencies also have a chilling effect on free speech. In May 1973 the CIA inspector general wrote a still classified report, nicknamed "The Family Jewels," detailing possible CIA violations of its charter prohibiting domestic activities. The "Jewels" were leaked in some form to the *New York Times,* whose story in January 1974 set off a new round of investigations by Vice-President Nelson Rockefeller, the House, and the Senate. They found that the CIA had illegally kept files on about ten thousand Americans, had committed burglaries and made illegal wiretaps, had reviewed income tax returns, had infiltrated antiwar organizations, and had tested LSD and other drugs on unsuspecting Americans, one of whom committed suicide as a result. The CIA claimed in its defense that it was trying to control leaks from within and to find connections between antiwar and black activities.[10]

The army spying operation was CONUS, running from 1967 to 1970. It reported on the activities of elected officials and eavesdropped illegally on citizen band radio at the Democratic and Republican national conventions, the Huey Newton trial, the march on the Pentagon, demonstrations in Washington, and the Poor People's March, all during 1967–1968. The army compiled 190 lineal feet of dossiers and card files on dissidents, covering financial affairs, sex lives, and psychiatric histories. Internal memos show the army was well aware CONUS was illegal; officers were very concerned not to get caught. They were caught but not punished.[11]

The FBI may be the greatest threat because its legitimate mission includes domestic operations for security and against crime. In the process of trying to find conspiracies to break the law, it necessarily becomes familiar with a large amount of irrelevant information. Many dissenters will break the law if they think it will advance their cause. Infiltrating and eavesdropping are essential to the FBI's task. The problems are the use of illegal means, the pursuit of more information when illegal activity seems unlikely, and the misuse of the information. From 1956 to 1971, the FBI carried out a counterintelligence program against the Right and the Left called COINTELPRO. Initially concerned with the Communist party, COINTELPRO added white hate groups in 1964, black "extremists" in 1962, and the New Left in 1968 to the groups it monitored. J. Edgar Hoover, the FBI chief from 1924 to 1972, also had some secret files of his own, in which he collected sensitive information about public officials. Neither system was careful about verifying information and collected it on an open-ended basis with no guidelines to protect privacy. Illegal wiretapping was especially common, so much so that in 1972 the Supreme Court had to rule that the FBI could not tap suspects without a court warrant. The FBI also conducted hundreds of housebreakings.

The government's systematic violation of the Fourth Amendment undermined its prosecution of many dissidents by making its evidence inadmissible. The FBI made matters worse by sharing its information with the CIA, the army, and the National Security Agency, an arm of the Pentagon using advanced technology for intelligence. In eavesdropping on overseas cable traffic, the National Security Agency picked up political information and relayed it outside of channels to the White House.[12]

Spying and privacy are pervasive problems. Even members of the elites have had their privacy invaded, as in cases of spying on members of the Supreme Court and the instances when the Joint Chiefs of Staff secretly copied papers written by Kissinger intended only for Nixon.[13] Corporations spy on each other for trade secrets and on government to find out about proposals for regulation. Retail Credit Inc. (now Equifax), the biggest credit investigation firm in the United States with three-fourths of the business, has personal files on 45 million Americans. An FTC investigation discovered a kind of quota system requiring enough bad news to lend credibility to its reports, but the victims were never told about it.[14] This and other abuses led to the 1971 Fair Credit Reporting Act, allowing people to get their ratings and challenge information in their file.

Suppression of Dissent

If government were responsible in its use of information, its invasions of privacy might not be so bad, which brings us to a third problem, governmental suppression of legal dissent. The government is not a theory; it is people, many of whom have strong political opinions going beyond their legally defined functions. The FBI's COINTELPRO's primary mission was disruption of dissenting organizations. A 1974 report detailed 2,370 acts of sabotage, mostly anonymous or fictitious letters or forged documents designed to confuse and undermine. Another technique was repeated questioning by agents during working hours, which could cost people their jobs. The FBI also harassed and intimidated people off the job. Provocateurs incited extremists within groups to undertake acts of violence.[15] For almost ten years, the FBI harassed Martin Luther King with no criminal or security purpose in mind. He was almost constantly under electronic or physical surveillance. The FBI used a mostly unintelligible tape recording as the basis for character assassination of King and attempted to disrupt his marriage and destroy his reputation. A monograph of false charges was circulated, and many false rumors started, some in an attempt to prevent King from receiving international honors.[16]

The high point for harassment of legal dissent occurred during the Nixon administration. Attorney General John Mitchell (himself later convicted for perjury, conspiracy, and obstruction of justice) illegally ordered a wiretap on Daniel Ellsberg. The FBI investigated Ellsberg for four years after he revealed the Pentagon Papers. Burglars acting on orders from the White House broke into his psychiatrist's office to steal his file. The CIA constructed a psychological profile of him despite its prohibition on domestic activities. The U.S. attorney initially told to prosecute Ellsberg refused to do so and was fired. While the case was being tried, Nixon offered the directorship of the FBI to the presiding judge. The government's case was weak because all substantive information in the Pentagon Papers had been published before in newspapers and in the memoirs of generals. Numerous witnesses from the defense establishment testified that the relevations had not damaged national security. When the government failed to reveal wiretaps relevant to the case, the case was dismissed. A poll of the jury indicated that they would not have convicted Ellsberg. But in the meantime, Ellsberg was forced to spend two years of his life raising funds and fighting in court.

Other cases involve IRS harassment, requested by the White House, of the Center for Corporate Responsibility, a research group, ended by a court order in 1973.[17] The Special Services Staff of the IRS, set up in 1969, audited 11,000 persons labeled "extremist," which included newsmen, politicians, actors, foundations, and established public-interest groups.[18] There is some evidence that a U.S. Army intelligence unit in Chicago worked with a rightist terrorist organization from 1969 to 1971 to beat, gas, and wreak havoc on antiwar activists. The Chicago police protected the organization and operated its own intelligence gathering.[19] In January 1975, a federal jury awarded $10,000 in damages to each of about 1,200 persons arrested during the May 1971 antiwar demonstrations in Washington, D.C. The arrests were ruled in violation of the First and Fourth amendments. Arrest records of 13,000 more persons were ordered expunged from the record.[20] The Justice Department was involved in setting up this harassment and also in at least a hundred investigations up to 1973. Over four hundred indictments were made, but only about 25 percent produced convictions, far below the usual conviction rate of 95 percent, and usually for unrelated minor offenses.[21] Ellsberg, the Chicago Seven, the Berrigan brothers, the Gainesville Eight, and others found their lives tied up in legal proceedings and fund raising for many months.[22] Many other examples could be cited, none of them part of legitimate criminal or security investigations, all of them aimed at suppressing legitimate dissent. This suppression is not the result of single individuals but of large and powerful institutions of many persons.

Illegal Dissent and the Role of Violence

The governmental threat from secret keeping, snooping, and suppression of legitimate dissent is encouraged by lawbreaking at the other end of the spectrum by a few extremists who engage in violence. Violence always seems to accompany change, including reformist change, and is so intermixed with other factors that it is hard to separate out its role. Sometimes it may seem to help success, other times to prevent it. The most useful kind of violence seems to be that which is carefully structured by reformists and comes from the elites. Three major examples include violence by police against women seeking the vote, violence by employers against workers seeking to unionize, and violence by police against civil rights workers seeking racial equality. In these cases, the attention of the mass media publicizes the violence, stripping the mask of pieties from the face of oppression. Public opinion shifts toward more concern and support for change.

Conversely, violence by those seeking change may lose sympathy and cause a reaction against the perpetrators. Black violence may have been a major factor slowing the civil rights movement. Antiwar violence may have provoked the election of conservative politicians, prolonging the Vietnam War and weakening civil liberties. Media magnification of the violence on the fringe reduces the effectiveness of peaceful demonstrations. Bombings are also relevant for civil liberties because frequently their political motivation provokes governmental overreaction and confusion in the public mind between legal and illegal dissent. In 1975 bombings killed 42, wounded 242, and caused $23.4 million in damages. In 1978 bombs killed 78 persons, injured 444, and caused $42 million damage. Homes and vehicles of police officers are often targets.[23] Activity is concentrated on the coasts, downtowns, and campuses.

Extremists seem to feel that antigovernmental violence for the people is justified by governmental violence against the people. Yet like others who feel strongly that they have the answers, they have a peculiarly restrictive way of defining people to exclude those they disagree with and of deciding what other people should think. The reality of our situation is similar to many other places and times: most people want personal security and will support counterrevolutionary efforts to get it. Counterrevolution is far more common than revolution in history. Politicians may well attain popularity by attacking unpopular dissent regardless of how legal it is. Thus, violence undermines civil liberties. If the center cannot hold, the extremes can feed on each other, destroying a system without producing anything better.

Public-Interest Groups

The ACLU. The American Civil Liberties Union has been the leading public-interest group domestically since its founding in 1920. It is one of the few large, old, still aggressive public-interest groups in America. (A tentative list of the others includes the Consumers' Union, the Sierra Club, the Audubon Society, Planned Parenthood, and the NAACP.) The history of the ACLU illustrates the theme of the durability of the central issues of this book even as the specific problems change, and hence the relevance of permanently organized citizen action.

The ACLU in its first decades was active in protecting the right of workers to unionize and the right of employers to propagandize against unions. It worked to prevent the illegal deportation of aliens and defended the right of John Scopes to teach evolution in Tennessee. It defended Sacco and Vanzetti and the Scottsboro boys, one of whom was finally released in 1976. In the 1940s, the ACLU helped conscientious objectors, draftees, and servicemen and did so again in the 1960s. It has fought against censorship, including action against the Customs Bureau to allow *Ulysses* by James Joyce to come into the United States. The ACLU tried to prevent the deportation of Japanese-Americans to inland concentration camps during World War II. Because of our wartime alliance with Stalin, the government began to prosecute his communist enemies, the Trotskyites, and the ACLU defended them. For years, the ACLU fought off the Mundt-Nixon bill, which eventually passed as the McCarran Act in 1950 over Truman's veto in the heat of the McCarthy Era. By 1979, all effective provisions of the act had been found unconstitutional. The ACLU has helped civil rights, opposing white primaries in Texas and poll taxes in Virginia. It has championed rights for Indians, homosexuals, children, students, women, hippies, the mentally ill, prisoners, and migrant workers.

In the 1950s, the ACLU fought against the excesses of McCarthyism and helped with the *Brown* school desegregation decision. It opposed censorship of birth control information and illegal detention by police. It won cases prohibiting prayer and Bible reading in the schools. In the 1960s, the ACLU helped defend the freedom riders and other civil rights activists. It won court enforcement of "one person-one vote." It worked for years against a vague and useless loyalty oath, which was eventually struck down, and also for years against the congressional committee most abusive of civil rights, the House Un-American Activities Committee, which was finally disbanded.

In the 1970s, the ACLU has continued to help indigent defendants get public defenders and other protections against forced confessions and illegal searches and seizures. It has worked for liberalization of abortion and marijuana laws, against discriminatory death penalties, and for the integration of juries in the South. There is hardly an area it has not touched.

The greatest historical challenge for the ACLU was its campaign to impeach President Nixon. Ultimately the Judiciary Committee would vote only a few of the articles of impeachment sought. In October 1973, the ACLU placed full-page advertisements in major papers citing Nixon's firing of the Watergate prosecutor; his approval of the Huston plan for illegal political surveillance; his creation of the Plumbers; his actions against Ellsberg; his use of private detectives to obtain personal information on his opponents; his attempts to harass dissenters; his use of the FBI to tap and harass reporters; and, finally, his claiming of an inherent power to violate the law.

In 1975, a less conspicuous but extremely important campaign was waged by the ACLU against a revision of the federal criminal code, which was used as an excuse to try to strengthen government secret keeping. When reformers wrote their version of the complex and overdue revision, it had over a thousand differences from the Senate bill. The ACLU's Project on

National Security and Civil Liberties has played an important role in the secrecy problem already discussed. It also has a Women's Rights Project and a National Prison Project. Only the U.S. government itself appears more often before the Supreme Court. The ACLU is active across a wide sweep of concerns because of the contributions of 250,000 citizens and the time volunteered by many lawyers. It has 350 local chapters dealing with a multitude of local issues.

Amnesty International. The relatively high level of enjoyment of civil liberties in the United States becomes clear when we look at most other countries in the world today, especially those with massive and barbaric violations of rights we take for granted. Our enjoyment is evident in the lack of fear of most people to speak up on those infrequent occasions when they feel threatened by governmental action. People of many other countries live in fear, accepting arbitrary exercises of power we would not tolerate. There seems to be no overall trend toward world freedom. Democracy and human rights, in fact, seem to be sliding backward; many countries have become dictatorships since the high point of democracy after World War II. There are positive cases: Mexico, Venezuela, India, Greece, Spain, and Portugal, some only recently and tentatively on this list. There is also the de-Stalinization of Eastern Europe and many smaller cases. But do they outweigh the many losses? We were involved when our CIA allowed Korean and Iranian secret police to operate outside the law in this country and when our policy of silence condoned their torture policies and those of our other allies.

What nation is the most barbaric? Was it Idi Amin's Uganda, where terror and genocide against subordinate tribes was the order of the day? Was it Cambodia, where a faceless new revolution probably killed far more of its own citizens than many years of war and foreign intervention? Or should we rank worst those countries whose extremes of torture are or were incredible—Brazil, Iran, and Argentina? Can we leave out the mass imprisonments of most communist countries and many autocracies? Extensive documentation of torture in Chile suggests its use as an illustration, all the more relevant because of U.S. influence in bringing the generals to power. People there are arrested at will, some several times. They are frequently tortured and often killed. Hundreds have disappeared. One man caught hiding in an attic was shot in front of his wife and small son. Common tortures include electrical shock to the genitals and other sensitive parts; sexual abuse, especially of women; and beatings with guns, sticks, and chains. Chile borrowed the *pau de arara* ("Parrot's perch") torture from Brazil, part of a trend of internationalization of torture techniques. The victim is hung for hours or days upside down from the knees with wrists and ankles tied together; this is often combined with electric shocks and cigarette burns.

Hundreds of people have testified to these and other tortures in detail and with monotonous repetition.[24]

Increasingly, the names of the torturers, the places, exact parts of the bureaucracy, and training schools are known. Such cruelty is largely gratuitous; it has never played an important role in the stability of the regime in Chile or elsewhere. Torture is used to punish people for their anti-government thoughts and for the haphazard and unreliable extraction of information.

Annual reports on human rights are issued by Amnesty International and by Freedom House, a private group concerned with human rights. In 1977, Freedom House found just one-third of the world's people living in freedom, but this was greater than the previous years largely because of the recovery of democracy in India for its 622 million people. Spain also improved, while freedom for 124 million people in nine countries declined.[25] Over a longer period, there are rises and falls in human rights. Once started, official violence tends to acquire a life of its own and becomes extreme before enough people become aware of what is going on and opinion forms to stop it. Violations in Chile, for example, have declined.

Up to 1977, U.S. policy was dominated by military security concerns. We downplayed violations in communist countries to improve détente and downplayed them in our allies to be stronger against communism. These concerns are still very influential. However, even within this framework, disregard for human rights may undermine our security. There comes a day of reckoning. If and when popular forces or counterelites overthrow a regime, how will they feel about the United States? Our influence, as shown by Indochina, is marginal in the affairs of foreign countries, but sometimes it can make the difference, as shown in Chile, and can be exaggerated, magnifying our responsibilities all the more. We have supported many of the repressers, such as the shah of Iran, with military and police aid, arms sales, training, economic aid, and diplomacy. In Chile we covertly financed the strikes that paralyzed the country and precipitated the military coup. We helped starve Chile of international credit, creating economic crisis on top of what was being created by copper prices and mismanagement. Other democratic countries have seen these actions, our Indochina involvement, and our support for repressive regimes in Greece, Spain, and elsewhere. American prestige has been falling slowly and steadily according to opinion polls sponsored by our government in foreign countries. Our excessive support for the shah of Iran is the major factor causing hostility toward the U.S. by the new Islamic regime.

In 1977 President Carter began a new emphasis on human rights in American diplomacy, with all the ambiguity, potential for self-righteousness, and ineffectiveness that such an effort must risk. Nevertheless, human rights advocates have welcomed it and feel it has done some good.

U.S. corporations pull us closer to certain regimes than we would otherwise be. Evidence from Brazil indicates that corporations will subsidize police operations not only against violent revolutionaries but against all dissenters, just as here in the 1930s they sought to suppress unions. Some corporations have contracted with security firms headed by Brazilian military officers. Some U.S. businessmen financed demonstrations against President João Goulart, helping his overthrow by the military in 1964.[26] U.S. corporate involvement and sometimes complicity in South Africa's apartheid system of racism is well established.

At Helsinki in 1975, the Soviet Union agreed to have "respect for human rights and fundamental freedom, including freedom of thought, conscience, religion or belief." They did not mean it as we would understand it, but they did open themselves up to more diplomatic pressure from the West. When the U.S. Senate made free migration of Jews an explicit requirement for improved trade, the Soviets cut back harshly on the limited emigration they had allowed. The U.S.S.R. has shown small trends of liberalization, but there have also been sharp repressive measures. *A Chronicle of Human Events,* an underground newspaper in the Soviet Union, has irregularly published on the abuses of the Soviet system for those few willing to see it. Typewritten manuscripts by dissidents pass from hand to hand secretly; a few are smuggled to the West and published. One example, Solzhenitsyn's monumental indictment, the *Gulag Archipelago,* is banned from the Soviet Union. Andrei Sakharov wrote *Progress, Coexistence and Intellectual Freedom* in 1968 and won the Nobel Peace Prize in 1975, the same year the KGB increased repression. Sakharov is allowed some freedom because of his international prestige; but other dissenters are treated less kindly.

Americans could greatly strengthen the cause of freedom by giving just a little time and money to others so that they can be high-level activists. The human rights area has an outstanding public-interest group, Amnesty International, winner of a Nobel Peace Prize in 1977.

Amnesty International was started in 1961 and in 1979 had grown to about 200,000 members throughout the world, with some concentration in northwestern Europe. American support has grown to 75,000 members in 155 groups. By 1976 Amnesty had taken about 13,000 cases and influenced the release of over 7,500 prisoners. It has files on about 4,000 political prisoners around the world, chosen because they are "prisoners of conscience" and do not advocate or use violence. Amnesty also protests torture of prisoners. Each Amnesty group adopts a few prisoners; it writes letters to and for its prisoners and seeks publicity for their cases. Its major weapon is publicity to influence world opinion in its favor. Many governments will release or exile a prisoner rather than put up with adverse publicity. Amnesty is influential because it is careful in its research, scrupulously nonpartisan, and therefore credible.

Money and Politics

Economic elites can use money to influence majority rule or to move into the vacuum created by lack of majority interest. They have enough money so they can use some to get power, and because they have power, they have money. Money is used to get power by buying the time of others with political skills, mainly lawyers, lobbyists, advertisers, accountants, business managers, scientists, engineers, technicians, and bankers. Good information, also expensive, improves the chances of success in the use of money for more directly political activities. A detailed, well-argued case can win a decision from a voter, reporter, elected official, bureaucrat, judge, or other holder of formal power and may do so independently of its merits. Money buys time to develop information to get influence.

Money influences voters through information and propaganda. Money means access to the media, themselves a type of vested interest. The media over time influence what we see as objective or biased. As compaign contributions, money elects friendly officials, and it then supports lobbying for favorable decisions. With this system, bribery is an unnecessary expense, although still occasionally used. Money buys access to the courts. The law regulates everything but is often ambiguous on specifics, allowing money to pay for lawyers to influence judges.

This section will concentrate on favors from politicians (elected officials and top appointees) to vested interests, from these interests to politicians, and from politicians to themselves. It will look at reforms to deal with abuses, such as lobby reform, conflict of interest reform, open meetings and records, campaign disclosure, public financing of campaigns, and enforcement machinery.

Favors to Vested Interests

Politicians help determine the profitability of all business. They legislate regulations, contracts, subsidies, and taxes that create markets and allow economic concentration. They create bureaucracies to implement the law and appoint top officials. Government is mostly a system of doling out favors and regulating conflict within the elites. Most subtle, even insidious, is the way officials control the development of information needed to control elites, creating knowledge needed by elites to perpetuate the system and avoiding it where needed for reform.

Some favors are not commonly known. Governments deposit tax collections in private banks, frequently at no interest, as a favor to bankers. At the federal level alone, bankers receive interest-free loans worth about $3 billion to $4 billion a year. The Federal Reserve System grants and revokes bank charters, decides the discount rate and money supply, and permits bankers themselves to control most of this system. Given uniform insurance rates, the choice of insurance becomes another opportunity to do a favor. Government buys or leases goods and services for its offices, motor pools, publishing, computers, and so on. Larger purchases by most governments are put to bid, but many smaller purchases (and in some states, even bigger ones) are made by political favor, either directly or by influencing the bidding process. Government buys and sells land and buildings and builds buildings for itself and for urban renewal, benefiting politically connected architects, realtors, and contractors.

Political appointees at top echelons of the Pentagon typically allow cost overruns, excess profits, and waste in advanced technology procurement. The Renegotiation Board, an independent agency outside the Pentagon, could recover the excess profits through legislated procedures but is not given enough staff to do the job. In 1975 President Ford rejected hiring more auditors.[27]

Some favors are not in terms of money for a business but rather go to individuals in the form of well-paying jobs. Judges are typically not selected by competitive examination, judicial qualifications commissions, or even by vote of the people. Merit is often important, but political connections are the key. Judges in turn do favors when they appoint receivers, guardians, trustees, referees, and appraisers in cases with large fees but little work. Most of government employment has become controlled by civil service systems, taking many jobs out of the hands of elected officials, but the spoils system still survives, and not just for judges. Many officials have a few appointments they can make, some governors have hundreds, and the president has a few thousand. Many cities lack any civil service. There are usually many advisory commissions and boards, some with real power, for which appointment is a political favor. Until recently, the U.S. Post Office was run by political appointees. District attorneys, their assistants, and marshals are still patronage appointments, and DAs, like judges, do favors in their turn by deciding what cases to prosecute. They may seek to protect their friends from citizen complaints, for example.

Local governments control many favors to business by general policies and land-use designations, specific zonings, site plans for buildings, conditional uses, business permits, building and grading and occupancy permits, and public investments in sewage, water, and roads. The biggest single favor giver is, of course, the federal government. Much has already been mentioned in this regard. It also influences agricultural prices, grazing rights, and timber harvesting. It gave $300 million in subsidies to farmers in 1974, a year of high market prices and an all-time high for farm incomes.

At the pinnacle of power is the president, whose decisions inevitably mean favors for vested interests. Presidential budget, appointment, legislative, and administrative decisions can radically affect whole industries. The president can influence airline routes, television channels, maritime subsidies, small business loans, antitrust prosecutions, and milk prices. An antitrust settlement favorable to ITT in 1971 for example, was a political decision at the presidential level.

In general, politicians let interests have excessive influence over the government that is supposed to control them. Their bias is evident not only in their decisions but also in whom they appoint to high office. Appointments are routinely cleared with moneyed interests, but the assent of public-interest groups is usually bypassed. Appointees very frequently come from the industry they are supposed to regulate and are therefore favorably disposed to industry thinking. While in government, they may continue to have a financial interest in the industry they are supposed to regulate. They leave government to join or rejoin the industry they regulated, if their decisions were friendly to it.

Systematic information has been collected in recent years by Common Cause, a public-interest group specializing in reform of the money and secrecy system. Its research discovered that over half of the 42 commissioners appointed to 15 regulatory agencies from 1971 to 1975 came from companies or law firms of the regulated industry, and 518 officials in 11 agencies own stock or other financial holdings in companies they regulated or in companies with which the agency had a contract. Information was lacking on an additional 619 employees who had failed to file required financial statements. Of 429 top employees of the Nuclear Regulatory Agency, 279 came from regulated or contracting firms. Over two-thirds of the NRA's 162 consultants were also working for such firms. From 1969 to 1973, 1,406 officers and employees left the Defense Department for jobs with defense contractors, many of them for contractors they had dealt with as public servants.[28]

Favors to Politicians

The favor system is reciprocal, with complementary favors going to the officials from the interests. Campaign contributions are the main example, but bribery and favors given without a specific goal are also important. Businesses, for example, give free meals, tickets to sports events, and discounts on merchandise to local police and inspectors. Bribery has greatly declined over the years, partly because civil servants are so much better paid than they used to be, but it has not completely disappeared. In Maryland, construction firms used to give back part of the payments they received from government to the government officials who gave them the contracts.

Considerable evidence implicated former Vice-President Spiro Agnew in bribery, extortion, and tax fraud, but in 1973 he pleaded no contest to a lesser charge and the case was dropped.[29]

Money for a campaign may be a bribe if the contributor gets a direct return favor. In 1971–1972, milk producers gave over $682,500 to Nixon's fund mostly in the form of checks for $2,500 made out to a multitude of spurious committees, all designed to hide the money and circumvent the law. They got a price increase of about $600 million a year. The milkmen were clear in their minds how the system was working and have said so in court. They believed they had to donate to the campaign to get their price increase. On March 12, 1971, USDA denied a price increase. On March 23, President Nixon met with the secretary of agriculture and sixteen top milkmen. On March 24, the Nixon campaign fund received the first checks from the milk association, as arranged in the White House but not in Nixon's presence. On March 25, the support price for milk was increased by the president, reversing the USDA decision. Ralph Nader sued but Nixon kept one hundred essential documents secret, claiming executive privilege. Nixon denied any direct connection between the contributions and the price increase.[30] Many similar though smaller cases could be mentioned.[31] Local elected officials, for example, typically receive campaign contributions from developers whose projects they later approve.

Elected officials often have businesses of their own before they go into politics and keep their old connections to some extent after they are elected. Thus, one way businessmen can do favors to officials is to do business with their law firm, buy insurance from their insurance firm, bank with their bank, and buy from their stores. Or they can give business to a close relative of the official.

Campaign Contributions. The primary mechanism for excessive elite influence is the giving of campaign contributions. It is the major part of the political system not yet paid for by taxes; it is a tiny part of the whole system, and it is the only part the vested interests need to control in order to have excessive influence in the system. Money is not the only influence over the outcome of an election, nor does all money come from antireform vested interests. However, money is the most important factor in initially winning major offices and in keeping a contested seat, and most of it comes from vested interests. Only presidential campaigns have been reformed and financed with mostly public money. Since about one-third of spending for all offices up to 1976 was for the presidency, we can say the system is about one-third reformed. About 23 percent of contributions and spending goes to congressional races, 22 percent to state races, and 22 percent for local races, and this distribution is one way of estimating the relative importance of the various offices.[32]

People running for office generally do not sell out. Rather, candidates critical of moneyed interests do not get contributions from them and cannot get their message across to the voters. Candidates who share views sympathetic to those of dominant vested interests can get contributions from them, get their message across, and win.

The costs of reaching voters are high and rising. In 1952 about $140 million was spent at all levels of government for over 500,000 elective offices, mostly local. By 1972 the costs were $425 million, a tripling over twenty years, and none of it from taxes. (Lest that seem expensive, over $23 billion was spent on advertising in 1972.)[33] This rate of increase is much faster than the rate of inflation. In 1976 the presidential race cost $114 million, of which $68 million was tax funds. Congressional campaigns that same year cost $105 million.

Incumbency. The primary problem for new politicians is raising funds to contest an election. Once elected, most politicians, especially if they cultivate their districts, can win reelection with much less money; others consider them to be likely winners, so the money is much easier to raise. Incumbent congressmen have the resources they need to win reelection. They have large budgets, large staffs, home district offices, travel expenses, and mailing privileges worth, by one estimate in 1975, $488,505 per congressman.[34] They can build name identification, important since most people do not know who represents them. Incumbents can make public appearances, announce federal spending in the district ("bring home the bacon" from the "pork barrel"), respond to letters, help people with problems with the bureaucracy, and send newsletters. They can, in fact, become free of commitments to vested interests, and many of them act free, but most share the general philosophy of the interests because of the initial selection process. Winning that first race depended on money, and the interests give money to candidates who agree with them. From 1968 to 1974, the average percentage of incumbents winning reelection to Congress ranged from 90 percent to 99 percent.[35]

Deaths, resignations, and incumbent losses allow each Congress an average of new members of about 10 percent in the Senate and about 15 percent in the House. Since most seats are safe (reelection is easy), many officials have long incumbencies. If a candidate wins by less than 55 percent of the popular vote, the seat is not considered safe. Over three-quarters of congressional candidates win by over 55 percent.[36]

In sum, money is important in two kinds of races: vacant seats and unsafe seats where the challenger can raise a lot of money. In 1974, there were fifty-two vacant House seats, which the average candidate spent over $94,000 trying to win. There were forty races in which challengers actually defeated incumbents (the number being higher than usual because of anti-

Republican sentiment after Watergate). Most of the successful challengers outspent the incumbents. Senate seats are more expensive: nine vacant seats were up for which the average candidate spent $400,000.[37]

Donors. There are many kinds of donors. Identifiable individuals giving over $10,000 each are usually the wealthy, corporate executives, and professionals; in 1972, there were 1,254 such "fat cats" who gave $51.2 million.[38] Political party groups who raised funds for congressional races from large and small givers gave $7.3 million; labor unions gave $8.5 million; economic interest groups gave $8.0 million; and other groups, variously labeled public interest, ideological, or special interest and often supported by smaller givers, raised $2.6 million, all in 1972.[39] Businesses giving goods and services are also important sources of funds, but figures are not available. About 8 to 12 percent of adults give in presidential election years; in 1972 an estimated 11.7 million gave, most of them small amounts.[40] Despite the large number of small contributors, large contributors gave much more money.

Big donors dominate not only in the amount they give but also because their money is more easily raised and given earlier in a campaign. It can be used as seed money for the important initial organizing and fund-raising efforts. Big donors are also more sophisticated at putting their money in key races for credible candidates.

Republicans have traditionally had more support from big donors than Democrats have. In 1972, fifty-one of sixty-three persons with fortunes over $150 million gave to a presidential candidate, a rate of 81 percent, far above the national norm. They gave over $6 million, and 91 percent of it to the Republicans. A separate study of thirty-nine newly rich persons (who owned $50 million or more) showed that 72 percent of them gave a total of $1.5 million, 77 percent of it to Republicans. Twelve prominent families in 1972 gave $3.7 million, 94 percent of it to Republicans.[41] Officers and directors of the American Medical Association, the American Bar Association, the Business Council, the National Association of Manufacturers, the U.S. Chamber of Commerce, and eight other top elite groups gave 90 percent of their money ($3.7 million) to the Republicans. Nixon got $2.6 million; McGovern, only $1,250. About 31 percent of these people gave, well above national levels. Contributions by officers and directors of the twenty-five leading contractors with the Defense Department, the Atomic Energy Commission, and NASA and of the top twenty-five of the Fortune 500 for industry (a total of seventy-two big firms) gave $3.1 million, 85 percent of which went to Republicans.[42]

The Democrats have done better in other years and in other races but generally have to make up for their lack of wealth and lack of social ties to business in other ways to get funding. In specific cases it seems to involve some corruption. Mayor Richard Daley's Chicago machine system was well known. In Alabama, businesses that sell asphalt, insurance, milk, road equipment, and other supplies to the state also turned out to be major contributors to George Wallace's campaign fund. Those who declined to contribute apparently did not win bids or secure favorable specifications. Liquor distributors, who sold only to state liquor stores, often seemed to provide kickbacks to Wallace supporters, says Jack Anderson, who has names, dates, details, and cancelled checks. When the IRS investigated, it found that Wallace's brother had some unreported income through his law firm. But in May 1972, after Nixon and Wallace conferred, the tax case was dropped.[43] Democrats in office also have the attraction of incumbency; many businesses contribute to campaigns just to keep access. It is important to distinguish among Democrats, however; conservative and moderate incumbents get the most money.

Democrats have been more favored by higher levels of party activism and small giving, although Barry Goldwater, Wallace, and Ronald Reagan have been able to tap the same kind of support. Small giving is generated by telethons, candidate appeals in the media, direct mail, and by public-interest groups, which depend on committed citizens. These groups were especially important in the late 1960s and early 1970s in the antiwar movement and in the 1970s for the environmental movement, both of which mostly supported reformist Democrats. The big, traditional standby for the Democrats, however, has been the labor unions, which are powerful enough in numbers and money partially to counterbalance Republican business, but which by the same token often have vested interests inhibiting their reformism. Both corporations and unions have proliferated political action committees under the new 1976 political reform law, assuring a continuation and even enhancement of their influence.

The big money bias could be easily overcome if average-income people were to give more. If 30 million people—about half the number who voted in 1974, a little over a fifth of the voting age population—had given $15 each for all races—local, state, congressional, and presidential—it would have raised $450 million, which is more than what was spent for all races in 1972. The fact that campaign money comes largely from vested interests cannot help but bias the system in their favor. Even a city council seat in a city of about 100,000 can cost $3,000 for an inexpensive campaign (and over $10,000 for a more expensive one). Nixon won by an eyelash in 1968; one critical factor was that he had $10 million more to spend than did his opponent, Hubert Humphrey.

Campaign money is increasingly spent on television. Excluding production costs, $60 million was spent in this way in 1972: it was 14 percent of total campaign spending.[44] Radio and television spots are simplistic in their appeals. A typical minute of national prime time in 1972 cost $50,000 and reached 13 million homes; it seems expensive but is cheaper than a mailing—$.038 per house versus $.163 for a mailing.[45] Moreover, 95 percent of homes have television, which are kept on an average of 5.5 hours a day, making it the most important leisure activity in America. The spot advertisement generally plays on simple hopes and fears, greatly oversimplifying the nature of the choice that voters have. This medium is probably effective in reaching the 10 to 20 percent of the population who vote but who are not well informed and are undecided. This group frequently determines the outcome of an election.

Like other professionals who provide the elite with skills aimed at profits, politicians tend to exaggerate the importance of their role. They emphasize the political problems a business faces and what they, the politicians, can do about them, and how much business needs to give to win the election. Few politicians were more adroit than President Nixon in 1972, who indicated to his supporters how much each was expected to give. (Mark Hanna used the same technique in the late nineteenth century.) Nixon succeeded in collecting a lot more than he needed, including the cash surplus that nurtured Watergate. The pressure was such that many executives gave from fear that Nixon would hurt them. Individually, many felt threatened and failed to realize their collective strength. The pressure induced illegal contributions on a scale unusual even in American history. The law prohibits direct contributions from corporations. The Watergate prosecutions of 1973–1974 produced forty-two guilty pleas for almost a million dollars in illegal contributions by corporate elite executives. They paid token fines and none went to jail.[46]

Nixon received almost $5 million from 413 top people in 178 oil companies, some of it illegally. The Watergate revelations led to others, and by 1975 many top firms were being investigated by the IRS, other administrative agencies, and Congress. Many have admitted to illegal actions.

The international dimension involves bribes and secret agents. Northrup, for example, was not confident that the merits of its planes would sell them. It had the vice-president of the French Assembly secretly on its payroll, a man who had also been chief of the French Air Force, who touted Northrup over France's own Mirage jets. Northrup secretly supported a Swiss firm to sell its planes and bribed Saudi Arabian and Iranian officials. Northrup sprinkled "agency fees" around Europe to influential people to promote its sales. Meanwhile, it made secret illegal cash contributions (totaling $250,000) to powerful Republicans and Democrats friendly to military spending. Northrup was one of three companies known to benefit from lack of adequate review by the Renegotiation Board, making 400 percent more profit on net worth than the industry average.[47]

In 1979 Lockheed Corp. pleaded guilty to concealing $1.8 million in payoffs to a former Japanese prime minister and to hiding additional sums given to other Japanese business and political officials. Lockheed pleaded guilty to four counts of wire fraud and four counts of making false statements to the government, both felonies, and to two misdemeanor violations for carrying excessive cash into and out of the United States. Four other corporations have made guilty pleas based on agreements with the Justice Department, which included not bringing criminal charges against individuals. Lockheed also admitted to the Securities and Exchange Commission making at least $30 million in secret payments to people in nineteen countries.

In 1978 a law took effect prohibiting payoffs to foreign officials; some problems are anticipated in interpreting the law.

Political investing by elites is geographically mobile within the country as well as internationally. Most people do not even give to a local candidate for Congress, but the elites give to any race of importance to them in the whole country. For example, oilmen had benefited from Senator Mike Gravel's (D-Alaska) work on the Alaska pipeline. Hess Oil and Dallas oil interests raised $60,000 as soon as they heard from his staff that he needed it to cover his campaign debts. Gravel, like other politicians, also gives speeches to companies that he helps and is paid large fees for this work.[48] This geographic mobility contrasts with restraint respecting function; each vested interest tends to stay within its particular business. Oil interests give to their key congressmen, for example, and bankers to theirs. Industrialist H. Ross Perot gave $57,900 to selected members of Congress in 1974; he was the biggest individual giver. He gave to those with the power to affect his Medicare-Medicaid data-processing business.[49] At the local level, taxi companies and builders support city council candidates that regulate them.

Contributions are also in the form of business favors. Contributors may buy advertising in the brochures of the political party conventions and loan office space, telephones, paper, printing, air travel, hotels, and vehicles for campaigns. These expenses can be written off immediately as a business expense or billed and written off later as uncollectable debts. (Indeed if the candidate loses, they may well be uncollectable.)

The system of bias is not perceived as such by the participants. The affluent are not more cynical than average; they have a way of thinking that preserves their feeling of integrity. Threats to particular businesses are easily translated into threats to whole economies, and sometimes with good reason. Elite members are specialized and often feel that "politics" is outside their expertise. They give with a sense of civic duty to people they feel have good judgment (like their own). They often think that the public is too apathetic, and if it understood better the problems of business, there would be more trust of it and less heavy-handed regulation and taxation. Like the general public, business elites believe that the system is beyond their influence. They are more aware of the limitations imposed on them over the years by waves of moderate reform and less aware that such changes have enabled them to survive basically intact. They are very much aware of their own internal divisions, which they are close to in their everyday life, and less aware of how similar they all are in their thinking and how their actions as a whole produce their predominance.

Favors to Themselves

Politicians also do favors for themselves. For example, they try to increase federal spending in the home district to ensure reelection, a kind of buying of popular votes. Most notorious are districts with heavy military spending represented by high-ranking congressmen on military committees. Fort Worth congressmen, for example, got Congress to spend $205 million on bombers not requested by the air force. Senior congressmen may use the power of the purse to control the bureaucracy and work closely with industry lobbyists. This Congress-interest-bureaucracy triangle is as important for the way government works as the Constitution.

Another example was Bob Sikes, a Florida Democrat whose district included Eglin Air Force Base, the Pensacola Naval Air Station, twelve other Defense Department installations, a Fairchild aircraft facility, and two other multimillion dollar defense contractors. Over half a billion defense dollars were spent there in 1972, a typical year. Sikes for years was chairman of the House Appropriations Subcommittee on Military Construction, and high in the army reserves. He holds substantial stock in defense corporations, a life insurance company that sells to servicemen, and a bank on a naval base. He promoted in Congress a big housing development on land he had leased, a clear conflict of interest. Sikes won every election with 80 percent or more of the vote until he retired in 1979.

People who receive federal spending want to continue receiving these funds, regardless of how unjustified the spending is. The intensity problem, as always, is at work: the majority of congressmen do not discipline the few who get excessive benefits, partly because the benefits of reform per congressman are too small to be perceptible. One person's "fat" is another person's "essential spending." The best way to handle the problem would be to prohibit a congressman from chairing any committee influencing federal spending over the national average in his or her home district. Self-interest should be removed from spending decisions to make them more objective, but such reform is virtually politically impossible because of public apathy on the issue. (Even attempts to reorganize along rational lines meet too much resistance.)

The favors politicians do for themselves include conflicts of interest, which occur when a public servant stands to gain monetarily in a private business from the decisions he makes. Weak disclosure laws prevent us from knowing enough (although sometimes examples, like the Sikes case, become known). More commonly, bankers serve on banking committees, lawyers keep outside practices, and so on. Research shows that many do not vote their economic interests, however, and some votes overlap public and private interests.

Legislators have the somewhat embarrassing authority to decide their own compensation and perquisites, but they succeed in overcoming their embarrassment. Congress has not adjusted its pay in terms of how well it is solving the country's problems, for example, lowering their pay if they cause inflation. Congress has proliferated nonessential perquisites of office: chauffeured luxury cars, deluxe tax-subsidized dining rooms, luxury carpets and other office decor, free medical checkups and all other health services, unlimited sick leave, gymnasiums, VIP facilities at National Parks, free air force travel, and so on. The style of self-indulgence is often more important than the actual costs: Why did the Ethics Committee subscribe to two St. Louis newspapers? Its chairman was from St. Louis.

Reforms to "Open Up the System"

A number of reforms deal with the links between money and politics:

1. Disclosure of who is *lobbying* for what, how much they are paid by whom, and what they spent on elected officials; certain easily kept records of lobbying contacts; and limits or prohibitions on campaign contributions, entertainment, and gifts by lobbyists to public officials.

2. Disclosure of *financial interests* of elected and top appointed officials, possible prohibition from holding office where substantial interest occurs, prohibition on voting where a conflict occurs, and regulation of future employment by an affected interest.

3. *Open meetings,* announced in advance, with agendas, recorded votes, and minutes.

4. *Open records,* or freedom of information.

5. *Disclosure of campaign contributions* and expenditures, including donors' names, occupations, neighborhoods of principal residence, and amounts given above a certain amount; and controls on amounts indi-

viduals can give, total amounts that can be raised and spent, and what the money can be spent on.

6. *Public money for campaigning,* except to preserve incentives for small private contributions.

7. Strong independent *enforcement* machinery to publicize requirements, make forms available, collect them, investigate possible violations, encourage voluntary compliance, prosecute when necessary, and to propose such additional reforms as may be needed for more popular participation.

The Watergate revelations provoked a strong reaction from media, elite, and popular concerns that reformers, particularly Common Cause, took advantage of to lobby for these seven reforms. They had much success at the federal level, especially with presidential campaign finance, campaign fund disclosure, disclosure and regulation of financial interests, open meetings in the House and Senate, open records, and enforcement, but less success in other federal areas, namely congressional public finance of campaigns and lobbying reform. As the concern generated by Watergate recedes, it may be increasingly difficult to get useful reforms. There are too many who think Watergate typical of politics and are cynical about changing any of it. Even more see Watergate as the exception. Relatively few see it as an exaggeration of an unhealthy system of excessive money influence, which needs basic reform. Even the reforms themselves lull some people into thinking enough has been done.

A major reform, the public finance of presidential campaigns under the Federal Election Campaign Act of 1971 (amended in 1974 and 1976), was successful in both its parts, the primaries and the general election. Most of the 1974 law was upheld by the Supreme Court, and Court requirements were met by the 1976 amendments. Primary candidates qualified for federal matching funds by raising at least $5,000 in each of at least twenty states in contributions of $250 or less. Even poorer candidates (such as Morris Udall or Jimmy Carter in 1976) can qualify in this way and get better funding than was previously possible. The success of funding primaries was tarnished in the spring of 1976 by the slowness of Congress and the president to reconstitute the Federal Election Commission as required by the Supreme Court, but that crisis is not likely to repeat itself. After the nominations, both presidential candidates chose to run with $20 million in public money rather than, as allowed by the law, raising all private money. The law encourages small private contributions in the primaries and mixes them with public, then disallows any mixing in the general election. The amounts proved to be too low, however, and should be raised. Fortunately, this will be easy to do because the fund has a $23 million surplus created by the one dollar tax check-off on the income tax form.[50] Also, about one-fourth of taxpayers are checking off, assuring enough money for a better-funded campaign.[51]

The checkoff itself is an interesting innovation, allowing those who file an income tax return to say where they want part of their tax money to go. Politics sometimes seems not to allow the accomplishment of one value, here public finance, without making another more difficult, in this case, tax simplification.

In 1976, $114 million was spent on presidential campaigns, less than in 1972, and 60 percent was publicly financed.[52] Over half of the private money came from small donors (less than $100), a radical departure from centuries of domination by the rich.

Case Study:

Free Speech versus Campaign Expenditure Limits

Previous case studies have lined up relative "good guy" reformers in light grey hats against relative "bad guys" in dark grey hats. Reform, however, also involves the balancing of positive values. This case study illustrates a conflict or tension between two values: free speech and free press versus campaign contribution limits and campaign expenditure limits. It also concerns conflict between two public-interest groups—the ACLU, emphasizing free speech, and Common Cause, emphasizing campaign finance reform. Both groups sympathize with the other's primary values, and they have many overlapping members. When James Buckley and Eugene McCarthy, candidates for federal offices, sued the federal government to stop enforcement of the Federal Election Campaign Act, Common Cause and the ACLU submitted briefs as amici curiae (friends of the court) on opposite sides of the issue.

Common Cause's research and attitudes led it to believe

that big donors had a controlling and corrupting influence over campaigns and that the way to control it was to limit contributions to campaigns and total campaign expenditures. The ACLU argued that any such limits were a restraint on free speech and free press.

The Supreme Court in January 1976 compromised those views and upheld most of the reform law. It agreed that free speech was threatened by expenditure limits and struck down the provisions of law limiting what a campaign could spend and what an individual could spend independent of a campaign. The Court held that free speech was threatened by expenditure limits because they "would appear to exclude all citizens and groups except candidates, political parties, and the institutional press from any significant use of the most effective modes of communication." However, the Court upheld the provisions limiting the amounts individuals and groups could give to campaigns. Contribution limits were valid because they did not directly limit what a person could say.[53]

The Court also ruled that if a candidate accepted public money, then he or she would also have to accept limits on campaign expenditures. This decision affected only presidential candidates in 1976 and meant that public funding is important not only for its own sake but also to set expenditure limits. Congress in 1976 had no limits and acted accordingly: an all-time record of $22.5 million was given by special interests, double the 1974 figure.[54] Individuals were also free to campaign independently for their presidential candidates, but relatively few chose to do so.

Without public-interest groups and the citizens behind them, it would be more difficult to balance these values. The conflict generated information that helped the Court make its decisions; reams of statistics were developed for the case. Common Cause, for example, spent $150,000 on the case, made possible by citizen contributions.[55]

In 1977 57 percent of the public supported public finance of congressional races, including a prohibition of private contributions like the presidential election. Only 32 percent were opposed, but the intensity problem makes this reform difficult to achieve. In August 1977, a Republican filibuster killed public financing for the Senate; fifty-two senators favored the idea, eight votes short of the sixty needed to cut off a filibuster. Liberal Republicans broke promises to support reform and fell in line under heavy pressures for party unity. They were joined by the ten southern Democrats. The Republicans feared the Democrats would get too much money; the Dixiecrats feared the Republicans would.[56] The intensity problem makes it extremely unlikely that any senator voting against reform would lose office because of not representing what people want. Campaigning, perhaps the most important public process, continues to be privately financed.

The cost of public finance is not great; in one scheme it was $.75 a voter. There are many possible techniques. Matching of small contributions is commonly proposed, and money for signatures by voters on pledge cards is another idea. Since many races involve low costs and candidates who are not political professionals, they should be kept simple. One way would be to provide qualified serious candidates (ones who can secure enough signatures or small contributions) with enough money for printing a brochure and with addressing and mailing by the election commission of the brochure to reach all voters. For larger areas covered by broadcasting, some free air time could be provided. Experimentation among the states could be very useful in finding practical schemes.

Other countries have much shorter and more regulated campaigns. In the United Kingdom, whose population is about a quarter of that of the United States, a seat in Parliament costs about $3,000. Campaigns last about three weeks. Each of three major parties is allowed five telecasts of ten minutes each. Each evening newscast gives balanced time to each candidate for prime minister. The parties are monetarily independent of vested interests.

Lobbying reform is also important. Lobbying is the activity in which the favors back and forth between money and politics are worked out. It is also an essential process of communication of information. Northrup, for example, lobbied by entertaining in its hunting lodge and by flying people around in its airplanes, and the air force does the same with its golf course and planes. Wining and dining are part of the game, but it takes money to play. A lobbyist who can get close to a congressional chairman may be able to work behind the scenes to weaken laws with slight word changes. At least eight states are ahead of Congress in lobby reform. Reform legislation was buried over a year in the same committee that impeached the president, although more than half of the members of Congress are on record for reform. In 1978 the House acted, only to have the reform blocked by the Senate Governmental Affairs Committee. In May 1979, the bill was back in a House Judiciary Subcommittee.

Lobbyists also work on the bureaucracy, part of the triangle that includes congressional committees and vested interests. In 1975 the Federal

Energy Commission, in cooperation with Common Cause, logged all contacts of its top officials. The administrator had 91 percent of his meetings with energy industry representatives; the other 9 percent were with state conservation agencies, nonindustry specialists, educators, consumer and environmental organizations, and media. The federal government has about 1,200 advisory committees, mostly dominated by affected vested interests. Most are useful or harmless, but many act as a government-sanctioned lobby with privileges denied reformers. They may have access to special files or can recommend against the collection of information needed to document proposed reforms. They work in secret. The government uses their information and does not have staff to verify it. Lobby reform thus ties into open meeting and records reforms. About 13,000 unregistered lobbyists spent about $2 billion in 1978 to influence congressional and public opinion.

The Federal Election Commission, which handles enforcement, is reasonably strong. It will have to grapple with probable abuses in corporate solicitation of funds through political action committees. (DuPont has a good system, for example, but Monsanto used undue coercion under the previous rules, indicating potential problems.)

Ethics are weakly enforced by committees of the House or Senate. The weakness of self-regulation common in so many other areas crops up here. In nine years, the House Ethics Committee investigated no one; it was really a protective committee. In 1976 Common Cause petitioned for an investigation of Congressman Sikes and was effective through its publicity to move the action along. Acting secretly and with no significant investigative effort, the committee recommended a reprimand, the minimal action, which carries no penalty. It refused to act on one of the charges not because what Sikes did was ethical but because the committee had not been created at the time of the offense. With minimum debate, the House approved the reprimand. Perhaps reform must start with tokenism. Common Cause succeeded where nine years of publicity against Sikes had failed. In 1977 real action was taken by the House Democrats, who ousted Sikes from his chairmanship by a two to one margin.[57]

Citizen Profile:

Monitoring Congressional Ethics

It's funny—I almost fell into it by chance. When I went to Alma College in Michigan, near my home town, I had an interest in going to law school. The prelaw adviser was also chairman of the history department, so I majored in history. One of the profs in the department, Mike Yavenditti, went to Washington, D.C., in May 1978 looking at internships for Alma students and was impressed with the Common Cause (CC) volunteer program. He told a friend, who told me; the prelaw people were all close to one another. I had the feeling that my learning was too tied up with school, that my studies weren't as important as the real world. I'd never been to Washington before, but I knew of its importance from studying history. I felt too sheltered at Alma. In September, I talked with my professor in detail, and he recommended Common Cause. I flew out to Washington in October and was reassured by my interview at CC headquarters. I was accepted.

Although the volunteer office at CC had a list of places to live in Washington, housing was a problem until one of the women who worked at Common Cause offered to rent out one of her bedrooms. The woman turned out to be Pat Keefer, one of the CC vice-presidents. Consequently, I wound up living in Glover Park above Georgetown and learning a lot from people who visited Pat's home.

As a legislative intern at Common Cause, my job was to monitor congressional hearings. I attended hearings on sugar policy, which involves quotas and price supports, which increase costs to consumers. With Mike Cole, a CC lobbyist, I attended a hearing on lobby disclosure, and I attended other hearings on funding resolutions for committee expenses, which involves how Congress spends money to oversee the executive branch.

There were many rewarding aspects of my internship, one of which was having the opportunity to see many important politicians. It was fascinating to observe Senator Kennedy chair a Judiciary Committee hearing, to hear Energy Secretary Schlesinger testify about the energy crisis, and to see Jerry Brown deliver an early campaign speech at Georgetown University. Living in Washington provided me with these opportunities and enhanced the richness of my internship.

My experience was not without its tribulations, however. A particularly frustrating incident occurred in March when the Senate ethics code sections pertaining to the limit on outside earned income was defeated. It was a surprise move: Common Cause had less than twenty-four hours notice that the measure would be voted on. Although implementation of the measure was promised for 1983, much of the work accomplished by CC had been undone. CC had lobbied for a raise for the senators because of the earnings limit; removing the limit broke the senator's part of the bargain.

Through incidents such as this I gained many insights during my internship in Washington. I discovered how isolated and unaware I was about politics and about the present problems that face our government. Problems similar to Watergate still exist at all levels of government, yet can be corrected through citizen interest and involvement.

In the future, I will probably go into law or business, but I have already become a CC member and I plan to follow closely the work of the organization. Common Cause has already made significant gains in governmental reform, and I believe it will continue to do so. Through an organization such as this, I've learned that the citizen really *can* do something.

Kathy Wolfe
Flint, Michigan

The states have a reputation for being less progressive than the federal government, but, except for public finance, they have forged a remarkable record of money and politics reforms. The Open Up the System campaign of Common Cause to get these reforms was carried by committed citizens to every state, and all fifty of them passed some legislation. One of the more severe reforms was in California, where legislative inaction forced a tough proposition to control lobbying and campaigning to be placed on the ballot. Despite opposition from big business and big labor, it won 69 percent of the vote. In at least one campaign after the new law took effect, the winner exploited newly public knowledge about who was contributing to his opponent's campaign. The states have not written flawless laws, and many are trying to adjust requirements to the realities of political life, especially to reduce the large paperwork requirements.

Money does not control politics. The problem is that it has excessive influence. Sometimes the influence seems obvious and self-serving, but usually it also involves a view of social reality able to coopt many people.

Nonradical reform-oriented candidates can win elections. Not all money is antireform money, and some wealthy donors are committed to reform, sometimes against their apparent private interest. Some reformist candidates have wealth of their own. A candidate can substitute work and skill for money. He or she may gain recognition by first winning a local office where money is not so important. Volunteers can give some time to campaign for someone, and that can make a big difference. Primaries can be won more easily than general elections because there are fewer voters to contact, and primary election voters are a little better informed. Party identification can help the winner of the primary of the majority party in a district. Incumbents have been knocked out in primaries or so weakened in them that they have lost general elections.

Events may set a public mood that a reformer can take advantage of, especially during movements that receive media coverage over many months. Many legislative bodies have sizable minorities of reform-oriented members without whom reform would be impossible. This legislative base, events, positive elite values, media attention, and public opinion may combine to create the temporary majorities needed to push through a reform. Money is not the only factor in politics, only the most important.

The fading of Watergate and of elite, media, and popular attention has reduced the impetus for money reforms. Few people without vested interests understand the system well enough to know why more reform is needed. We can hope such procedural reforms will lead to reforms of substantive policy, as in the oil depletion case study, but there is no guarantee. The 1976 presidential election, however, showed that money ties can be supplanted by other ties, which also have problems. President Carter, for example, owes nothing to the moneyed elites, but he has big debts to many organizations—city, labor, environmental, ethnic—whose work outside the South was critical to his victory. The money reforms themselves have to be defended against a backlash and have to be adjusted based on experience. These activities take time from getting new reforms. Because of the reforms we did manage to get, we now know much more about campaign and lobby money than we used to, but exposure alone will not create participation. The disclosure laws work so that we can keep better score, but unless we pay attention, it is still the same old game.

Institutional Reform

Once officials are elected and appointed to top positions of the various levels and branches of government, how democratically and efficiently do they make decisions? How well are the institutions structured? While democracy and efficiency are in tension with each other, there are too many cases where neither value is achieved. For example, legislative procedures may grant such excessive rights to individual members that they can, independently of the merits, slow down, diminish, and even stop legislation, hindering both efficiency and majority rule. The kind of delay that has to be criticized slows the legislative process even after much relevant information has been developed and the majority are ready to act on it.

Both efficiency and democracy suffer in another case: local governments in urban areas whose boundaries are meaningless in relation to the problems that flow across them. There are limits on intergovernmental coordination, especially when the interests of a locality go against those of its region. This section will look at Congress as an example of legislatures in general, at work-place democracy, and at bureaucracy. These problems are especially difficult because they are so complex, because they are often so far removed from the daily experience of most people, and because most people concerned with such machinery are mainly interested in making more money or keeping their jobs.

Congress

Congress is central to the national system of government; it is generally more important than the president or the Supreme Court. Its potential is to represent the majority and to protect the minority; it is 535 people overseeing a nation and a government too big for one person to control. Congress is the symbol of democratic decision making, while the president is the symbol of one person speaking for a majority. Historically, the trend is on the side of strong chief executives, and the American Congress until recently surrendered important powers in war making, budget making, and initiating new legislation. The excesses of the Nixon administration finally caused a reaction to that historic trend. The problem has not been presidential leadership in a time of war, when high consensus and necessity produce a near one-man rule. The problem has been in times of peace, when domestic crises seemed to require strong central leadership. Congress has tended to wallow in its unworkable procedures and lack of discipline, making it easy for presidents to set and decide agendas.

Fortunately, the Constitution was written during a period of high distrust of political executives. The Constitution also mistrusted majority rule and so created a system difficult for either one person or all the people to control. But it put more power in Congress than elsewhere (two major examples are the war-making and the budget powers), and it was these powers that Congress reasserted in the 1970s.

One of the problems with the war in Indochina was the way we made decisions about it. As Congress turned against the war, it discovered that the president had all of the information and could manipulate it at will. It discovered that its own laws allowed the president too much legal and budgetary flexibility. In September 1973, a Senate committee reported that there were 470 emergency power provisions granting sweeping powers to the president. The war was being prolonged by a prowar president and Congress's own cumbersome procedures. Congress finally did find a way to end the war, and it also passed the War Power Act over President Nixon's veto in 1972. This act revoked previous grants of power and required quick presidential consultation with congressional leaders in an emergency. Other legislation has repealed other grants of power. Unfortunately, the first test of the new law, the Mayaguez affair under Ford, was ambiguous. The president consulted Congress a little more than usual, but not within the letter or spirit of the law. A Congress jealous of its power would have immediately impeached the president, an extreme penalty but one that would have gotten the message across. Nor was the impunity of the president much commented upon at the time. Congress did, however, cut off U.S. involvement in Angola, leaving the results of this reform ambiguous but hopeful.

As for budget and taxes, the basic documents had for decades been prepared by the Office of Management and Budget in the Executive Office of the President, and it reflected presidential priorities. Congress had no committee to set overall policies or targets; the appropriations committees, which might have done the job, considered each money bill separately from all the rest and were mainly concerned with budget authority rather than outlays. (*Budget authority* refers to permission to spend in a future fiscal year or years; *outlay* refers to money actually being spent in a given fiscal year.) Taxes were under another committee, and decisions on deficits were handled separately from budget and taxes. There was no way to determine fiscal policy (total revenues, total spending, size of deficit). What finally provoked reform was the impoundment of billions of dollars by President Nixon in his fight against inflation. Nixon claimed statutory authority, and the courts were too slow to overrule him. Considering the importance of spending in the home district, Nixon was hitting where it hurt. Congress could not get information about what was going on.

In 1974 Congress drastically overhauled the budgetary machinery in a major reform too little noticed at the time. A new fiscal year starting in October was created, along with new procedures, strict schedules, a new Congressional Budget Office, and strict limits on impoundments (renamed "recissions" and "deferrals"). A powerful new committee, the Committee on Budget, was formed, composed of chairmen of other major committees, to decide fiscal policy and spending limits within fourteen major spending categories, including defense, education, and revenue sharing.

The Pentagon put the system to a severe test in 1975 by requesting amounts well over the congressional limits. In August, the Senate voted forty-eight to forty-two to reject a conference report breaking the budget, and in subsequent negotiations the compromises came out close to the limits. The Congressional Budget Office keeps score on how close the limits are adhered to and also projects economic impacts of deficits on employment and inflation. These two sets of reforms helped redress the balance of power with the president and improved Congress's ability to carry out its functions.

Other problems have concerned the ability of congressional minorities to delay or stop action by the majority. Frequently committee chairmen, the House Rules Committee, or filibusterers in the Senate can stop legislation that, if brought to a vote on the floor, would probably be approved or would at least put Congress on record. Chairmen have great power because most of the work of Congress is done in committees and most of the power of committees is in the hands of their chairmen. Subcommittees, almost as important, are similarly run.

Junior members of Congress tend to be powerless. In 1958 in the House, reformers and moderates formed the Democratic Study Group to provide an organizational home not available in the conservative-dominated party caucus, speakership, and majority leadership. The DSG documented the problem of conservative influence: the seniority rule made the Democrat with the longest continual service on a committee the chairman. Long service was found in safe seats whose incumbents did not aspire to higher office. Most of these seats were in the South, creating a conservative, racist group of older members with excessive influence over a northern, younger, more liberal party. Except for two years, the Democrats have controlled the House since 1933, yet for only five or six of those years have Democratic programs in significant numbers been approved. The Dixiecrats, representing about a quarter of the population, were able to control about half of the committees. In the late 1960s, 34 of 114 Democratic chairmen had better "Republican" voting records than the average Republican and helped defeat much progressive legislation. Age was also a problem; at one time the ten most powerful chairmen averaged seventy-four years old, compared with top corporate executives averaging fifty-seven.

The DSG alone was unable to reform seniority until it was helped by Common Cause, formed in 1970 for the purpose of organizing citizens to fight money and secrecy. They did not make much progress until 1975 when seventy-five new freshmen Democrats finally tipped the scales within the Democratic caucus. Holding unprecedented secret elections, the caucus voted on each chairman, and three lost their power. The three lost not because of their conservatism but because of their arbitrary exercise of power. About the same time Wilbur Mills, a powerful chairman, resigned from the Ways and Means chair due to alcoholism, and about a year later the autocratic Wayne Hays was forced to resign the Administration Committee chair because he had put a mistress on the payroll. With the reelection of most of the freshmen in 1976 and all of the chairs on notice to be responsive, the House is entering a new and creative period after decades of stagnation. The efficient way it handled the energy bill in 1977 outclassed the much slower Senate.

Other reforms have also lessened minority rule: the expansion of the House Rules Committee to include a few more liberals (but it still can and does kill some progressive legislation), electronic voting in the House, the granting of more chairmanships to younger members, the reduction of the Senate filibuster cutoff from sixty-seven votes to sixty (though filibusters can still kill legislation), and open-meeting, open-record reforms. Common Cause played a vital role in most of these changes. But Congress still has antiquated procedures not tolerated in progressive state legislatures. Committee jurisdictions have been difficult to reform. Voting in the Senate is inefficient. Scheduling problems keep congressmen walking back and forth among their offices, committee meetings, and the floor. Poor scheduling also produces an end-of-session logjam of legislation. Congress has tended to handle its bigger workload by increasing its staff—which rose from 26,000 in 1965 to 37,000 in 1975.

Reformers hope that procedural reforms will lead to substantive reforms, but there is little guarantee. The depletion allowance case study showed the importance of procedures to reform, but there is a conservatism evident in the conservative coalition, a voting alliance of Republicans and Dixiecrats that frequently blocks reform. For example, the Ways and Means Committee even with a new chairman voted in 1975 to emasculate a tax reform bill. The bill initially proposed closing $2.6 billion in tax loopholes but was reduced by $1.7 billion, and much of what was left did not make it through the Senate. Over a hundred special-interest lobbyists attended the tax sessions but only two public-interest lobbyists (Common Cause and Nader's Tax Reform Research Group). One study showed how many of each major group voted for tax reform—about 18 of 88 Dixiecrats, about 156 of 167 northern Democrats, and about 9 of 180 Republicans, adding up to about 183, far from a majority. Similarly, a mood of disillusionment with liberal programs grew in the late 1970s, strengthening regressive forces opposed to any regulation and any welfare. Procedural reforms are important; elections are more important.

Work-Place Democracy

A second specific problem area of institutional reform is work-place democracy. Too often the topic has been relegated to the fields of industrial sociology, interest groups (labor unions), or economic policy. In the past, society was dominated by smaller work organizations where face-to-face relationships existed. But with the growth of large business, large government, and other large institutions, we are dependent on others whom we do not know. One kind of response is unionization, and one of their concerns is wages. The problem of work-place democracy is much broader in both organizational responses and concerns; it concerns the quality of our major adult activity, our work, across a wide range of interests, and thus is a problem of general government. In this context, unions are not private-interest groups but part of the government of the work place. Unions are particularly important because they are the only formal means devised so far to deal with representation on the basis of where we work rather than on the basis of where we live. The politics or democracy of the work place is underdeveloped compared with that of the living place. Historically, owners and top officials had complete authority.

Residentially based governments (vote based on residence) have attempted to regulate the work place, especially from the federal level, starting in 1935 with the Wagner Act creating the National Labor Relations Board (NLRB), the right to organize, and the right to strike. In 1947 business pressure produced the Taft-Hartley Act, legalizing state right-to-work laws, creating ninety-day injunctions against strikes, and forbidding secondary boycotts. In 1959 the Landrum-Griffin Act strengthened requirements for union democracy and accounting of union funds. The NLRB conducts elections to see if workers want a union and which one, and it regulates labor practices along with the Labor Management Services Administration of the Labor Department.

Four important problems affect work-place politics: corruption of some older unions, lack of union protection for some categories of workers, destructive union-employer conflict, and worker participation in decision making.

The United Mine Workers was a major example of union corruption. This case and many others show that union leaders can fall into the same abuse of power as other top elites and for many of the same reasons: the union members are not paying enough attention to what is going on. Labor leaders have successfully discouraged enforcement of the laws by the Labor Department.[58] The UMW was an exception in which enforcement occurred mainly because of the murder of a union leader and his family. The investigation led to massive Labor Department intervention and the election of a new reform leadership. Current news focuses on the Teamsters, and protection is needed for courageous dissidents in that union. Irregularities in the management of pension funds and infiltration by organized crime are suspected. In too many older unions, leaders pay themselves high salaries, force through dues increases as needed, fill lower positions with loyal supporters, control the union newspaper, connive with employers to fire dissident workers, link to political party machines, use intimidation and violence, and discriminate against women and minorities.[59]

Some categories of workers, particularly workers in the South, farmworkers, and public employees, find union organizing very difficult. Domestic workers, retail clerks, and many service workers are low paid, but their situation is not conducive to unionization. They are generally low-skill, entry-level workers in small units, such as the family, a small store, a fast-food franchise. They have more face-to-face relations with employers and better working conditions than the farmworkers.

A similar problem exists for public employees, whose strikes may be no more destructive than those of private workers. Public workers are organizing in sanitation, hospitals, and civil service offices. Only public safety services—police and fire—have convincing arguments that strikes should not be allowed, and these can still have binding arbitration. Public workers face the same problems and have the same desires as private workers. The public perceives a direct threat to its pocketbook, but the same threat occurs with private strikes, in which corporations typically pass on to the consumer the cost of higher wages.

Many private workers covered by the NLRB are unable to exercise their rights due to illegal employer resistance and delaying tactics, a major case being Stevens textiles. Organized labor and the Carter administration are trying to improve the law. In 1978 a moderate reform to improve procedures was defeated in the Senate. Ultimately all groups could be organized in some way so that we can get past the stage where each newly organized group wages economic warfare on the rest. Unions should be seen as a legitimate and necessary mechanism for workers for dealing with powerful employers.

A third problem of the work place is destructive union-employer conflict, which can have two major results. One is that prices can be increased so much that overall levels of economic activity are lowered, as may have happened in the construction industry. The other is that prices grow so high that imports and substitutes capture a higher share of the market. In both cases, employment is reduced because of miscalculations by union and corporate leaders. Stockpiling in anticipation of a strike may create an artificial boom-bust cycle. All of these things happened in 1971 to the steelworkers, who decided in 1973 to negotiate a no-strike contract with management and to try to increase their own productivity. Arbitration is used to settle disputes during the three-year life of the contract. Other unions have yet to follow suit. Some have moderated their demands; others do not face import competition or substitutes. In the railroad industry, Congress has had to intervene frequently in destructive conflict situations, which have helped put many railroads out of business. And some on both sides would rather go out of business than yield to the other. The social gulf between worker and manager leads the one to resist productivity improvements and to demand excessive pay, and the other to resist profit sharing and to ignore worker complaints about conditions. Unions that abuse their power tend to lose it. The seventeen building trades unions represented 70 percent of the construction industry in 1973, but only 40 percent in 1979.[60]

A fourth problem, worker participation in decision making, has two goals—improved efficiency and higher satisfaction with the job—and involves more informal kinds of relationships than unions. Worker dissatisfaction is frequently evident in rejection of contracts, absenteeism, wildcat strikes, sabotage, featherbedding, rigid job classifications, and hostility toward management and even union leaders. Workers often feel ignored and unappreciated, and these feelings are at least as important as physical work requirements and conditions. Discontent can lead to productive union efforts to improve pay, training, and job status. Management can engage in job enrichment by giving workers more control and also by increasing their productivity. Consideration for workers has long been part of the Japanese managerial style and a major reason for Japan's economic success. Research shows that job satisfaction is correlated with the degree of control over the job. Many experiments have shown that jobs can be restructured to increase worker responsibility, improve morale and productivity, increase profits, and thus achieve efficiency and democracy at the same time.

Bureaucracy

The problem of bureaucracy is more general than the two cases of Congress and work-place democracy. It is a kind of necessary evil, so our success in dealing with bureaucracy will always be relative.

This story is about something popularly called bureaucracy. A couple of graduates of the University of California at Berkeley wanted to sell hot, salty pretzels from a pushcart in San Francisco. In May 1974, they found they needed licenses. In anticipation, they took a load of pretzels to a busy corner on a nice day and sold out in a couple of hours. At the police station, they learned they would need a special permit from the Department of Public Works for temporary occupancy of a public way, but they also found that such permits are given only to construction companies. They could go to the Board of Permit Appeals, but only if the police turned down their application, but the police would not even accept the application in the first place. A ballot proposition that had passed had allowed street artists but not food vendors. They had been selling pretzels illegally, dodging cops as necessary, but soon got an artist's license and sold "baked sculptures." But that does not end the story.

They were next cited for violating the rules of the Department of Health; but, to get a health permit, they needed a peddlers' permit from the police, which in turn depends on a DPW permit. The undaunted peddlers put up a new sign, "Not intended for human consumption." The problem began to move up in the health and police bureaucracies. The police said the street artist permit was also good as a peddlers' permit, removing the need for the DPW permit, and opening the way to the health permit. But the Health Department refused a permit. After some effort, they discovered someone selling pretzels as "hearth-baked rolls," which under the state Bakery Sanitation Act of 1928 were exempt from Health Department rules. And a call to the state confirmed that pretzels qualify as a hearth-baked roll. But the Health Department refused to give a permit until the vendors had hot and cold running water, a stainless steel sink, a Formica food surface, Plexiglas around the cart, and a receptacle for chlorinated water. The pretzel kings ripped apart a mobile home and attached various parts to their cart, such as a battery and a motor to run a pump for the water, a propane water heater, and so on.

The Health Department finally granted the permit, but the next day the Police Department revoked the street artist permit. A news story had prompted the police to hold a hearing, which overruled the lower echelon police who gave the permit. This newest action meant that the vendors had an official denial of their application, allowing them to go to the Board of Permit Appeals. During delays, they were expanding, opening a bakery downtown, and getting permission to sell on the San Francisco State campus. On December 2, 1974, the board approved their permit. By August 1975, they had five pushcarts and twelve employees. They were no longer selling on the public streets, but they were on state park land, the campus, and private property. Their street license, which they wanted to keep, was denied when it came up for renewal and the Health Department was requiring that the carts qualify as "fixed location restaurants."[61]

Bureaucracies generally suppress internal dissent and penalize people who are inconveniently competent and productive. The inspector who finds too many violations gets inspected. A critic of his or her own organization or a persistent inspector may be threatened with transfer, a technique known as "exile." Elite pressures on regulatory agencies are especially effective. Examples do not make the case, but they are the scuttlebutt that encourages timidity.

Red tape and gobbledygook are the hallmarks of bureaucracy. Red tape results when fear of making a mistake becomes more important than getting a job done; the forms and steps proliferate so much that, for example, some small towns find it costs more to process applications than they can get in federal grants. Business is often stifled by more than a dozen approvals being needed for minor projects. Frustration and contempt for law grow; the system cannot be made to work. Gobbledygook is a protective device; if no one can understand what the bureaucracy wants, the bureaucracy has more power (and lawyers have more work). Once created, a bureaucracy frequently becomes its own justification, independent of its effectiveness in solving the original problem. Vested interests build up around the money being spent, reinforced by the intensity problem.

How can bureaucracy be made humane? How can well-intentioned programs have the results of their intentions? Formal mechanisms are helpful for the sophisticated, but only 10 to 30 percent of public administrative processes involve adminstrative law adjudication, rule making, and judicial review. Most bureaucracy is informal and unreviewed discretionary actions, and creating formal processes would probably not help the average citizen.

An inefficient business in a competitive market is disciplined by bankruptcy, takeover, or stockholder revolt. Tiny local governments are disciplined by having too little money to waste. Bureaucracy occurs where these disciplines are lacking—in the firms and unions with market power and in the bigger governments. Their discipline comes often from exposure; hence free access to information is important as a check on bureaucracy. Bureaucracies must also be probed actively. Exposure becomes the equivalent of red ink. Unfortunately, the less established muckrakers and whistle-blowers have a hard time keeping their jobs.

Less dramatic but equally important are local citizens who take a durable interest in how governments work. Interested people can get appointed to various citizen advisory groups as in the mental health citizen profile. Public-interest groups can monitor government and recommend changes; an outstanding example of such a group is the League of Women Voters.

Another attack on bureaucracy can be made through education in public administration and business management. Bureaucracy itself has become a profession. If we must have such things as the Joint Funding Simplification Act of 1974, undistributed offsetting receipts, and interfund transactions, then we will have to train people about them. In 1974, the federal government spent $100 million to train local city workers in program management, helping less expert governments learn how to take advantage of federal money.

Complication, unfortunately, makes government harder for most citizens to understand. They are intimidated by its incomprehensibility, unable to apply their good common sense to the tangles. They give up and trust the experts. We passed that point a long time ago and now face a new frontier of bureaucracy: the experts cannot understand it either, at least not more than their small piece. Bureaucrats get frustrated trying to deal with other bureaucrats. HEW alone publishes about 5,000 regulations per year in the *Federal Register,* often changing previously issued regulations.

The great ideal of the rule of law becomes the petty ideal of the law of rules. At some point, the costs of complication outweigh the marginal gains it achieves. Hence a major reform theme of our time, first voiced by Republicans and conservatives and increasingly echoed by Democrats and liberals, is to simplify government, to make it comprehensible and controllable, to make it realistic about what it attempts to do, and to concentrate federal government on a few, simple, big programs. It means professionalizing people on the front line, risking some mistakes rather than putting them in a straitjacket of rules and delays.

Revenue sharing and bloc grants, which replace categorical grants-in-aid, are major examples of this kind of bureaucratic reform. Hundreds of grants-in-aid programs with separate and complex applications and tight federal controls have been or may be replaced by simpler programs, which allow localities greater discretion and have simpler review by the federal government. The horrendous paperwork, innumerable complaints, and a preference for state and local government where possible led to these reforms. A number of other reforms simplifying paperwork and requirements could be mentioned; simplifying becomes itself an almost routinized function of government.

Reformers, generally Democrats, have been overly optimistic about what reform can do. Liberalism, or mild ambiguous reform, has been fairly successful in increasing social spending even during Republican administrations. We now have much more familiarity with the strengths and weaknesses of bureaucracies and we can do a better job of designing bureaucracy, which, for all its weakness, is the only instrument for implementing policy reform.

Bureaucracies can outlive their purpose or get sidetracked from it. Legislatures have the responsibility of oversight and do accomplish it to some extent, but legislators tend to become part of the system they are supposed to oversee. One remedy is *sunset laws,* legal provisions that limit the number of years any legislation is in effect. For example, if several tax loopholes or the Interstate Commerce Commission's trucking regulations were automatically terminated, there is little chance that Congress would reenact them. Programs would have to be reviewed and be reenacted only if found effective. Common Cause has been promoting sunset legislation as a major new tool to control bureaucracy.

Reform is concerned with national security, the economy, the environment, and social justice, which are affected by the substantive policies of government. Reform is also concerned with the machinery of government, both for its impact on substantive policy and for its own sake in achieving values on democracy and efficiency. The major aspects of the machinery include civil liberties, majority rule, and the institutions of government. A major civil liberties problem is for citizens to get the information they need to control government. Elites tend to use valid reasons for keeping secrets as excuses for excessive secrecy. These secrets become exposed through leaks, whistles, and investigations, all resisted by the elites, which use economic sanctions against revealers of secrets. Government also sometimes invades privacy and suppresses legitimate dissent. Nonviolent civil disobedience can help reform, but antigovernmental violence can lead to a climate of supression. Historically, the American Civil Liberties Union has defended civil liberties with citizen support. Amnesty International in recent years has worked around the globe to free political prisoners and stop torture. The major majority rule problem is the excessive influence of money, particularly campaign contributions. Seven structural reforms can deal with the problem. Much has been accomplished, but public financing of campaigns below the presidency and lobby reform remain to be achieved. Respecting institutions, the Congress has made many reforms in recent years. Work-place democracy has problems of union corruption, organizing new workers, destructive union-employer conflict, and worker participation in decisions. Bureaucracy needs exposure, citizen participation, professional training, simplification, and sunset laws.

Notes

1. David Wise, *The Politics of Lying* (New York: Random House, 1973); Morton Halperin and Daniel Hoffman, *Top Secret* (Washington, D.C.: New Republic, 1977); and Norman Dorsen and Stephen Gillers, eds., *None of Your Business* (New York: Viking, 1974) cover this general area. Jonathan Schell, *The Time of Illusion* (New York: Knopf, 1976), and Leon Jaworski, *The Right and the Power* (New York: Reader's Digest Press, 1976) cover the Nixon phenomenon.
2. *San Francisco Chronicle*, February 26, 1973, column by Jack Anderson.
3. Ibid., February 23, 1973.
4. Ibid., November 19, 1975.
5. *San Francisco Chronicle*, April 17, 1974.
6. Ibid., October 3, 1974, July 10, November 11, 1977. See Charles Peters and Taylor Branch, *Blowing the Whistle* (New York: Praeger, 1972) for details on many other cases.
7. *New York Times*, December 6, 1977.
8. *San Francisco Chronicle*, October 18, 1974.
9. Ibid., April 2, 1974.
10. Edward Roeder, "Rocky and the CIA's Family Jewels," *New Republic*, November 1, 1975, pp. 5–7; *San Francisco Chronicle*, January 16, 1975; see also *New Republic*, November 8, 1975.
11. *San Francisco Chronicle*, August 30, September 1, 1972.
12. Ibid., October 13, 30, 1975.
13. *San Francisco Chronicle*, January 17, 1974, column by Jack Anderson.
14. Ibid., December 19, 1973.
15. Ibid., May 5, 1976.
16. Ibid., November 19, 20, 1975.
17. Ibid., December 12, 1973.
18. Ibid., October 3, 1975.
19. Ibid., April 13, 1975.
20. Ibid., January 27, 1975.
21. Ibid., November 10, 1977, column by Jack Anderson.
22. *Time*, August 20, 1973.

23. *San Francisco Chronicle*, November 23, 1975; January 2, 1979, from the Bureau of Alcohol, Tobacco and Firearms.
24. Ibid., October 15, 1975; February 11, 1976; Amnesty International, *Matchbox*, most issues in the 1970s.
25. *Hayward* (Calif.) *Daily Review*, December 27, 1977.
26. *San Francisco Chronicle*, September 25, 1975.
27. Ibid., October 21, 1975.
28. Ibid. See also various issues of *In Common* published by Common Cause.
29. Herbert Alexander, *Financing Politics* (Washington, D.C.: Congressional Quarterly, 1976), pp. 177–178.
30. *San Francisco Chronicle*, July 21, 1973; Alexander, *Financing Politics*, pp. 118–120.
31. Alexander, *Financing Politics*, pp. 87–90, 113–118, 120–126, 194–195.
32. Ibid., p. 18.
33. Ibid., p. 17; *Statistical Abstract of the United States, 1975*, p. 790.
34. Alexander, *Financing Politics*, p. 55.
35. Ibid.
36. Ibid.
37. Ibid., p. 227.
38. Ibid., pp. 85–86.
39. Ibid., pp. 211–216.
40. Ibid., p. 81.
41. Ibid., pp. 79–84.
42. Ibid., pp. 108–110.
43. *San Francisco Chronicle*, March 20, 1972.
44. *Statistical Abstract, 1975*, pp. 454–455.
45. Alexander, *Financing Politics*, p. 92.
46. Ibid., pp. 112–118.
47. Admiral Hyman G. Rickover, testimony of July 12, 1975, to the House Subcommittee on General Oversight and Renegotiation, in *Oversight of the Renegotiation Act Hearings*, June 5, 10–12, July 29, 1975, pp. 264–293. See also *Hearings Part 2*, September 19, 25, 1975, and *Evaluations of Proposals to Extend and Amend the Renegotiation Act of 1951*, Report by the Staff of the Joint Committee on Internal Revenue Taxation, September 30, 1975.
48. *San Francisco Chronicle*, February 20, 1975, column by Jack Anderson; June 2, 1978, on Lockheed.
49. Alexander, *Financing Politics*, pp. 229–230.
50. *San Francisco Chronicle*, November 7, 1976.
51. Alexander, *Financing Politics*, p. 251.
52. *San Francisco Chronicle*, June 5, 1977.
53. Ibid., January 31, 1976.
54. Ibid., February 15, 1977.
55. Common Cause, *Frontline*, March–April 1976, p. 3.
56. *San Francisco Chronicle*, August 3, 1977.
57. Ibid., January 27, 1977.
58. Wilfrid Sheed, "What Ever Happened to the Labor Movement?" *Atlantic Monthly*, July 1973, pp. 60–61.
59. Ibid; Gilbert Burck, "A Time of Reckoning for the Building Unions," *Fortune*, June 4, 1979, pp. 82–86.
60. Burck, "A Time of Reckoning."
61. Walter Blum, "This Story Isn't About Pretzels," *San Francisco Chronicle*, August 10, 1975.

7

Reforming: A Complex Commitment

Chapters 2 through 6 discussed reforms topic by topic. Some connections were made among them to show overall compatibility, frequent complementarity, and occasional conflict. There can be a coherent rationale behind this array of reforms. This chapter will discuss net social welfare as such a unifying concept, giving some coherence to an otherwise amorphous idea. What specific reforms show the most promise? We need a way to judge proposals among each other; this chapter will discuss several disciplines to whip a reform into pragmatic shape. We will also discuss how reform thinking fits into the world of "isms." Other parts of the chapter will look at public-interest groups because they are the major tool of citizen effectiveness, and at the dimensions of personal action and commitment.

Coherence, Complexity, and Discipline

Net Social Welfare

We need a way to measure how well we are doing on the whole. We could use something called *net social welfare* (NSW). Such a measurement must necessarily be an approximation for several reasons. The concept itself is somewhat mystical and elusive. It reflects certain values and perceptions, which others may reject. It will have to mix together very dissimilar goals, such as national security and health. Although many numerical indexes exist in the various policy areas, they are not available for all policies, and some miss the point. At this time, there are no accepted measurements of NSW, but there are some partial approximations. NSW seems likely to be developed by researchers using the same data but different ways of analyzing it, possibly leading to "liberal" or "conservative" versions, or environmental optimist or pessimist versions. The development of some concept of net social welfare could clarify debate and stimulate firmer measurement of how well we are doing.

NSW would imitate the development of gross national product and replace it as the key concept of policy debates. GNP measures in dollars the total output of the economy. In a larger context, it refers not to size alone but to a series of concepts—inflation, unemployment, industries, input–output relationships, investment, savings, interest, debt—that make it up, and to the general system of ideas that now dominates debate. GNP-based thinking has pros and cons. On the positive side, it provides a systematic and fairly objective system of understanding important features of our national life and international situation. It is complex, highly developed, and intellectually rigorous. It has developed strongly over the last several decades into a powerful, sophisticated instrument of analysis. But, negatively, it tends to be used by policy makers in a way that exaggerates what it really can do. It is too narrowly economic and materialistic. Exciting ideas are being developed by breaking out of the narrower economic mold and applying the same kind of thinking to larger issues. GNP does very well at money values and physical quantities but very poorly at quality. While economists consider GNP valuable because of its objectivity, it fails as an overall measure for that very reason. It measures objects, not the quality of life experienced by people; it hides its assumptions about values.

More and more economists are asking questions about quantification. How do you measure the value of the national parks? The value of the skills and education people have? The invisible asset of a brand name created and sustained by advertising? The economic meaning of campaign contributions?

Uncritical acceptance of GNP thinking leads to an emphasis on growth to maximize GNP, which can harm environmental, social, and even certain economic goals. For example, life-styles and technologies could radically change, resource and energy consumption drop, income be redistributed, and patterns of urbanization and transportation change with no change at all in GNP. NSW, however, would be designed to show such changes as dramatic improvements.

Fifty years ago, a proposal to create the GNP system now existing would have been called visionary at best and impossible, dictatorial, and wasteful at worst. Now it is a fact of life. The same development can occur with NSW and is a logical projection from GNP. Some examples exist of the kind of thinking required. The National Wildlife Federation for several years has published its environmental quality index. In 1973, the Urban Institute ranked eighteen urban areas on fourteen diverse indicators. Some corporations have attempted monetary measures of their impacts on people and the environment. Environmental impact studies on large issues require NSW-style thinking. The American Institute of Certified Public Accountants has a Social Measurement Committee. After four years of work, federal statisticians published *Social Indicators, 1976* in 1977, providing raw material for an NSW analysis. One fairly simple international comparison giving equal weight to GNP per capita, health, and education ranked the United States in sixth place, tied with Finland. Sweden placed first, followed by Denmark, Norway, Canada, and France.[1]

Discipline

While NSW develops, we need ways of sizing up proposed reforms. Reforms must grow from the forces of the unreformed system and be spliced into a complex, ongoing, ambiguous system. We mold the future better from the present worse. Reforms have to be disciplined to fit into this reality. We have to think whether the program will achieve its goals and how it fits in with other values and programs. The few proponents cannot think of everything; their ideas have to be shaped by debate involving many interests. Specifically, four disciplines can be applied to reform proposals: budget, economy, administration, and skills.

Budget. The federal budget is as close as we come to a national statement of priorities and commitments. It usually has a deficit, but that does not make it much easier to pay for programs. State and local governments are even more disciplined because they must make their budgets balance. A summary of all governmental revenues and expenditures can be found in the annual *Statistical Abstract of the United States*. The federal government publishes budget documents each January. The Brookings Institution each year produces a widely respected critique of the federal budget. One of the most progressive proposals was *Counterbudget,* an attempt by the Urban Coalition to get consensus among a large number of reform activists in different fields.

Counterbudget expressed ideas about how to reach its six major reform goals in terms of proposed federal budgets over a five-year-period.[2] (It was prepared as a counter to President Nixon's budget.) Each goal needed a realistic budget and schedule. The Urban Coalition staff had position papers prepared in each policy area. People from many backgrounds and special interests participated, working out compromises among conflicting needs. In twenty-one basic categories of outlays, *Counterbudget* presented new programs, reforms of old programs, and shifts of emphasis. Its reforms were not radical; they have been widely debated and are already law in many other countries. *Counterbudget* was not implemented, is now somewhat dated, and did not cover well several issues of great concern today, but it still stands as a good example of the kind of thinking that can be done about realistic coordinated approaches to a number of problems. "Realistic" means socially, economically, and environmentally feasible, not necessarily politically acceptable to dominant elites.

Economy. Reforms must also be disciplined in terms of their impact on the general economy. A major example is the question of how much of our economy should be controlled by government. The portion has increased steadily over the years, mostly for very good reasons, and we are still well below that of most European countries. We are far ahead of Japan, but in their system, corporations perform many of the functions of government, reducing the need for state spending. We are neither Japanese nor European, but their experiences indicate the amount of latitude we have. We need not fear lowering government spending if the private economy picks up the burden, and we need not fear a loss of democracy if the public sector increases. The problem is one of balancing values, with the rich generally favoring less taxation and the disadvantaged favoring more programs. Other things being equal, there should be a presumption in favor of the freedom of private decisions and against control by government. Government should not make decisions for us, but be the way we make decisions. Reform is commonly misunderstood or misrepresented as meaning a much bigger tax bite and much more government. In fact, the *Counterbudget* reforms make the federal budget rise from 21.2 percent to 23.7 percent of GNP, and that almost entirely due to national health insurance (NHI). Under NHI, money now flowing through private insurance schemes for basic health would flow through government. The United States went through a similar process when social security was implemented, and most European countries have programs bigger than our proposed NHI. *Counterbudget* reforms other than NHI do not increase the budget because increases in one area are balanced by decreases in others.[3]

There are, however, long-term trends, which cannot continue. Expenditures by all three levels of government have risen steadily over the years, from 7 percent in 1902 to over 10 percent in the 1920s, about 20 percent in the 1930s, to 23 percent by 1950, to 29 percent in 1960, and 33 percent in 1970, finally reaching a recession high of 40 percent in 1976.[4] The burden is not military defense, which has declined since 1968 and is now about 6 percent of GNP, nor has the increase come in nonwelfare domestic spending, which has stayed fairly constant. The big increase has come in the broad welfare category, which helps "those with income below a certain level and [establishes] minimum levels of health, education and housing." [5] The amount has gone up in both Democratic and Republican administrations. It was about $65 per person in 1929, $163 in 1940, $211 in 1950, $316 in 1960, $630 in 1970, and $935 in 1975 (adjusted for inflation).[6] Generally we paid as we went, but not enough to prevent serious increases in debt and in interest payments. Without tax increases, the spending is either inflationary or its financing crowds out businesses that need loans critical for investment and jobs. This is a sensitive and complex issue with disagreements among competent disinterested economists, but what is clear to specialists and educated laymen is that the trends cannot continue. Great Britain and Italy have heavy tax burdens to pay for big debts, and they have slow to zero growth. Other European countries have high welfare burdens but paid as they went in taxes and have higher growth rates than ours. Specific recommendations have already been formulated to bring social security under control. We will have to reform the reforms, in a sense, to pay enough taxes and to prevent benefits from growing as they have in the past. The challenge is to change direction within the general limits of the existing economy.

What would the impact be of a hypothetical comprehensive reform on the economy? *Counterbudget* was tested on an econometric model using 330 variables and was compatible with a dynamic economy. Its problem was being somewhat inflationary, an interesting projection in view of the fact that we had a very high inflation without *Counterbudget* after 1971.[7] Also, *Counterbudget*'s impact on the distribution of income was healthy, with substantial increases for lower income, some for the middle, and decreases for the affluent, especially those earning over $35,000 per year in 1971.

Administration. A third discipline of reform is administration—specific activities people can perform to attain the policy goal. Many reforms we would like to accomplish cannot be done through government. We have enough experience, however, to assess the costs and benefits of several kinds of systems, mainly regulation, transfer payments, direct services, and social services. Regulation can be the most cost-efficient kind of administration because it affects a large amount of private activity for a minimum public cost. To work, regulation must have a strong legal base. The most difficult phase of regulation is initial implementation; a whole bureaucracy must be trained, procedures must be developed, and responsibility assigned. Also, affected parties have to change the way they do business. Charges of arbitrariness and court tests are common, but in time the changes are accepted. Regulation suffers when it has weak enforcement mechanisms and when the intensity problem leads to decay of budgetary and political commitment. Regulation, for all its weaknesses, is usually more efficient than average citizens' trying to defend their interests one at a time. Regulation is especially important for market power control, consumer protection, environmental regulation, health and safety regulation, race and sex discrimination, and labor unions. In a few cases, deregulation is needed, especially to allow more competition.

Transfer payments are fairly cost-effective because a small bureaucracy can transfer a huge amount of money, maximizing the benefit with a minimum overhead. In 1971, 73,000 social security employees sent out checks for $54 billion, or $740,000 per employee. These systems are most important for income poverty. As with regulation, they can be inefficient—in this case when there is too much complication in qualifying for transfers and too many levels of government, each with its own set of rules. Techniques to prevent abuses need not be too complicated and expensive. Transfers to government—taxes—are another example and also in need of simplification. Such simplifications can reduce the size of the bureaucracy or increase compliance and fairness.

Direct services are a third kind of administrative system. Examples include services like businesses (the Post Office, local bus services, and the TVA). Other direct services are tax supported (firefighting, physical health services, scientific research, and public lands management). The military is still the biggest in this category. Direct services need to expand in public transit, sewage treatment, and solid waste processing. Direct service bureaucracies are harder to create than the other two but easier than the fourth type, social services.

Social services are designed to help people individually. Examples include police, criminal rehabilitation, mental health, education, and consumer and health education. Social services are partly a matter of knowledge and technique, but they are also a matter of personality. We know that inadequate resources are likely to fail, but enough resources are not enough to succeed; there must be a commitment, a caring that people cannot get paid for, a family spirit, a kind of leadership. Similarly, it is more difficult to measure the success of social services. Social service institutions have to be built gradually to get caring, capable people as employees. The boom-bust cycle of the War on Poverty provided many examples of how not to administer social services. There is great danger of governmental paternalism in social services. Many oppose them, believing instead in self-help and private market mechanisms (but these are equally difficult). If successful, such services help people be more productive and lower costs of institutionalization. However, trying to save costs can undermine the effectiveness of the services; the people needing help are typically the weak of our society who often cannot provide for themselves.

Skills. A fourth discipline of reform is its demand upon skills available in the labor force, paralleling the analysis of the economy. Manpower planning is much less advanced than economic planning. Without competent people, reforms cannot be implemented. We now face the need for energy conservation in building, for example, but have relatively little competence in the building industry or government. Also, our training may not match market job opportunities. We have produced too many schoolteachers and too few sewage plant operators. Many reforms require low-skill work, and these tie directly into the reform of public-service jobs. But higher skills require that time and money be invested in vocational and higher education programs aimed at shortages. Besides simple availability, another job impact is the cost of the job created. Defense spending, for example, creates very few jobs compared with industry and social services, which in turn create fewer jobs per budget dollar than public-service jobs do. Environmental protection jobs to clean up existing industry may be on a par with the cost per job of industry.

In general, reform will deemphasize increases in private disposable income while improving income distribution; it deemphasizes materialism. Increased productivity is instead allocated to technology changes, environmental quality, and improving the quality of life. Some redistribution of wealth will end involuntary unemployment among those with low incomes.

The current system diverts money from many jobs that need to be done; reform would create those jobs and even reveal a shortage of workers. The gradual rehabilitation and redesign of our cities alone will take decades of time and talent. Whole new industries in energy, recycling, and pollution control are coming into existence. The end of conventional growth is not no growth but new growth, more productive of world peace, environmental quality, social justice, and democracy.

Ideology

These ideas about reform do not fit comfortably into the notions popularly used by the participants in the system, notions such as liberalism and conservatism, and socialism and capitalism, which are in a loose sense ideologies—sets of related ideas about general policy and the nature of society. Reform is not an ideology for attaining pure values. It is more of a pragmatic response to conditions balancing an array of values. Reform seeks to ameliorate many problems, not solve any one problem. Solutions inevitably develop problems of their own, so reform is a continuing process.

On the whole, reformers have leaned more toward liberalism in this century. Liberals generally see the major pervasive problems of society as the control of corporate power and the redistribution of wealth to create equality of opportunity. Conservatives are more likely to believe that we have enough equality of opportunity and that competition checks corporate power. They are concerned with preserving incentives to invest and reducing governmental regulation. Liberals want government to play an active role in asserting equality before the law, expanding social programs, and taxing the wealthy. Conservatives think that free markets are the best remedy for problems and the most meaningful freedom and that taxes detract from the vital, productive part of the economy, the private sector. Liberals are generally environmentalist, consumerist, pro-union, pro-poor, pro-minority, and pro-women; conservatives may also be environmentalists but are less concerned with social issues and are mistrustful of governmental activism. In foreign policy, liberals are antimilitarism, pro-arms control, pro-human rights, pro-foreign aid, and in favor of the United Nations. Conservatives are pro-military spending, less concerned about the liberal issues, and more fearful of socialism-communism.

Conservatism emphasizes some values that liberals too often overlook, such as self-reliance, self-discipline, and limited government. But conservatives can be criticized for defense of the status quo and its benefited vested interests, fear of change, militaristic anticommunism, and intolerance toward the disadvantaged. Liberals can be narrow also; they may be so pro-union that they overlook defects in the way that conservatives overlook corporate abuses.

Certain corporations and unions are particularly antienvironment, making the liberal-conservative distinction less clear on these issues. Also, principled liberals and conservatives have many overlaps, such as on civil liberties. Yet even here the conservative is most likely to emphasize rights of victims and punishment of those who violate the rights of others, while liberals are more concerned with defending the rights of the disadvantaged and with rehabilitation. Liberals have pushed federal power to attain economic justice and to end discrimination, while conservatives have emphasized states' rights.

Clear differences exist over property rights. Conservatives emphasize the sacredness of private property, and liberals assert the authority of the majority to regulate property in the public interest. The notion of private property has a mythic grip on the American mind, making it easy for elite conservatives to translate threats to their property to the much smaller property of average people.

The socialism-capitalism concern comes in here as a major battleground within the larger liberal-conservative debate. The more radical liberals embrace socialism; the more radical conservatives tout capitalism. Most liberals want to regulate private property; socialists want to eliminate large private holdings altogether. Socialists believe that the profit motive necessarily rides roughshod over public values, corrupting the political process. They think that public ownership would eliminate that influence because public administrators, they believe, would have no motive but the public good. The problem is that socialist regimes need surpluses just as much as capitalist systems do; essentially a multiplicity of owners is replaced by one, the top governmental elite. The Soviet Union and China, for example, could prohibit cigarette smoking, but in both countries tobacco profits are so high that the elites are unwilling to do so. To the extent that socialist enterprises are not profit oriented, they may become wasteful, inefficient, and unresponsive to the need for change. Liberals find it hard enough to regulate enterprises outside the government; it might be even harder if they were part of the government itself. Worker-owned and consumer-owned enterprises are improvements on the same theme but have other problems. No "ism" yet has found a way to deal with the propensity of individuals to work in their own personal, family, or group interest. On the other hand, ideology, like religion, can inspire some people to identify with the larger group of the whole nation or world of nations, so that they work for some conception of the public interest. The profit motive is, in a real sense, part of human nature, ignoring capitalist or socialist labels. Regulating it is a universal problem, transcending the ideas by which people think their societies operate.

Socialism is compatible with democracy, as evident in Europe, although even there most of the economy is private. Many enterprises in the United States are public yet could be private, such as public transit, municipal utilities, federal reclamation and power projects, federal uranium processing, health services, the Army Corps of Engineers (a construction firm), state liquor stores, vast public lands and their resources, financial services to small business and housing, insurance services for banks, the Government Printing Office, the post office, education, and government-owned military plants. Some of these enterprises are big, some small; some are efficient, some inefficient. If they are inefficient, it is not because they are publicly owned but because of the competency of the people running them and the situations within which they work. Private enterprises are just as prone to be inefficient.

Both public and private enterprises are likely to get reformed as adverse publicity rises, yet both kinds have been given subsidies when bankruptcy was seen as too socially expensive. Public enterprises have, as most moderate liberals would expect, been difficult to regulate. The TVA, for example, sold cheap electricity to big aluminum companies and bought strip-mined coal without restoring the land for many years. Both capitalists and socialists find it easy to hide personal materialism in nationalistic and public-interest rhetoric.

Socialism also connotes a redistribution of the wealth, yet socialist countries differ only in degree in their use of material incentives, and as a result they have social classes. Socialist managers become a new quasi-capitalist class, which is the reason that the somewhat more egalitarian Chinese are so critical of the somewhat more elitist Soviets. Many European countries have shown that significant redistribution can be accomplished within a basically capitalist and democratic system. Life constantly undermines simple theories. Communist countries are not more successful in dealing with their problems than we are on the whole; they are simply more able to hide their problems by suppressing freedom.

Less needs to be said about capitalism because it has so completely disappeared, at least in its original forms. It has been superseded by massive governmental intervention in the economy and by the growth of market power. We have regulated monopoly capitalism, with capitalists focusing attention on "capitalism," socialists on "monopoly," and liberals on "regulated." Sometimes, in an ironic turn of events, socialists discover the quaint advantages of small-time capitalism, the most ruthlessly capitalistic part of our economy. They may even take refuge in cooperatives and private property to set up their alternative life-style experiments, getting a private socialist island in a sea of capitalists. Capitalism has been modified because it failed to live up to the brighter promises of the early theory. Reformers are not overly concerned about capitalist and private ownership versus socialist and public ownership. They are concerned more with competency, with structuring of markets, and with regulation in the public interest.

Liberal Reformism: Ambiguity versus Meaning

Liberals have been in the ascendant since the New Deal, but the ascent is slow. People easily forget how much ground the elites held and still hold. Have liberals only saved conservatives from radical reform? Or have they been essential in helping people get more of what they want than ever before?

Liberalism, always diverse, is evolving. There is a new pessimism about the ability of government to solve problems. The new liberalism condemns the old, yet as it looks around for solutions, it comes up mainly with more liberalism.

Liberal reform forces have also usually been weak. To get programs sold to moderates, they promise more than can be delivered. Making matters worse, they must usually also weaken them, reducing the impact. Reform in small increments produces a hodgepodge needing reform itself, but the basic changes are not dismantled; they are too popular.

The tensions and ambiguities built into liberalism are mostly those built into the rest of life. To move toward a better society, we must somehow work with the people who are the reasons we have the problems. Ideologues tend to reject the humanity of one or another social class or group; reformist liberals see no black or white hats. They condemn and accept at the same time, neither fully for nor against the system. With a complicated world view, they look to compromise solutions—not the capitalism of the conservatives or the socialism of the radicals but a mixed system using regulation. Similarly, conservatives seemingly expect the poor to applaud the rich for their success; radicals would gladly equalize wealth holding and income. Liberals balance rewards for achievement against avoiding disparities that undermine opportunity and the sense of community.

In an undoctrinaire way, liberal reformists do claim a lighter shade of grey for their hats. However complex and ambiguous the world may seem and however much they may question and change their ideas, they have some confidence in the value of what they propose.

Public-Interest Groups

In a society as complex as ours, we cannot observe and participate directly in all that we need to influence. If we work hard on one policy, it takes so much time we cannot be influential elsewhere. The media and elected officials communicate distant realities to us with unavoidable selectiveness, bias, and self-interest, usually not giving us the information we need to be influential.

Public-interest groups can carry out many citizen functions that we do not have the time, money, and ability to do ourselves: research, inform, take direct action, lobby, campaign, and litigate. Some depend on endowments, foundations, and wealthy donors; others depend heavily on citizen contributions. To survive as groups, they have organizational features: fund-raising, membership, and policy-making procedures. In general, they pursue some concept of a public interest with no clear monetary self-interest at stake. Other types of groups—such as professional associations concerned with the issues—may also act for the public interest. Public-interest groups vary greatly by function, size, geographic level, issue area, wealth, vigor, and historical relevance. Some are opposed to reform as we have defined it.

The appendix to this book lists about 100 groups that seem to be reformist interest groups, broken down by area of interest. Some are membership organizations; others are sources of information. There are many more at the state and local levels. Relatively few are multi-issue and national: Common Cause, the Nader groups, the League of Women Voters, Americans for Democratic Action, Ripon Society, the Friends Committee on National Legislation, the National Committee for an Effective Congress, and a few other fund-raising efforts for reform candidates.

Research is a major public-interest group activity. The groups create detailed information about abuses, what can be done, and the politics of reform. Common Cause, for example, used its staff and activist members to compile the most extensive information on campaign finance now available. It also polled legislators on their position in various areas and discovered existing majorities for certain reforms of the system. Ralph Nader and others produce volumes of research; Nader's groups (called Nader's raiders) have covered many areas. Research includes pulling together existing information on a problem and presenting it in a dramatic way that calls for action. Facts are more persuasive than rhetoric because politicians are constantly pulled by conflicting rhetoric. Unlike most other citizens, they are constantly being exposed to both sides. Sometimes research proves that existing information is inadequate and stimulates improved data collection. Reformers are oriented to rational, scientific analysis and may overemphasize it in relation to the more difficult task of getting people involved in the decision-making process.

Disseminating information is another major activity. It can take the form of a magazine, like *Consumer Reports* from the Consumers Union. It can be books; over twenty-five have been published by the Nader groups. Common Cause press releases, reports, and articles in its newsletters condense its research findings. Audubon has an extensive outreach educational program, as well as an excellent magazine. The League of Women Voters educates its members by publications and in meetings. Groups commonly use press conferences, bulletins, magazines, and newsletters to let people know about government actions and legislative voting records. Special occasions may lead to full-page newspaper advertisements or even television spots. Some groups gain strength from an appearance of impartiality; they do not lobby but are commonly called upon to testify at hearings. However, public education is like a sponge that can absorb any amount of effort, and most activists concentrate on the media, government, and other activists, where results are more visible.

Direct action has been a minor activity at the national level with the ending of direct American involvement in Vietnam, but it retains its potential and is still used at the local level on occasion. Direct action is dramatic (media coverage is a major purpose), disruptive, sometimes illegal, but always nonviolent. It is aimed at educating and forcefully helping people to pay attention to a problem. Direct action can convert a situation into an event. The media found it easy to ignore decades of routinized injustice to blacks, but they found it impossible to ignore freedom rides and sit-ins. Martin Luther King, Jr., was the master of direct action. He and his followers broke the Jim Crow laws and could thus test the constitutionality of them. Racist violence against peaceful integrationists, tragic though it was, created the media attention and thus national awareness and willingness to act. Direct action was also used against the Vietnam War, including the unauthorized release of classified information. But too often the media's preference for violence distorted the message intended. A primarily middle-class nonviolent movement became confused with radical, violent fringes. Local action has included such efforts as dying the effluent of an industry that claims it is not polluting; then dye shows up quite visibly where it is claimed not to be. It includes boycotting meat because of high prices, or Gallo wines to support farm workers. Wildcat strikes and picketing are typical direct actions of labor unions. Greenpeace has taken direct action against whalers by maneuvering its ships between the harpooners and the whales.

In May 1979 Mark Dubois of Friends of the River (see the case study in chapter 3) bolted himself to a rock in a secret location near the edge of the gradually rising New Melones Reservoir in California to protest the death of the river. This direct action, risking drowning, induced the Army Corps of Engineers to promise to stop filling above the Parrotts Ferry Bridge, the end of the river run and the only point of public access to the area. Governor Brown promised that the state will police the water level. It was an important if interim victory pending settlement of the larger issue.

Direct action is difficult; it must be dramatic but stop short of violence, which tends to backfire. The line between an outraged citizenry and an outrageous mob is not always clear.

Lobbying is probably the major activity of most public-interest groups.[8] There are about 8,000 practicing lawyers in Washington, D.C., most of whom work for profit-oriented interests. Fewer than a hundred work full time for consumer and environmental interests. An additional 7,000 lobbyists work in Washington, a very small percentage of whom work for reform. About $1 billion is spent to influence Washington and another billion on the rest of the country.[9]

The most publicized aspect of lobbying is testifying at hearings, but most lobbyists say that the most important aspect is talking personally with officials and their key aides. Most lobbying consists of coordination among those who are in general agreement about specific goals and actions and, secondarily, convincing those who are undecided. Lobbyists usually do not try to convert the opposition or even complain about weak friends. However, it happens; Common Cause, for example, criticized a congressman to his constituents for his absenteeism. Stung, he showed up for a key committee vote; his vote was the deciding one.[10] Such criticism is a major way to make delay and inaction on needed reforms more visible.

Lobbying includes citizen contacts through letters on public issues. Common Cause calls its member its "outside lobby" (outside Washington); many groups inform their members when to write and explain why the issues are important. Surprisingly few people actually write letters on legislation, so most congressmen are very sensitive to letters whose writers have taken a reasoned position on an issue.

Campaigning is probably the next most important public-interest group activity, usually taking the form of raising funds nationally for distribution, concentrating on a few key races. This is a far more effective method for citizens than supporting a local candidate where the outcome is not in doubt. Groups tend to split between those who support candidates and those who do not. Common Cause, the League of Women Voters, and the Nader groups analyze and report votes but are nonpartisan, while others specialize here, including the National Committee for an Effective Congress (NCEC) and the Council for a Livable World. Environmental Action (which also has other activities) and the League of Conservation Voters have been effective in recent years in electing environmentalists. Environmental Action's "Dirty Dozen" campaign has already been discussed; the League of Conservation Voters publicizes voting records. The analysis of votes and ratings of elected officials is one of the most important functions performed by public-interest groups. Too few voters are members of groups; most are unaware of even how to find out where legislators stand.

Most people vote without knowing the candidates' stand on issues, although relatively little money is needed to give them information to connect their values with candidates positions. Such information often builds on concern generated by mass media trends and closes a gap left by the media. Antiwar activists defeated a number of hawks, who were sometimes also the antienvironmentalists opposed by Environmental Action. NCEC in 1970, emphasizing the war, helped elect eleven of its nineteen candidates. In 1974 when turnout was down, reform voting was up, electing seventy new congressmen, mostly NCEC-supported progressives, and defeating twenty-three incumbents. NCEC spent only $125,000 for all the races, but it also gave professional advice on campaigning, which proved to be of great value. Considering how few people actually work in campaigns and how few people give money with a public interest in mind, it is surprising that these groups are so successful. Much reform lobbying fails because it does not appeal to enough politicians. It is often easier to persuade voters to change the politicians than to change the minds of politicians. In a procedural democracy, elections are the major way to change the context within which policy is made.

Litigation is probably the third most important public-interest group activity. We have a disingenuous way of passing laws and then ignoring them. Yet we also have a fairly honest, able, and independent judiciary, which will usually enforce the law eventually. The judiciary does not, however, get very far ahead of what is politically acceptable, and for decades it supported the suppression of blacks. There are still a surprisingly large number of abuses, fought by the NAACP Legal Defense Fund, the Southern Poverty Law Center, and others. In recent years, several new types of public-interest legal practice have been developed: poverty law, women's rights, environmental law, and consumer law. Some public-interest groups like the ACLU specialize in litigation across a wide range of issues; other groups, such as Common Cause, have many activities, of which litigation is only one. Unfortunately, environmentalists have been so successful that the Supreme Court greatly reduced their ability to use class actions. The courts do not generate their own cases; they must be brought to court by litigants, which takes money, which can be supplied by committed citizens.

The organization and finance of public-interest groups vary. In many cases, a national membership costs $15 to $25. Local groups are likely to cost even less. It is a cheap price to pay for political influence. Most people say they believe in peace and justice but spend nothing to get it. We employ professionals for medical, legal, and other purposes. Why not employ them for the public interest? It is well within the means of most American families to contribute $100 or more to political causes; it is less than 1 percent of most families' incomes. Success in the past and the requirements of the future indicate that such spending is worthwhile.

Support from the average American is not essential; reformist groups have never had such support in the past and are not likely to get it in the future. They depend, rather, on a relatively small number of committed citizens. Our problem is to think of ourselves as having political needs as urgent as other needs.

Common Cause, one of the most successful and sophisticated groups, has about 215,000 members, less than 0.14 percent of the adult population. Dues of $15 produced in 1976 about $3,750,000, with additional contributions adding up to over $5 million. Common Cause budgeted 35 percent for membership development and processing, 13 percent for governance and management, 26 percent for national lobbying, 23 percent for state lobbying, and 3 percent for litigation. Common Cause employed seventy-six people and mobilized volunteer talent equal to another seventy-six.[11]

Some organizations are controlled organizationally by their members; sometimes elections are competitive, with short sketches of candidates; others have only enough nominees to cover the vacancies. Sometimes members must attend an annual meeting to vote, but more and more mail ballots are being used. Some are conscientious about reporting financial information to members in summary form and supplying details on request. A few, like Consumers Union or Common Cause, poll their members to find out what issues are important. Most public-interest groups have a magazine, report, bulletin, newsletter, or regular fund-raising letters to keep members abreast of events and ideas. Some, like the Sierra Club, Audubon, and the League of Women Voters, have strong local chapters. Others are centered in Washington, D.C. Some are strictly political; others have strong educational or other programs.

To survive, public-interest advocates must continually raise money. The primary technique for finding new supports is mailings. Groups with similar goals exchange lists so those who are members of a few groups are likely to receive mailings from many. It is difficult to evaluate groups on the basis of their mailings alone, yet there are no easily available sources of independent information about the honesty and effectiveness of the group. Some guidelines can be suggested, such as using the newspapers and knowledgeable friends for information. Appeals that seem oversimplified, emotionally extreme, dehumanizing in their treatment of any group, or crass in offering possible winnings or gifts to contributors should be avoided. Appeals that present a lot of specific information on their issues and its politics are likely to be more trustworthy. Groups that make available detailed information on their finances, poll their members for their opinions, or have competitive elections of officers by the membership may be more worthy of support than those that do not do these things. Comparing appeals against each other is also useful.

Direct mail appeals of all kinds have increased greatly in the 1970s. In 1976, for example, the average household received eighty-five mailings costing about $12 each. Americans mailed back $20 billion in contributions, about four times the combined giving of corporations, foundations, and all other sources. In 1978 almost $40 billion was given, close to half going to religious causes and a small fraction to public-interest groups. (This sum was about equal to what was spent on movies, cosmetics, and liquor.) Nonprofit organizations of all types are probably the largest kind of business in the United States that is not regulated. Often more than half the money raised is spent on fund raising and administration, and some groups are rackets for self-dealing swindlers. In 1978 a fund raiser for the Pallotine Fathers pleaded guilty to misappropriating $2.2 million in contributions. Only 3 percent of the $20 million raised by the Pallotine Fathers went to hungry children. Some large, independent, evangelical churches using television to get money have kept their finances secret, and some are being probed by governmental agencies. The Council of Better Business Bureaus established standards for solicitations in 1974, but many groups have not met them. Many people hold back, feeling suspicious; others give not knowing how well their money will be used. Donations are dropping as a percentage of disposable income.[12]

Several hundred evangelical Christian groups have set up a council to regulate themselves. The American Institute of Certified Public Accountants in 1979 was preparing principles for accounting and disclosure for the nonprofit sector in general. Secular charities have supported legislation to require disclosure of how much of the amounts raised by mail go for the purpose advertised. Religious groups have opposed such a law, fearing governmental interference with religion.

The biggest fund raiser of them all is United Way, which uses its usually exclusive access to places of employment and payroll deductions. United Way usually excludes from its membership controversial groups no matter how worthy, risking irrelevancy but keeping broad community support. Reform issues are controversial, so advocacy groups for the environment, women, minorities, and the old tend to be excluded. It would not, in fact, be desirable to have a United Way for advocacy groups, but it would be desirable for businesses to give access once a year to literature from a multiplicity of groups, creating a competitive market for political giving.

The choice between direct service charities and political-interest groups is difficult. Direct services provide the satisfaction of meeting a specific need. They can pioneer programs later taken over by government and can fill in the gaps left by government. Political giving risks failure and is several steps removed from the actual rendering of a service, but historically it has been far more effective than charitable giving. Inexpensive advocacy can lead to large commitments of resources through government to deal with a problem. Government has steadily taken over functions previously performed by charity and on the whole has reached more people more effectively. Political giving is obviously necessary to get regulatory reforms, which can be implemented only by government.

Conflict and Cooperation

Sometimes reformers have problems working together. The general goals of reform are easier to state than the specifics, and reformers often squabble among themselves within their general values.

One chronic division is between, on the one hand, the purists, the ideologues, the part-time activists, the radicals, the emotionalists, and the idealists seeking big changes, and, on the other hand, the moderates, the pragmatic infighters, the compromisers, and the full-time politicians. The first are intensely aware of how much needs to be done; the second are happy that anything gets done. The second group, close to the action, feels that it gets half a loaf often enough; the first feels that those half loaves are only slices, or crumbs.

Conflicts occur over balancing values, too. What kind of national health insurance should we have? If campaign contributions should be restricted to control the influence of money, then what about our freedoms of the press and speech? On this issue, the ACLU battled Common Cause, and the Supreme Court produced a compromise ruling. Common Cause and the Sierra Club have wrangled over reorganization of the jurisdictions of House committees and over lobbying disclosure reform. Environmentalists generally want oil to be more expensive to encourage conservation, and consumerists want prices lowered to limit oil oligopoly profits. Environmentalists may want tax breaks for home insulation while tax reformers want to simplify the tax code. Environmentalists want to stop certain projects damaging to the environment, while unions want jobs. Consumers want lower prices; unions, higher wages. For each narrower concern, convinced of the centrality of its own approach, the differences may seem more compelling than the common ground.

Yet usually there is a way to work out the disagreements. This is one of the disciplines of reform. For example, more public finance can trigger constitutionally valid contribution limits. A lobby reporting compromise is possible for that conflict. A petroleum tax would encourage conservation without windfalls to big business, mollifying consumers. The tensions are inevitable, but there is much cooperation among public-interest groups. Coalitions have frequently formed for lobbying for civil rights, women's rights, and the environment and against military projects and the Indochina war. The breadth of the coalitions demonstrates some kind of reform consensus at work.

Public-Interest Groups in the System

It is difficult, perhaps impossible, to catch in a few words the nuances of power possessed by reformist groups. They play a vital role and have some power. It is hard to separate their effectiveness from the forces with which they work closely—the media, reformist legislators and aides, progressive bureaucrats, and liberal presidents. Given our tendency toward presidency worship, we can start there.

Public Actors and Reform. Americans have never elected a radical president, either conservative or liberal, and outside of war and depression, few presidents have been radical in their exercise of power. Since World War II, the most radically conservative candidate, Barry Goldwater in 1964, and the most radically liberal, George McGovern in 1972, were badly beaten at the polls. On the other hand, moderate losing candidates have come very close to winning: Thomas Dewey in 1948, Richard Nixon in 1960, Hubert Humphrey in 1968, and Gerald Ford in 1976. (Eisenhower's personal popularity from his wartime generalship made his election in 1952 and 1956 special cases.) The positions of moderate presidents are acceptable to most elites, so presidents will not push too strongly for reform. By the same token, they tend not to oppose a reform that reformers and the progressive part of the elite want strongly to implement.

Within these broad constraints, the liberalness or conservativeness of a president makes a big difference as to what reform legislation Congress will pass and what is signed into law. President Carter, part of the mildly liberal elites, is more supportive of moderate reform than were Nixon and Ford, who were members of the more conservative factions. The media exaggerate the difference a president can make, however. Congress, and especially its bipartisan collection of middle-of-the-roaders who hold the balance of power on many issues, has a mind of its own. In terms of the broader political forces at work, presidents are extremely limited. They exercise power within the context of existing elite and active citizen opinion. It is the reformist groups that play a major role in changing the context of opinion, which in turn changes what presidents and Congress can do.

A president can get a reform in some limited area of personal interest, but across a wider range of concerns, the groups can take more initiative. Typically, reformers work closely with each other at lower levels of the system to gather as much support as possible before going public. They have the same triangular power relations that characterize elites: groups, bureaucrats, and congressmen. Since they must mobilize opinion, they also have close links with friendly people in the media. The network of people behind any given reform is hard to predict; for example, a generally conservative congressman may back a particular reform. Congressmen and bureaucrats acting alone usually do not have enough resources to get a reform; the extra energy that makes for success comes from reformist groups.

The judiciary has a less autonomous role, but the law is vague enough to make it very important. Nevertheless, judges cannot use that power without cases, which require money and talent to push. Once again the groups play a key role.

These same general observations apply to state and local governments, except that their political forces occasionally produce more radical politics, both Right and Left. Also, with less public attention being paid, they tend to be controlled even more by elites than the federal government is. There are greater variations in local situations, so what might be a reform in one place is accepted fact in another. Although they receive little attention in the national media, local groups play, or can play, as important a role at their level as the more publicized national groups play at theirs.

Private Actors and Reform. There are many private actors: corporations, unions, occupational associations, the media, academia, and political parties, among others. Large corporations are probably most opposed to reform because it so often conflicts with short- to medium-term monetary self-interest. Corporations are established to make profits for stockholders, a legitimate function, but the viewpoint is usually carried by corporate executives from their business roles to their citizen roles. The important aspect of business opposition to reform, and what so clearly distinguishes it from the far

Right, is the good sense with which it argues its case. Business people often have a much better understanding of the practical difficulties of their particular operations than do outside reformers. Their prestige and their ability to employ expertise add to their persuasiveness. It is too easy for reformers and others in general to blame business for the problems that would exist in similar form under public ownership. It is the responsibility of elected officials, not businessmen, to make decisions in the public interest; only the politicians have the formal responsibility to do so. When the money of the few and the apathy of the many distorts this representative function, public-interest groups emerge as a major means to redress the balance, lobbying against business and campaigning for more representative politicians. Once a reform is implemented, it generates new vested interests, which help keep it going, yoking corporations to the public interest. For example, social spending is so great that many businesses depend on it, and a significant reduction could precipitate a recession. Environmental reform businesses are likely to have similar characteristics.

Business does not speak with one voice and on certain issues can play a useful role in reform. Some business groups, for example, are intelligently and seriously concerned with public policy. The Committee for Economic Development, composed of mildly progressive businessmen, produces a steady stream of moderate, often useful studies. The business-financed American Enterprise Institute has risen in esteem in recent years because of the sophistication of its economic studies. *Fortune* magazine, despite its bias for the top corporate elite, can be useful for policy issues. Several top businessmen lent their names to *Counterbudget*. Many businesses cooperate with often onerous reporting and regulatory requirements; many find creative ways to link the private with the public interest. The corporate business world is so big and complex that it is not useful to have simplistic attitudes toward it. Reformers too often blame business when they should be working on the voters to change the politicians to change the way business is done.

Labor unions are generally much more progressive than business, although there is quite a range of attitude within organized labor, and it is less progressive than it used to be. The more progressive unions include the United Auto Workers, the United Mine Workers, the American Federation of State, County, and Municipal Employees, and the Communications Workers. In 1972, 35 of 116 AFL-CIO unions broke away from the neutrality of the official federation and supported McGovern for president. Without strong labor support, a progressive Democrat cannot win the presidency, and Carter was no exception. As with business, labor develops blind spots respecting its own income and power.

Occupational associations also run a gamut of political complexions. The high-income, high-prestige professions like medicine and law are indistinguishable from the corporate elites. More liberal and reformist are educators, social workers, welfare workers, probation and parole officers, and health workers. Organized action by these groups reflects their position on the front lines dealing with the problems of this book, and it is usually as progressive as the public-interest groups.

The media play a central role in reform. Muckraking journalists have historically exposed the problems of the system, communicating the facts that motivate others to work for change. Exposure is sometimes enough in itself to precipitate corrective action; other times the learning process seems impossibly slow. The media function includes books. Recent important reporters include Bob Woodward and Carl Bernstein, who broke the Watergate story; I. F. Stone, the patron saint of leftist journalism; Ralph Nader; Rachel Carson, exposer of the danger of pesticides; Michael Harrington, writing on poverty; Gloria Steinem and other feminists; and Jack Anderson. While reform may be precipitated by an event, like the crash of an airliner, more often the problem is to dramatize conditions and trends to make them newsworthy. For better or worse, public relations with its overtones of manipulation of public opinion is as important for reform as it is for the rest of the political process.

Academia—colleges, universities, and research institutes—are in many ways the ideal institutions to formulate and work for reform. Faculty members have far more time to think about problems than people in other occupations. They usually have little financial stake in the outcomes of policy. They are usually intelligent. Their jobs are usually protected from politics by tenure. However, traditional academic concerns are not directly related to reform and take up most faculty time. Academic specialists sometimes have expertise of value to business and, through consulting work, absorb probusiness policy positions. Too many academics equate objectivity, considered desirable, with lack of controversy, which may not be objective. Academics are often so immersed in their specialization that their small world becomes the only important one to them. As citizens they may be less effective than less educated people who read newspapers and are involved with their communities. Some academics are concerned but lose touch with practicalities. Nevertheless, much useful policy thinking comes from academia, which is well tied into the reformist groups. It is also a means of disseminating the fundamental understandings that profoundly influence elite and active citizen opinion, which in turn sets the boundaries within which policy alternatives are debated.

Political parties are not exactly private actors; they are rather loose confederations of most participants in the system. Party leaders are highly committed to the idea that parties are important. For most participants, however, the parties are weak. In 1978, for example, special interests gave $40 million to congressional elections while the parties gave only $30 million. Their functions are to meld together on a temporary basis the minimum agreement necessary among many diverse interests to win a presidential election and to organize legislatures into voting blocs on certain issues. The Republican party is in trouble as far as popular support is concerned, and a majority of their leaders are opposed to significant reform. However, it is still viable wherever it can avoid overly conservative candidates and where the Democrats nominate overly liberal ones. Democrats and Independents have voted Republican enough to show how superficial party identification can be. The Democrats are the larger party, but internal divergences are seriously undermining their tentative unity. The party is so weak that it will not discipline a member who constantly votes against the party program; only actively campaigning for the opposition's presidential candidate draws censure.

The parties, especially the Democrats, are fairly open to serious outsiders. Most reformist politicians are Democrats, but like others they get little help from the party itself. They must develop their own supporters and prove themselves in primaries before they can use the label. These campaign organizations are a kind of public-interest group. They contest primary elections, which are a key point of leverage in the system. If they win the primary of the major party of their district, it is often fairly easy to win the general election. Nonparty interest groups, such as the National Committee for an Effective Congress, specialize in helping such reformist candidates.

Citizens can be bureaucrats, legislators, reporters, academics, corporate executives, labor leaders, and so on, but as citizens (that is, as people with limited time and money for most issues) they have to use public-interest groups. Such groups perform functions the citizen, acting alone, cannot: research, inform, lobby, campaign, litigate. There are enough committed citizens already that reformist groups have been able to figure prominently over the last few decades. Radical change is probably impossible, but piecemeal implementation of great change over time is possible; it is, in fact, the reality of how positive change has been accomplished. The energy of reformers and the issue-processing capability of our institutions are both limited. Still, moderate reform can be exciting because it is possible.

Reformist groups have essentially adopted elite methods of influence and use them for different purposes, taking advantage of the openings allowed by procedural democracy. The elites use the system largely to benefit themselves, but reformers uphold the procedures of the system to change its evils: its militarism, its abuse of economic power, its materialism, its environmental destructiveness, its inequality of opportunity, its lack of compassion, its inefficiency, and its antidemocratic features. Reformers can use their limited resources with maximum leverage and move the whole with a small force.

Activities for Committed Citizens

Being an ideal citizen—reading enough, participating enough, voting right—is impossible. It takes too much time, too much intelligence, and too much money. What is your image of the good citizen? It is probably like the image of clergymen among people who do not know one. "Good citizen" suggests a do-gooder, a moralistic person who does boring things. But there is an alternative, more realistic image: the committed citizen. The committed citizen does not try to live up to the abstract ideals of high school civics but *reacts to reality*. A person does not start off as committed; rather, over time we understand better a real problem and how our *action* is relevant for dealing with it. Many problems are more or less personal, like education, work, and family-related problems, but the line between these and the more political problems is an analytical one not necessarily experienced in real life. Maturing involves becoming aware of larger communities in which our face-to-face relations are embedded. To go from personal to political action is a natural process, yet it is also natural to learn passivity. Our families, the schools, the media, and the general culture tend, without really meaning to, to teach passivity and minimal involvement. We can overcome that inertia by learning, which deepens our understanding and helps us rehearse mentally the kinds of actions we might take. One common pattern is for college students to be fairly inactive but to lay the groundwork mentally for effective participation in later years. Understanding the connections between problems and ourselves compels us to act.

The personal activities of commitment encompass information strategy, work, and citizen activities.

Information Strategy

All of us, consciously or unconsciously, have an information strategy. We systematically ignore most sources of information because of ignorance of them, lack of time to read them, or lack of money to buy them. We disbelieve some information because it conflicts with what we have decided to believe and similarly we believe distorted versions of events because they fit in with the way we think things are. We pay attention to very few sources. Over time these sources affect profoundly our conception of the world and of our personal responsibility for events. Typically, Americans attend to television news and newspaper front pages, both of which are oriented to events about "them." We are spectators, commenting on but not playing the game. We neither ask nor are told why the game is being played, why the rules are the way they are, or anything about the larger framework of events. We learn to blame "them" for problems.

Most people's information strategy does not protect their interests, but who is going to tell them what they need to know to do so? The media have no reason to relate events to the way we might act, to explain our choices to us. Politicians do not win votes by criticizing people or even by educating them. Social scientists as objective observers see neither good nor bad; it is simply the way things are. They are reluctant to criticize for reasons similar to why most people do not criticize others.

In a pro forma way, we complain about the media, but in a practical way, we believe it. How do we find better sources? Or is it easier to believe that something is not our fault because we are ignorant about it? Information is vast; time is limited. But what have we done to increase our chances of finding out what we need to know? Little research has been done on these questions. Some informal surveys of students indicate that they spend about four to ten hours during a typical week in information seeking, and a few people spend more than fourteen hours a week in this way. Some of this reading tends to be general, and some tends to be specialized, reflecting our particular interests and involvements. General reading is relevant for voting and campaigning; specialized reading is helpful for supporting lobbying through public-interest groups and contacts with officials.

A good information strategy touches several kinds of sources: conventional news; investigative reporting on public policy; summaries of the results of research by academic, governmental, and other reliable sources; reviews of books and other publications; and analysis and opinion from a variety of informed viewpoints. An information strategy is not just news; most people probably overemphasize events. It is also analysis and opinion, which help us understand what is behind the news and make us aware of what is not in the news. A good strategy is a kind of continuing education. It can use conversation as a major source. If you know someone who is well informed in a given area, you can pick up the main ideas from him or her and put your reading time in on other areas. Similarly, if you specialize, people may rely on you to alert them to problems they need to know about.

A good strategy saves time. For example, many elections have foregone conclusions and are not worth a lot of effort to study, while others are being contested by candidates with important differences. Or your strategy may tell you that an officeholder is doing a poor job, leading you to work with others to mount a challenge and letting all the other elections go with much less attention.

No source is perfectly objective, of course. You need to know the strengths and weaknesses, to see through and adjust for bias, and to read for the persuasive facts (or lack of them). There is not enough time to do the job right; you are better off trying to do a little better than in the past, and as your background improves, your use of sources becomes much more efficient. Disagreement among trusted sources, unexpected agreement with sources you usually disagree with, and information that clashes with your operating beliefs are signals that you need to get more information and do more thinking. Again, conversation becomes a way of working out problems.

Since there is too much to read, you need to avoid sources that tell you more than you want to know or need to know. Good sources have synthesis, continuity, brevity, currency, frequency, general coverage, and low cost. Books do not have this; magazines and newspapers do. You can use book reviews to eliminate reading most books; only then will you have time to read those few that are the most valuable to you, usually in your specialization. Reading includes skimming and selective reading. You can develop strategies for reading newspapers, using headlines and news indexes or summaries to guide you. A good strategy usually has to include a local paper whatever its quality because it is likely to be the only source of local news.

Printed sources are far better than commercial broadcasts because they can be read at any time, at any speed, with great selectivity, and over a much wider range of subjects reported. They lend themselves to clipping files on topics of special interest. How we read is important, too; with a little thought we can improve our news reading skills.

Newspapers are abundant and inexpensive. In 1979 there were 9,710 in the United States, most of them weeklies; only 80 had over 200,000 daily circulation. The nation's leading newspapers are the *New York Times,* the *Washington Post*, the *Wall Street Journal* (which specializes in business), and the *Los Angeles Times* (although primarily regional), about in that order. They can be extremely valuable but tend to be expensive outside their local areas. Many libraries subscribe to the *New York Times,* the *Washington Post,* and the *Wall Street Journal.* Lower-ranked papers also can be excellent sources, often because they reprint stories from the leaders and from the conventional wire service, mainly United Press and Associated Press.

Magazines and other periodicals can be important, but of 9,719 (1979) published in the United States, only a relative handful deal with policy issues for a citizen audience. There are 111 U.S. magazines with circulations over 450,000 per issue.[13] They are a strong witness to the nonpolitical nature of most Americans and to the vitality of their interests. Badly undercut by television, many general interest magazines have stopped publication or lost circulation, leaving one giant, the *Reader's Digest,* which with 17.8 million has the highest circulation of all types. Its short, simplistic, overstated articles are fun to read but are hardly adequate for policy reading, and they are generally conservatively biased. To its credit, though, the *Digest* does have a few reform-oriented articles in most issues and is factually reliable.

All other magazines have much lower circulations: in order, for 1978, come *National Geographic, Family Circle, Woman's Day, Better Homes and*

Gardens, McCall's, Ladies Home Journal, Good Housekeeping, and *Playboy,* ranging from 8.6 million down to 4.5 million. The first with much politics is *Time,* thirteenth in circulation. If your only sources of information are a lower-quality newspaper and television, then subscription to a newsweekly like *Time* or *Newsweek* may be essential. However, with a good daily and a few magazines, the newsweekly may be redundant. A good information strategy also involves experimentation; switching around can be stimulating.

Other mass magazines are mostly nonpolitical or moderately to strongly conservative and do not contribute to the debate because they derive their information from other sources and usually do no political research themselves. Mass magazines that can have value for an information strategy include the *New Yorker, Ms., Playboy, Today's Education, Fortune,* other business magazines, *Jet, Saturday Review, Scientific American, Rolling Stone,* and *Money,* each for very different reasons.

Below 450,000 circulation is a rich proliferation of magazines best approached by using Katz's *Magazines for Libraries,* with its interesting annotations and useful subject organization. There are about a hundred listings under "Politics" alone.

What guidance is available in the citizen-policy area? None. Social scientists have made no effort to help people with the information explosion; they have not yet recognized this part of the problem. In 1970 some careful research established who was in the intellectual elite and asked them what magazine best expressed their views on policy and which they considered influential among other intellectuals. The leader was the *New Republic,* chosen by somewhat less than half the group for both questions. The other magazines receiving some ranking were, in order, the *New York Review of Books, Commentary, Nation, Harpers, Daedalus, Dissent, Newsweek, New Yorker, Saturday Review, Atlantic, Public Interest,* and *Foreign Affairs.*[14] Three of these are also mass circulation. The quality and reputation of magazines vary considerably over the years, and there are many more that could be mentioned. Browsing through the library and talking with others are good ways to discover interesting sources. A good guide has yet to be written.

A few other sources are worth suggesting. The *Wilson Quarterly* has several policy-related articles, reviews of books, and summaries of selected articles from over five hundred specialized journals and reports from research centers. In many areas of concern, specialized periodicals are found that still appeal to the general reader. *Urban Affairs Abstracts,* although too expensive to subscribe to, can be found in libraries and covers about fifty policy areas; it describes briefly what articles are about from many different periodicals. *Society* describes social problems and other research by social scientists. The *Bulletin of the Atomic Scientists* and *Science* have policy articles relevant for science and technology. *Environment* covers environmental issues; *Challenge,* economic issues; *Ms.,* women's issues;

Foreign Policy, foreign policy issues. Other sources are not oriented to issue areas or academic disciplines but to still other concerns. *Washington Monthly* explains how the federal bureaucracy, Congress, the press, and the presidency work behind the scenes. Muckraking journalism from the Left is still alive in *Mother Jones* and the *Progressive.* More academic approaches are taken in *Policy Studies,* a social science journal; *Skeptic,* which treats one issue in depth each issue; and *Policy Review,* a thoughtfully conservative journal. *Sojourners* is a Christian magazine as concerned with the social and political implications of faith as it is with the personal. There are many others; public-interest group periodicals have been listed in the appendix rather than here.

Once you become involved, you will receive all sorts of publications through the mail, including fund-raising letters, political newsletters, agendas and minutes of governmental agencies, environmental impact reports, planning documents, and hearing reports. An information strategy is highly personal and variable. Some people are able to find time to browse in a library; others will not read something unless they subscribe to it.

Another kind of information problem occurs when you need to do research on a particular topic. You should be familiar with the various reference works that guide you to relevant books, articles, news stories, and governmental documents. Reference librarians can be extremely helpful. Library orientation courses are useful. In about four hours or less, you can locate references to your topic. Local experts can help you find initial sources and provide their own perspectives.

An information strategy includes being aware of the kind of materials that are available. At the national level, key sources are *The Almanac of American Politics* (biennial), the *Washington Information Directory,* the *Statistical Abstract,* the *U.S. Government Manual,* and the *Budget of the U.S. Government,* all annuals and *C Q Weekly Report.* General Accounting Office reports, Congressional Budget Office studies, and other agency and congressional documents can be very valuable too.

So much is published that just finding relevant information is a problem. National government sources in addition to the above include the *American Statistics Index, CIS/Index to Publications of the U.S. Congress,* the *Guide to U.S. Government Publications* (for federal agencies), and the indexes of the *Code of Federal Regulations,* the *Congressional Record,* the *Federal Register,* the *Monthly Catalogue of U.S. Government Publications,* and *Public Papers of the Presidents.* Most major cities have Federal Information Centers or toll-free tielines to such centers. About twenty cities have General Printing Office bookstores. The *Consumers Guide to Federal Publications, The Consumer Information Catalogue,* the monthly *Selected U.S. Government Publications,* and almost three hundred subject bibliographies are available free.

A good information strategy is grounded on a liberal education. College courses and books are available to deepen understanding of all the subjects we have discussed.

It is easy to feel overwhelmed by all the information available and by your own ignorance, and easy to be bored or uninterested in difficult reading and by unstimulating teachers. However, your questions and concerns, not your knowledge, make you important. Your commitments can give you self-confidence. If you cannot understand something, it may be that it is written in jargon by people who are themselves ignorant or who fear offending anyone. Ask common-sense questions until you understand the answers. Hang onto a reasoning process that takes you to the facts and analysis you need. Amateurs often have an unbiased, fresh, and holistic perspective that professionals may lack. Being informed is always a relative process. You will gain understanding gradually and will never know enough. You will also get a sense of how much others know. Without being absolutely certain of your own rightness, you can often justifiably develop a strong feeling that others are incorrect. You will discover that they do not have bad intentions but that they do what they can for what they believe. As your background improves, you will develop an ability to move through intimidating stacks of reading material and to talk knowledgeably about a special interest. People will approach you as if you were an expert. A good information strategy leads naturally at some point to action based on knowledge.

Work

Our work provides our second major social role after the family, and it always has a political dimension. At the most basic level, the kind of people we are at home and at work contributes greatly to the quality of life of others.

Work varies greatly in its political content and its relationship to reform. Most college students are headed for careers rather than jobs. A *career* is a continually developing occupation, with a cumulation of skills and reputation leading to higher and different levels of performance. *Jobs* require less ability and may be well paid but do not lead to much more. Gourmet cooks, for example, have careers; short-order cooks have jobs. A career is not a straitjacket unless you make it so. Most people generally enjoy their work, but some sense an inner self going one way and the demands of work going another. Some switch careers, going, for example, from stock brokerage to tree farming. Some people switch gradually over a period of years without a conscious plan; others join one company or agency and stay with it for a lifetime. Some people follow established patterns; others define their own careers. There is an infinite variety. Two common desires most of us have is to do good and to do well, balancing the community good (with its indirect benefits) with the more obvious private benefit of income. We also want to do something personally satisfying. It is surprising how many people are able to accomplish all three goals.

Most college students are headed toward professional, technical, managerial, certain sales, farming, and protective services work. (See table 7.1.) Students generally get some help from their colleges in the transition from school to work, but the major burden is on the student to learn about the huge variety of opportunities. Major ways to start are to visit a college placement office and to read the *Occupational Handbook* of the U.S. Department of Labor. Most opportunities can be eliminated from lack of interest or lack of adequate academic qualifications. Graduate schools, medical schools in

Table 7–1 Occupations and College Education

	1950	*1978*	*% College* [a]
Professional and technical [b]	4,490	14,252	64.7
Managers, proprietors [c]	6,429	10,026	29.0
Clerical	7,632	16,600	8.4
Sales	3,822	5,795	18.7
Craftsmen, foremen	7,670	11,853	3.7
Operatives, including transport	12,146	14,026	1.8
Service workers	6,535	12,608	3.6
Laborers, excluding farm	3,520	4,217	2.2
Farm laborers, farmers	7,408	2,469	5.6
Total	56,648	91,846	17.4

Note: The figures for 1950 and 1978 are in millions.

[a] Percentages of workers in occupation with four or more years of college in March 1976. These percentages would be about the same for 1978.

[b] Professional and technical: accountants, architects, computer specialists, engineers, lawyers and judges, life and physical scientists, physicians, dentists and related, pharmacists, health technicians, religious workers, social scientists, teachers, draftsmen and surveyors, electrical or electronic related technicians, airplane pilots, writers, artists, entertainers, others; librarians, nurses, dieticians, therapists, actuaries, social and recreation workers, psychiatric workers.

[c] Managers, proprietors: buyers, purchasing agents, sales managers, school administrators, public administration, salaried managers, self-employed managers.

Sources: *Statistical Abstract of the United States, 1975,* p. 359; *Statistical Abstract, 1978,* pp. 418–420; U.S. Department of Labor, "Education Attainment of Workers," *Special Labor Force Report,* March 1976, table B–9.

particular, are heavily overapplied and turn down many who have the ability to do well. Preparation during college can make entry into an occupation much easier, helping you to take the right courses, to apply for the examinations or schools you need, or to develop contacts in the business. Low-level jobs, part-time volunteer work, and internships are a few ways to help you get started. Generally, more advanced education yields more interesting and challenging work opportunities, a wider range of job choice, better compensation and security, greater chance for advancement, and more opportunities for influence and reform. Every problem discussed in this book has a variety of careers dealing with it. Anything you have a special personal interest in can usually lead to a job.

Most of these careers involve the idea of professionalism, a powerful and generally positive force in our society today. (Our discussion will focus on the professions, but any job can be approached with a sense of professionalism.) Professionals measure themselves not only by the money they make but also by how well they are doing their jobs. Professional ethics involves a commitment to the long-term good of the community and a sense of service and discipline. For example, a professional manager is concerned with long-term profits and with anticipating, rather than fighting, the need for regulation. These sensitivities make the ideal capitalist manager little different from the ideal socialist manager. Indeed, profits are not so much a motive but one of a number of measurements of performance. Given the impossibility of regulating everything all of the time, professional ethics of the elites act as the first line of defense in protecting the public interest. Most people do not appreciate the importance of personal character and integrity in doing business. Historically, such ethics have been rooted in religious convictions through personal belief and church activities; more recently socialization and enforcement have partially shifted to graduate schools and professional associations, a weaker foundation. In this context, reformist action is a second line of defense, attacking specific abuses that even most elite members can see as such.

Professional roles place high demands on our thinking ability. Over the years, even centuries, a body of knowledge and practice has evolved. A profession emerges slowly from similar occupations, gradually establishing its own rules for entry and behavior and its particular institutional mechanisms integrating it with the rest of society. Professionals are always students of their profession. Social norms usually include membership in a professional association, taking one or more specialized periodicals, and attending annual meetings. Friendships develop, knitting the professions together. Each profession has its own special vocabulary, which is often incomprehensible to outsiders. Professionals have fairly fixed geographical or institutional bases but associate on a worldwide basis. Hierarchies of internal specialization develop, as well as prestige for recognized accomplishments.

Professionalism has played a major role in transforming our society because professionals have the expertise, the ability, and the organization to work for change over a long period of time. Research shows the established professions to be the most satisfying of all occupations. ("Urban university professor" is at the top.) Generally 80 to 90 percent of professionals are satisfied with their work, while both white collar and skilled blue collar are in the 40 to 50 percent range. Less-skilled workers come in at 15 to 25 percent. Satisfaction correlates with income, control over one's work, and even how long one lives.[15] The professions also dominate the choice of work people prefer as a career if they were free to choose.[16]

There are, however, three problems with professionalism. One is the strength of institutional or organizational needs in overcoming professional scruples or narrowing them at the cost of other values. The Pentagon, for example, is the only important employment for military professionals, which greatly increases the pressures for conformity. By contrast, most other professionals have many potential employers. Another example is the multinational corporation, where so many court convictions have occurred concerning illegal contributions and bribes. Obviously professional goals were subdued by desires for corporate profits or political protection. Organizational loyalty frequently overcomes professional scruples.

A second problem is the weakness of the strength of specialization. Professionals are rewarded by knowing more than other people about a small subject. Such narrowness may mean that important perspectives and concerns outside the profession are overlooked. A conventional professional wisdom that is destructive of the public interest can develop. Professions can develop their own agendas independent of what society really needs. Reform-oriented professionals often see this problem most clearly and work to generate outside pressure for change. Dissident experts are a fertile source for citizens oriented to reform. The affluence, prestige, and power of many professionals make them insensitive to some problems. Corporate law may provide ethics for preventing corporate war but not prevent civil war. Academics may love to research tiny problems, but they lose student interest and public support. To be really good as professionals, many say they have not had time to be committed citizens. Apathy is not confined to less educated people.

A third problem is that the professions, dominating the kind of work available to college students, are likely to be biased toward the status quo respecting many of the problems discussed. Students and young professionals have to make a special effort to seek out work beneficial to the public interest, and it is to their credit that many do so, often sacrificing income for service and satisfaction. We can't all decide to be a certain occupation, but the number who choose it can expand or contract somewhat independent of market demand. The VISTA and Peace Corps programs are open-ended; they take about as many as apply with basic qualifications. These and other volunteer jobs are too low paid and too temporary to be careers, but they can provide valuable experience and contacts that lead to careers. Law is a flexible career. The barriers to entry are not as great as in medicine, and there are many reform applications. The number of reform-oriented legal jobs has increased greatly in recent years, but there is still a limit, and reform lawyers may find themselves "starving." (Crusading farmers, at least, can grow their own food.)

Many nonprofessional or subprofessional occupations are moving toward professionalization and can be very rewarding. There are many technical and administrative careers, as well as social service jobs. One of the most important is police work, which has become quite complex. Law enforcement involves two professions—law and social work. Police work in cities and suburbs shows signs of being underprofessionalized; too often, jobs are not properly defined, training and education for the job are inadequate, job holders do not have enough opportunity for recognized upgrading of their skills, unskilled job holders aggravate the problems they are supposed to solve, working conditions are poor (although inherent to some extent in police work), and jobs are underpaid and underrecognized.

Political Activities

How can you be effective within the very limited time allowed by other commitments? We need to knit special citizen activities into the larger fabric of everyday life so they become part of our way of thinking rather than episodic. We need better information strategies; then voting and other activities take little time and flow naturally from an awareness of their importance. One thing should be clear: political action is essential. We cannot solve our problems by good thoughts and changes of our personal habits alone. Much of the job has to be done through government.

Voting is important because so few people do it, especially in nonpresidential elections, and because so many elections are close. The problem for the citizen is to figure out quickly and accurately which elections are important and which are not and, for the relatively more important races, to determine candidate differences. Unfortunately, information on candidates is not generally handy. The media do not review an incumbent's record in depth in most cases nor do they develop information on challengers, except to present, perhaps, a candidate-dominated interview. To get voting records, key votes, and ratings, and more general information about congressional candidates, the *Almanac of American Politics* is the best single source. Other information can be obtained from public-interest group mailings, attendance at a candidates' night in a local race, and opinions of active people. Do not assume that candidates are alike and use that as an excuse for not voting. This work may take a little time shortly before an election. Just remember how few vote and how many elections turn on one or two votes a precinct. Only you can protect your own interest.

Memberships in most organizations take only the time needed to write a check and mail it in. With thousands of likeminded other people, you can move the system with your own lobbyists. Contributions to candidates can work in the same way, only instead of trying to lobby a possibly unfriendly power holder, you are electing a friendly one. Lobbying has a marginal influence on policy; elections have a major influence.

Letters are an easy activity, but an off-the-cuff effort is likely to be a waste of time. You need to know when to write, to whom, and about what—information your media will not give you but your interest groups will. So few people write timely, intelligent letters on legislation that officials usually pay some attention to the ones they receive. Letters of this sort frequently have been important for legislative and administrative decisions.

Other activities include trying to persuade others how to vote, signing petitions, and boycotting selected products. Some personal activities have direct private benefit, like exercise and other health practices, using consumer information and product ratings, recycling much of our trash, insulating our homes and otherwise conserving energy, getting a better education or training, guarding against crime, and so on.

Activism

There is a rough distinction between the active citizen and an activist member of the secondary elite. As you move toward higher levels of activism, you become *activist,* which takes much more time than being a *citizen.* Activism tends to be cyclical among volunteers, with intense activity building up to an election, a scheduled governmental hearing or decision, or an important meeting and then rapidly dying down. At higher levels, activism begins to resemble a job because of the long, steady hours required. The first rule for activists is specialization following personal interests. Citizen specialization need not be as narrow as professional specialization, but public policy is so complex that some is necessary. Specialization is also important in forming durable personal relationships with others of similar interests; they are the basis for organization. Specialization makes the information proliferation problem just a little more manageable and brings you more quickly to the heart of a decision-making process.

A first level of activism is simply going to meetings of citizen groups, work-related groups, and governmental bodies dealing with your interest and reading more periodicals and writing more letters. It means participating at a low level in a campaign by working in the office, registering voters, going door to door with literature, and getting out the vote. It means giving a little more money, going to candidate receptions, and being a minor officer in small organizations. These activities involve self-recruitment. If you do not do them, they probably would not get done. Local groups and local chapters of larger groups are excellent places to start.

A second level of activism is more of the same, plus holding more important offices in more important groups. It means taking responsibility for some part of a campaign, committee work, preparing for the programs of a meeting of your groups, and organization work like collecting dues, passing petitions, and so on. Many people are active in addition to their home and work roles, but they are usually not oriented toward politics and even less toward reform. Churches, hobby groups, social clubs, and work-related associations are especially common.

At the third level, you hold a leadership role in an important public-interest group for which you were chosen by others, by election or appointment. Your word-of-mouth communications become especially important for information, and you will know personally a number of elected officials, bureaucrats, and other activists. You will be organizing campaigns, writing newsletters, doing research, preparing testimony, organizing others and trying to motivate them (which means getting them to do the things they said they would do). You will spend a fair amount of time on the telephone and frequently wish you had someone to tell you the answers instead of having to think so much yourself. If you get this far, you will probably be hooked for life on the importance and fascination of politics. You will be influential, but you probably will not feel influential because you will know how difficult it is to get anything done. In fact, you may find that often your major task is to prevent the problems you are attacking from worsening.

Activists at the third level usually require some source of outside financial support; for this reason, many are housewives without preschool children, retired, or independently wealthy. College teachers, clergymen, and independent business and professional persons may also be included because of the way they can schedule their time or manage to make a living without working full time. Such people also share another important characteristic: they usually cannot easily be fired from their job for their activities. People who are paid for working for reform are not activists but professionals. There is an intermediate category of people (between volunteers and well-paid professionals) who accept lower pay than their ability requires so that they can do worthwhile work.

Attitudes of Committed Citizens

One of the most important attitudes for committed citizens is a combination of persistence and low expectations. Too many people suddenly get excited about how the world is falling apart, and, filled with determination to help, they volunteer, join a group, or attend a meeting. They expect the group to appreciate their efforts and give them something meaningful to do. There are two things they should realize: the activists in the group have seen too many others before who did not do what they volunteered to do, who stop coming to meetings, and who disappeared. The activists will be friendly, but they are often unwilling to spend their limited time trying to find work for new volunteers.

Second, the best volunteer is self-organizing. They listen and talk with members, go to a few meetings, and figure out for themselves what needs to be done. They tell the leaders what they will try to do, they do it, and they tell the leaders what they have done. It is difficult enough for activists to organize their own time, let alone others.

Activists are very human people with many limitations. Personalities easily become more important than issues. Time is dissipated into impractical activities, or too many things are attempted, none well. Purely organizational affairs and procedural problems can take up an incredible amount of time. Reform is not just working for goals but working with people, balancing participation against pushing things through. Most activists are not wealthy, overly ambitious, or outstandingly intelligent. Activists receive little coverage in the news media and in many other ways fail to meet the criteria for success held out by secular materialism, power politics, and social fashion. But they have a sense of real values, which gives them the strength to care, not to be defeated by the magnitude of the challenge, not to be discouraged by their own weakness, not to be enervated by the length of the struggle and the uncertainty of the outcome. Intimidated but not beaten, they persistently work in a productive direction. Frequently outnumbered, outmaneuvered, outvoted, and overcompromised, they nevertheless keep trying and succeed in ways sometimes difficult to measure.

Losing

By the rules of the world in their time, Edgar Snow, Frank Graham, and Norman Thomas were all losers. Edgar Snow in the 1930s went past the court reporters around China's Chiang Kai-shek and reported on Mao Tse-tung and a few other revolutionaries who had retreated over a great distance to a remote province. His book, *Red Star over China,* and his other reporting were perhaps somewhat too uncritical in some respects, but they captured more accurately than other public sources what was happening and why. During the McCarthy era, he and other accurate reporters were labeled communists and generally ignored. Shortly after Snow's death in 1972, Richard Nixon, one of the most fervent of the red-baiters, followed the trail Snow had blazed thirty-five years earlier.

Frank Graham, president of a southern university, was appointed to complete a term in the U.S. Senate. He worked for equal job opportunities and decent wages for all. He held a competitive examination to decide his selection to the U.S. Naval Academy at Annapolis. He appointed the winner, unusual because the cadet was black and the year was 1950. Graham was called a pro-communist, un-American, and a traitor to the South. He lost his bid for reelection.

Norman Thomas, a Socialist, ran for president four times from 1928 to 1948. He advocated unemployment insurance, Social Security, and the rights of unions to organize and strike. A rich aristocrat, Franklin Roosevelt, implemented so much of what Thomas was advocating that most of the Socialist following went Democratic. Thomas's lifelong commitment to civil liberties led him to help found the American Civil Liberties Union. He opposed Ku Klux Klan terror at home and mass bombing abroad. He opposed Stalinism in the Soviet Union and McCarthyism in the United States. Consistently opposed to militarism, he was an early opponent of the Indochina war. He was an excellent speaker but not much of a political operator. Thomas never counted for much among people who really held power. For him, as for the others, politics was not the art of the possible, that is, working within existing constraints. It was, rather, the art of changing the possible, of moving opinion and agendas toward what was desirable. Thomas did win one thing: the Nobel Peace Prize.

Winning

Reformers, of course, do not always lose. The purpose of reform is not to hit our heads nobly against brick walls; the purpose is positive change. It is one thing not to reach a goal and another to fail to make any progress toward it.

Reviewing the problems facing us, we can see from a certain viewpoint great progress. The Indochina war became the object of the most important peace movement in American history, one that gradually increased its influence until it controlled the Congress and forced a reluctant president step by step to withdrawal. Defense spending is drastically below cold war levels and unlikely to rise to previous levels. Presidential power for war making has been carefully restricted. In 1975–1976, we stayed out of the Angola conflict; we stuck close to budget guidelines on defense. The security reform movement is growing, armed with increasing expertise and logic. The United Nations, for all its weaknesses, has proved its usefulness in many important ways. Militaristic anticommunism is ebbing as a force in domestic politics. Tentative steps toward peace have been made in the still explosive Middle East, especially the 1979 treaty between Egypt and Israel.

The income tax, despite its loopholes, is strongly progressive, and combined with federal transfer programs we have substantial redistribution of wealth and a proportional income-tax-transfer system. The massive oil depletion allowance loophole was greatly reduced, and others have been narrowed. By 1979 more people were working, even as a percentage of adult population, than in most of our history. Huge transfer systems have created deficits, but they have also sustained demand during a recession, preventing depression and helping recovery. Market power is a problem, but the economy is still mostly competitive, and antitrust efforts, though well below desirable levels, have been useful in sustaining competition. Never before have so many people enjoyed so high a standard of living. Serious unemployment persists, but it is less than indicated by the unemployment rate. Gradual improvements in the funding and organization of federal-state job training efforts have been made and much useful experience gained with public-service jobs. Regulatory reforms to protect consumers and responsible performance by most companies have produced high levels of consumer satisfaction and opportunity, a fact not realized by many Americans until they go abroad.

Enormous progress has been made in the environmental area, which promises to be a dominant policy area of the coming decade. Popular awareness and education has expanded significantly. Dozens of major laws, especially NEPA, have been passed and are generally being implemented. Despite problems of standing, major court cases have generally gone to the environmentalists. The surge of popular interest has strengthened many older conservation groups and helped create new ones. Protected wilderness and parkland have been expanded, and efforts to protect species have been effective. Environmentalists have been winning elections. Air and water quality measures and regulations have had notable success in many areas and produced many new jobs in the process. Prodevelopment city councils and county boards in many areas have given way to environmentalists and careful land-use planning. Dams, freeways, and other destructive public works are being stopped. Other projects have been substantially modified by newly required procedures and environmentalist pressure. Suburbanization and highway building are slowing down, and older neighborhoods are organizing to defend themselves against high rises and excessive use of cars. Respecting population, we are unlikely to reach zero growth but have made tremendous progress in moving toward it, in abortion liberalization, and in providing family planning services. It is increasingly recognized that environmentalism is not antigrowth or antijobs but against past destructive growth and in favor of new kinds of growth, which will protect and enhance the quality of life. Environmental reform has already created about a million jobs, and effective reform would create millions more.

Economic growth and poverty programs have so reduced the amount and changed the nature of poverty that it is not a major economic or social problem. Social security, SSI, cost-of-living escalators, benefit increases, food stamps, Medicare and Medicaid, AFDC and other welfare, unemployment benefits, veterans' benefits, and other transfers have helped the economy and have benefited millions of middle- and low-income people. Never before had so many been out of work with so little suffering as in 1975. Substantial reorganization and simplification and some additional money could eliminate income poverty. Sexism and racism are still serious problems, but tremendous progress has been made. For women, the revolution is just beginning; for minorities, the revolution is well on its way. For southern blacks, who still have some of the most serious problems, most progress has been made.

Great progress has been made in protecting constitutional rights of criminal defendants, and some progress in reducing victimless crime. Crime prevention efforts are improving, and police forces generally are becoming more professional. Substantial progress has been made in health regulation, and there is increasing recognition of the need for health education. Health finance took a big step forward with Medicare and Medicaid, and national health insurance is on the national agenda. Health maintenance organizations have proven their worth and continue to grow. The Hill-Burton Act has created an abundance of hospitals, and medical schools are expanding. Health research is well funded, and advancements in treatment are constantly being made. Mental health institutions have greatly improved staff-patient ratios, and help of this sort is reaching more people than ever before. Community mental health services are steadily expanding. Legal actions are helping to improve state institutions for the mentally handicapped. Drug and alcohol abuse programs are gradually expanding.

Regarding education, never before in history have so many people been given so much opportunity, and taken advantage of it. The United States has the most educated population in the world. Tax-supported higher education provides a major path toward self-fulfillment from a liberal education and from attaining qualifications for worthwhile careers. A rich array of resources for continuing education is also developing.

The United States has a high level of civil liberties and is just emerging from a severe test of politically important rights to know what the government is doing, to privacy, and to freedom of legal dissent. Leaks, whistle blowers, and investigations have proven more powerful than a president who tried to put himself above the law. Illegal political violence has decreased also. Respecting majority rule, a large number of significant reforms affecting money and secrecy have been implemented at the state and federal levels. Congress has made substantial progress in recent years, gaining many new and able members and disciplining its chairmen. It has improved its budget procedures, made other internal reforms, and asserted its power in relation to the presidency. New workers have made progress in organizing; reform movements are active in some older unions. Many work places have experimented to improve the quality of the work experience.

Most nations are striving to achieve our levels of living standards, welfare, justice, and freedom and with little hope of attaining them in the foreseeable future. Most of the rest of the world has neither freedom nor abundance. A global Gallup Poll asked people about their degree of satisfaction with ten aspects of the quality of their lives. The United States came out ahead of Western Europe, Latin America, Africa, and the Far East on thirty-nine of forty comparisons. Even when the lower-income portion of the United States is considered separately, we still come out ahead on thirty-eight of forty comparisons. On some of the aspects for Europe and Latin America, the gaps are fairly small; for Africa and the Far East, the gaps are large.[17]

It would be a mistake to attribute all of these improvements to reformers because probably most of them result from forces beyond the influence of a small number of reformers. The proportion of adults belonging to reformist interest groups, for example, is probably about 1 percent. The major causes of these successes (as well as the failures, which have been our major concern) are the characteristics of the elites and the people. The important fact, however, is that reformist activists and citizens have had influence far out of proportion to their money or their numbers.

Ambiguity and Inaction

The world is complex enough to allow optimism or pessimism, each viewpoint selecting what it wants to see. The complacent optimists emphasize the winning; their actions are not needed to win. The alienated pessimists emphasize the losing; their efforts would do no good. Both stances can be used, thus, to justify inaction. People reveal themselves when they think they are describing an objective reality. We find it difficult to live with uncertainty and (without realizing it) come to believe things without much basis in fact.

This ambiguity of situations is paralleled by ambiguity in the power of reformers and in accomplished reforms. Are reformers so powerful that the system has been steadily modified to serve the public interest? Or are they weak or misguided, so that their reforms are minor and only serve to strengthen the power elite? Most of us want an answer one way or the other, but the reality may be partial reform in a modified elitist system. Consider the cases. The oil depletion loophole was closed, but only halfway. Kaiser Ridge was saved, but a big piece on the far side was lost. The Stanislaus River run may be lost, but others are being saved. Employment discrimination cases are usually won, but the backlog of cases is too large. More people can afford health services than ever before, but costs have escalated, there is too much abuse and fraud, and some are still not adequately covered. Can we have free speech and control the role of money in campaigns at the same time? Are reformers failures because of their failures? Successes because of their successes? Powerful because of what they did do? Weak because they did not do what really needed to be done? Most of the time reformers are simply too weak to accomplish what really needs to be done, yet we are generally better off for what they were able to do. This assessment is complicated by the fact that the definition of reform is constantly evolving as conditions change and our insight develops.

Reform ebbs and flows through history, beginning with a few voices, building a core of committed people, exploiting dramatic events to lobby for laws, and lobbying and litigating for law enforcement. Some changes can be made in crises; in brighter periods, many changes become possible. Breakdown affects the elites as well as the rest of us, and progressive members of the elites are willing to pay the price of some change to have continued preeminence. The ambiguity of reform enters early, for half-measures can easily lower the importance of a problem, lessening chances for stronger solutions.

Now there is a new generation of reformers and a new momentum. An unimplemented agenda has been laid out in this book. These programs will be implemented in bits and pieces because reformers have little power. Constantly the momentum toward reform is interrupted by war, conservative presidents, procedural delays, and conservative majorities in elections and legislatures. Reformers have had to appeal to the middle of the road, compromising their ideal to achieve some progress. A recent example is the Legal Services Corporation. Initially a strong program in the Office of Economic Opportunity, it was rendered largely ineffective by President Nixon. It was showing that whom lawyers worked for was as important as the law, a reality that elites would prefer to obscure with the myth of equal justice. Yet the legal elite believed in its rhetoric enough, and reformers were strong enough, so that legal services were not destroyed, and the Legal Services Corporation was permanently established to do half the job it should do. The reformers win often enough to be part of the game and even when they are losing, other players have to take them seriously.

Commitment to reform is highly personal. It should arise out of our deepest personal concerns and not out of some sense of externally imposed duty. Reform is a sophisticated form of selfishness. A desire for peace in the world also involves a desire not to be killed in a nuclear war and not to spend more money on the military than necessary. Fair taxation will save most of us money and improve services that we need. Stopping inflation, encouraging competition, stopping concentration, and protecting consumers all benefit our pocketbooks. Environmental reform is essential for the health, beauty, and continuity of our standard of living and quality of life. Protection from crime, better health, and more education benefit most of us. Ending racism, ending poverty, and rehabilitative concern for criminals and the mentally disabled seem to have more altruism, since few in number are directly helped, but there is also the fact that these goals will increase our security, productivity, and sense of community and reduce our welfare costs. It is hard to pursue any goal without in some way pursuing a private good, and the real arguments are over how to balance the many values we seek and how to get them most efficiently. The problem is to be intelligent about the trade-offs that must be made.

Religion and Reform

Religion here means our real commitment in life. We face choices that test our good intentions. If we came into some money, would we donate it to an interest group or take a vacation? With a little money, would we give it to a cause or have dinner in a nice restaurant? With a little extra time, would we read about a problem or watch television? The point is not to eliminate enjoyable diversions but to bring them into balance with our commitment to community values.

We say that we believe in peace, a good economy, environmental reform, social reform, and political reform. If an outsider were to try to define what we stand for based on how we spend our time and money, what would they say? Would we recognize the persons described? Is it the description we want? Many people, especially younger people, have very little money indeed and need feel no embarrassment about how they spend it. But it is a fact that most of us are far above the poverty line and still have a long list of things we would like to do for ourselves narrowly defined and very little for ourselves broadly defined. We are protected by our anonymity. No one is going to call our behavior into public question; we do not risk embarrassment. It is up to us to decide what we really believe in and start bending our habits in that direction. It is how we live day to day that constitutes our religion more than any set of religious beliefs or nonbelief.

There has been some weakness in our formal religious commitments. We blame elites rather than ourselves for the problems. Even members of one elite blame the others. But elite members are about as virtuous as the average person. It is because of their greater influence that their failings do greater damage.

Rabbis, ministers, priests, and church stalwarts support political reform vaguely but rarely specify what it means in particular, which might actually require us to do something. The emphasis on the accepting aspect of love is valuable but can make religious practice anemic, robbing it of substantive worth. Yet too often the voices of the judgment aspect are concerned with the assertion of narrow doctrinal beliefs, devoid of real political meaning, and pronounced in a way that emphasizes the letter of belief over the spirit of faith. It is hard work to think through the implications of our religious commitments for our citizenship role, but the alternative is what we already have in abundance: hypocrisy, the religious common cold of the middle and affluent classes.

Religion has played a prominent historical role in the quest for a better society. The major formal religions of American history—Catholicism, Protestantism, Judaism—have traditions of support for reform and for public service. Other religions have been important, such as the native American reverence for an unspoiled environment. Religious revivals, such as that of John Wesley and the Methodists, have had extensive political results. The Society of Friends and the Unitarians have perhaps the longest history of sustained reformism. The social gospel of social reform has long been part of the Protestant tradition and is increasingly important for Catholicism, exemplified in the support for farm labor unionization. Jews have long had a tradition of advocacy of tolerance and reform. Current movements, seemingly secular, have a strong religious overtone, evident in the commitment of the feminists and the environmentalists, and in the speeches of Ralph Nader and John Gardner. The intimate link between vital religion and political activism has been especially evident in the career of Harold Hughes, an alcoholic, who became governor and then senator of Iowa, and retired from the Senate to pursue religious work full time.

The commitment to reform should spring from a certain wholeness of self, which is inherently a religious quality. We need to think of our citizen role in terms of our commitment, which is unique to each person, and has to be thought through by each person alone. Our citizen activities become personal activities when they flow from that personal commitment. Reform politicians and activists will do what is possible; it is up to citizens to make reform possible, to change the forces to which politics responds. It would be easier if we could know we were right in some scientific sense, but it is not in the nature of life to allow such certainty. On the other hand, it is all too easy to let uncertainties lead to self-doubt and paralysis.

Our first steps lead to experience, from which we can develop a sense of judgment about when to study and when to act. The commitment can grow from the long conversation we should hold with ourselves about what is really so important and worthwhile that it transcends uncertainty, self-consciousness, and possible failure. That personal commitment, combined with the fascination of politics and ideas, the importance of the issues, a sense of community with other reformers, and some hope for success, can lead us into a lifetime of personal growth and effective action.

Gross national product analysis dominates general policy making today yet is inadequate. The concept of net social welfare needs to be developed using existing indexes and developing new ones and may have variants to reflect differences in values. Reforms aimed at improving NSW have to be disciplined by budget constraints, economic impacts, administrative feasibility, and skills available in the work force. Many reforms meet these tests and have worked in other countries but are not implemented in the United States for political reasons. Reformers include many diverse kinds of people characterized not so much by ideology as by pragmatism, by a perception of problems and an effort to attain a number of values. Ideologies seem to be losing their relevance as modern societies with different concepts of themselves face similar problems. Reformers have generally come from a liberal and democratic world view, but the content of liberalism is always changing, and conservatives also make contributions. Liberal reformism is an ambiguous process. Public-interest groups are one of the most important tools for citizen effectiveness. They can research, inform, take direct action, lobby, campaign, and litigate on our behalf and give us the information we need to be effective. Advocacy groups often work with each other, though occasionally there is conflict. Working with other parts of the system, they can often attain reform. Committed citizens seek out better understandings of reality through effective information strategies. They often have reform-related jobs and usually vote, join groups, and write letters. Activists dedicate even more time. Committed citizens are realistic and persistent and are not much influenced by traditional definitions of success. They have contributed greatly to what successes the system has had. With sophisticated selfishness and religious commitment, they continue their work. Huge impersonal forces seem to control our destiny; the elites still exercise the most power and average Americans still let them. Yet our history is ultimately made by individuals who have the power to change the possible upon which politicians practice their art.

Notes

1. Ruth Leger Sivard, *World Military and Social Expenditures, 1978* (Leesburg, Va.: WMSE Publications, 1978), pp. 24–32.
2. National Urban Coalition, *Counterbudget* (New York: Praeger, 1971).
3. Ibid., pp. xiii, 8, 20.
4. James L. Clayton, "Fiscal Limits of the Warfare-Welfare State," *Western Political Quarterly,* Spring 1976, p. 377 (1967 dollars).
5. Ibid., pp. 374, 381.
6. Ibid.
7. National Urban Coalition, *Counterbudget,* chap. 21.
8. Jeffrey Berry, "Citizens Approach Government" (Paper presented to the Midwest

Political Science Association meeting, 1974). See also Berry, *Lobbying for the People* (Princeton, N.J.: Princeton University Press, 1977).

9. *San Francisco Chronicle,* April 17, 1977; Common Cause, *Lobby Disclosure Reform,* May 1979.
10. These and some other examples are taken from Berry, "Citizens Approach Government."
11. *In Common,* December 1975, p. 6.
12. *San Francisco Chronicle,* April 17, December 5, 1977; January 7, June 13, 1978; April 15, 1979.
13. *1979 Ayer Directory* (Philadelphia: Ayer Press, 1979), p. vii. The number published excluded those of Canada and any publications less frequent than weekly. For a list of mass magazines, see the *World Almanac & Book of Facts 1978* (New York: World Almanac, 1978). For a description of most magazines of interest, see *Magazines for Libraries* (New York: R. R. Bowker, 1972).
14. Charles Kadushin et al., "How and Where to Find Intellectual Elite in the United States," *Public Opinion Quarterly,* Spring 1971, pp. 1–18.
15. *San Francisco Chronicle,* December 22, 1972.
16. Ibid., December 3, 1973.
17. Ibid., November 8, 25, 1976.

Appendix

Selected National Associations

The following list is based on *The Encyclopedia of Associations* (Detroit: Gale Research, 1979), the *Washington Information Directory* (Washington: Congressional Quarterly, 1976), *Jobs in Social Change* (Philadelphia: Social and Educational Research Foundation, 1975), and numerous mailings I have received. To qualify for this list, an association had to be politically active in 1979, concerned with national issues, take a generally reformist position, and engage in one of the activities of an interest group: research, education, direct action, lobbying, electioneering, or litigation on public policy. I generally excluded contract research institutes like RAND (Santa Monica CA) and SRI (Menlo Park CA), foundations and the groups they support, government-supported groups, labor unions, professional and occupational associations, governmental associations, church groups, business associations, and other nonpolitical or economically self-interested groups. I included groups that derive support from citizens through memberships, subscriptions, or donations and put the more important of these in capital letters. "R" indicates that the group reports key votes or rates congressmen. The name of the group's publication is in italic. If no city is given, the group is located in Washington DC.

The *Encyclopedia of Associations* has listings of thousands of groups of all different kinds and useful information about them. The *Washington Information Directory* is an excellent reference for other kinds of groups, committees of Congress, and executive branch agencies organized by subject. *Jobs in Social Change* lists about 175 groups and describes student internship opportunities in Washington DC. Public-interest groups are continually changing, with some becoming inactive while others are created. They generally have to have a Washington DC office to have a national impact, so the current Washington telephone directory is useful and available in most libraries. Reference librarians can be useful in locating groups and sources of information in specialized areas.

Multi-Issue Associations

Nonelectoral, Citizen Based

COMMON CAUSE, 2030 M St. NW, Washington DC 20036. R. *In Common, Frontline*. Public finance of congressional campaigns, lobby disclosure, sunset laws, tax loophole closures, trucking deregulation.

PUBLIC CITIZEN, 1346 Connecticut Ave. NW, Washington DC 20036. R. *Public Citizen*. Run by Ralph Nader and includes or supports others: Congress Watch, Public Citizen Litigation Group, and groups listed separately below for media reform, nuclear power, health care, tax reform, and visitors to Washington.

LEAGUE OF WOMEN VOTERS, 1730 M St. NW, Washington DC 20036. R. *National Voter*, state and local *Voters*. Women's rights, urban issues, foreign policy, institutional reform, health, energy, economic issues, voter education; emphasizes member participation in local Leagues.

FRIENDS COMMITTEE ON LEGISLATION, 245 Second St. NE, Washington DC 20002. R. *FCNL Washington Report*. The Quaker lobby against militarism and for social justice, the best example of a reform-oriented religious lobby in Washington. Also of interest, though relatively nonpolitical, are the National Council of Churches, the National Conference of Christians and Jews, the major denominations, and a multitude of smaller religious groups in Washington DC concerned with social service and related policy.

CLERGY AND LAITY CONCERNED, 198 Broadway, New York NY 10038. Nuclear power, food for Vietnam, multinational corporation abuses in Africa, human rights; religious activists.

INSTITUTE FOR POLICY STUDIES, 1901 Que St. NW, Washington DC 20009. *In These Times*. Liberal-radical think tank; did a *Counterbudget*-type study in 1978 but not as concise.

Also of interest are Business Executives Move for New National Priorities, Baltimore MD, a liberal business group; and Conference on Alternative

State and Local Policies, progressive elected officials looking for new ways to improve local government.

Electoral, Citizen Based

NATIONAL COMMITTEE FOR AN EFFECTIVE CONGRESS, 10 East Thirty-ninth St., New York NY 10016. R. *Congressional Report.* Raises funds for reformist congressional candidates, gives them technical aid.

COUNCIL FOR A LIVABLE WORLD, 100 Maryland Ave. NE, Washington DC 20002. R. Raises funds for reformist Senate candidates, lobbies for security reform.

AMERICANS FOR DEMOCRATIC ACTION, 1411 K St. NW, Washington DC 20005. R. *ADA World.* The quintessence of liberalism, usually reformist.

Also of interest are the DSG Campaign Fund (DSG is Democratic Study Group, which is composed of moderate and liberal House Democrats); the Ripon Society, a group of progressive Republicans critical of big government and big business; and the New Leadership Fund, which raises money for progressive Republicans.

Corporation Emphasis

COUNCIL ON ECONOMIC PRIORITIES, 84 Fifth Ave., New York NY 10011. *CEP Report, CEP Newsletter.* Researches corporate pollution, defense contracting, investment in South Africa, environmental advertising, minority employment, nuclear power, Indian lands leasing.

CORPORATE ACCOUNTABILITY RESEARCH GROUP, 1346 Connecticut Ave. NW, Washington DC 20036. A Nader-inspired group.

AGRIBUSINESS ACCOUNTABILITY PROJECT, 1000 Wisconsin Ave. NW, Washington DC 20007. Researches the effect of big business on food.

INTERFAITH CENTER ON CORPORATE RESPONSIBILITY, 475 Riverside Dr., New York NY 10027. *The Corporate Examiner.* Supported by 14 denominations and over 150 Roman Catholic orders, researches and advises on shareholder actions, lobbying, and investments.

Economic Emphasis

PUBLIC INTEREST ECONOMICS FOUNDATION, 1714 Massachusetts Ave. NW, Washington DC 20036. *Public Interest Economics.*

BROOKINGS INSTITUTION, 1775 Massachusetts Ave. NE, Washington DC 20036. Academic research by the moderate liberal establishment; publishes a useful critique of the federal budget each year.

AMERICAN ENTERPRISE INSTITUTE, 1150 Seventeenth St. NW, Washington DC 20036. *Public Opinion; Regulation; AEI Economist;* others. Academic research from a free enterprise viewpoint.

COMMITTEE FOR ECONOMIC DEVELOPMENT, 477 Madison Ave., New York NY 10022. Policy studies by businessmen and academics. Also of interest is the Institute for Contemporary Studies, San Francisco CA; to the right of AEI and CED.

Accountants for the Public Interest, San Francisco CA. Does accounting studies for nonprofit organizations.

Legal Emphasis

CENTER FOR THE STUDY OF RESPONSIVE LAW, PO Box 19369, Washington DC 20036. A Nader group; includes Freedom of Information Act Clearinghouse.

Also of interest are the Center for Law and Social Policy; Student Legal Action Organization, George Washington University Law Center, supports projects of law students based on ASH (see Health, Prevention Emphasis below); and the Center for Law and Behavioral Science, University of Wisconsin, Madison; researches public-interest law and law and public policy.

Media Emphasis

NATIONAL CITIZENS COMMITTEE FOR BROADCASTING, 1028 Connecticut Ave. NW, Washington DC 20036. *Media Watch.* Headed since 1978 by Nader, seeks to encourage competition, popular access to the media, stronger public television, improved public affairs coverage, regulation of advertising aimed at children, quality ratings of programs.

Also of interest are Accuracy in Media, reviews complaints and publicizes errors; Citizens Communication Center for Responsive Media; Media Access Project, legal actions, under the Center for Law and Social Policy; National Citizens Communications Lobby; and the Fund for Investigative Journalism.

Science Emphasis

CENTER FOR SCIENCE IN THE PUBLIC INTEREST, 1755 F St. NW, Washington DC 20006. Mostly interested in food additives and energy issues.

FEDERATION OF AMERICAN SCIENTISTS, 307 Massachusetts Ave. NE, Washington DC 20002. Especially active on military issues. See also Union of Concerned Scientists below under Nuclear Power.

Security Reform Associations

Although related issues are not covered in this book, these groups are an integral part of the public-interest scene and can provide a starting point for interested students. There are many regional and functional groups, most of which have been omitted. Many of the groups already named have international interests.

NEW DIRECTIONS, 305 Massachusetts Ave. NE, Washington DC 20002. *New Directions*. A citizen lobby modeled on Common Cause for foreign affairs: security reform, effective aid, control of multinational corporations.

FUND FOR PEACE, 1995 Broadway, New York NY 10023. Sponsors Center for Defense Information, which publishes the *Defense Monitor* on military policy; Center for National Security Studies, concerned with abuses by U.S. intelligence agencies; Center for International Policy, which studies U.S. aid and human rights policies; Institute for the Study of World Politics, which awards fellowships; and In the Public Interest Media Service, which broadcasts corrections to right-wing extremism on the radio.

COALITION FOR A NEW FOREIGN AND MILITARY POLICY, 120 Maryland Ave. NE, Washington DC 20002. R. Coalition of twenty organizations; critical of military, supportive of third world and human rights.

UNITED NATIONS ASSOCIATION OF THE U.S.A., 300 East Forty-second St., New York NY 10017.

Also of interest are the American Peace Society; Arms Control Association; SANE (National Committee for a Sane Nuclear Policy); Women's International League for Peace and Freedom, Philadelphia PA; Institute for World Order, New York NY; Council on Religion and Foreign Affairs; Military Audit Project; for the Middle East, Americans for Middle East Understanding, New York NY; American Jewish Alternatives to Zionism, New York NY; American-Arab Relations Committee, New York NY.

Economic Reform

Tax Reform

TAX REFORM RESEARCH GROUP, 133 C St. SE, Washington DC 20003. R. *People and Taxes*. A project of Public Citizen.

TAXATION WITH REPRESENTATION, 6830 N. Fairfax Dr., Arlington VA 22213. *Taxation with Representation Newsletter.*

Also of interest are Tax Analysts and Advocates, Movement for Economic Justice, and Committee of Single Taxpayers.

Inflation, Unemployment, Market Power

See Economic Emphasis, Corporation Emphasis.

Consumer Protection

CONSUMERS UNION, 256 Washington St., Mount Vernon NY 10550. *Consumer Reports; News Digest.* Brand research plus political action.

CONSUMER FEDERATION OF AMERICA, 1012 Fourteenth St. NW, Suite 901, Washington DC 20005. *News.* A coalition of 220 groups.

Also of interest are National Consumers League; Consumers' Research, *Consumers' Research Magazine,* Washington NJ; Cooperative League of the U.S.A.; Peoples Business Commission; Aviation Consumer Action Project.

Environmental Reform

General

SIERRA CLUB, 530 Bush St., San Francisco CA 94108. *Sierra;* international, Washington, and chapter newsletters. Includes Sierra Club Legal Defense Fund and Sierra Club Foundation.

NATIONAL WILDLIFE FEDERATION, 1412 Sixteenth St. NW, Washington DC 20036. *National Wildlife; International Wildlife; Conservation Report; Conservation News.* Largest membership among conservationist groups; mostly educational, with wildlife emphasis.

ENVIRONMENTAL ACTION, 1346 Connecticut Ave. NW, Suite 731, Washington DC 20036. *Environmental Action.* Lobbies and campaigns, Washington focus.

FRIENDS OF THE EARTH, 124 Spear St., San Francisco CA 94105. *Not Man Apart.* Advocates sweeping reforms; environmentalism as ideology.

LEAGUE OF CONSERVATION VOTERS, 317 Pennsylvania Ave. SE, Washington DC 20003. R. Raises funds, gives endorsements for candidates.

IZAAK WALTON LEAGUE, 1800 Kent St., Suite 806, Arlington VA 22209.

Outdoor America. Most active in eastern United States; emphasis on protection and rehabilitation of watersheds.

Also of interest are Concern, Inc., educates on personal actions; Environmental Policy Center; American Committee for International Conservation; International Institute for Environment and Development; Worldwatch Institute, research, publicity; Resources for the Future, research.

Wilderness

WILDERNESS SOCIETY, 1901 Pennsylvania Ave. NW, Washington DC 20006. *Living Wilderness; Wilderness Report.*

CONSERVATION FOUNDATION, 1717 Massachusetts Ave. NW, Washington DC 20036. *Conservation Foundation Letter.* Research, education.

NATURE CONSERVANCY, 1800 N. Kent St., Arlington VA 22209. *Nature Conservancy News.* Buys and accepts endangered land from private owners for eventual public ownership; has 660 of its own preserves. The Trust for Public Land, San Francisco CA, is similar.

NATIONAL PARKS AND CONSERVATION ASSOCIATION, 1701 Eighteenth St. NW, Washington DC 20009. *Environmental Journal.* Works to expand park land and protected land in United States and abroad, plus other environmental concerns. A related professional association is the National Recreation and Park Association.

Also of interest are Center for Natural Areas and American Rivers Conservation Council.

Wildlife

NATIONAL AUDUBON SOCIETY, 950 Third Ave., New York NY 10022. *Audubon;* chapter newsletters. Education and protection of wildlife and habitat, has many sanctuaries, active membership.

FUND FOR ANIMALS, 1765 P St. NW, Washington DC 20036. Active lobby on seals, whales, dolphins, African wildlife, commercial abuse, zoo reform.

GREENPEACE, 860 Second St., San Francisco CA 94107. Direct action to save whales, seals.

WORLD WILDLIFE FUND, 1601 Connecticut Ave. NW, Washington DC 20009. A major effort, among others, is to save the Bengal tiger.

CENTER FOR ENVIRONMENTAL PROTECTION, 2100 M St. NW, Washington DC 20037. Runs the Whale Protection Fund, educates and lobbies.

Also of interest are Project Jonah, San Francisco CA, and General Whale,

Alameda CA, both concerned with whales; Defenders of Wildlife, protects wolves and other endangered species and opposes steel leg traps; African Fund for Endangered Wildlife, saves giraffes in Kenya; African Wildlife Leadership Fund, saves mountain gorillas.

Litigation

ENVIRONMENTAL DEFENSE FUND, 475 Park Ave. S., New York NY 10016.

NATURAL RESOURCES DEFENSE COUNCIL, 122 E. Forty-second St., New York NY 10017. See also the Sierra Club above.

Nuclear Power

CRITICAL MASS ENERGY PROJECT, PO Box 1538, Washington DC 20013. *Critical Mass*. A Nader-supported project.

Also of interest are the Union of Concerned Scientists, Cambridge MA; Clamshell Alliance, Portsmouth NH, for the East Coast; Abalone Alliance, San Francisco CA, for the West Coast. Friends of the Earth is also actively antinuclear.

Pollution

Of interest are the Cousteau Society, New York NY, and the Oceanic Society, San Francisco CA, both concerned with the oceans and their pollution and emphasizing research and education; Rachel Carson Trust for the Living Environment, concerned with pesticides; Crusade for a Cleaner Environment, working on bottle bills. Relevant business and professional associations include American Academy of Environmental Engineers, Rockville MD; Air Pollution Control Association, Pittsburgh PA; Water Pollution Control Federation.

Urban Affairs

Of interest are the Urban Land Institute, emphasizing research and development; the Institute for Local Self-Reliance, promoting small-scale technologies for food, energy, waste, and so forth, and local control in urban areas; Highway Action coalition, opposing freeway expansion and supporting mass transit; Walking Association; American Pedestrian Association, Forest Hills NY; National Association of Railroad Passengers. A relevant governmental association is the American Public Transit Association. The social reform groups also have an interest in urban environments and are listed below.

Population

PLANNED PARENTHOOD FEDERATION OF AMERICA, 810 Seventh Ave., New York NY 10019. *News*. Closely related are the International Planned Parenthood Federation and the Alan Guttmacher Institute for research; the institute publishes many periodicals, including *Planned Parenthood Washington Memo*.

ZERO POPULATION GROWTH, 1346 Connecticut Ave. NW, Washington DC 20036. *ZPG National Reporter*.

NATIONAL ABORTION RIGHTS ACTION LEAGUE, 825 Fifteenth St. NW, Washington DC 20005.

Also of interest are Population Crisis Committee; Population Reference Bureau; Population Institute; World Population Society; Environmental Fund; Religious Coalition for Abortion Rights; Negative Population Growth, New York NY; Pathfinder Fund.

Social Reform

General

NATIONAL URBAN COALITION, 1201 Connecticut Ave. NW, Washington DC 20036. *Exchange; Washington Update*. A coalition of thirty groups.

LEADERSHIP CONFERENCE ON CIVIL RIGHTS, 2027 Massachusetts Ave. NW, Washington DC 20036. *Memo*. A coalition of 147 organizations.

Also of interest are the Lawyers' Committee for Civil Rights Under Law; the National Sharecroppers Fund, Charlotte NC, runs the Frank Graham Center, a demonstration farm and training center; Rural America Inc.; Center for Community Change; National Association for Community Development; Urban Institute, research; Council on Municipal Performance, New York NY, for better local government and community development. Relevant professional associations are the National Association of Social Workers, *Social Work* and other publications; and American Public Welfare Association.

Poverty and Welfare

Of interest are the American Freedom from Hunger Foundation; the Institute for Research on Poverty, University of Wisconsin, Madison, *Focus:*

Southern Poverty Law Center, Montgomery AL. A relevant professional association is National Legal Aid and Defenders Association.

International Poverty

OVERSEAS DEVELOPMENT COUNCIL, 1717 Massachusetts Ave. NW, Washington DC 20036.

SOCIETY FOR INTERNATIONAL DEVELOPMENT, 1346 Connecticut Ave. NW, Washington DC 20036.

Also of interest are International Voluntary Services; Friendshipment, New York NY, food and medical aid for Vietnam; Bread for the World, New York NY, a Christian group concerned with improving the effectiveness of American aid. Some multi-issue and security reform groups are also concerned with international poverty, as well as many international voluntary service agencies and groups concerned with particular regions and countries.

The Young

CHILD WELFARE LEAGUE OF AMERICA, 67 Irving Place, New York NY 10003. *Child Welfare Journal.*

CHILDRENS' DEFENSE FUND, 1520 New Hampshire Ave. NW, Washington DC 20036. Litigation and other activities for children's rights.

Also of interest are the American Parents Committee, R. *Washington Report on Federal Legislation for Children;* Day Care and Child Development Council of America; the Children's Foundation; Coalition for Children and Youth; National Association for the Education of Young Children; American Humane Association, Englewood CO, concerned with cruelty to children and animals. A relevant professional association is the Council for Exceptional Children, Reston VA.

The Old

AMERICAN ASSOCIATION OF RETIRED PERSONS, 1909 K St. NW, Washington DC 20049. *Modern Maturity*; *News Bulletin.* Mostly non-political, offers services; includes the National Retired Teachers Association.

GRAY PANTHERS, 3635 Chestnut St., Philadelphia PA 19104. *Network.* Lobbies on savings interest, pensions, Medicaid-Medicare.

NATIONAL COUNCIL OF SENIOR CITIZENS, 1511 K St. NW, Washington DC 20005. R.

Also of interest are the National Alliance of Senior Citizens and a relevant professional association, the National Council on the Aging.

The Disabled

AMERICAN COALITION OF CITIZENS WITH DISABILITIES, 1346 Connecticut Ave. NW Room 817, Washington DC 20036. *Coalition; Newsletter.* Coalition of sixty groups representing people with physical, mental, or emotional impairment.

Also of interest are the National Association of the Deaf, Silver Springs MD; American Council of the Blind; National Association for Retarded Citizens, Arlington TX; National Federation of the Blind, Baltimore MD; United Cerebral Palsy Association, New York NY; National Easter Seal Society for Crippled Children and Adults, Chicago IL; many other disability-related groups. A relevant professional association is the American Association on Mental Deficiency.

Housing

NATIONAL HOUSING CONFERENCE, 1126 Sixteenth St. NW, Suite 211, Washington DC 20036.

Also of interest are the Community Associations Institute, helps self-government of condominiums and cooperative housing; a governmental association, the National Association of Housing and Redevelopment Officials; and a professional association, the International Federation of Housing and Planning, The Hague, Netherlands. The Urban Coalition, Urban Institute, and Urban Land Institute listed above are also interested in housing.

Sexism

NATIONAL ORGANIZATION FOR WOMEN, 425 Thirteenth St. NW, Suite 1048, Washington DC 20004. *National NOW Times.*

NATIONAL WOMEN'S POLITICAL CAUCUS, 1411 K St. NW, Suite 1110, Washington DC 20005.

WOMEN'S LOBBY, 201 Massachusetts Ave. NE, No. 116; Washington DC 20002. R.

Also of interest are the Women's Legal Defense Fund; Women's Equity Action League; Human Rights for Women; American Association of University Women; Women's Campaign Fund, R; and National Women's Education Fund.

Racism, Native Americans

AMERICANS FOR INDIAN OPPORTUNITY, Plaza del Sol Bldg., Suite 403, Albuquerque, NM 87102.

Also of interest are the Native American Rights Fund, Boulder CO, for litigation; Coalition of Eastern Native Americans; Association on American Indian Affairs, New York NY, gives legal and technical aid to tribes, has several publications; National Indian Youth Council, Albuquerque NM, opposes coal stripping and power plants on Indian lands; Arrow, Inc.; National Congress of American Indians, researches and lobbies on resource and social issues; American Indian Development Association, Bellingham WA, has eleven projects promoting development in harmony with Indian culture.

Spanish-speaking Americans

NATIONAL COUNCIL OF LA RAZA, 1725 Eye St. NW, Suite 210, Washington DC 20006. *Agenda.*

Also of interest are the Mexican American Legal Defense and Educational Fund, San Francisco CA; and American G.I. Forum, Albuquerque NM. A relevant labor union is the United Farm Workers, Keene CA.

Black Americans

NATIONAL ASSOCIATION FOR THE ADVANCEMENT OF COLORED PEOPLE (NAACP), 1790 Broadway, New York NY 10019. *Crisis.*

NAACP LEGAL DEFENSE FUND, 10 Columbus Circle, New York NY 10019. Not part of NAACP; litigates, gives scholarships; educates.

NATIONAL URBAN LEAGUE, 500 E. Sixty-second St., New York NY 10021. *Urban League News.*

Also of interest are the National Council of Negro Women; National Committee against Discrimination in Housing; National Neighbors, for integrated housing; Medgar Evers Fund, New York NY, to help Fayette MI; Southern Christian Leadership Conference, Atlanta GA; Black Child Development Institute; Joint Center for Political Studies, *Focus,* does research on black political participation; Voter Education Project, Atlanta GA, to register blacks and defend black participation in the South.

Social Institutions

Crime

NATIONAL COUNCIL ON CRIME AND DELINQUENCY, 411 Hackensack Ave., Hackensack NJ 07601. Research and training related to rehabilitation.

NATIONAL COALITION TO BAN HANDGUNS, 100 Maryland Ave. NE, Washington DC 20002.

Also of interest are the National Council for a Responsible Firearms Policy; National Council to Control Handguns; National Alliance of Businessmen, finds jobs for ex-offenders, youths, and veterans in big cities; Fortune Society, New York NY, for penal reform. A relevant professional association is the American Correctional Association.

Health, Prevention Emphasis

ACTION ON SMOKING AND HEALTH, 2000 H St. NW, Suite 301, Washington DC 20006. *ASH Newsletter.*

Also of interest are the National Association for the Prevention of Blindness, New York NY; National Jogging Association; Center for Auto Safety; Federation of Homemakers, Arlington VA, concerned with food additives. Many consumer protection groups are active in the area of health regulation. A relevant business group is American Seat Belt Council, New Rochelle NY.

Health, Care Emphasis

HEALTH RESEARCH GROUP, 2000 P St. NW, Suite 708, Washington DC 20036. Sponsored by Public Citizen.

HEALTH SECURITY ACTION COUNCIL/COMMITTEE FOR NATIONAL HEALTH INSURANCE, 821 Fifteenth St. NW, Suite 801, Washington DC 20005.

Also of interest are the Health Policy Advisory Committee (Health-PAC), New York NY; American Cancer Society, New York NY; American Heart Association, Dallas TX; American Lung Association, New York NY; other disease-related groups. Relevant professional associations include the National Health Council, New York NY, and the American Public Health Association.

Mental Health

MENTAL HEALTH ASSOCIATION, 1800 N. Kent St., Rosslyn VA 22209.

Also of interest are Al-Anon Family Group Headquarters, New York NY, to help family members of alcoholics; National Council on Alcoholism, New York NY; American Schizophrenia Association, New York NY.

Education

Of interest are the Council for Basic Education, *Bulletin;* Association for Childhood Education International, *Childhood Education;* National PTA (National Congress of Parents and Teachers), Chicago IL. Relevant professional groups include the National Education Association, *Reporter, Today's Education,* R; American Federation of Teachers, *American Teacher, American Education,* R; American Association of University Professors. Relevant institutional associations include the American Council on Education, for higher education, and the American Association for Higher Education.

Political System

Civil Liberties

AMERICAN CIVIL LIBERTIES UNION, 22 E. Fortieth St., New York NY 10016. *Civil Liberties; Civil Liberties Review.* Includes several projects for the death penalty, prisons, women, mental health, and other concerns.

AMNESTY INTERNATIONAL, 2112 Broadway, Room 405, New York NY 10023. *Matchbox.*

FREEDOM HOUSE, 20 W. Fortieth St., New York NY 10018. *Freedom at Issue.* Compares nations on human rights.

Money and Politics Reforms, Institutional Reforms

Of interest are the Fair Campaign Practices Committee and the Citizens' Research Foundation, University of Southern California, Los Angeles CA, researches money and politics. See also Common Cause and the League of Women Voters listed above.

Public Interest Related

PUBLIC CITIZEN VISITORS CENTER, 1200 Fifteenth St. NW, Washington DC 20005. Helps visitors find politically important hearings, other events, sources of information; advises how to lobby one's representatives.

Also of interest are the National Center for Voluntary Action, encourages voluntarism; Commission for the Advancement of Public Interest Organizations; Association of Voluntary Action Scholars, Chestnut Hill MA, does research on all kinds of voluntarism; National PIRG Clearinghouse (PIRG is Public Interest Research Group), helps organize PIRGs around the country.

Index